IMPRINT

Nelles Guides ... get you going.

AVAILABLE TITLES
Australia
Berlin and Potsdam
Brittany
California
The Caribbean:
 Greater Antilles
 Bermuda, Bahamas
The Caribbean:
 Lesser Antilles
Crete
Cyprus
Egypt
Florida
Hawaii
Hungary
India North
India South
Indonesia West
 (Sumatra, Java, Bali, Lombok)
Kenya
Morocco

Nepal
New Zealand
Paris
Provence
Spain North
Spain South
Thailand
Turkey

IN PREPARATION
Bali / Lombok
China
Laos / Cambodia
Malaysia
Moscow / St Petersburg
Munich
New York
Philippines
Rome

MEXICO
©Nelles Verlag GmbH, München 45
 All rights reserved

First Edition 1993
ISBN 3-88618-384-X
Printed in Slovenia

Publisher:	Günter Nelles	**Translation**:	Roger Rosko
Chief Editor:	Dr. Heinz Vestner	**Cartography:**	Nelles Verlag GmbH, München
Project Editor:	Volker W. Radke		
Editors:	Angus McGeoch, Marton Radkai	**Color Separation:**	Priegnitz, München
		Printed by:	Gorenjski Tisk, Kranj

No part of this book, not even excerpts, may be reproduced without prior permission of Nelles Verlag

MEXICO

**First Edition
1993**

TABLE OF CONTENTS

Imprint 2
List of Maps 7

HISTORY AND CULTURE

The Origins of Mexican Culture 13

TRAVELING IN MEXICO

THE MEGALOPOLIS 52

Mexico City 53
Teotihuacán 68

COLONIAL SPLENDOR AND TEMPLE PYRAMIDS 74

Tula 75
Taxco 81
Puebla 83
Toluca 86

IN THE CENTRAL HIGHLANDS 94

Morelia 95
Querétaro 102
San Miguel de Allende 104
Guanajuato 106
Guadalajara 109
León 111
Aguascalientes 112
San Luis Potosí 113
Zacatecas 114

MEXICO'S WILD NORTH 120

Monterrey 120
The Border States 121
From Los Mochis to Chihuahua 123
Baja California 129

SUN, SAND, SEA 134

Acapulco 135
Ixtapa-Zihuatanejo 138

Manzanillo	139
Puerto Vallarta	140
Mazatlán	141

INDIGENAS AND TOURISTS 146

Oaxaca	147
Chiapas	153

ALONG THE GULF COAST 162

Veracruz	162
Tabasco	172
Campeche	174

THE MAYA RUINS AND BEACHES OF YUCATAN 180

Mérida	182
Chichén Itzá	186
Uxmal	189
Cancún	196
Cozumel	201
Quintana Roo Coast	202

FEATURES

Mexican Cuisine	210
Mexican Music	214
Folk Art	216
Mural Art	220
Literature	222
Fiestas	226
Bullfights and Mounted Games	226
Voladores	228
Machismo	230
Viva la Muerte	232
Social Conflicts	234

GUIDELINES

Travel Tips	238
Authors	250
Photographers	251
Index	252

MEXICO

LIST OF MAPS

LIST OF MAPS

Mexico	6/7
Mexico City	54/55
Metro	57
Teotihuacán	68
Environs of Mexico City	77
Central Highlands	96/97
Querétaro	103
Guadalajara	108
Northern Mexico	122
Baja California	128
Acapulco	136
Pacific Coast I	138/139
Pacific Coast II	140
Oaxaca/Chiapas	148/149
Monte Albán	150
Gulf Coast	164/165
Veracruz	166
Yucatán Peninsula	182/183
Mérida	184
Chichén Itzá	189
Uxmal	190

HISTORY AND CULTURE

THE ORIGINS OF MEXICAN CULTURE

The history of what is now known as Mexico had its beginnings many millenia ago. During the most recent Ice Age (the period starting some 35,000 years BC), wandering tribes came from Asia over the then-frozen Bering Sea into the region of present-day Alaska in small nomadic groups. They subsisted as hunters and gatherers. From there they moved southward and settled the entire region, extending into South America. Among the numerous peoples that developed and flourished, two high cultures are worthy of note: One in Meso-America, which extends, roughly speaking, from central Mexico to western El Salvador and Honduras; the other, that of the Incas, became established in the central Andean region of South America.

Until the emergence of what we now call "Indian" peoples and high cultures (the expressions Indio and Indian are avoided in Mexico, therefore in the following text the designation *Indígena* = indigenous or aboriginal will be used), the historical development of Meso-America can be divided into three periods. During the paleo-Indian or Early Hunter Epoch (35,000 to 7000 BC), nomadic tribes populated the regions from Mexico to Costa Rica. The *hombre de Tepexpan*, a skeleton discovered near Mexico City, has been roughly dated to 8000 BC. About 12,000 years ago the continent began to warm after the retreat of the most recent Ice Age. Swamps were transformed into semi-deserts, and as a consequence of the changing vegetation numerous prehistoric animal species became extinct, including the mammoth and the mastodon. Impressive archeological discoveries from this period are found in the Museum of Anthropology in Mexico City.

During the Neolithic period (roughly 7000 to 2500 BC) cultivation and harvesting of crops began. The development of maize, the bean, various types of chilies and the pumpkin and gourd took place during this period, which also saw cotton being cultivated and woven into material for clothing. The previously nomadic peoples became increasingly sedentary. Due to the fact that seeds and the harvested produce had to be stored, the first vessels of clay appeared. Advanced methods for working stone, the keeping of domestic animals, agriculture and permanent settlements evolved during the fifth millenium BC.

The development of the high cultures began during the Formative or Pre-Classical Epoch (roughly from 2000 BC until the beginning of the Christian Era). The production of ceramics was refined, agriculture became more efficient and permanent settlements were expanded. This resulted in members of society being freed for construction work, clerical functions, leadership tasks and the arts. This development was a precondition for the development of high civilization.

Pre-Columbian Era

The Olmecs, whose civilization is considered the precursor of the rest of Meso-American culture, constructed the first pyramid-like hills on the Gulf of Mexico, initially of mud and clay with only a slight angle of incline. They created altars of granite, sculptures of basalt and figures of clay. Presumably their early temples were constructed of wood. These relics have given us some indication of their first religious beliefs and rituals – a simple fertility cult connected with

Previous pages: Music plays a very important role in Mexican life. Relief in Chichén Itzá. Children immaculately dressed to participate in a fiesta. Left: Olmec sculpture.

HISTORY AND CULTURE

elemental deities (earth, rain/water, the underworld) and the jaguar, who was supposed to have played a role in the birth of the human race. The Olmec culture wielded decisive influence over the remaining Meso-American peoples. This society, whose influence can still be found in La Venta (Tabasco), Tres Zapotes (Veracruz), Monte Albán (Oaxaca) and Guerrero, had already left the gulf region before the beginning of the Christian Era.

What we now know about the cultures of early Mexico is due, first and foremost, to the pre-Columbian monumental buildings. In addition, considerable knowledge has been deduced from the sculptures, vessels, wall-paintings, stone inscriptions, decorative motifs, jewelry and *codices*, or chronicles, that managed to survive the destruction by the Spaniards. The records and reports of the con-

Above: Pre-Columbian hieroglyphics. Right: The negroid features of Olmec sculptures still present a riddle for archeologists.

quistadors and the priests who accompanied them are of a certain value, although they must be viewed with great caution and reservation, since they were written to justify the conquest and missionary activities. The flourishing art and sciences of the Meso-American cultures, with their mathematics, astronomy, historical documentation and calendar technology were almost completely destroyed by the conquerors and the representatives of the Catholic church. For us, information on the organization and structure of the community and on the relationships between various tribes, peoples and cultures, is primarily derived from their architectural creations, including pyramids, temples, palaces, fortresses, observatories, residential structures, ball-playing courts, burial places and even complete cities of the dead. With their help, it is possible to define the boundaries and pick out some of the relationships between the major cultural regions of ancient Mexico. Of approximately 11,000 archeological sites only

HISTORY AND CULTURE

about 100 have been excavated and scientifically investigated to date. Nevertheless, we have learned about the life of the ancient peoples – the Olmecs, Mayas, Teotihuacans, Zapotecs, Mixtecs, Aztecs and many others.

Around the 15th century BC, the formative epoch for the Olmecs began on the gulf coast, for the inhabitants of Monte Albán in Oaxaca and for the Mayas in Yucatán. The Olmecs erected their first larger buildings at some time around 1200 BC. The residents of Monte Albán (under Olmec influence) followed 200 years later, at about the same time as the Mayas and the Central Americans. The Olmecs were named after the region of their origin, the latex cultivation areas in Tabasco and Veracruz. In Nahuatl, the language of the Mayas, the name means "rubber people".

In the swampy primeval forests of La Venta (in the state of Tabasco), at the beginning of this century, archeologists at oil drilling sites had already made their first discoveries of an enigmatic culture. Beginning in 1941, systematic excavation and research began, and the culture of the Olmecs came to light and into the limelight. Monoliths of granite and basalt, altars, sculptures and small figures of clay and jade were unearthed.

The Olmecs had constructed a ceremonial center here, surrounded by a flourishing community. A pyramid of compressed earth measuring 130 meters by 60 was erected, 35 meters in height and thus with an incline of only 30 degrees. Next to the pyramid, the Olmecs constructed two burial mounds and a main plaza surrounded by buildings as well as a court on which a type of ballgame was played that later spread throughout Meso-America.

Today it is believed that the community in the religious center's surrounding area numbered some 20,000 inhabitants. The agriculture they practiced served to feed the great numbers of construction workers and stone-cutters. These workers were urgently needed, since the colossal heads of basalt and monumental granite

15

HISTORY AND CULTURE

altars (weighing up to 30 tons) were carved from single blocks of stone, which furthermore had to be transported between 60 and 120 kilometers from the quarries to the places where they were set up and later discovered. The floors of some graves consist of stupendous mosaic pavements of serpentine stone depicting stylized jaguar masks.

The jaguar theme reappears in a variety of forms in many sculptures and figures. It symbolizes rain and water, and was passed on as a cult figure and the focus of worship in many subsequent cultures. Some time around the year 400 BC La Venta was destoyed by an unknown catalysm, and its inhabitants were dispersed throughout Central America. 200 years later the same fate befell Tres Zapotes in the state of Veracruz.

Above: Hundreds of stone masks clad the facade of a Mayan temple in Kabáh. Right: Mayan relief of the sun-god Kinichthan (Anthropological Museum, Mexico City).

During the classical epoch of ancient Mexican culture (250-900 AD) the Mayas expanded from the Guatemalan highlands and Chiapas into the Yucatán lowlands. The "Greeks of the Americas", as they have been designated for their extraordinary cultural achievements, constructed tremendous city-states which developed independently at first, and only later began influencing each other. At the apex of a city's administration was a theocratic ruler, who reigned over the temples to the gods that stood on the pyramids, the priests' palaces and houses of nobility as well as the cult-based ball courts. Around the periphery of the religious center were the bamboo huts of the farmers and the craftsmens' workshops. The most renowned cities from this period are Palenque, Uxmal and Chichén Itzá.

The Mayas recorded significant events with a type of hieroglyphic script. They chiseled them in stelae and temple walls and even wrote chronicles. Sadly, however, these documents bearing portrayals

HISTORY AND CULTURE

of their lives, religious rituals, astronomical calculations, history, depicting the pantheon of gods and describing the philosophies of their people, were almost completely destroyed by the Spaniards.

The development of more efficient cultivation methods for maize gave Mayan laborers, artists, priests, scientists and architects more leeway for cultural (i.e. religious) pursuits. Their most important deities were Itzam Na (the god of creation), Kinich Ahau (the sun god), Ix Chel (the moon goddess) and Chac (the god of rain). Mayan religious rituals followed a calendar with 13 months of 20 days each, while worldly events were documented according to the solar calendar (with 365 days). After a cycle of 52 years, both calendars began once again on the same day, on which the population braced itself for crises and oblivion. If no catastrophe occurred, then the pyramids were added on to and furnished with yet more splendid ornamental plasterwork. This led to the growth of extraordinary complexes with pyramids up to 70 meters in height and elaborately decorated temples surrounded by immense palaces.

For reasons not yet clear, the Mayas departed their cities in the ninth century, leaving structures on which building had already begun incomplete. During the post-classical epoch (from 900 AD onward) several groups migrated to the north under Toltec influence, where, at Chichén Itzá, a Mayan city flourished once again for a brief period.

Situated at an altitude of 2300 meters, 50 kilometers to the northwest of Mexico City, is a pyramid complex of unparalleled size and beauty, Teotihuacán. As early as 150 BC, a people of which little is known today constructed a sun-pyramid which towers over the site, forming its core. In the course of the next 600 years, the entire city emerged, only one-tenth of which is still visible. Around 750 AD, the city was set ablaze and abandoned; probably it was the Chichimecs, pushing into the region from northern Mexico, who destroyed this strange and threatening realm of the gods. To date, re-

HISTORY AND CULTURE

search on the inhabitants of Teotihuacán has yielded precious little. The Aztecs pointed out the burned-out city to the Spaniards, calling it the "place where gods are born". This gigantic cultural fulcrum influenced many peoples of ancient Mexico. Its geometrically planned center consists of an immense ceremonial road hemmed by pyramids, temples, palaces and platforms. Its wall-paintings were highly elaborate (the jaguar appears once again) and the ingenious design of a type of slanted wall construction, the so-called *Talud-Tablero* system, reached its highest perfection. Jewelry and ceramic wares from Teotihuacán were traded throughout Meso-America. We can still see some of the relics of this great culture, though we know hardly anything about its priests and rulers, their deities and beliefs or of the countless people who, as farmers, craftsmen, laborers or brilliant architects, created and maintained the city's en-

Above: The "Plumed Serpent", symbol of the god Quetzalcóatl (Teotihuacán).

ormous wealth. Thus one of the greatest legacies of ancient Mexico is still a mystery. Future excavations may reveal from which region of North America the Teotihuacaños came to this lofty Mexican valley and what the reasons were for the later abandonment of their cultic center.

The folk-hero of the Zapotec people is Benito Juárez, the initiator of key Mexican reforms. The history of his ancestors had its beginnings around 1000 BC, when the first preparations were undertaken for the construction of Monte Albán. There, on the Isthmus of Tehuantepec (Mexico's narrowest section between the Pacific and the Caribbean) they flattened off the summit of a mountain at a height of 2000 meters and created a "heavenly" citadel. The peak served as a religious center and residence of the priests, while the common folk lived on the mountain's slopes and in three adjacent valleys, supplying the center with food and water, which was lugged up the mountain in jugs during the dry season. After preparatory work to make the

HISTORY AND CULTURE

mountain top suitable for building, which continued for centuries, a Zapotec site of unrivaled splendor came into being.

Sweeping staircases lead upward to the temples. The complex, covered with painted plasterwork, must have been a gorgeous spectacle indeed. The Zapotecs maintained a custom of burying their rulers and priests with valuable gifts in colorfully painted burial chambers whose roofs were designed in a particularly intricate fashion. In the vicinity of Monte Albán, cultic centers were established, including the fortress of Yagul and the future capital city of Zaachila. After the original inhabitants had transformed their residences into burial facilities, these were taken over by the Mixtecs.

To the northeast of Mexico City, in the primeval forests of Veracruz, are about 100 mounds as well as an excavated acropolis and the Pyramid of the Niches in El Tajin, the capital city of the Totonacs. Construction started around the beginning of the Christian Era. In their use of material, stone sculptures and ornamental style, the Totonacs closely resemble the Olmecs. By the sixth century, these sites had finally reached their full bloom, though only 100 years later they were abandoned by their inhabitants. Researchers are still puzzling over the reasons for this.

Around 1000 AD, El Tajin blossomed anew, this time under Toltec rule. Apparently the Toltecs made their way from Tula via El Tajin to Chichén Itzá. In Cempoala, a Totonac culture developed that was subjugated by the Aztecs around 1460 (this was also the reason why the Totonacs were quite willing to aid the conquistador Cortés in battle against the Aztecs). There are ten ball-playing courts in El Tajin, several of them with outstanding bas-reliefs. By the way, this people of stone-cutters, potters and pyramid-builders invented a unique ritual in their efforts to earn the favor of their gods: the Dance of the Flying People, today known to every tourist as the *voladores* spectacle.

Tula (once called Tollan), the capital city of the warlike Toltecs, was founded in the ninth century. At first, roofed-over assembly plazas were erected consisting of halls whose roughcast beamed roofs were supported by numerous columns. A magnificent pyramid was decorated with feathered serpents, with human heads projecting out of their mouths, eagles clutching human hearts in their talons, and coyotes and jaguars. These symbols of their military Jaguar and Eagle Orders are found again in Chichén Itzá. Tollan's temple roof was also supported by mighty pillars, including four warrior sculptures, the Atlantes of Tula. The Toltec's architectural design of pillar-supported hall construction was taken up by many other cultures. 100 years after the construction of their city the inhabitants sustained the first attack of the Chichimecs, an ethnic group from northern Mexico that was advancing into the region. A number of them emigrated, moving under the leadership of their god-king Quetzalcóatl ("Feathered Serpent") first to El Tajin and then further to Chichén Itzá. During the 12th century, another Chichimec onslaught sealed Tula's fate once and for all.

The culture of the Mixtecs is usually and erroneously viewed simply as the successor to the Zapotec culture. In fact, it is surmised that the Mixtecs had settled in Yagul as early as 400 AD, and the first structure on which a date was left is from 692 AD, when their precipitous ascent began. They were skilled craftsmen, producing the finest of gold jewelry, fashioning many other metals into everyday utensils, carving bone and wood, and considered unexcelled masters in the art of stone-cutting.

Around 1100 AD the Mixtec culture, and pre-Columbian architecture alongside it, reached its zenith: The white palaces of Mitla, arranged into five

HISTORY AND CULTURE

groupings, were furnished with a mosaic like stone decor which, in just one of the numerous palaces of this type, consists of more than 100,000 individual pieces, all of them elaborately carved and fitted together in a great variety of geometric designs. After the Zapotecs had left Monte Albán, the Mixtecs transformed the mountain city into an immense burial grounds. They expanded the graves that were already present, turning them into cross-shaped sites, painted the interior walls, installed small temples at the entrances. The dead were buried along with valuables that included jewelry, gold, mosaics and carvings.

Archeologically, western Mexico is the country's least researched region to date. The Tarascans, who lived in comparative isolation from the other peoples of Meso-America, primarily in the region of the present-day state of Michoacán, are by far the best-known people of the region. They were successful in defending themselves from attempted conquests by the Aztecs. Their origins are, however, unclear. One generally accepted hypothesis suggests that they emigrated into the area from the north during the 13th and 14th centuries, as did the Aztecs, although other researchers place this event at a considerably earlier point in time. The Tarascans distinguish themselves in a number of characteristics from other indigenous ethnic groups. They developed techniques of unsurpassed mastery in the areas of pottery, jewelry production and portrayal of the human figure. The designation *Tarascan* can be traced back to the Spaniards, who were called *tarasco* (brother-in-law) by the native population after the conquerors had taken their daughters as wives. By some inexplicable means this name was transferred to the Indigenas themselves, whose actual name was *Purépecha*, or "simple man".

The basis of the Tarascan temple structure is the *yácata*, a truncated pyramid

Above: The giants of Tula once supported the roof of a temple. Right: The remains of Yácata in Tztintzuntzan.

HISTORY AND CULTURE

combining a rectangular and circular layout. The core of the edifice is formed of natural rock consolidated with pebbles, clay and soil. Today in Tzintzuntzan, which is said to have once had between 30,000 and 40,000 inhabitants, there is a platform 20 meters high, 400 meters in length with a width of 250 meters. A 100-meter-wide (former) flight of stairs led upward in westerly direction, that is, toward the sea. At the top was a platform with five 12-meter-high *yácatas,* each featuring a staircase on its eastern side. Temple buildings of perishable materials stood on the rounded *yácatas.* They were probably dedicated to nature deities such as fire, sun, moon and earth. Scarcely any stone sculptures or other hewn rock have been found at the site to date.

As concerns ceramics, the discoveries have included jugs with handles and spouts, elaborately worked and decorated bowls, some of them with feet; rattles, toys, whistles and a great variety of representations of the human body. Some of the clay work has a fine black glaze. Musical instruments were produced from bone. Jade is rarely found, but there are many pieces of jewelry made of obsidian and quartz crystals as well as gold, silver and particularly copper. The preferred production method was the "lost wax" principle, though even copper-work often featured a gold overlay.

The known centers of Tarascan culture are Pátzcuaro, Quiroga and Tzintzuntzan, its capital city during the 14th century. In 1479, the final major Aztec attack was successfully fended off. The last king of the Tarascans, Zuanga (1479-1519), died of smallpox. The disease had been transported to the region from the West Indies by a black slave in servitude to Pánfilo de Narváez. When the Spaniards advanced into western Mexico, the Tarascans abandoned their city and retreated into the mountains. Not until Vasco de Quiroga made Pátzcuaro an episcopal see and became a vehement champion for their rights did some of them return.

The Aztecs were the last of the pre-Columbian cultures to appear. This war-

HISTORY AND CULTURE

like people extended their area of influence from the high valleys of Mexico over almost all the ethnic groups in Central America. In pre-Columbian manuscripts there are reports that during the 14th century the *Mexica* tribe had settled on an island in Lake Texcoco, where they founded Tenochtitlán. It was connected to the mainland by three causeways, and an aqueduct brought water to the settlement. At the time of the Spaniards' arrival, more than 200,000 people are believed to have lived in what had become the capital of the Aztec empire. Its settlers were named Aztec because they came from the mystical *Aztlán* (in northern Mexico). Within 100 years, they had subjugated the Chichimecs and Toltecs of central Mexico, and then the Zapotecs and Mixtecs in the southern reaches of the land as well as the Totonacs and Huaxtecs on its eastern coast.

Above: Market in Tlatelolco. In the background is of the Aztec lake-city of Tenochtitlán (mural by D. Rivera).

Aztec architecture incorporates the styles and forms of the cultures they had subjugated. The same applied to their deities: The "Plumed Serpent" and the gods of the wind, rain and sun as well as the jaguar and maize gods had already been revered in the preceding pre-Columbian cultures. The daily lives of the Aztecs were strongly influenced by these deities, to whom constant sacrificial blood-offerings had to be made. Solely for the consecration of Tenochtitlán's main temple in 1487, 20,000 prisoners are said to have had their heart cut out of their living bodies with obsidian knives. The famous Aztec calendar stone, today on display at Mexico City's Anthropological Museum, was used at the main temple as the sacrificial altar. The blood of the people killed there, offered to the sun god Tonatiuh, was supposed to insure the deity's survival, and thereby the Aztecs' as well.

There were certainly forerunners of the double-temple among other peoples, but with the Aztecs this became a predominant architectural principle. They built on top of extant pyramids and temples several times, enlarging the uppermost platforms, and erected twin temples ascended by two flights of stairs. They elaborated the calendar system, polished the construction of circular temples and perfected their urban planning, which used astronomical data for its basic orientation. Unfortunately, the majority of edifices left to us are only religious ones in nature. The aqueducts, residences, palaces, bath-houses, and markets, which received such glowing reports in the Spanish conquistadors' logbooks, have all disappeared, destroyed to the last.

The Conquest

Moctezuma II's reign over the Aztec empire began in 1502. He succeeded in fortifying and expanding it even further. More than 30 tribes paid him tributes. In the year 1519, at the height of his power and wealth, he received the report that men with white skin and beards had landed on his realm's eastern coast.

The 34-year-old Spanish officer Hernán Cortés was among those who set off on exploratory voyages after hearing Columbus' reports of the New World's riches. By 1504, he had already come to Hispaniola (the present-day Dominican Republic) and had become a major landowner on the island of Cuba by 1517. At roughly the same time, the first Spanish expeditions had reached the Yucatán coast under the command of Francisco Hernandez de Córdoba and Juan de Grijalva, discovering the white city of Tulum standing high above the sheer coastline. Cortés also sailed from Cuba to Yucatán, where he vanquished a Mayan tribe and liberated Father Gerónimo de Aguilar, who had been held prisoner for seven years and had meanwhile acquired mastery of the Mayan language. In the future he was to serve Cortés as an interpreter. At another landing along the coast of Tabasco they engaged in battle with the indigenous folk, whose chief relinquished a Nahua princess by the name of Malinche. She knew several languages, including Nahuátl, the Aztec language, and a Mayan dialect as well. She learned Spanish from Aguilar and also came to be an interpreter for Cortés. In the course of the Conquest she performed invaluable service, and soon became Cortés' confidant and lover.

Cortés landed with ten ships (500 men, 14 cannons and twelve horses) at Antigua, in the vicinity of the present-day city of Veracruz. One week later more than 100 bearers sent by Moctezuma brought him welcoming gifts in great measure, gold, silver, precious stones and pearls. Instead of moving the Spaniard to depart the land, these gifts merely revealed the country's wealth. But Cortés was bent on advancing into the country's interior. To prevent his crew from simply returning to Cuba and Spain with the "presents", he had nine of the ships scuttled. With the help of his interpretess he learned of the hostility between the Aztecs and their subjected peoples who desired to reestablish their independence from Tenochtitlán. This was valuable information which he used to his advantage. He immediately found allies ready and willing to support him in his march on the Aztec capital. In the Totonac city of Cempoala, Cortés enjoyed a peaceful reception and was provided necessary equipment. The advance on Tenochtitlán began in the summer, with indigenous bearers guiding his small army into the highlands. En route, the first resistance from the native population was met in the city of Tlaxcala, 150 kilometers to the east of the Aztec capital. They were no match for Cortés' army. Thousands lost their lives, while the remainder joined the victor as auxiliary troops. The reception in Cholula was friendly, but the Spaniard nonetheless had some 5000 of its inhabitants slaughtered, presumably so that

HISTORY AND CULTURE

rumor of his invincibility would rush on ahead of him. Moctezuma once again sent gifts to the approaching troops, but to no avail. Cortés reached the Aztec capital in late autumn of 1519, but for inexplicable reasons Moctezuma's 60,000 warriors did not put up any resistance. On the contrary, the Aztec emperor received Cortés with all honors and once again generously showered him with gifts. (Cortés sent a portion of these treasures back to Europe.)

Bernal Díaz, a nobleman in Hernán Cortés' entourage, authored *The True Story of the Conquest of New Spain*. He reported on the first meeting between Cortés and Moctezuma: "When Cortés saw the great Moctezuma approaching, he jumped from his horse and both demonstrated high respect for each other. Cortés gave Moctezuma a necklace... It was made of multicolored ornamented glass beads, threaded onto a golden cord and perfumed with musk". Afterwards Cortés was guided to the palace of Moctezuma's father, where he took up quarters. His army moved into the city of Tenochtitlán, placing the cannons in position. Moctezuma was taken hostage. Once again, there was no resistance.

In the spring of 1520, 20 Spanish ships under the command of Pánfilo de Narváez landed on the Mexican coast from Cuba. Narváez had been ordered to call Cortés to account and bring him back to Cuba, for having undertaken his march on the Aztec capital of Tenochtitlán without the approval of the Cuban governor. Cortés left his cannons and a few troops to guard Tenochtitlán, and headed out with an army to meet Narváez. He succeeded in defeating Narváez due to treachery in the latter's own ranks. The greater part of the newly-arrived troops allied themselves with Cortés, lured by promises of land ownership and gold. Cortés returned to Tenochtitlán bringing

Above: Aztec ruler Moctezuma receives Cortés with great pomp. Right: Frenzied destruction of the ancient Aztec capital by the Spaniards.

HISTORY AND CULTURE

an additional 100 mounted troops, 700 men and 20 cannons.

Pedro de Alvarado, the notorious future conqueror of Guatemala and El Salvador, had been in command of the Spanish troops which had remained in Tenochtitlán during Cortés' absence. Without authorization he had interfered with the Aztec's religious ceremonies and killed several dignitaries. This finally caused the dam to burst. An Aztec rebellion under the command of Moctezuma's brother seriously threatened the Spaniards, and Cortés' return failed to defuse the situation. Skirmishes broke out repeatedly, in the course of which even Moctezuma's fate caught up with him. The Spaniards, heavily outnumbered by their Aztec hosts, were ultimately forced to flee Tenochtitlán. In the course of this hasty retreat, two-thirds of the invaders lost their lives, an event which has gone down in Spanish history as the *noche triste*. Cortés' troops were reduced to a mere 450 men, now without their cannons, which were lost in the flight.

Now Cortés had to withdraw to his allies in Tlaxcala in order to recruit more reserves. Coincidentally, four new Spanish ships landed, laden with troops, horses and weapons; they had not gotten wind of the recent defeat. The new arrivals joined forces with Cortés. With a force of 600 men and 100 riders they advanced against Tenochtitlán once again, facing off against the Aztecs under the leadership of their new emperor Cuauhtémoc. The Spaniards surrounded the city and began a three-month siege, cutting off water and food supply-lines. The Aztecs were further weakened by a smallpox epidemic, introduced by the Spaniards, which took a great number of lives.

In the summer of 1521, the Spaniards forced their way into the capital city and destroyed it. Some 100,000 Aztecs were killed, and emperor Cuauhtémoc was taken hostage.

The tribes of central Mexico, which had been forced to paying tribute to the Aztecs accepted the Spaniards immediately. With the support of auxiliary

HISTORY AND CULTURE

troops, Cortés advanced into western Mexico as well as Oaxaca and Yucatán, subjugating the peoples who settled in these regions. The Spanish conquerors committed the most gruesome atrocities against the population, recording even the smallest details of many of their misdeeds. On the taking of a city, as many as possible of the indigenous people were killed, even when they put up no resistance. The soldiers were followed by the priests and monks of the Catholic church, who sponsored a further series of bloodbaths.

It is thus a matter of record that in the summer of 1562, 4500 Mayas were tortured to their deaths in one town in Yucatán because they confessed to having worshipped "foreign gods". 6300 more of the town's inhabitants were inflicted the gravest injuries. Burnings, roasting, crushing and breaking of limbs, upside-

Above: Spain's conquest of Mexico brought sickness, slavery and death to the native inhabitants.

down hangings, setting bloodhounds onto infants and children and other methods of torture applied by the priests and soldiers simply defy description.

In this manner, Mexico became *Nueva Hispania*, or New Spain. An enigma which has scarcely been explained to this day is how Cortés managed, with just 700 men, to conquer all of Mexico and Central America, an area comprising more than 20 million inhabitants. His troops were equipped with muskets and cannons, whose use proved devastating against Moctezuma's and Cuauhtémoc's warriors, who fought with bow and arrow, obsidian knives and swords. Nonetheless, their hosts numbered in the hundreds of thousands. Even if one takes into account that Cortés repeatedly succeeded in recruiting allied troops from the native population, this scarcely explains his victory over the vast armies of central Mexico, who were themselves well versed in the arts of waging war. Two factors certainly contributed to the astonishing success of the Spaniards:

HISTORY AND CULTURE

Firstly, the horse was unknown to the populations of Central America. This large beast, to which the rider appeared to be firmly attached, must have seemed like some sort of supernatural creature to the natives, who simply became paralyzed with fear initially. Another possible factor might have been the legend of the god-king Quetzalcóatl, who had departed Tula in the 10th century and, it was believed, would return one day in the shape of as a white-skinned, bearded man. Did the Aztecs and other native peoples believe that the great deity had indeed come back? Battle had never been waged against gods during the pre-Columbian epoch; on the contrary, they had been given everything of value that might have served to placate them – in some cases even human lives.

The Colonial Period

Even after the conquest of Mexico, the Spaniards continued waging their campaign of destruction, demolishing countless palaces and temples. On their sites colonial buildings were constructed from the old stones. Indigenous slaves were forced to work under the supervision of Spanish master builders and architects. The stonecutters' skill and art served the Spaniards' aims neatly. The elaborate Baroque ornamentation on the colonial edifices was, by and large, the work of indigenous artists.

New cities were established steadily, uniformly laid out in a chequerboard pattern. The city center featured a large plaza, the *plaza de armas*, around which stood the colonial rulers' most important buildings: the governmental palace *(palacio del gobierno)*, the city hall with the local administrative functions (*palacio municipal*), the church, the residences of the priests and/or bishop, a hospital and a school. In the immediate vicinity further administrative buildings and businesses were constructed, followed by residences. The state buildings and the larger residences included a *patio*, surrounded by colonnades with galleries in the upper level. Many of these interior courtyards were laid out with elaborate gardens and graced with a fountain.

All of this splendor stands in sharp contrast to the actual origins of the new Mexican "nobility". Almost without exception they were Spanish immigrants with few means who achieved their wealth and titles by means of unscrupulous business dealings and exploitation of the native population.

Anybody who opposed the Spanish was killed. This fate befell not only the indigenous chiefs (*kazics*), but the native clerical elite as well. The Spanish administrative system was established and Christianity raised to the status of state religion. The conquerors and Catholic church worked together hand-in-hand. The Christian Orders, first and foremost the Franciscans (from 1523) with the Dominicans, Augustinians and Jesuits in train, were never far behind the conquering soldiers. In just a century after the Conquest, hundreds of churches, cloisters and monasteries were erected, accompanied by the achievement of an almost total christianization. This process received an enormous boost from the appearance of the dark-skinned Madonna (or Virgin) of Guadalupe, who was said to have been seen by a baptized native in 1531 and thereafter rapidly became the patroness-saint of Mexico and later all of Central America.

The earliest church edifices were massive fortress-like affairs, windowless and surrounded by thick walls since attacks and rebellions could be expected. At the same time, in the early phases roofs were omitted from the houses of worship; the altars stood under the open sky, an accommodation to the natives, who were unaccustomed to enclosed ceremonial places. In the distribution of the expropriated lands the Spanish rulers didn't

HISTORY AND CULTURE

forget their clergymen: Immense swathes of land, altogether some 30 percent of the conquered territories, became the property of the Catholic Church over the course of time.

Several bishops, among them Vasco de Quiroga in Michoacán and Bartolomé de las Casas in Chiapas, turned against the enslavement, exploitation and inhuman treatment of the indigenous peoples. Bartolomé de las Casas was born in 1474, the son of an aristocratic family that had originated in Limousin and achieved wealth in Andalusia. Entirely a child of his epoch, las Casas was at first enthusiastic about the expeditions of the conquistadors Cortés, Pizarro and Alvarado. The youthful theologian took part in several conquest campaigns as an interpreter for native dialects, during which he met Cortés and Alvarado. The heinous deeds committed by the conquistadors against the Indıgenas left him unmoved in the beginning. Not until the second half of his life did the clergyman las Casas take notice of their suffering. "And as much as I might study, in every book I read, whether in Latin or Spanish, I found only more arguments and established teachings speaking for the rights of these West Indian peoples against robbery, outrages and injustices that were being committed against them".

Don Bartolomé became the legal advocate of the exploited Indigenas. Countless interventions and petitions addressed to the royal dynasty were aimed at liberating the enslaved natives. It was, however, a political battle that couldn't be won. In 1552, las Casas' *Report on the Devastation of the West Indian Lands* appeared, a no-holds-barred work on both the material and spiritual exploitation of a colonized people.

In fact, legislation for protection of the Indigenas was enacted quite early (1542) though in practice it had little effect. For

Above: Hernán Cortés (right) and Bartolomé de las Casas, first champion of native rights.
Right: A typical example of the integration of "heathen" temples into Christian churches.

HISTORY AND CULTURE

example, as of 1550, the *encomiendas*, whereby the only "compensation" for slave labor was conversion to Christianity, were superseded by *repartimientos*. Now the Indigenas had to be paid wages, although they were still compelled to perform their labors. This system remained in effect until 1632, after which the natives could seek out employment on their own. The Spanish rulers also reacted to this change without hesitation: They encouraged the workers to incur debts, so that in this manner they became bound to one *hacienda*.

The leading officers of the *conquista* received huge landed estates. Cortés became *Marqués del Valle de Oaxaca*, Count of the Oaxacan Valley, where more than 20,000 slaves toiled under him. At first, he was vested with rule over Mexico, becoming governor of New Spain. Within a short time he conquered the country's entire southern reaches and founded a capital city, La Ciudad de México, on the rubble of Tenochtitlán. Thus, laying beneath the cathedral and the zócalo, are the Aztec's ancient religious sanctuaries, while the National Palace stood atop the former palace of Moctezuma.

From 1524 to 1526, Cortés was gone on a journey to Honduras because Cristóbal de Olid, who had been put in charge of exploring the country, seemed to be acting autonomously and had not returned. Cortés took Cuauhtémoc along on the trip as a hostage. He left Malinche, his interpretess and lover, behind when passing through her homeland Tabasco, giving her to a Spanish officer as wife. In the winter of 1525, he had Cuauhtémoc hanged in Honduras. Two years later Cortés was relieved of his duties by the Spanish Crown and replaced with a five-man governing board, the *audiencia*, which also assumed jurisdiction of the realm and supreme command of the army. Cortés undertook further maritime journeys in the Pacific regions, exploring the peninsula of Baja California with little success (though it should be mentioned that the body of water between the

29

spit of land and the mainland was later named the Sea of Cortés). He also returned to Spain to take up his defense against the reproaches against administration of his office. He returned to Mexico once again, and finally died in 1547 during a stay in Spain.

In 1530, Nuño de Guzmán succeeded in bringing western Mexico and the Pacific coast under Spanish hegemony after stiff resistance from the native population and rebellions that flared up time and again. He became the founder of Guadalajara. In Yucatán, the Conquest lasted another ten years; not until 1540 did Francisco de Montejo manage to decisively subjugate the peninsula and found Mérida, its first Spanish city. As for the Mayans, they held out longest in the town of Petén, Guatemala, where Spanish rule was only firmly established in 1697.

In 1535, Spanish Emperor Carlos V, a Habsburg, named Antonio de Mendoza as first viceroy of New Spain. He was to govern the land for the coming 15 years. He expanded his capital city once again. The country was divided into provinces which were ruled by governors, who in their turn established local administrative offices.

Judges and priests were sent to every village, so that through administration of justice and missionization a rapid adaptation of the indigenous population to the new rulers, their system of government and religion was made possible.

In order to ease this process, the Indigenas were gathered together in centers (*reducciones*), the forerunners of the Spanish settlements and cities. The viceroy was in charge of governmental administration, juridical matters and the army, which increasingly gave rise to conflicts with the powerful Catholic church over the administration of the colony. Mexico was governed by 62 (!) viceroys by the time it gained independence from Spain in 1821.

The waves of immigrants rolled in steadily. Just 50 years after the Conquest there were already 70,000 Spaniards in Mexico. However, their dreams of finding quick riches didn't come true, because the motherland collected enormous taxes, duties and interest. After the land had first been plundered by the conquistadors, yielding gold and jewels that were sent off to Spain, the new arrivals' wealth was now to be found in agriculture and silver mining. Various useful European plants, grain varieties and cattle were imported.

The Indigenas worked in the fields and mines. Their numbers were reduced from more than 20 million to only 3 million during the battles of conquest, rebellions and wanton killings; the Inquisition, by which the conversion to Christian beliefs was enforced, often killed the prospective convert, as did the diseases brought in by the Spaniards.

The dissemination of Christianity was the Spaniards' declared goal, though their greed for gold and wealth stood in stark contrast to their lofty intentions. The practice of human sacrifice they so heartily condemned, (they scarcely even recognized that it was a religious ritual), was pursued by themselves, in manner of speaking, through slavery, forced labor and indentured servitude. However, the only people who became wealthy were a few large landholders able to call their immense haciendas their own and those merchants who engaged in business with Spain.

Since the Spanish immigrants were almost exclusively men, extramarital cohabitation (concubinism) was tolerated. The Mexican people was in fact born in this fashion, out of a special ethnic group, the *Mestizos*, descendants of the Spaniards and Indigenas. By the end of the

Right: The cathedral of Mexico City – an imposing symbol of the Church's power during the colonial days.

HISTORY AND CULTURE

18th century, Mexico already had 6 million inhabitants again. Of these, some 3.5 million were Indigenas, 1.5 million Mestizos and one million Creoles (*criollos*), i. e. white, Mexican-born descendants of the Spanish settlers.

Power and wealth lay concentrated in the hands of the roughly 30,000 *peninsulares*, as immigrants from Spain named themselves; called *gachupines* in Mexico, these Spanish-born whites considered themselves the supreme and true rulers of the land.

Alexander von Humboldt, who traveled through the country in 1800, described them as follows: "The most miserable European, lacking upbringing and general education, believes himself superior to whites born in the new continent. He knows that through the patronage of his fellow countrymen he can one day achieve a position to which access is forbidden for the native-born, even when they distinguish themselves for their talent, their knowledge and their outstanding moral qualities."

The Struggle for Independence

The new territories of Spain expanded ever further, by 1800 encompassing to the north the regions of the present-day US states of California, Arizona, New Mexico and Texas. Influenced by the American independence movement and the new US constitution, the first groups of conspirators had already begun to form in the late 18th century. Their members pursued the establishment of Mexico's independence from Spain. Riots broke out in 1804 when the Spanish Crown, influenced by the ideas of the Enlightenment, expropriated a large portion of Church properties. The clergy and Creole population were particularly outraged by this action. Four years later, Napoleon conquered Spain and installed his brother Joseph as king. Ferdinand VII was overthrown. Thus, in the view of the Creoles and the clergy, there was no longer any legitimate Spanish government capable of exercising power in Mexico. The Creoles pressed the Mexi-

HISTORY AND CULTURE

can viceroy to remain loyal to the deposed Ferdinand and to govern Mexico autonomously and independently until the reinstatement of the Spanish king. However, the Spanish *peninsulares*, who were charged with the orderly administration of their colony, were fearful of such a development since it would in fact constitute the first step on the way to Mexican independence. For this reason they deposed the viceroy, giving Ferdinand up as it were, and pledged loyalty to their motherland's French occupants. The antagonism between the Creoles and born Spaniards intensified.

The *gachupines*' wealth and claims to power had always been a thorn in the side of the Creoles, and now they came to the fore once again, loud and clear. In addition, the notions of the French Revolution also reached Mexico. Enthusiasm for these new social and political ideas was particularly strong among liberal circles. Groups began to form throughout the country that served as political clubs, where people could debate the pros and cons of Mexican independence from the "Motherland" Spain.

In Querétaro a Creole rebellion took shape at whose core was the city's mayor (*El Corregidor*, the Judge), his wife Josefa Ortíz de Domínguez (*La Corregidora*), Ignacio Allende, an army officer from San Miguel, and the priest Miguel Hidalgo y Costilla from Dolores. They championed the complete abolition of slavery, an end to the principle of indentured servitude, a just set of land reforms and the abolition of the Spanish monopolies. The rights of the Mestizos and Indigenas were to be strengthened relative to the Creole upper classes and the *gachupines*. Besides performing his duties as a parish priest, the 57-year-old Hidalgo, who had received a liberal Jesuit education, drew up plans for the redistribution of land and other social re-

Above and right: Reminders of the struggle for independence – in a painting by Diego Rivera and in a stage play.

HISTORY AND CULTURE

forms. The group decided to take a change at revolt in the beginning of December 1810 and took the necessary steps of arming sympathizers.

The movement was at risk because the colonial rulers had learned in advance of the group's plans for revolution. The *Corregidora* managed to warn Hidalgo that the conspiracy had been uncovered. He took immediate action: On September 15, 1810, the bells of his church in Dolores (in the state of Guanajuato, 200 kilometers to the northwest of Mexico City) were rung, and he proclaimed the revolution: "Long live Mexico! Long live the Virgin of Guadalupe! Death to the *gachupines*!" (this *Grito de Dolores* is repeated annually on the evening of September 15 by the incumbent president from the balcony of the National Palace and by all the governors and mayors in the country). An eleven-year-long war of independence thus began. Hidalgo was able to mobilize first 20,000, later 80,000 armed men and almost completely rid the state of Guanajuato of major Spanish landholders and silvermine owners. He released the prisoners from the penitentiaries and locked up the *gachupines*. His troops didn't have many scruples in the liberation of the Spanish towns; many of the *peninsulares* lost their lives. However, the *insurgentes* (insurgents), as the rebels were called, ran into a threatening situation during the second year: Allende and Hidalgo were taken prisoner and executed in Chihuahua. Aid was sent up from the south by the priest José Maria Morelos, who was able to assemble an army and push forward to Guerrero. There, in the city of Chilpancingo, in 1813, a National Assembly was called to order for the first time, and the independence of Mexico was proclaimed. Morelos submitted a new constitution one year later. In 1815, however, the Royalists gained the upper hand once again when their military commander Agustín de Iturbide managed to defeat Morelos at Valladolid (the city was later renamed Morelia in the hero's honor). Ferdinand, who had regained power in

HISTORY AND CULTURE

1814 after ousting the French occupiers, had sent reinforcement troops to Mexico to support the fight against the revolutionaries. Morelos was also arrested and later executed.

In Spain, Ferdinand put the Constitution of Cádiz into effect in 1820. It was liberal in spirit, guaranteeing equal rights for Spaniards, Creoles and Mestizos in New Spain. This led, on the one hand, to a revival of the independence movement. On the other, it didn't please the *gachupines* much, since it encroached on their privileges. A conservative conspiracy came into being, under the leadership of Iturbide, which pledged itself to maintaining the privileges of the Creole upper-classes and set itself against social reforms. It cunningly concluded a pact with Vicente Guerrero, who came from the south with a rebel army. Together they promulgated the Plan of Iguala, which provided for Catholicism as the state religion, the granting of equal rights to all Mexicans, and called for an independent Mexico (with a king from Europe). With this, the war of independence came to an end, having cost a total of 60,000 lives. Arriving from Spain in 1821, Viceroy Juan O'Donojú (he had Irish ancestors), was forced to sign the Treaty of Córdoba, by which Mexico became independent. (This severance from the mother country wasn't recognized by the Spanish Crown until 15 years later.) In 1822, Iturbide had himself crowned Emperor Agustín I and proclaimed ruler of the "United States of Mexico". Iturbide's goals were far removed from those of the social movement inspired by Hidalgo, Allende, Morelos and Guerrero. The Creole upper-class, wealthy landlords, the clergy and the bourgeoisie now had the power in their hands and retained their old privileges. Things were just as bad as ever for the majority of Creoles and the indigenous population.

Chaos and Reforms

Iturbide already abdicated in 1823 in the face of increasing resistance to his imperial rule, and retired to Europe. Mexico became a republic, with Guadalupe Victoria, one of Iturbide's opponents, becoming the country's first president. When Spain's final remaining stronghold, Fort San Juan de Ulúa in Veracruz, fell in 1825, the last Spaniards also left the country. However, the chaos increased: The laws enacted in Mexico City to protect the rights of the Indigenas were flouted on the estates of the major landholders. During the first 30 years of independence no less than 50 governments were established. One of the most prominent figures of this period was General Santa Ana. From his hacienda in Veracruz, he directed armies of mercenaries and piloted rebellions. Ultimately he even had himself elected president, and that a total of eleven times!

During his period in office, Santa Ana fought bitterly against the American army. Because increasing numbers of American settler families in Texas had been refusing to pay taxes to the Mexicans since 1821, he launched punitive military expeditions against the territory. The Americans, however, managed to capture him. In order to save his own skin, Santa Ana promised Texas independence. In 1845, the Americans unexpectedly declared Texas a US state. For the Mexicans this was grounds for war. They prepared for an invasion over the Rio Grande. US troops occupied Mexican California and advanced toward Mexico City. In September 1847, General Winfield Scott seized the Mexican capital. The resistance put up by six young cadets has gone down in history. When the *Niños Heroes* (Valiant Children) realized that the battle had been lost,

Right above: Eleven times president – General Santa Ana (left). The first president of native descent – Benito Juárez (right).

HISTORY AND CULTURE

they wrapped themselves in the Mexican flag and jumped to their deaths from the tower of the castle in Chapultepec Park. By the terms of the Treaty of Guadalupe Hidalgo, on February 2, 1848, the Mexican government ceded to the Americans nearly half of their country's area, namely the territories of Arizona, California, New Mexico and Texas for all of 15 million dollars...

In order to defend themselves against the advances of American soldiers into the Yucatán Peninsula, the region's major landowners also supplied firearms to the Mayan tribes. However, the Indigenas wasted no time turning these weapons against their true enemies, their wealthy Mexican masters. Thus began the three-year-long "War of the Castes". It ultimately cost the lives of nearly half of the Yucatán Mayan population. Some of them managed to take refuge in the jungle, from where they continued their battle with relatively little success.

In 1857, a truly towering personality entered the Mexican political stage for the first time: Benito Juárez, a pure-blooded Zapotec and former governor of the state of Oaxaca.

In the beginning, Juárez, who as a lawyer had become renowned for offering his services free of charge to the poor and needy, worked as minister of justice under President Ignacio Comonfort. The list of his planned reforms was impressive, including securing the legalization of civil marriage, the separation of church and state, the nationalization of church holdings and a guarantee of religious freedom. By 1858, Benito Juárez had already acceded to the presidency, although due to a rebellion of conservative Mexicans he was unable to move into Mexico City and get his reformist legislation passed until two years later.

When, under his government, delays arose in the repayment of foreign debts, he played right into the hands of his opponents, who requested the European countries of France and Spain as well as Great Britain to dispatch troops; the French actually succeeded in occupying the capital city. Thanks to the assistance of Archbishop Labastida they were able to install the Austrian Maximilian of Habsburg on the throne in 1863. Once again, Mexico had become a monarchy. In the meantime, Benito Juárez had gone into hiding in the inaccessible reaches of northern Mexico. From there he organized resistance against Emperor Maximilian with the aid of the USA. In the beginning, the youthful emperor and his wife, Charlotte Amalie of Belgium, enjoyed great popularity among Mexican conservatives. But Emperor Maximilian proved to be more than a pleasure-seeking ruler intent on preserving aristocratic conventions. His supporters came to the alarming realization that he was pursuing an increasingly liberal course, allowing many of Benito Juárez' reforms to stand. Then, when the French troops withdrew, things became critical for the progressive Habsburg: The Mexican-born conservative elite had closed ranks against him. He also suffered defeat in military conflict with Benito Juárez, who once again assumed the office of president. By a plebiscite, the population decided in favor of executing the 35-year-old Maximilian. The four-year-long French interlude in the New World, beginning with splendor, glory and hopeful expectations of the young emperor, once again made room for a Mexican republic.

Juárez was re-elected in 1871. As he had been four years earlier, he was victorious over his antagonist Porfirio Díaz, general and hacienda-lord in Oaxaca. One year later, Juárez died, of a heart attack. Not even he, the peoples' hero, had succeeded in bringing the country's social and economic problems under control. He had started the process of abolishing the great haciendas, but was unable to reserve the general frend towards pauperization of the country. Mexico's social and economic problems were becoming acute. The landless Indigenas and Mestizo day-laborers couldn't scrape together enough pesos to purchase the church holdings that had been put up for sale. The state treasuries were empty, and foreign financiers were not prepared to float any loans.

Juárez' successor, Sebastián Lerdo de Tejada, transformed the Mexican parliamentary system into a bicameral arrangement with a Senate and lower chamber.

The Dictatorship of Porfirio Diaz

By means of a coup d'état, the 47 year-old Porfirio Díaz finally managed to take the reigns of power in 1877. This political figure from an impoverished background was fanatically convinced of his mission to rescue Mexico. With the exception of a brief interruption, he was to rule Mexico for more than three decades. The "Porfiriat", as the era of his dictatorship is called, was at first marked by a time of peace and prosperity that Mexicans had longed for. The economy enjoyed an enormous upswing. New industries were established and the production of silver and gold was substantially increased. The railroad network grew from 500 to 19,000 kilometers and the telephone network was developed and expanded. By 1892, the state's revenues were already larger than its expenditures. Since foreigners were able to ring up hefty profits, outside capital streamed into Mexico. Economic relations with the USA were increasingly intensified, and the northerly neighbor advanced to become the most important trading partner. Simultaneously, Díaz, who appointed his legislators personally, introduced censorship of the press. Critical journalists were taken into custody. The land reforms started by Benito Juárez were not continued. Instead, Díaz abolished the existing collectives *(ejidos)* for the most part and transferred the land back into the

Right: The execution of Emperor Maximilian of Mexico in 1867 (E. Manet).

HISTORY AND CULTURE

hands of wealthy hacienda owners. Nor did Díaz want to lose favor with the Catholic church, though as a pragmatic tactician he did not return the clergy's former properties. He was convinced that the church's higher dignitaries would be satisfied if they were to regain only a few of their old privileges. The Jesuits were also allowed back into the country, and pilgrimages to the Virgin of Guadalupe resumed. Díaz' second marriage, to the wealthy daughter of a Don Romero Rubio, a major Catholic landholder, was also considered as a skilled move on the political chessboard.

The dictator turned a blind eye to the resulting increase in social injustice. Not only did the rich accumulate ever more money and properties until ultimately only a couple of thousand families owned half of the land in Mexico, but the situation of the village communities of indigenous folk and the landless Mestizo farmers became increasingly bleak. Rural mounted police proceeded brutally against those who tried to flee from their indentured servitude. Labor unions were forbidden, but the plantation owners were even vested with their own jurisdictions. In 1904, Díaz stood for his fifth re-election. There was still no more than a small minority daring to register their protest. Nevertheless, the dissatisfaction of vast classes of the population grew rapidly, but due to the fatalistic mentality of the Indigenas (who comprised nearly half the population of 13 million) no revolt broke out for the time being.

In an interview on February 20, 1908, the dictator declared to an American journalist that Mexico was finally ripe for democracy. "It is my irrevocable intention to step down from power when I turn 80 years old, regardless of the opinions of my friends and followers, and no longer to remain president..."

At roughly the same time the major landowner Francisco Madero authored a book entitled *The Presidential Succession in 1910*. In the publication, which rapidly became popular in Mexico, the liberal idealist championed free elections.

HISTORY AND CULTURE

He also demanded that the corrupt Ramón Corral not be installed anew as vice-president. Instead he proposed himself for the office. Madero was then nominated as the new presidential candidate by his "Anti-Re-election Party". Evidently, however, the dictator's bold words turned out to be nothing more than lip service designed to appease the American public. The meanwhile 80-year-old Díaz stood once again for re-election. In order to influence it in his favor, he simply had the results manipulated.

Madero was thrown in prison and not set free until after Díaz' re-election, whereupon he fled to Texas. From this safer distance Madero laid claim to having been the rightful winner of the election. He drew up a program of reforms (the Plan of San Luis Potosí) and issued an appeal for rebellion against the dictator. On November 20, the rebels opened their attack, and surprisingly meeting only weak resistance.

The Revolution

In the North, Madero joined forces with the former bandit leader Francisco ("Pancho") Villa, whose *Division del Norte* was composed of the most diverse groups. In addition to impoverished agricultural workers and small farmers there were miners, members of the socially critical middle classes and so-called bandits. They called for Díaz' resignation.

In the country's southern regions a revolt of farmers and Indigenas emerged, whose battle cry *tierra y libertad*! (Land and Liberty!) helped reinforce their determination. They were lead by Emiliano Zapata.

In February 1911, Madero returned to Mexico from Texas. When uprisings were reported in both Morelos and Mexico City, Díaz was compelled to resign. In Ciudad Juárez, Madero reached an agreement with Díaz and his military on a pro-

Above: F. Madero enters Cuernavaca in 1911. Right: Revolutionary troops embarking horses in Aguascalientes, 1914.

visional government with Madero at its head. In return, he offered the disarmament of the revolutionary groups and armies. Díaz traveled by way of Veracruz to Paris (where he died in 1915). Madero took office as president in June. The Revolution appeared to have succeeded.

In reality, however, it had only just begun. Zapata refused to disarm his forces as promised. In the interest of his followers, he first wanted a thoroughgoing set of land reforms. To this end he submitted the "Plan of Alaya" in November 1911, in which he demanded the return of the village land holdings (the *ejidos*) from the major landowners; the expropriation, with compensation, of one-third of all hacienda lands as well as the non-compensated expropriation of land holdings from active opponents of the Revolution. Zapata began to translate his demands into action in the state of Morelos, distributing conquered lands to the farmers and agricultural laborers of his army. The village cooperative holdings were re-established and administrated by democratic village councils. These reforms went decidedly too far for Madero, a liberal reformer beholden to middle-class tenets. He proved unsuccessful at restoring social tranquility. The situation escalated, and then Madero called his military into action against Zapata's militia of farmers. However, this move was also to go without success.

In the beginning of 1912, General Orozco, a former confederate of Pancho Villa, revolted against Madero in northern Mexico. The latter succeeded in suppressing this resistance but only with the help of Pancho Villa and Victoriano Huerta, formerly of General Díaz' cadre. Madero then raised taxes on landowners and, still in 1912, permitted the formation of the first Mexican trade union. At this point conservative powers rose up, even receiving support from General Huerta, who had switched camps.

In February 1913, Huerta instigated a coup and had Madero shot. The exact circumstances surrounding this deed have never been fully clarified. According to

Above: The legendary meeting of the revolutionary leaders, Vasconcelos, Pancho Villa, Gutiérrez, Zapata and Villarreal (l. to r.) in 1914. Right: Federal troops being transported by train (1915).

Huerta's version, Madero was "shot in flight". Huerta proclaimed himself president of Mexico, in essence disposing of the Revolution, since once again Mexico was under the sway of military dictatorship, suppression and corruption.

Almost immediately, Huerta had a civil war on his hands. His adversaries had gathered with varying motives around Venustiano Carranza, Pancho Villa, Emiliano Zapata and Alvaro Obregón. Carranza was governor of the state of Coahuila, and he had been minister of war during the brief period of Madero's regency. He promulgated the "Plan of Guadalupe", which called for Huerta's overthrow, demanding that the *constitución* in force under Madero be reinstituted. From then on his followers were referred to as the Constitutionalists. Carranza was, like Madero, an adherent of bourgeois-liberal reforms, also rejecting Zapata's sociocritical movement. Seeing no other alternative, Huerta fled to Central America.

At this point, antagonisms flared up once again. In November 1914, Carranza's and Obregón's armies had already begun fighting against Pancho Villa's motley bunch and Zapatas armed farmers. Obregón reached Mexico City, but he was then forced to retreat to Veracruz. Villa and Zapata "captured" the capital city and occupied the presidential palace, had themselves photographed in the president's chair and met for a breakfast (which was to become famous) in the *Casa de los Azulejos*. These pictures created a stir around the world. But the pair weren't able to hold their ground in the capital because their conceptions and plans didn't correspond to those of the urban bourgeoisie. Zapata returned to Morelos, while Pancho Villa headed off for the lengthy journey into the North.

HISTORY AND CULTURE

It may sound unbelievable, but in order to get the money he so urgently needed to maintain his army, Pancho Villa, the revolutionary hero, didn't exactly shrink away from some unorthodox ideas from time to time. On the third day of January, 1914, in other words, at a point in time when relations with America were still on an even keel, he put his signature to a contract with the Mutual Film Corporation which guaranteed him a sum of US $25,000, whereby he was obliged, from then on, to carry his battle forward before running movie cameras! Hollywood director Raoul Walsh recalled that Villa exchanged his old uniform for a new one, specially tailored and rather befitting of Tinseltown, and even allowed himself to be talked into not waging his battles before seven in the morning "due to the better light conditions"...

In 1915, Pancho Villa, whom the respectable Obregón still viewed as a bandit and didn't want to see in the president's chair, was defeated in the Battle of Celaya by Constitutionalist troops. Villa took flight to Chihuahua. There he got wrapped up in a variety of skirmishes, even tangling with the USA, and was shot in his automobile (from behind) in 1923. In 1916, Carranza was recognized as president by the USA; he brought a large portion of Mexico under his rule. He worked on a new constitution based substantially on that of 1857. It provided for the elimination of the huge private haciendas as well as the nationalization of all mineral resources. It contained further clauses for the protection of farmers and the labor force, as well as limiting the president's term of office to four years, without possibility of re-election. The constitution was proclaimed in Querétaro, taking effect in 1917.

Zapata continued his efforts at resisting Carranza, but in 1919 he was the victim of a dirty trick, murdered in an ambush arranged by the president. The land reforms and improvements in working conditions would still have to wait, however. In 1920, Carranza prohibited the unions Madero had permitted in 1912. This aroused resistance from within his own ranks, with the outcome that Alvaro Obregón was elected president. Carranza was shot while on his way to Veracruz. Obregón managed to tackle the land reform question. He stimulated industrial development and set workers' social security on legal foundations. The Revolution had finally achieved its goals, but it had cost more than one million human lives.

The Consequences of the Revolution

During his term in office, Obregón succeeded in further realizing the goals of the Revolution. He pressed forward with the land reforms and transferred the expropriated properties to village cooperatives. Measures for the protection of workers were broadened, while the union movement continued to gain momentum. The education system was also taken up

HISTORY AND CULTURE

in the program of reforms, starting with the expansion of schools. Increasing limitations were placed on the power of the Catholic church, though at first the displeasure and resistance to this change was loud and clear.

As of 1924, these reform efforts were continued by President Plutarco Elías Calles, who also acted to further limit the clergy's privileges. This led to a confrontation between conservative Catholics and the government which soon took on on all the aspects of another civil war, with the so-called *Cristeros* rebellions (1926-29): Under the instigation of the priests, armed Catholic farmers moved against government representatives.

Calles put through a change in the constitution by which the president's period of office was lengthened to six years; a re-election also became permissible so long as it didn't take place immediately subsequent to the first term. This cleared the way for Obregón's second election, though shortly after entering office he was assassinated by a Catholic fanatic. In 1929, Calles founded the National Revolutionary Party (in 1946 renamed the *Partido Revolucionario Institucional*, or Party of Institutionalized Revolution, abbreviated PRI), which has since provided Mexico with all its presidents in spite of sporadic opposition.

In 1934, President Lázaro Cárdenas took office and immediately set about further advancing the interests of labor and small farmers. Calles, who could still count on considerable influence in the country, disagreed with this movement to the political left, particularly in view of the fact that Cárdenas was chipping away ever further at Calles' primary power base, the military. This led to tensions, in the course of which Cárdenas removed Calles' adherents from high official positions and ultimately expelled them from Mexico altogether in 1936. The high point of the Cárdenas administration was the 1938 expropriation and nationalization of the American and British oil companies, a measure that met with broad approval within the population, especially in view of the developing national consciousness.

A new political course began in 1940, when President Avila Camacho undertook a cautious counter-movement, slowing down land reforms, attracting foreign capital into the country, and encouraging the growth of private property. During his term Mexico declared war on Germany and Japan (1942) although it didn't engage in battle. A large number of socialist and communist intellectuals and antifascist as well as Jewish emigrants from Europe were readily granted asylum.

Economic development experienced an enormous upswing under the presidency of Miguel Alemán (1946-52), the first civilian to hold the office since the Revolution. Alemán placed special emphasis on the advancement of agriculture and the country's transportation network. At the end of his tenure, Mexico found itself at the highest state of economic development it had ever known, a condition that Presidents Ruiz Cortines and López Mateos were able to maintain until 1964. At that point, however, the problems of rising inflation and growing corruption set root; they have persisted to the present. Gradually, a stratum of the population developed that was excluded from the benefits of economic growth. It suffered the typical pains of an industrializing society: insufficient housing, unemployment or underemployment, and a lack of land even for its own subsistence.

During the government of Díaz Ordaz (1964-70), Mexico twice landed in the spotlight of worldwide publicity: In 1968 the Olympic Summer Games were held in Mexico City, as was the World Soccer Championship in 1970. In October of 1968, a large crowd turned out on the

Right: A trade union meeting of campesinos (farm workers) around 1928.

42

HISTORY AND CULTURE

Plaza of Three Cultures in the nation's capital to demonstrate against the huge expenditures devoted to the Olympiad, while the gouvernement consistently ignored the needs of the poorest social classes. The protesters demanded a more reasonable appropriation and application of public finances. The police moved against the demonstrators by force of arms, shooting to death some 250 people. In protest, the author Octavio Paz, winner of the 1990 Nobel Prize for Literature, resigned his post as a foreign diplomat.

Mexico Today

During the presidency of López Portillo (1976-82), immense petroleum deposits were discovered in the Gulf of Mexico. By 1980, the country had already become one of the world's largest oil exporters. Mexico's future seemed secured, since by 1981 the annual income from oil sales had risen to $US 14 billion. In order to reduce dependence on the USA, investments were made in the national economy. There was money on hand, and foreign bankers readily advanced funds to cover shortfalls. Mexico was considered a rich country and a reliable debtor. However, the foreign debt shot up rapidly, reaching $US 100 billion in just a couple of years. An equivalent in capital investments has to date failed to materialize. Huge sums were in fact swallowed up by corruption and mismanagement. When collapse of oil prices hit the Mexican economy, export revenues sank rapidly and debts could no longer be serviced. Then inflation once again began its devastating escalation. Whereas in 1976, a tourist received just ten pesos for a dollar, today the figure is nearly 3000. High inflation, a considerable national budget deficit, the all-too-pervasive corruption and empty foreign exchange coffers induced López Portillo to nationalize the country's banks at the close of his term. But even this measure was no longer of much use.

In 1982, Miguel de la Madrid took on a difficult office. At first he devoted his ef-

43

HISTORY AND CULTURE

forts to reducing the foreign debt, setting up a debt conversion program with the International Monetary Fund (IMF) that provided his insolvent state some temporary relief. He made special repayment agreements with US and Japanese banks that cut the actual debt load considerably.

All these restrictive economic measures brought some first signs of success. The foreign debt declined perceptibly; reserves of certain foreign exchange began to accumulate, inflation fell and the budget deficit was reduced. However, the problems of mass under- and unemployment could not be brought under control quite as rapidly.

A new economic setback caused the annual inflation rate to soar again in 1987, this time to 160 percent. This development was successfully confronted with a national solidarity pact be-

Above: Arduous manual labour still typifies Mexican agriculture. Right: The earthquake of 1985 caused serious damage in Mexico City and surroundings.

tween employers, unions and state authorities, which included a wage and price freeze. By 1988, the inflation rate had already sunk considerably. New blueprints for debt restructuring with the USA and IMF brought further relief to the precarious situation.

While Mexico was suffering economically, it was, nevertheless, able to consolidate its position on the international stage. It began to play an important role in Central American peace negotiations, quickly winning the respect of the involved countries by virtue of its democratic tradition and cautious approach as well as its proposals, which were balanced with a view to consensus.

In September of 1985, a formidable earthquake shook Mexico City and several regions in the neighboring states. The official figure was 10,000 dead, although the real total was probably very much higher. Great numbers of "earthquake-safe" buildings collapsed and buried their occupants, and the authorities responsible were accused of not having

HISTORY AND CULTURE

invested the funds required to make the buildings safe.

As a result, several hundred thousand people became homeless. Total damages were estimated at several billion US dollars. The catastrophe cast a long shadow over the 1986 World Soccer Championship held in the city.

Dissatisfaction with the unity party PRI, which permitted only a few small opposition parties, had already cropped up under Lopez Portillo. New parties were now allowed to form, with one-fourth of the seats in the lower house being reserved for the opposition. But the traditional system remained in place: The party chiefs selected the succeeding president by themselves, with the "election" being nothing more than a confirmation of that choice. Then in 1983/84, the conservative party PAN achieved electoral victories in several regions. The PRI, fearful of this opposition, resorted to rather obvious means of rigging. Two years later, riots broke out in several states, in the aftermath of which Cuauhtémoc Cárdenas, son of the legendary president (who the people still respectfully called "Don Lázaro"), split away from the PRI and joined the left-wing coalition FDN (*Frente Democrático Nacional*). In 1988, he even entered the presidential race against Carlo Salinas. The election of Carlos Salinas de Gortari, who still holds the office of president today, has been declared invalid by the opposition. The PRI total of 50.74 percent, the poorest result in the history of the party, was once again achieved by fraud, so that in actuality the PRI doesn't have an absolute majority at all, at least according to many Mexican voters.

Salinas began a thoroughgoing re-privatization program, which included both the Mexicana and Aeromexico airlines as well as the majority of the once state-controlled banks.

With bated breath, observers both foreign and domestic followed the president's announcements of plans to carry out long overdue, far-reaching agricultural reforms. In the opinion of leading

HISTORY AND CULTURE

economic experts the matter is extremely urgent, since the Mexicans are far from being able to feed themselves on their own. In 1990 alone, staple foods had to be imported at a cost of two billion US dollars. This had to be paid in foreign exchange that the heavily indebted land was lacking, at any rate, for other areas of the budget. Nevertheless, to date no head of state has ventured a change in the traditional property ownership arrangements or the implementation of measures to increase efficiency in agriculture. Then, for the first time for more than 50 years, limbs were to be hacked off of article 27 of the Mexican Constitution. Originated by President Lázaro Cárdenas, its provisions guaranteed that nearly half of all agriculturally usable lands were to be granted to landless farmers. This had proven to be an unprofitable system, since nearly three quarters of the land so distributed and worked were tiny parcels which, moreover, could be neither used as collateral, nor leased out, nor could ownership be transferred. According to Salinas' plan, the *ejidos* could continue to be operated as before if the majority of holders decided in favor. Otherwise they could opt to acquire the lands they worked as individual property. Critics of this agricultural scheme were certain that the farmers, most of whom were poor, would then sell their land immediately, thus producing new large estates that might even be owned by foreigners.

Salinas had also set his sights on improving relations with the Catholic church, at least since the visit of Pope John Paul II in 1990. Conflict between state power and the clergy had been on the rise for a long while, more precisely since the Revolution and the Constitution of 1917, in which a series of articles had been included that sharply limited the rights of religious communities. In Mexico, of course, this affected the Catholic church in particular. It had always sup-

Above: Demonstration by campesinos in Mexico City. Right: Every year, 1.6 million children are born in Mexico.

ported politically conservative groups and used every means at its disposal to work against supporters of the Revolution. It now appeared as if the old animosities were a thing of the past. Thus the church-schools, which, despite constitutional prohibition, had been established and tolerated, were officially legalized; the Church could once again possess capital, and since the end of 1991, priests have also been allowed to wear their cassocks in public again, a demonstration of religious affiliation that had previously been forbidden. To be sure, though, their tax-exempt status was also abolished, and the Catholic clergy was even less pleased by the fact that these liberalizations also applied to the Protestant competition, whose congregations are growing ever larger in Mexico.

As regards tourism, Mexico has been wooing the European market. In 1990, 6.5 million tourists visited the country, producing a foreign exchange surplus of $US 1.4 billion. Only three percent of the visitors were European, although they supplied six percent of the foreign exchange. Salinas has opened the gates wide: Today any airline or travel organization can operate "completely freely" in Mexico, because the government assigns high priority to international tourism as an important factor in the country's continued economic development. On the one hand, it brings foreign exchange into the land, on the other it serves to reduce unemployment. Salinas' government has appropriated $US 3.5 billion for the promotion of tourism, a sum that will probably have been paid back quite soon, since goals of ten million tourists and a foreign exchange surplus of $US five billion have been set for 1994.

Mexico has concluded a free trade agreement with the states of Central America, where it has, of course, a strong interest in the region's political stability and hopes to advance the peace process with the accord. A further economic upswing is anticipated following the meanwhile existing trilateral agreement with the USA and Canada (NAFTA). Mexico hopes to carry more weight among foreign investors, since it will be of greater interest as a production center because of low labor costs, supplying products to the other two signatories. After long discussions, the North America Free Trade Association (NAFTA) was officially founded on August 13, 1992.

Since 1990, real wages and income have been on the rise once again, and capital is flowing back into the country. Inflation is sinking year by year, and Salinas has also had success in the question of foreign debt. In tough negotiations with the IMF and foreign creditors, he brought their total significantly below $US 100 billion.

At the beginning of 1992, Salinas was confident that by obtaining the remission of debts, privatizing state corporations and stimulating tourism, he can rehabilitate the Mexican economy in the two remaining years of his term.

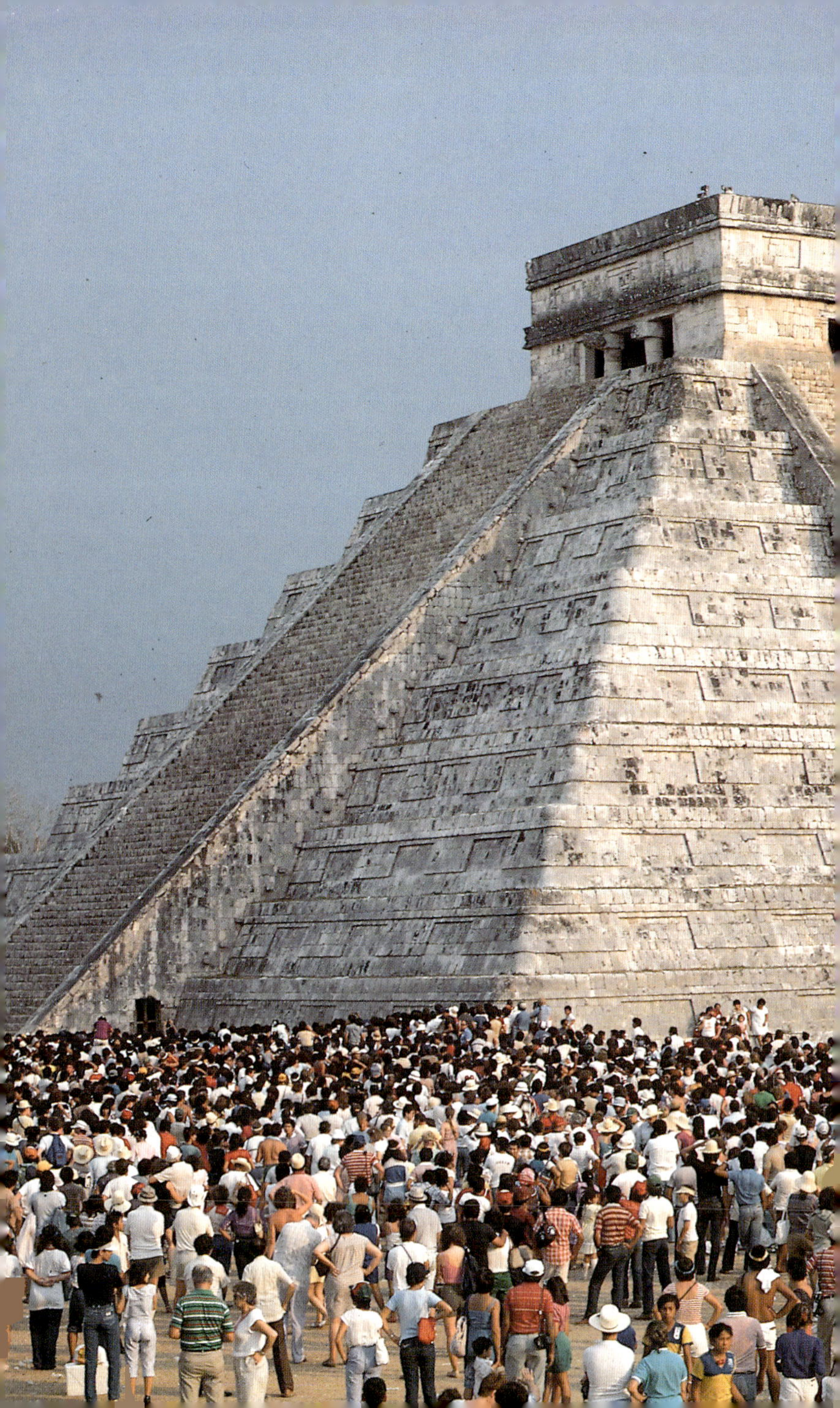

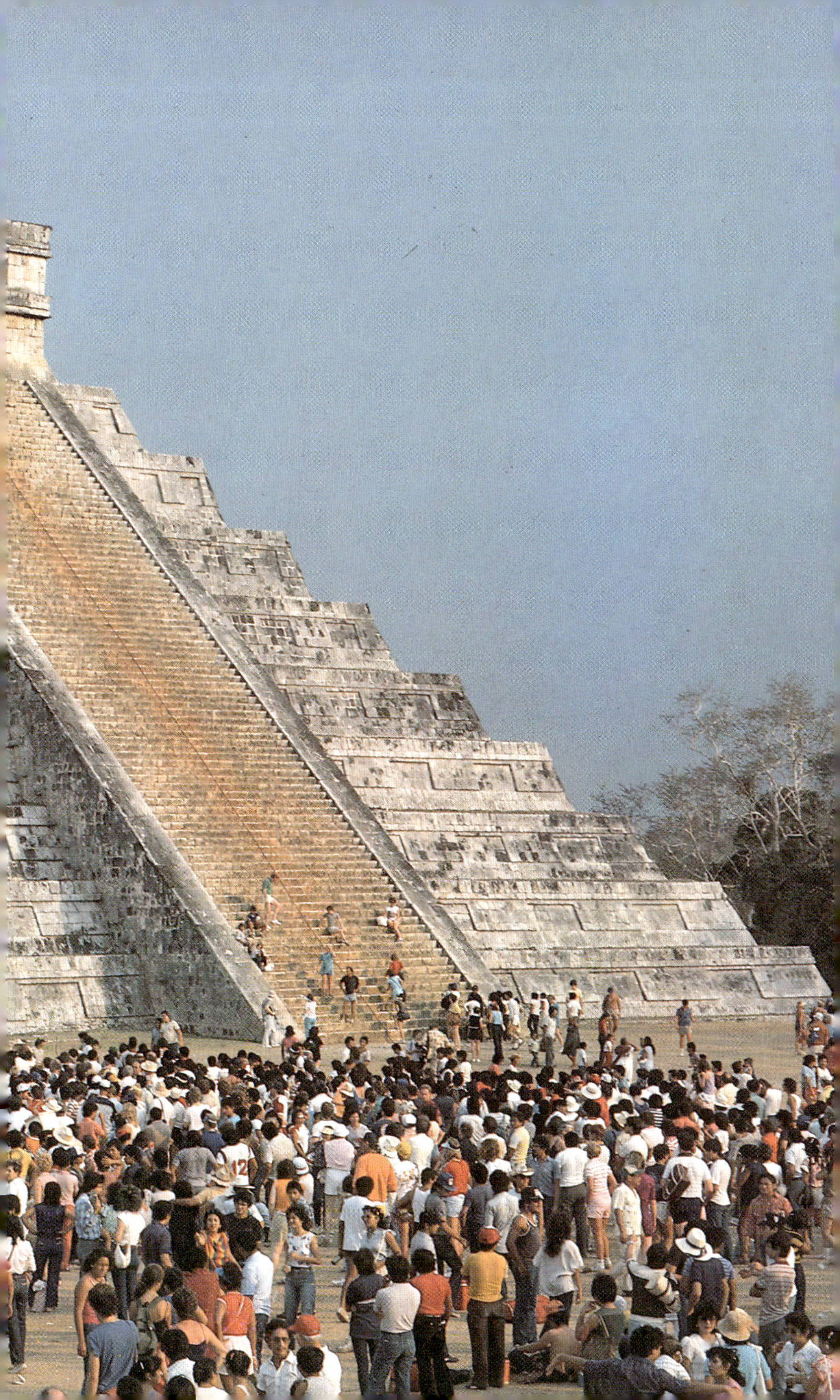

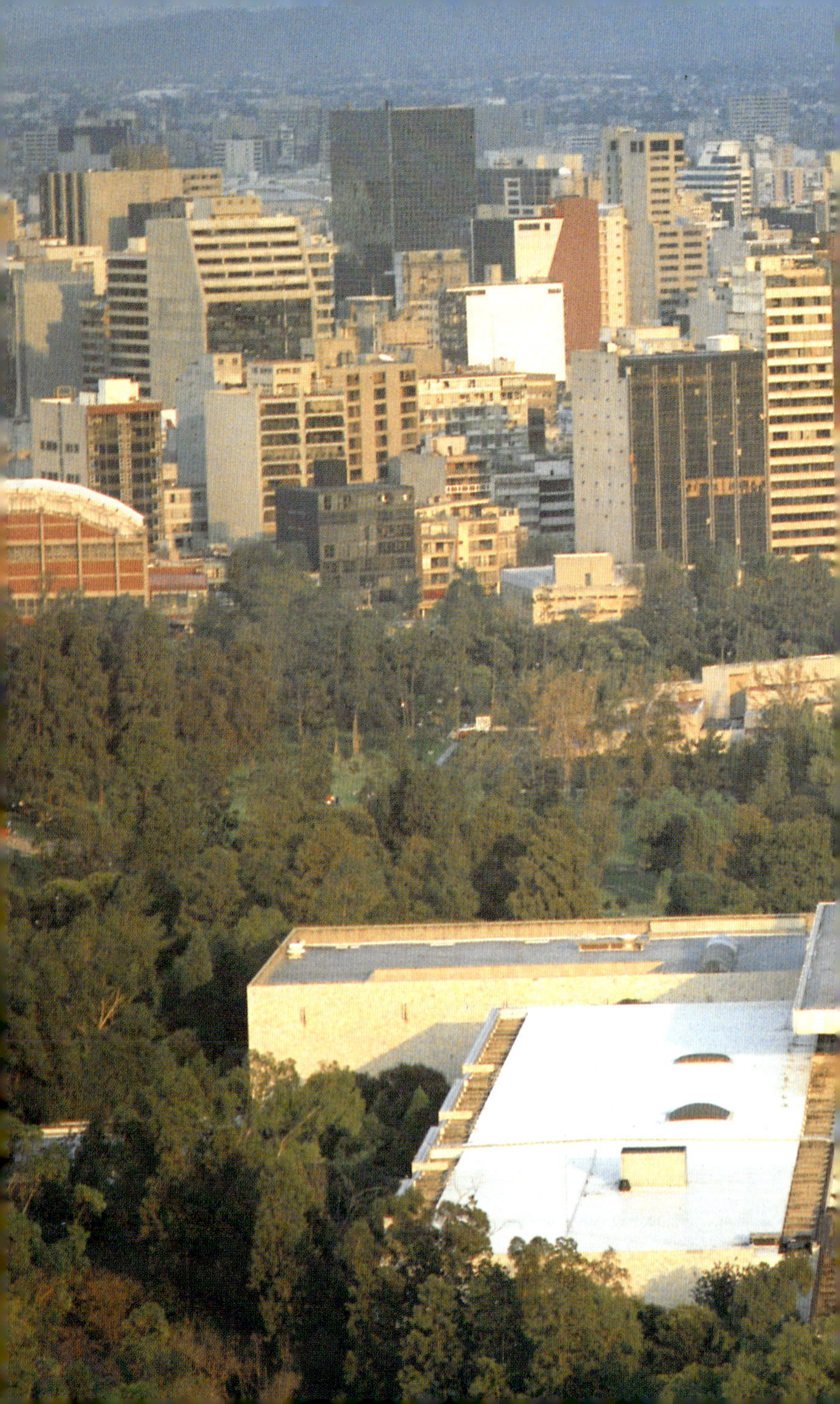

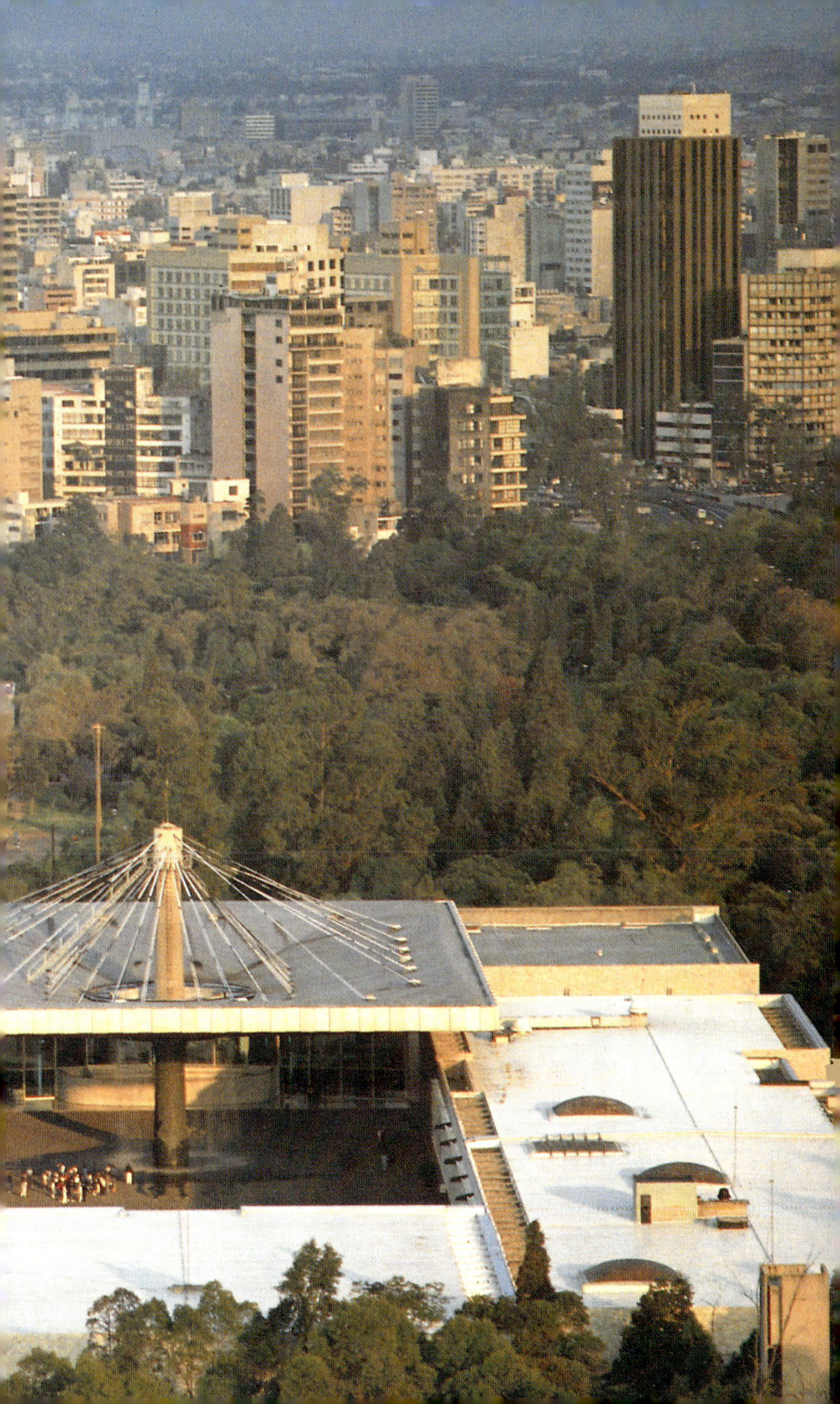

MEXICO CITY

THE MEGALOPOLIS

**MEXICO CITY
TEOTIHUACÁN**

MEXICO CITY

Founded by the Aztecs around 1325, **Mexico City** is the oldest capital in the New World. It is also one of the world's largest and highest, lying in a valley that was once a lake bed 7500 feet above the sea. Three cultures – Aztec, Iberian and modern Mexican – have melt within its bounds where modern skyscrapers tower over colonial churches and the ruins of pre-Columbian temples.

The metropolitan area takes in more than 1000 square miles. Technicallly, there is no Mexico City. This is the *Distrito Federal*, governed by the President of the Republic through an appointed mayor, the Chief of the Federal District. The 9.8 million residents (*capitalinos*, as they style themselves, or *chilangos,* as they are scornfully dubbed by their less respectful fellow citizens) call it simply Mexico (pronounced Me-hi-co), as if everything of importance in their country is to be found in this metropolis. To a large extent they are right. This is the

Previous pages: Celebrating the equinox in Chichén Itzá. Mexico City – the National Museum of Anthropology and skyline beyond the Chapultepec Park. Left: El Angel, the Independence Monument on the Paseo de la Reforma.

political and the cultural center of the nation. Decentralization is the current buzzword as the capital, embarassingly oversized, struggles to trim its size but has yet to find a workable diet. Some 20 million or more people live in the metropolitan area that includes several *municipios* in the neighboring State of Mexico. With roughly 1000 rural migrants moving in daily and 373,000 babies born every year, the population eruption shows no sign of abating.

Mexico City is a Third World capital of hovels mingled with palaces. The altitude can be dizzying and the smog suffocating as 3.5 million cars and some 30,000 factories pump 12,000 tons of poisonous fumes into the air daily. Still, the climate delights. Really cold days are rare and the warmest are never really hot. Summer rains fall fiercely but seldom for very long, although they can briefly flood downtown streets an inundate poor outlying neighborhoods.

Although the metropolitan area covers a scant one percent of Mexico's territory, it is home to nearly a quarter of the nation's inhabitants. And a miserable home for most. About a third of the families sleep in a single room, and an estimated 40 percent of the homes lack adequate plumbing. Crime is rampant in spite of the threat of unpleasant prison condi-

MEXICO CITY

MEXICO CITY

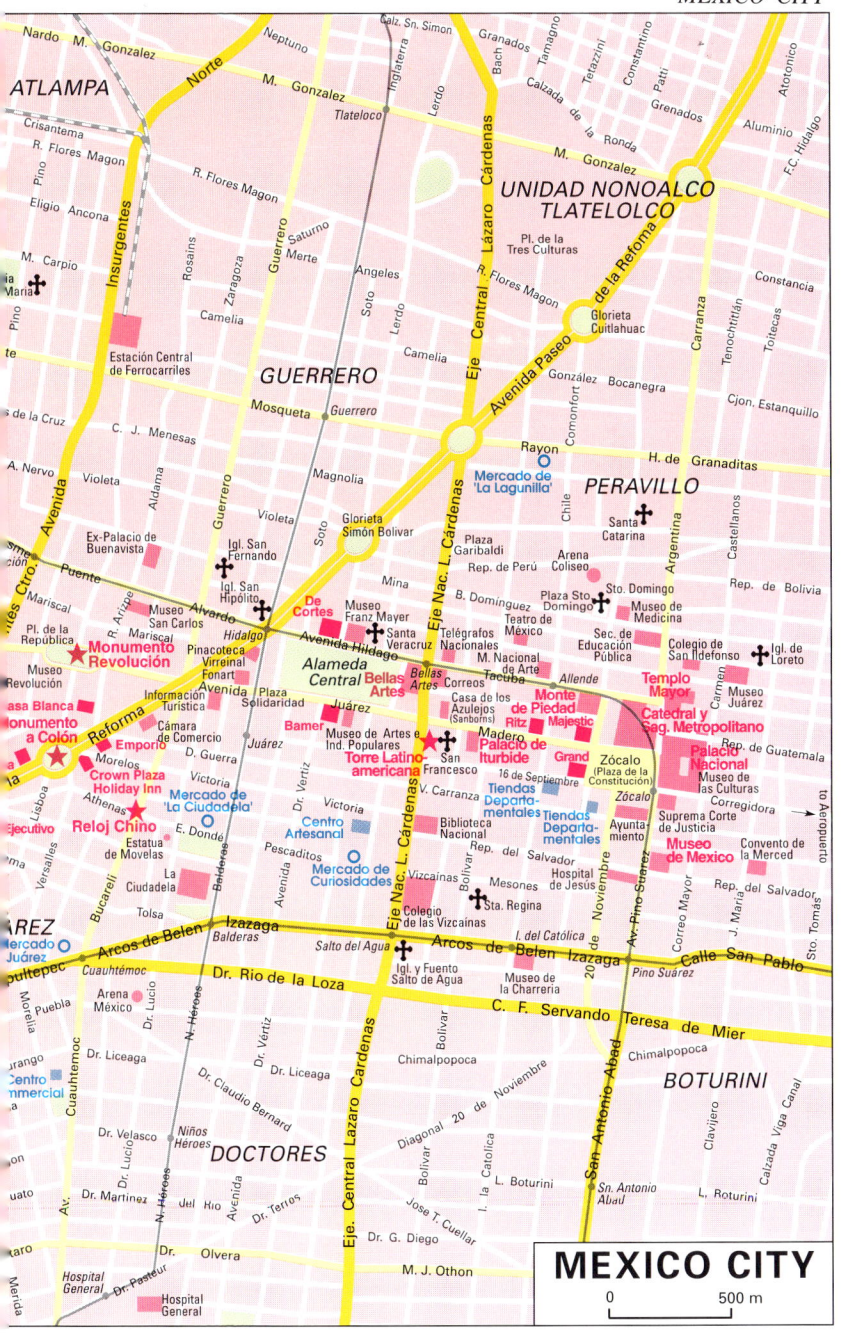

tions. Employment is difficult to come by, and when so, it is generally poorly paid: The minimum wage in Mexico is around $US 4 per day. And traveling to and from work in the city is a daunting experience. Buses and subways are intolerably overcrowded – though the fares are very cheap. Those who travel by taxi or private car still must deal with endless traffic jams.

Best time for arrival is after dark when the valley seen from the air is a sea of light and the city takes on a magical air. By day the wrinkles show. While the trip in from the airport is blessedly brief (depending on traffic, 25-40 minutes to most hotels), the road passes through the more dreary, dusty, dirty, smoggy areas of the city. Most big hotels in Mexico City stand on or near the **Paseo de la Reforma**. This majestic boulevard that leads from Chapultepec Park, the world's largest inner-city park, into Avenida Juárez, Avenida Madero and finally to the **Zócalo**, which, in a city with so many superlatives, is the largest plaza in the Americas. It also is a concentrate of Mexican history. It is bordered today by three important buildings: the National Palace, commissioned by Hernán Cortés and built from the rubble of old Tenochtitlán, the huge Metropolitan Cathedral and the ruins of the Great Temple of the Aztecs. The Halls of Moctezuma once stood around the Zócalo, which indeed was the core of the mighty Aztec empire.

It was the Aztecs who founded the city in the 14th century while searching for new pastures. Legend has it, that having landed on a vast island on Lake Texcoco, they spotted an eagle perched on a cactus while eating a snake. The Aztecs interpreted this as a signal that they had discovered a promised land. And it was, until the Spaniards destroyed both their capital and empire. The Aztecs made their last stand about a mile to the north at Tlatelolco where the modern Foreign Of-

Above: Shoeshine boy and client in Mexico City – a symbol of the contrast between rich and poor throughout the country.

ZÓCALO

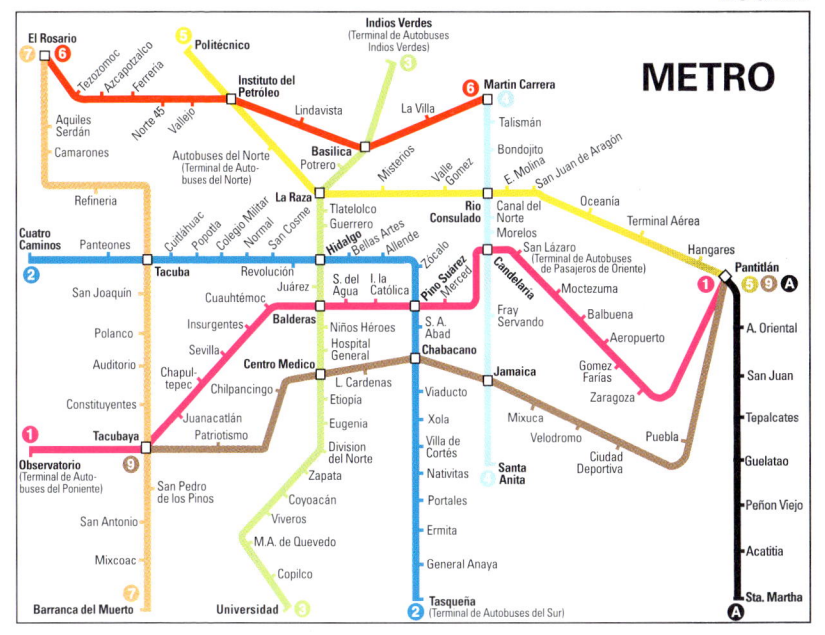

fice towers over a 17th-century church and the remains of ancient temples and pyramids at what is called the **Plaza of the Three Cultures**. "Neither triumph nor defeat", reads a plaque marking the battleground. It was the painful birth of the Mexican people. On October 2, 1968, ten days before the start of the Olympic Games, Tlatelolco saw a bloody confrontation between students and the army so that lately it has come to be called Mexico City's Tiananmen Square.

But we are still standing on the Zócalo. The ruins of the **Great Temple of the Aztecs** (Templo Mayor) just off the Zócalo are about all that remains of this grandest of the pre-Columbian cultures. The Great Temple – two temples atop a pyramid, actually – was destroyed by the Spaniards, and the covering of the pyramid chipped away leaving what appeared to be a huge earthen mound that, over the centuries, sank into the muddy subsoil as the lake around the island where the city stands was drained. In 1978, a power company crew digging a cable ditch came upon a huge altar stone buried where the temple had stood. Archeologists, convinced to find more treasures lay below, persuaded the government to launch a massive excavation project in the heart of the city. The efforts were rewarded. The Aztecs, it was revealed, built new pyramids and temples on top of old ones. The Great Temple had been reconstructed 20 times and the Spaniards had destroyed only the most recent version. Yet for all the hype, once it was opened to the public, the Great Temple disappointed tourists. The old walls and ancient steps along with platforms protected by tin roofing resembled more a construction site than a grandiose place of worship.

The **Temple Museum**, inaugurated in 1988, changed everything. On display are a great number of artifacts unearthed from the Great Temple of the Aztecs during the past decade. Lifesize figures of eagle warriors are displayed along with the skulls of their sacrificial victims. A handsome modern building of granite and marble, it is designed theatrically. Labeling – in Spanish only – is etched on glass, the exhibits dramatically lit by blue spots. The galleries are dark without being gloomy. "We saw such wondrous sights we knew not what to say or whether they were real," wrote one of Cortés' soldiers about his arrival in Tenochtitlán. "Canoes filled the lake, causeways led from shore to shore and in the distance shimmered the great City of Mexico."

When the Spaniards seized the city in 1521, they proceeded to raze it and build their version of an Iberian capital in its place. The **National Palace** (Palacio National) was among the first structures to go up on the Zócalo. Among its most prominent features are the murals by Diego Rivera, who painted the history of Mexico over the central staircase. Being of Indian extraction he had little fondness for the Spaniards. Cortés is shown as a knock-kneed, popeyed syphilitic and there is no sign of the Aztec ritual of cutting out hearts from live human beings, one of the sacrifices the Aztecs were particularly fond of. Rivera also tried to predict the future of Mexico when he took brush in hand back in the 1930s. He proved to be a better painter than a prophet, for he envisaged a country united under Marxism. As it turns out, Mexican presidents these days are Harvard MBAs. Rivera once painted a mural at New York City's Rockefeller Center showing Lenin as a savior of mankind. John D. Rockefeller, who was footing the bill, had it sledgehammered into dust in 1934. Rivera, however, repainted it at the Palace of Fine Arts in Mexico City. It is called *Man at the Crossroads*.

The National Palace is the presidential office, although Mexico City's traffic being what it is, Mexican presidents prefer to work at home. They may show up a couple of days a week for ceremonials, receiving ambassadors and the like. The presidential part of the palace is closed to the public, but you can wander all about through the rest of the place. For 300 years, Spanish viceroys made this their home. Later it became an imperial palace for the emperors Augustín Iturbide and then Maximilian of Habsburg. Both monarchs ended up before firing squads, but Maximilian left his mark. His monogram appears on the base of many of the more elegant lamps, his bust gazes down on clerks behind bronze tellers' cages in the old treasury office; the palace itself still has its "imperial" stairway and "imperial" garden.

The **Metropolitan Cathedral**, close by the ruins of the Great Temple and across from the National Palace, dominates the Zócalo. It is imposing and boasts something of a mishmash of architectural styles – it took three centuries to build it – with the **Sagrario Church** (Sagrario Metropolitano) next door, a separate church built to blend in with its neighbor. Within the Cathedral, the **Altar de los Reyes** (Altar of the Kings) is considered one of the finest examples of Mexican colonial art, Baroque to end all Baroque. It was built for use by Spanish monarchs who never came. Perhaps the **Altar de Perdon** at the end of the nave was carved to forgive them. What fascinates about the cathedral is its life. Along with baptisms and first communions, it serves as a kind of employment agency. Plumbers and carpenters squat by the gates, a sign identifying the specialty of each by one foot, tools by the other. Locals who need a roof patched or a wall plastered head for the Cathedral.

Across the way stands a sanctuary for those who fail to find work, the *Monte de Piedad* (National Pawn Shop). Originally a private charity, it now is operated by the Federal Government which alone is allowed to loan money in this manner. Built more than two centuries ago, the

Right: The Cathedral of Mexico City and the Zócalo by night.

"Monte" is not particularly interesting from an architectural point of view, but it remains a favorite with visitors ever hopeful of finding a bargain (few do).

The Zócalo is the heart of the capital and part of an area comprising 600 blocks that have been designated as the **Historical Center** of Mexico City. Officially the square is designated *Plaza de la Constitución*; in colonial times it was the *Plaza de Armas*. Zócalo is a uniquely Mexican term, for in Castillian it refers to a socle, which is to say a base or a pedestal. Following independence, a statue of Spain's King Charles IV was removed from the square but the base remained for decades, giving the plaza its popular name. Today, town squares all over the country are known to the citizenry as *zócalos* and anyone seeking the center of a city needs merely inquire for it.

A place to get the feel of how the capital was when the Zócalo got its name is the **Museum of the City of Mexico** (Museo da la Ciudad de México), three blocks east of the National Palace on Pino Suarez. This splendid mansion dating back to 1528 (a bit of Aztec sculpture serves as the cornerstone), which was once the seat of the Counts of Santiago, houses the museum which tells the story of Mexico City from prehistoric times to the present, giving considerable space to the 300 years of Spanish rule. Strolling around the streets near the Zócalo shows Mexico City at what some would call its most authentic. Save for the architecture, these streets are what they might well have been had Cortés failed in his bid for conquest. Crowds teem, vendors with their stalls block sidewalks, sending pedestrians scurrying into traffic-snarled roadways where everyone seems to be lugging, pushing or pulling something.

Wanderers can stroll from the City Museum along Pino Suarez to where it becomes Republica de Argentina beyond the Zócalo and, at the corner of San Ildefonso drop into the **Ministry of Education** to see the first murals Rivera ever painted. A block away is **Plaza Santo Domingo**, heart of the old university dis-

59

trict, where the former School of Medicine has been turned into the **National Museum of Medicine**. Across the way public scribes – old men sitting before ancient typewriters – practice a profession dating from viceregal times. At one time, they usually help less fortunate citizens fill out the rather complicated forms issued by the Mexican government.

The main street of the Historical Center is **Avenida Francisco Madero**. Once known as the "Street of the Silversmiths", Madero, since colonial times, has been a thoroughfare of elegant shops, although in recent years the elegance has begun wearing thin. With its period street lamps and oldfashioned paving stones, Madero remains, however, a joy to explore. The original Sanborns – now a national chain of upscale stores and coffee shops – started out on Madero in a viceregal palace known as the **House of Tiles** (Casa de los Azulejos).

The building dates back to the late 16th century and at one time served as home to the Counts of Orizaba who brought in the blue tiles that adorn the facade from the Orient. This *Sanborns* is one of the good places to pick up a souvenir. The coffee shop located in a Moorish-style patio can be a nice place for a snack or a meal.

The **Iturbide Palace** (Palacio Iturbide), a block toward the Zócalo, is another aristocratic mansion from the viceregal era and in some ways the most magnificent of them all. Now owned by a bank which holds art exhibits in the public areas, the mansion served as an imperial residence during the brief reign of the first ruler of independent Mexico, the self-styled Emperor Agustin Iturbide.

The **Latin American Tower** (Torre Latinoamericana), 43 stories of blue-tinted glass, on the corner of Lázaro Cárdenas, marks where Avenida Madero and the Historical Center begin. This is now the third tallest skyscraper in Mexico City, both the PEMEX Building and the World Trade Center being higher, but view from the observation platform or restaurant on the top floor can be excellent – weather and pollution permitting. The snow-tipped Popocatepetl and Iztaccihuatl volcanoes are visible along the horizon on days when the smog is under control. Built nearly four decades ago, the tower has withstood some of Mexico City's most devastating earthquakes without so much as a cracked window. Below, looking somewhat like a fried egg when seen from up high, squats the **Palace of Fine Arts** (Palacio de Bellas Artes) which, since its completion in 1934, has sunk some 15 feet into spongy subsoil. A monument to Art Deco, the palace is both an art gallery and opera house, a place to admire paintings by Rivera and his two outstanding contemporaries, Josè Climente Orozco and David Altaro Siqueiros, as well as many others. Symphony orchestras usually perform at the palace during the season, but it is the remarkable *Ballet Folklorico,* with its stylized renderings of regional dances, that attracts most tourists.

The home of real *mariachi* music lies just four blocks north along Lázaro Cárdenas at **Plaza Garibaldi**, an unlikely name for the gathering place of *mariachis*. Here from time immemorial lovelorn swains have sought out a band to serenade a sweetheart while the rejected drown their sorrows to ranchero tunes. A square lined by "topless" bars, no longer quite as naughty as it pretends to be, Garibaldi is a favorite final nightcap stop for the slumming wealthy. In spite of a fairly strong police presence, it nonetheless remains a likely spot to have a pocket picked or a purse snatched.

During daylight hours, the nearby streets belong to those some would call the culture vultures. At the Palace of Fine Arts, Avenida Madero becomes Avenida

Right: The Palace of Fine Arts seen from the Latinoamericana Tower.

HISTORICAL CENTER

Juárez and passes **Alameda Park**, once fashionable, now a shade dingy. Many of the open spaces in the neighborhood recall where the 1985 earthquake struck. A small museum in **Solidarity Park,** by the park, houses "Sunday Afternoon in the Alameda", a Rivera mural rescued from the ruins of the old Del Prado Hotel. The **Pinacoteca Virreinal** comprises a collection of paintings from the colonial era, while on the far side of the park along Avenida Hidalgo is the **Franz Mayer Museum**, a handsomely presented eclectic exhibition of applied arts. Further west, where Hidalgo becomes Puente de Alvarado (rarely do streets in Mexico City retain the same name for more than a few blocks) stands the **San Carlos Museum**, home of some of the best classical European art to be found in Mexico. It was originally an arts academy (Rivera studied there). It is, incidontally, one of the few museums in the capital open Mondays (Tuesday it is closed).

The **National Art Museum**, east along the same street, now named Tacuba, shows some of the best works done by Mexican artists over the centuries, all in a palatial setting. Manuel Tolsa's equestrian statue of Spain's Charles IV is one of the best-known works here. Mexicans simply refer to it as *El Caballito*, "The Little Horse," ignoring the monarch sitting on it. Having stood on many sites over the years, this was the statue for which the *zócalo* (socle) was built on the Zócalo.

At the far end of Avenida Juárez, what looks like a dome without a building is just that. It is all that was completed of what was to have been the capitol building. The 1910 uprisings kept it from being finished and it now stands as the **Monument to the Revolution** (Monumento a la Revolución). Juárez leads into **Paseo de la Reforma**, an avenue laid out in the 1860s on instructions from the Emperor Maximilian. Once little more than a broad country lane, Reforma has become Mexico's most famous street. On traffic roundabouts (*glorietas*), stand shrines to Columbus and Cuauhtémoc,

PASEO DE LA REFORMA / CHAPULTEPEC

last of the Aztec emperors, as well as the **Monument to Independence** (Monumento a la Independencia) known to everyone as *El Angelito. El Angelito* marks the entrance to the famed **Pink Zone** (Zona Rosa), once trendy, now a bit tawdry, a neighborhood of boutiques, shops, cafés, restaurants and discotheques. Reforma, one of the few Mexico City avenues that keeps its name, cuts through **Chapultepec Park** (Bosque de Chapultepec), "Grasshopper Hill" in the tongue of the Aztecs), a park which served as Moctezuma's royal hunting grounds. Here the viceroys ordered **Chapultepec Castle** (Castillo de Chapultepec) built as a summer retreat, but Mexico declared independence before the builders finished. The castle became the National Military Academy, site of the final U.S. victory in the 1847 Mexican-American War. Later it served Emperor Maximilian as his palace and than became official residence of Porfirio Díaz whose 30-year dictatorship ended with the outbreak of the Mexican Revolution.

After 1949, the Mexican presidents moved the executive mansion to **Los Pinos**, also in the park. Chapultepec Castle today houses the **National Museum of History** (Museo Nacional de Historia). While it paints a picture of the past from the Conquest to the present, guides often concentrate on the woeful tale of Maximilian of Habsburg, which could easily serve as an opera libretto with all its tragedy, the beautiful empress dying a madwoman after her handsome, idealistic husband was executed. Chapultepec, 2100 acres of woods, fields, lakes, playgrounds and a zoo, is packed with museums. Most famous is the **Museum of Anthropology** (Museo Nacional de Antropología) but others include the **Museum of Modern Art** (Museo Nacional de Arte Moderno), the **Tamayo Rufino Museum** (Museo de Arte Contemporáneo Internacional Rufino Tamayo), the

Above: Acrobats perform at a red light for a few pesos. Right: Dozens of mobile stalls cater to every need in Chapultepec Park.

Natural History Museum (Museo Nacional de Historia) and the **Museum of Technology** (Museo Tecnológico).

The park itself edges **Polanco**, a smart, polished neighborhood that includes the Nikko and Stouffer Presidente hotels, numerous restaurants, cafés, boutiques and department stores for the upwardly mobile. And in order to be horizontally mobile as well, one really needs a car with chauffeur, since few establishments are within walking distance of each other and parking spaces are as scarce as diamonds.

The **Avenida Insurgentes** is Mexico City's other grand street with name that never changes. It slices through the heart of the city. One takes Insurgentes north to the **Guadalupe Basilica** and south to the Plaza Mexico Bullring, colonial San Angel, Coyoacán and University City. The basilica marks the spot where on December 12, 1531, a decade after the Conquest, the Virgin Mary appeared to one Juan Diego, an Indian convert, and to prove it imprinted her image on his tunic. That tunic is now enshrined in what to some is a rather garish sanctuary opened in 1976 to replace a crumbling, non- descript colonial chapel that could no longer handle the crowds. The Guadalupe image was used on Mexico's first flag, and it is still an important icon on house altars and in workplaces throughout the country. It is perhaps no coincidence that the first Mexican to win the Miss Universe contest is named Guadalupe.

Off in the other direction (Insurgentes not only retains its name, but is the only street that actually crosses Mexico City from one end to the other), the avenue leads to some of the more fascinating areas of the capital. First landmark, two miles south of the Cuauhtémoc Monument and the Reforma intersection, is the not-yet-complete 51-story **World Trade Center**, a building originally designed as a hotel but which stood unoccupied for some two decades.

Part of the project is the **Polyforum Cultural David Alfaro Siqueiros**, presenting one of the last works of one of

Mexico's master muralists. The mural here, *The March of Humanity,* is a three-dimensional "sculpto-painting" of metals and acrylics on asbestos-covered concrete, stretching over 27,000 square feet. All this surrounds a theater, an art gallery and exhibition of folk art, giving meaning to the term Polyforum.

The next few miles in southerly direction is what might be called Mexico City's restaurant row. Here office towers soar over the **Sunken Gardens** (Parque Hundido) with its replicas of prehispanic sculptures. Just off Insurgentes is the **Plaza Mexico**, the largest bullring in the world, seating 50,000 (the soccer stadium virtually next door seats 64,000 and is only the third largest in the city, one indication of bullfighting's declining popularity in favor of soccer). The bulls draw the crowds on Sundays; the day before,

however, people head to **San Angel** and the **Saturday Bazaar** (Bazar Sabado), arguably the best place to shop for crafts in the entire country. San Angel has retained the gracious air of its colonial past and has become something of a ghetto for successful intellectuals – artists, writers, filmmakers and the like. The house where Diego Rivera lived – and died in 1957 – is now a little museum.

Perhaps a mile to the east, on the other side of Insurgentes, in the equally captivating, old-fashioned Coyoacán district, is the shrine to Rivera's wife, the **Frida Kahlo Museum**. Coyoacán reminds one of Paris' Latin Quarter a touch more bohemian than upscale San Angel. Indeed it is where many students at the National University find living quarters. The shady twin plazas are adjoined by bookstores serving espresso and cafés appealing to the scholarly. Hernán Cortés settled briefly in Coyoacán following the Conquest and Leon Trotsky died in exile here, murdered by a Stalinist agent. Trotsky's home is now the **Trotsky Museum**.

Above: The University serves as an open air gallery of muralismo (Mosaic by D. A. Siquieros) Right: Traditional weekend entertainment – a boat-party in Xochimilco.

As for the **National Autonomous University of Mexico (UNAM)**, founded in the 1550s, it now straddles a southern stretch of Avenida Insurgentes in University City. With its magnificently muraled buildings and avant-garde architecture, **University City** in the late 1950s was one of the capital's prime tourist attractions, but of late has become more of an add-on for visitors with an extra day in town and nothing better to do. The outdoor works by Rivera and Siqueiros, along with the Juan O'Gorman mosaics covering the library, are striking, but the graffiti and mob ambience (some 300,000 students are registered at the university, although a scant 30% ever manage to graduate) lessens the appeal. As a center of learning, UNAM long ago was eclipsed by other colleges in the capital and the provinces.

Less than a mile south along Insurgentes lies the **Cuicuilco Archeological Zone** with its curious circular pyramid. While not as impressive as one might imagine, it dates back perhaps 3000 years and represents all that is left of the oldest known settlement in the Valley of Mexico. All around stand the modernistic suburban homes of **Pedregal**, acres of rock garden formed by lava and, not far off, glittering **Perisur**, Mexico City's most lavish shopping mall.

The **Floating Gardens of Xochimilco** lie a few miles east of Insurgentes, a reminder of Mexico City the way it was in Aztec times. Actually, the gardens do not float, but once they did. Over five centuries ago, the pre-Columbian inhabitants in these parts, needing more farmland, placed earth-covered rafts in these swampy regions, on planted vegetables in the soil. Over the years, roots extended down to the bottom through the shallow waters. Now flat-bottomed flower-bedecked barges ferry passengers along the canals amid boats loaded with *taco* vendors and *mariachi* bands. Weekends are especially festive with hordes of Mexican families coming for an outing. Xochimilco also is a standard treat on Sunday excursions that feature a morning

MUSEUM OF ANTHROPOLOGY

performance of the *Ballet Folklorico* and bullfights in the afternoon. Tour packages, while they may not seem especially sophisticated, are the most efficient, effective and usually least costly way of getting to see Mexico City.

National Museum of Anthropology

Mexico's appreciation of its archeological discoveries has grown hand-in-hand with the awakening of its national consciousness. The Spaniards by and large destroyed Mexico's indigenous heritage. After the Revolution, at the beginning of the 19th century, awareness of this vanished cultural heritage began to germinate. In 1825, at a time when Europeans were also investigating their "roots" as it were, work began on a collection, which Emperor Maximilian later

Above: Jade mask from a grave in Palenque. Right: From the Pyramid of the Moon you can survey the whole archeological site of Teotihuacán.

had installed in a palace in 1865 – the new country's first national museum.

A century later the number of exhibits had grown so large that there was no room left to warehouse them properly. The **Museo Nacional de Antropología** in Chapultepec Park was opened in the autumn of 1964, after a 19-month construction period, at a cost of $US 20 million. Architect Pedro Ramírez Vásquez created a modern structure, timeless in its simplicity, which is now among the most significant museums of its kind in the world. A visit to it is a must for the anthropologist and layperson alike.

At the entrance, visitors are received by an uncompleted seven-meter-tall, 165-ton sculpture of the rain-god Tláloc. Orientation in the two-level museum is simple. Individual halls are devoted to each cultural complex. They are arranged in such a manner that one can always return to the central patio instead of having to make a complete tour. Visitors in a hurry can thus take the shortest path in pursuit of their particular interests, punctuated by breaks under the open sky.

Hall I offers an introduction to the interrelationship between anthropology and other scientific branches. Hall II presents **Central America** from the perspective of its common cultural bases. Hall III informs the visitor about Mexico's **original inhabitants** from the nomads to the sedentary livestock breeders. The **Pre-Classical cultures** in hall IV are subdivided into four epochs, distinguished by the forms of their pottery. Also worthy of special note is a *Chipicuaro* figure dating from around 1000 BC. Hall V is devoted to **Teotihuacán**, which features an impressive full-size replica of the Temple of Quetzalcóatl and its serpent heads, painted in the original hues.

The culture of the **Toltecs**, whose name means "craftsman and scholar", is a so-called acculturation; in this case the residual culture of the fallen Teotihuacán Empire. Tula (formerly Tollan), the Tol-

MUSEUM OF ANTROPOLOGY

tec capital city, was founded around 900 AD. In Hall VI one can get an impression of its chief architectural landmark, the Atlantes colossal temple statues over 4.5 meters in height. The people of Tula also revered Quetzalcóatl, whose characteristic symbol, the feathered serpent, is everywhere to be seen. Hall VII, titled **Mexica** (Aztecs), leaves the visitor with some enduring impressions. The *Mexica* were the most widely known and politically significant ethnic group of pre-Columbian Mexico. The hall features the commanding, subtly illuminated Aztec calendar stone, four meters in diameter and weighing 24 tons. In the center of the tremendous basalt slab is an image of the face of Tonatiuh, the sun-god, with his tongue sticking out. He is surrounded by symbols arranged in a circle, a representation of the universe. The third circle from the center gave the stone its name. The Indigenas' calendar-cycle, a complicated combination of solar (or working) calendar, was composed of 18 periods of 20 days plus five "nameless" or "superfluous" days, and the ritual calendar, consisting of 20 periods of 30 days. The years ended simultaneously once every 52 years, at which times the pyramids were over-built and everyday articles were destroyed. Afterward, a new life was symbolically begun. Moctezuma's head ornament is a facsimile (the original is in Vienna).

Hall VIII, which concentrates on **Oaxaca**, encompasses the Zapotec and Mixtec cultures. Central emphasis is placed on their cultural centers in Monte Albán and Mitla (with frieze reproductions) in the Oaxacan highlands. The abundance of exhibits (mostly burial gifts) made of gold, silver, jade and sea-shell display a high level of craftsmanship. The Olmecs, Totonacs and Huaxtecs, cultures of the **Gulf Coast** in present-day Veracruz region, are treated in Hall IX.

The museum's richest section from the perspective of both artistry and art history is in Hall X devoted to the **Mayan Empire**. The models of various Mayan centers provide a good overview of their ar-

TEOTIHUACÁN

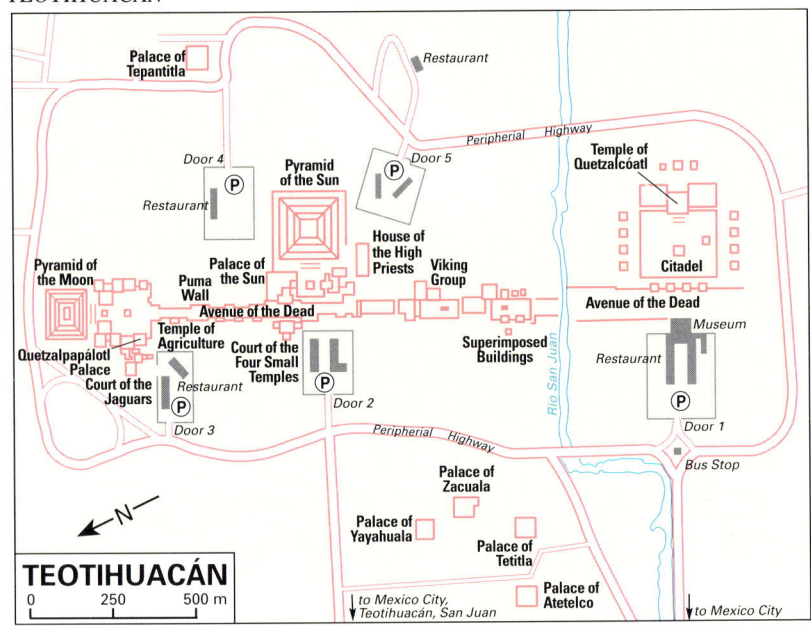

chitectural achievements; nor should one miss a descent into the pyramid crypt of a Palenque priest-king. The nomadic cultures of **Northern Mexico** (Hall XI) and the cultures of the **West** (Hall XII) round off a tour of the ground level.

The **ethnological collection** on the upper level (Halls XIII to XXI) features true-to-life model portrayals of the lifestyles of Indigenas' through the whole of Mexico. Hall XXII is a presentation on the **Nahua**, who lived scattered throughout the Mexican highlands.

TEOTIHUACÁN

Upon the Aztecs' arrival in the Mexican highlands, **Teotihuacán**, 50 kilometers to the northwest of Mexico City, was a desolate, nameless place long since abandoned by its inhabitants.

In *Nahuatl*, the Aztec language, Teotihuacán means "Place where the Gods are born". According to Aztec mythology, the gods assembled here following the death of the Fourth Sun to create the Era of the Fifth Sun. Then, after the downfall of Teotihuacán (and the accompanying death of its inhabitants), the gods were filled with despair, because they no longer had anybody to worship them. So, the deities Nanauatzin and Tecciztecatl dove down from the void of the universe into a blazing pyre, in order to reappear as the sun and moon after their self-sacrifice. This legend explains why the Moctezuma II made a pilgrimage each year to Teotihuacán, where he had a temple erected next to the Pyramid of the Sun. In doing so he wanted to pay homage to the gods. Aztec rulers told the Franciscan monk Bernardo de Sahagún (1499-1570) that Teotihuacán became the burial place for Aztec kings, who were then resurrected as a *teotl* (god) after their deaths.

When the Spaniards discovered this field of ruins, which had been overgrown with vegetation for some 750 years, they were unable to imagine its significance as one of Meso-America's largest cultural, intellectual and religious centers. In 1889, motivated by vague conjectures, the Mexican-born archeologist Leopoldo Batres initiated the site's first excavations. To this day far from all the site's mysteries have been unraveled. The site is located some 50 kilometers to the northwest of the capital and consists of an area of some 4 by 2.1 kilometers (unearthed so far). The myths and legends surrounding it remain in a haze that will most probably never clear.

Teotihuacán was founded around 150 BC in a fertile valley with a strategically advantageous situation. The pile-dwellings in the Valley of México, the regions around Puebla, Cholula and the coast of Veracruz were all relatively easy to reach. By the beginning of the Christian Era there were already some 10,000 people living there on an area of six square kilometers.

While the society here must have been purely agrarian during its first centuries, it wasn't long before it was profiting from a monopoly: In its workshops, obsidian was fashioned into a variety of articles. Soon, Teotihuacán had developed into a formidable center of trade and culture. Shortly after the beginning of the Christian Era, the city had grown to a population of around 30,000, spread out over 20 square kilometers. Execution of a general architectural plan was begun; it had been largely completed by 450 AD. During the first 200 years, the **Pyramid of the Sun** was constructed, with a height of 63 meters, a basal surface of 225 by 225 meters and a total of 365 steps; the **Pyramid of the Moon** (height 43 meters, 112 steps, basal surface area 120 by 150 meters) as well as 23 **temples** and **palaces** on an east-west axis 42 to 44 meters in width and nearly four kilometers long. The Spaniards named it *Calzada de los Muertos* (Avenue of the Dead) because they surmised that it concealed the graves of the *teotihuacaños*. Heading toward the east, the level of this "avenue" between the citadel and the Pyramid of the Moon drops 27 meters terrace-style. This creates the optical effect that the Pyramid of the Moon appears to be the dominating edifice.

Only a portion of this one-time metropolis is open to viewing by the general public, although it includes the most important and beautiful complexes of the inner city along the Avenue of the Dead. They are, from east to west**,** the **Citadel**, the **Temple of Quetzalcóatl** and the **Viking Group**; next to the Pyramid of the Sun is the **House of the High Priests** and the **Palace of the Sun**; across from these the **Court of the Four Small Temples**; after that the **Temple of Agriculture** and opposite it the **Puma Wall**. Extending along the base of the Pyramid of the Moon is the **Quetzalpapálotl Palace** with the **Court of the Jaguars**.

During its Golden Era, between 200 and 650 AD, the theocratically governed society became a religious, economic and ultimately a military superpower. By 700 AD, Teotihuacán had passed its zenith. Some indications of the decline have been identified from the final Metepec epoch; signs have been found of a great conflagration, and there is unmistakable evidence of the ceremonial center's violent destruction. Around 750 AD the city was abandoned by its inhabitants. Teotihuacán's demise is still unexplained. One hypothesis suggests that, toward the end of the sixth century, trade with the rest of Meso-America had declined, while the raw materials necessary to make their own export products were lacking. Other conjectures include epidemics or a popular rebellion which aimed at ousting a military dictatorship down, leaving chaos in its place. Yet another theory proposes that the city's growth (in the end covering about 120 square kilometers) fostered the development of a bureaucracy that ultimately made unscrupulous abuse of its power, until it simply exhausted the motivating force of its society's intellectual and cultural energies.

MEXICO CITY
Accommodation

Rates for a double room in the *LUXURY* category range from 65 US$ to more than 100 US$ per night, *MODERATE* 40-65 US$, *BUDGET* 30-40 US$. Hotels with very basic accommodation – little to no comfort – start at 20 US$.

LUXURY: **Camino Real**, Mariano Escobedo 700, Tel: 203-2125. **María Isabel Sheraton**, Paseo de la Reforma 325, Tel: 207-3933. **Nikko Mexico**, Campos Eliseos 204, Tel: 203-4020. **Presidente Chapultepec (Stouffer Presidente)**, Campos Eliseos 218, Tel: 250-7700.
Aristos, Paseo de la Reforma 276, Tel: 211-0111. **Century Zona Rosa**, Liverpool 152, Tel: 584-7111. **Clarion Reforma**, Paseo de la Reforma, Tel: 207-9075. **Crowne Plaza Holiday Inn**, Paseo de la Reforma 80, Tel: 566-7777. **Del Prado**, Marina Nacional 399, Tel: 254-4400. **Fiesta Americana Aeropuerto**, near the airport, free transport, Tel: 762-0192. **Flamingos Plaza**, Av. Revolución 333, Tel: 271-7044. **Galería Plaza**, Hamburgo 195 (Zona Rosa), Tel: 211-0014. **Holiday Inn Aeropuerto**, at the airport, free transport, Tel: 762-0192. **Howard Johnson Gran Hotel**, 16 de Septiembre 82, Tel: 510-4049. **Imperial**, Paseo de la Reforma 64, Tel: 566-4879. **Krystal Zona Rosa**, Liverpool 155, Tel: 211-0092. **Marco Polo**, Amberes 27 (Zona Rosa), Tel: 207-1893. **Plaza Florencia**, Florencia 61 (Zona Rosa), Tel: 211-0064. **Royal**, Amberes 78 (Zona Rosa), Tel: 525-4850. **Sevilla Palace**, Paseo de la Reforma 105, Tel: 566-8877. **Suites Amberes**, Amberes 64 (Zona Rosa), Tel: 533-1306. **Suites Niza**, Niza 73 (Zona Rosa), Tel: 511-9540/48. **Suites San Marino**, Rio Tiber 107 (near the Zona Rosa), Tel: 533-6680.
MODERATE: **Ambassador**, Humboldt 38, Tel: 518-0110. **Bristol**, Plaza Necaxa 17, Tel: 533-6060. **Calinda Geneve**, Londres 130 (Zona Rosa), Tel: 211-0071. **Corinto**, Vallarta 24, Tel: 566-6555. **Del Angel**, Rio Lerma 154, Tel: 533-1032. **Del Bosque**, Melchor Ocampo 323, Tel: 545-6429. **De Cortés**, Hidalgo 85, Tel: 585-0322. **Gran Hotel Ciudad de Mexico**, 16 Septiembre 82, Tel: 510-4040. **Majestic**, Madero 73, Tel: 521-8600. **Plaza Reforma**, Insurgentes Centro 149, Tel: 535-0556. **Reforma**, Paseo de la Reforma, corner Paris, Tel: 546-9680. **Ritz**, Madero 30, Tel: 518-1340. **Romano Diana**, Rio Lerma 237 (near the Zona Rosa), Tel: 211-0109.
BUDGET: **Bamer**, Juárez 52, Tel: 512-9060. **Casa Blanca**, La Fragua 7, Tel: 566-3211. **Diplomático**, Insurgentes Sur 1105, Tel: 563-6066. **El Ejecutivo**, Viena 8, Tel: 566-6422. **Edison**, Edison 106, Tel: 566-0933. **Emporio**, Paseo de la Reforma 124, Tel: 566-7766. **Fleming,** Revillagigedo 35, Tel: 510-4530. **Isabel,** Isabel de Católica 63, Tel: 518-1213. **María Cristina**, Rio Lerma 31, Tel: 546-9880. **Metropol**, Luís Moya 39, Tel: 510-8660. **Monte Carlo**, Uruguay 69, Tel: 585-1222. **Park Villa**, Gomez Pedraza 68, Tel: 515-5245. **Prim**, Versalles 46, Tel: 592-1609. **Regente**, Paris 9, Tel: 566-8933. **Del Valle**, Independencia 35, Tel: 585-2399.

Restaurants

Mexico City offers an extremely varied culinary palette, from the typical Mexican *cantina* to luxury restaurants and specialities from all parts of the world. Therefore, the following list of restaurants is by no means complete; the town quarter is given in brackets.

INTERNATIONAL: Top-quality cuisine: **Cicero**, Londres 185 (Zona Rosa), Tel: 525-6130. **Delmonicos**, Londres 87 (Zona Rosa), Tel: 514-7003. **Estoril**, Génova 75 (Zona Rosa), Tel: 511-3421. **Hacienda de los Morales**, Vázques de Mella 525 (Los Morales), Tel: 540-3225.
Los Irabien, Avenida de la Paz 45 (San Angel), Tel: 660-2382. **Isadora**, Molière 50 (Polanco), Tel: 520-7901.
Les Moustaches, Rio Sena 88 (Cuauhtémoc), Tel: 533-3390. **El Olivo**, Varsovia 13 (Zona Rosa), Tel: 511-4225. **San Angel Inn**, Calle Palmas 50 (San Angel), Tel: 548-4514.

Good international cuisine: **Andersons**, Paseo de la Reforma 382 (Juárez), Tel: 525-1006. **Los Puertas**, Pedro Luis de Ogazón 102 (San Angel), Tel: 550-7489. **Isla Victoria**, Monte Kemerún 120 (Lomas de Chapultepec), Tel: 520-5597. **Passy**, Amberes 10 (Zona Rosa), Tel: 511-0257. **Rivoli**, Hamburgo 123 (Zona Rosa), Tel: 525-6682 and 528-7789.
MEXICAN: **Fonda del Recuerdo**, Bahía de las Palmas (Anzures), Tel: 545-1652, elegant. **Fonda el Refugio**, Liverpool 166 (Zona Rosa), Tel: 528-5823, high standard, expensive. **Bellinghausen**, Londres 95 (Zona Rosa), Tel: 511-9035. **Café de Tacuba**, Tacuba 28 (Centro), Tel: 518-4950. **Danubio**, Uruguay 3 (Centro), Tel: 512-0912. **Focolare**, Hamburgo 87 (Zona Rosa), Tel: 511-2679. **Fonda Don Chon**, Regina 159 (Centro), Tel: 522-2170. **Fonda el Pato**, Dinamarca 9 (Juárez), Tel: 546-2272. **Hostería de Santa Domingo**, Domíguez 72 (Centro), Tel: 510-1434. **La Cazuelas**, Colombia 69 (Centro), Tel: 563-3956. **Lincoln**, Revillagigedo 24 (Centro), Tel: 510-1468. **Majestic Hotel Roof**, at the Zócalo end of Madero, rooftop restaurant with unique view across the Zócalo, Tel: 521-8600.
SEAFOOD: **Costa Dorada**, Avenida Ejército

GUIDEPOST MEXICO CITY

Nacional 648 (Polanco), Tel: 545-3086, elegant. **La Marinera**, Liverpool 183 (Zona Rosa), Tel: 511-3568. **La Trucha Vagabunda**, Londres 104 (Zona Rosa, in the Jacaranda Arcade), Tel: 533-3178. **Prendes**, 16 de Septiembre 10 (Centro), Tel: 521-1878.

Museums

Among the 63 museums of Mexico City the following deserve a special mention:

HISTORICAL CENTER: **Museo de la Alameda,** Plaza de la Solidaridad, Tue-Sun 10 am-4 pm. **Museo Nacional de Artes e Industrias Populares**, Av. Juárez 44, Tue-Sun 10 am-4 pm. **Museo Franz Mayer**, Av. Hidalgo 45, Tue-Sun 10 am-5 pm. **Museo del Palacio de Bellas Artes**, Av. Juárez / Lázaro Cárdenas, Tue-Sun 10.30 am-6.30 pm. **Museo Postal**, Av. Lázaro/ Tacuba, Mon-Fri 8 am-3 pm, Sat 9 am-1 pm.

Museo Nacional de Arte, Tacuba 8, Wed-Sun 10 am-6 pm. **Museo de la Ciudad de México**, Pino Suarez 30, Tue-Sun 9.30 am-7.30 pm. **Museo del Templo Mayor**, behind the cathedral, opposite Argentinia, Tuesday-Sunday 9 am-5 pm. **Museo Nacional de las Culturas**, Calle Moneda 13, Tue-Sun 9 am-5.30 pm, Sun 9 am-4 pm. **Museo de San Carlos**, Puente de Alvarado 50, Mon-Sun 10 am-6 pm, closed Tue.

DISTRICT SAN ANGEL: **Museo Estudio Diego Rivera**, Diego Rivera corner Altavista, Tue-Sun 10 am-6 pm. **Museo de El Carmen**, Av. Revolución 4 and 6, Mon-Sun 10 am-5 pm.

Museo de Arte Carrillo Gil, Av. Revolución, Tue-Sun 9 am-6 pm.

CHAPULTEPEC PARK: **Museo Nacional de Antropología**, Paseo de la Reforma/Gandhi, Tue-Sun 9 am-7 pm, Sun and public holidays 10 am-6 pm. **Museo Rufino Tamayo**, Paseo de la Reforma/Gandhi, Tue-Sun 10 am-6 pm. **Museo Nacional de Historia**, Castillo de Chapultepec, Tue-Sun 9 am-5 pm. **Museo Technológico**, Bosque de Chapultepec 2 A, Tue-Sat 9 am-5 pm, Sun 9 am-1 pm. **Centro Cultural Arte Contemporáneo**, Campos Eliseos/Jorge Eliot, Tue-Sun 10 am-6 pm. **Sala de Arte Público Siqueiros**, Mon-Fri 10 am-5 pm, Sat 10 am-1 pm. **Museo de Arte Moderno**, Paseo de la Reforma/Gandhi, Mon-Sun 10 am-6 pm.

DISTRICT COYOACAN: **Museo Nacional de Culturas Populares**, Hidalgo 289, Wed, Fri, Sat 10 am-8 pm, Tue, Thur 10 am-4 pm, Sun 11 am-1 pm. **Museo Frida Kahlo**, Londres 247, Tue-Sun 10 am-2 pm and 3-6 pm. **Museo León Trotsky**, Viena 45, Tue-Fri 10 am-2 pm and 3-5.30 pm, Sat and Sun 10.30 am-4 pm.

DISTRICT REFORMA-INSURGENTES: **Museo Nacional de la Revolución,** Plaza de la República, Tue-Sun 9 am-1 pm. **Museo de Cera de la Ciudad de México**, Londres 6, Mon-Sun 11 am-7 pm. **Museo de Instrumentos Musicales**, Liverpool 16, Mon-Fri 9.30 am-2.30 pm.

Post / Telecommunication

Central Post Office, Lázaro Cárdenas/Tacuba opposite the Palacio de Bellas Artes, Tel: 521-7394, Mon-Sat 9 am-8 pm. **Telegrams**, Tacuba 8, opposite the Central Post Office, Tel: 519-0216, national and international service, telegrams abroad can take several days to arrive, daily from 8 am-8 pm. **Telephone** (long distance calls): Best connection from the hotels, but very expensive. There are 16 phone-boxes for long-distance calls (*Casetas de Larga Distancia*) in Mexico City, for instance at the airport Sala E (6.30 am-9.30 pm). Airport Sala A (7 am-11 pm). Buenavista Station (8 am-9 pm). Central de Autobuses del Norte / Metro-Station Terminal del Norte (5), 8 am-9 pm. Local calls are free of charge from old phone-boxes and hotels, otherwise phone-boxes take 100-, 500- and 1000-Peso-coins.

Transportation

Metro (underground): 9 lines - fast, clean and cheap, one train every 30 seconds during rush hours. Lines 1-2-3 run weekdays from 5 am-0.30 am, Lines 4-5-6-7 from 6 am-0.30 am, all lines Sat 6-1.30 am, Sun 7 am-0.30 am.

Buses: Buses run every 10-15 minutes, along the main roads buses stop at official bus-stops only, on smaller roads they can be hailed by hand signs. **Taxis**: Constantly in motion - no official stops with the exception of *limousines* or *turismo*-taxis in front of the hotels (fare ca. three times higher than ordinary taxis, must be agreed on before departure!). All taxis must have a working taximeter, cheapest are the yellow-orange VW-beetles. For "better" taxis at the airport and all bus terminals tickets at fixed prices. *Sitios* are radio-taxis, numbers are listed in the Yellow Pages, i.e. COTAVI, Tel: 563-8618. *Peseros* or *colectivos* are minibuses running on fixed routes, slightly more expensive than buses. **Rental Cars**: Avis, Tel: 571-3483. Hertz, Tel: 511-5686. Smaller car-rental agencies have their offices in the Zona Rosa.

Tourist Information

Federal Tourist Office, Amberes 54 (Zona Rosa), Tel: 525-9380, 9 am-9 pm. **Secretaria de Turismo**, Presidente Mazarik 172, Tel: 250-8555 for general information, Tel: 250-0123 for tourist information, Tel: 545-4613 for tourist help, Tel: 250-4618 for complaints, all numbers Mon-Fri 8 am-8 pm. **Department of Tourist Security**, Tel: 250-0151, 250-0493 and 250-0589, information, emergencies, complaints, 24-hour-service.

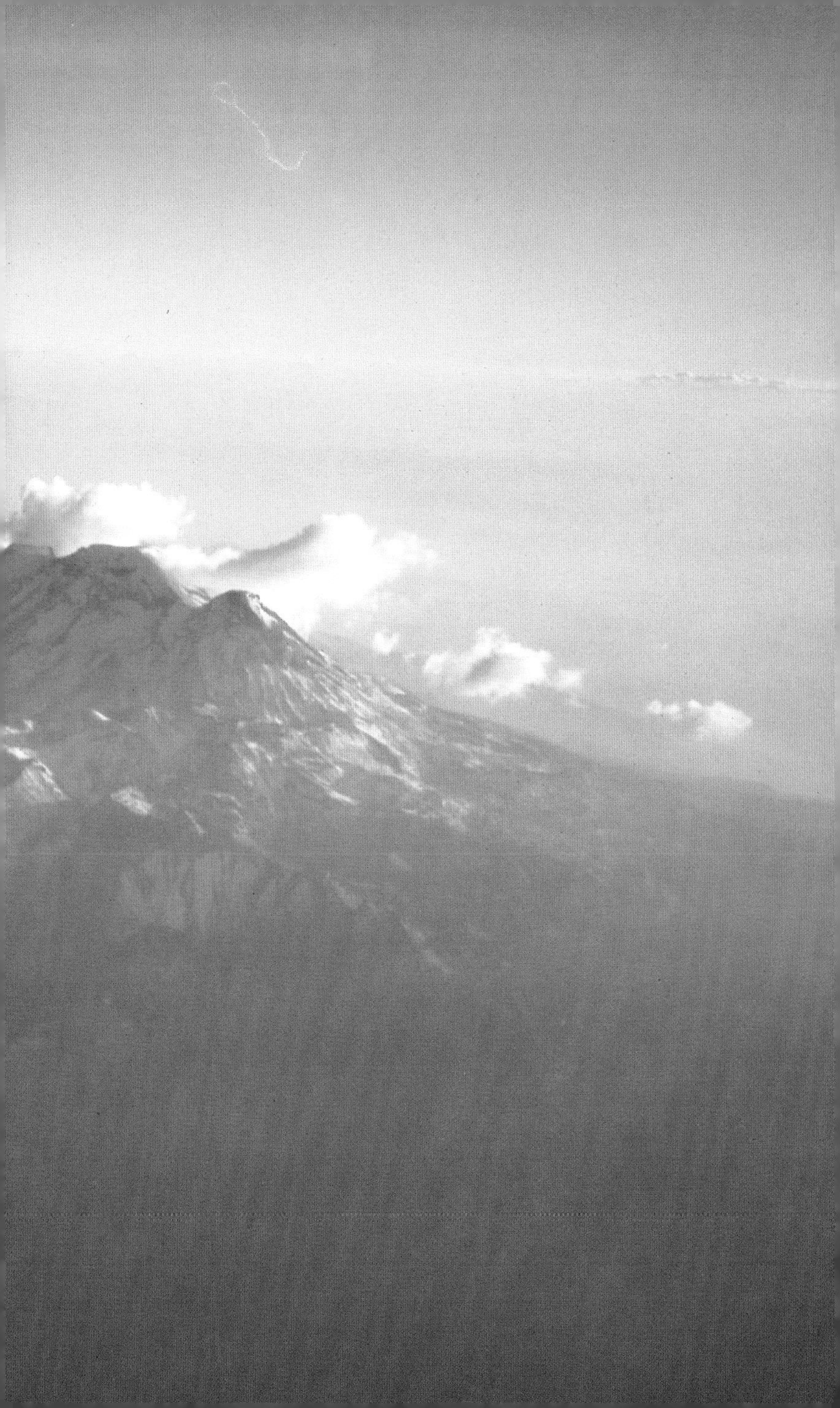

TULA

COLONIAL SPLENDOR AND TEMPLE PYRAMIDS

TULA
TAXCO
PUEBLA
TOLUCA

TULA

Driving north out of Mexico City, past all the squalor in the outskirts, you climb into the rocky mountains along the same route taken by the natives of Teotihuacán. These early Indians, probably Toltecs, one of the great Indigena civilizations to inhabit Mexico, built their capital called **Tula** (80 kilometers northwest of Mexico City and 30 kilometers north of Tepotzotlán), which flourished until 1156. It was during this time that Quetzalcóatl (the "Plumed Serpent") ruled in a time of peace and prosperity.

As the traveler moves across the treeless terrain he should be on the lookout for signs of the earlier civilizations. Here and there stand three-meter-high, weather-worn statues that lead to the entrance of the site where the Toltecs once dwelled. The complex of pyramids cannot be overlooked. The main pyramid rises shear from the earth in the midst of pastel shades of pinks and yellows and deep reds. Climb to the top and look out over the flat prairie below that seems to spread forever. Almost five-meter-tall statues of giant men stand next to you

Previous pages: Popocatépetl, the "Smoking Mountain", is a landmark of Mexico. Left: Statue of Quetzalcóatl in Tula.

atop the **Templo de Tlahuizcalpantecuhtli** – a tongue-twisting word meaning "Morning Star" in Toltec. This platform high above the world is a photographer's dream, but do not expect a sea of ruins.

To the west of the temple is **Palacio Quemado** – the Burnt Palace – which blends in with the earth-colored walls that spread out like a mural of subtle shades. On its pink, red and magenta wall the visitor will see the reclining statue of Chac Mool, one of the most important Toltec gods who is wearing a high rounded headdress, and with his face portrayed in a remarkable profile. Below, next to the ball court, are several sharp reliefs of the classical feathered serpent, eagles and jaguars.

Tula was a thriving capital city for the Toltecs, but it was overrun by the Chichimecs in 1156. However, within 40 years, a drought that baked the central highlands destroyed all crops year after year and finally drove the Chichimecs south. Well over a century later, the Aztecs reached Tula and tried to reconstruct it. And by 1519 it was in Spanish hands. But the place never again saw the riches that it had known during the Toltec reign.

Near the large temple is a tiny museum with a scattering of Aztec pottery found in this area. Here, too, are two stone figures archeologists believe were stand-

TEPOTZOTLÁN

ard holders for a Toltec king. The museum is open daily from 8 am to 6 pm, and there is a small admission fee.

Tepotzotlán

A two-kilometer side-trip off Highway 57, the toll highway to Querétaro, leads to **Tepotzotlán**, a pretty town with a population of 23.000. The main square, **Plaza Hidalgo**, cannot be overlooked. Its most important feature is the huge Baroque church, **Iglesia de la San Francisco Javier**, built in 1682. It is considered one of three finest examples of Churrigueresque architecture in Mexico, the other two being Santa Prisca in Taxco and La Valenciana in Guanajuato. The church has a majestic quality as it towers over the little town. Its ornamentation is as elaborate outside as inside. Almost every square inch is filled with gilded

Above: The architecture and decoration of the Monastery of Tepotzotlán is a treasuretrove of Mexican Baroque.

flourishes; a host of grinning cherubs welcome the visitor. On the walls of the church are 22 paintings by Cristóbal de Villapando, showing the various steps in the life of San Ignacio de Loyola, founder of the Jesuit order.

Next to the church is the **National Viceroy's Museum** (the Museo del Virreinato), once the novitiate of the Society of Jesus in 1585. Here the Jesuits studied language, art, theology and mathematics. The treasures gathered by the Catholic church during its colonial tenure in Mexico are displayed in the rooms of the museum, which is operated by the National Institute of Anthropology and History. The collection here includes a great number of fine religious paintings and statues. Among the special items are relics, one of which is displayed in a silver chalice with coral inlays crafted in Italy. The museum also boasts a relic alleged to be a bone of Saint Peter himself. At the center of the museum is the **Chamber of the Virgin**, a room dating to the early 18th century, with an altar under a pretty cupola ringed with a freeze. Mirrors enable visitors to take a closer look at the ornamentation on the ceiling. There are depictions of the moon, the sun and stars, and a host of gambolling cherubs. In the very center of this chamber is the Virgin Mary in a lantern, surrounded by the apostles in the scene from the Pentecost, with the Holy Ghost descending from the heavens. The Jesuits, who ran the church as well as the novitiate, were expelled from Spain and its colonies in 1767 for supporting the Enlightenment. The church and the buildings were to become a school for priests, but the plan was abandoned. When the order's rights were reinstated at the beginning of the 20th century, the Jesuits re-took possession of their property. The government took over the novitiate in 1964, turning it into a museum.

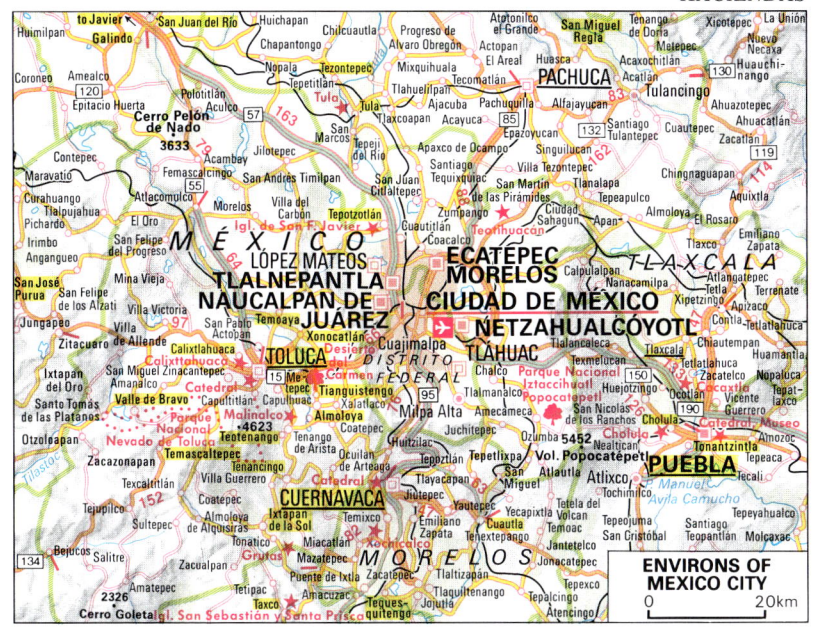

Haciendas: Small States-within-States

Quite soon after the arrival of the Spaniards, the haciendas had developed into agricultural production sites on a colossal scale. Hernán Cortés, for example, owned an estate that today covers four Mexican states. He claimed to own 23,000 serfs. In those days, only the old paths of the Indigenas and the *caminos de herradura*, the Spaniards' "horse-hoof routes", gave access to these estates.

As protection from attacks by the native population, fortress-like building complexes were erected in several strategic places creating veritable states-within-states. Because of the underdeveloped – indeed, non-existent – transportation lines, the haciendas had to be self-sufficient, independent of imports and outside food supplies. Furniture and bricks were produced on the estates; they had blacksmiths for the making of tools, agricultural implements, wagon wheels and the like. The type of hacienda generally developed from the areas' agricultural potential as well as the technologies at its disposal. Many hacienda owners invested gigantic sums in the installation of irrigation systems and the processing of their raw products. In the hot climates of the states of Veracruz and Morelos sugarcane haciendas developed, while cattle haciendas were established on the dry central plateau and southward to the lowlands of Chiapas and Veracruz, *henequén* (sisal hemp) haciendas in the arid parts of the Yucatán, and cotton was cultivated all over Coahuila. Profitable haciendas also developed where iron ore was mined.

Some of the owners of silver mines were so wealthy that they could afford to mint their own silver coins with their family's coat-of-arms. They were not merely the lords of their properties, rather also rulers over the lives and deaths of their serfs. Both the Spaniards and the *criollos* (Creoles), people of mixed European and native blood, assumed ever-increasing privileges and rights for themselves. They ruthlessly expanded their possessions further onto the Indigenas' communal lands. The clergy

Above: The bridal suite in the Hacienda Vista Hermosa.

played a key role in this brutal expropriation. Consequently, there was not a single hacienda without a chapel, a kind of token reward for the Catholic church. The Revolution of the beginning of the 20th century, although chaotic and somewhat ineffective, did lead to a spate of land reforms. The former day-workers took possession of the abandoned manorhouses in their own way: They took building materials for their cottages from the walls. In this way it was only a matter of a few decades before these symbols of feudalism had fallen almost completely into ruins.

Once Mexico had been discovered by tourists, several of the haciendas came back to life as exclusive lodgings steeped in a very special historical ambiance. Film star Anthony Quinn wrote in the guest-book of the **Hacienda Vista Hermosa**: "Whoever has dreams that aren't fulfilled here ought to leave dreaming alone." Indeed, this hideaway 75 minutes by automobile from Mexico City off of the N 95 toward Acapulco at Tequesquitengo, is a very special sort of refuge. The hacienda, originally a sugarcane mill, was constructed by Hernán Cortés in 1529. When engineer Fernando Martínez found it in 1944, it was a ruin. He bought the parcel and created a luxurious refuge, an oasis of peace with an architectural and artistic tradition stretching back over 450 years. Halls, barrel-vaults, subterranean dungeons, stables, workers quarters and the former aristocrats' chambers became reception halls, restaurants and suites. More than a dozen of the latter possess a private, discreetly shielded pool. One can get married in the colonial Baroque chapel, while the "honeymoon suite" is conveniently located right next-door. By the way, the complex has also been the backdrop for many films. Robert Redford and Paul Newman "died" here in the bloody conclusion of *Butch Cassidy and the Sundance Kid.*

With its 300 rooms, the **Hotel Hacienda Cocoyoc** near **Cuautla** is the largest of all the guest-haciendas. In the mid-16th century, Isabel, a daughter of the Aztec ruler Moctezuma II, selected the "Place of the Coyotes" as her domicile. This well-tended complex does indeed have a predominance of old structures, but it is considered overrun (particularly on weekends) by well-heeled Mexicans on outings from the capital.

Two highly recommended colonial residences can be reached on the N 57 en route to Querétaro. **La Estancia** (late-16th-century with 108 guest rooms) is situated eight kilometers to the north of **San Juan del Río**. The **Hotel La Mansión Galindo** at **San Gil**, in its original condition a gift from Hernán Cortés to his lover Malinche, was remodeled in 1975 into a luxury hotel with 166 rooms (of which 17 have private terraces and small *jaccuzzi*) as well as 19 deluxe suites. With its present-day colossal free-standing buildings, Galindo is representative of the feudalism of the late colonial period, and its combination of generous spaces and extremely luxurious amenities have rendered it the last word among all establishments of this sort in Mexico.

The **Hacienda Jurica**, 9 kilometers to the northwest of Querétaro, has also retained the charm of the colonial period. Its 190 rooms and suites are distributed over a paradisiacal park-like grounds. Antique furniture, precious paintings and carpets underline its ambiance of feudal elegance.

Not all haciendas are located in the country. There are, at least according to their names, urban haciendas as well. The **Casa de Sierra Nevada** in **San Miguel de Allende** must be considered the best facility in this category. In 1982, its 18 suites were incorporated into the Swiss-managed Relais-et-Château hotel chain as their first Latin American facility.

Cuernavaca

Cuernavaca, the capital of Morelos state, is located about 80 kilometers to the south of Mexico City. Its current population is over 250,000. It was already known to the conquistadors as a pleasant place to live: Hernán Cortés had a palace built on the steep slope of the valley where Cuernavaca now sprawls. Mexico-City's well-heeled, and foreign tourists of course too, already enjoyed the fresh air of the "city of eternal spring", as it has been nicknamed, for over a century. During his brief tenure, the Habsburg emperor Maximilian had a mansion built for himself, where he used to come to bathe and sun far from the maddening politics of the big city.

It was Cortés who introduced sugarcane to the region and developed the plantation system whereby huge farms govern the lives of the peasant farmers. It was these poor laborers, disgruntled, disillusioned and disenfranchised from years of quasi-slavery, who formed the rank and file of the army of Emiliano Zapata during the Mexican Revolution of

1910. Their battle cry was *Tierra y Libertad!* (Land and Liberty!) At the northern entrance of his one-time palace stands the statue of the great revolutionary hero astride his horse. The triptych also shows a group of young girls holding a candlelight vigil over the corpse of Zapata, who was assassinated in 1919.

Cuernavaca has become the refuge for the wealthy who continue to enjoy the peace and solitude behind its walls. Nobel Prize-winning novelist and poet Gabriel García Marquez, champion prize fighter Muhammad Ali, movie star Mary Martin and many others have bought or built mansions here.

The great **zócalo**, the center of the city, consists of two *plazas,* the largest of which is the **Plaza de la Constitución** (also known as Plaza Morelos or Plaza Principal). The **Palacio de Gobierno** (the state's administrative offices) and the **Palacio de Cortés**, the fortress built by Cortés on the base of an Aztec pyramid, are nearby.

The Palacio now houses the **Museo Cuauhnáhuac**, a gigantic historical, archeological and anthropological museum, showing the histories of the Toltec, Olmec, Aztec and Mayan people who have occupied the territory south of Mexico City.

On the western gallery of the second floor of the palace is a magnificent mural by Mexico's most internationally famous artist, Diego Rivera. Commissioned by the U.S. ambassador to Mexico at the time, Dwight D. Morrow, the father-in-law of the American aeroplane pioneer Charles Lindbergh, it depicts the Mexican Revolution of 1910 and the Mexican history since the beginning of the 20th century. The second plaza on the zócalo is **Jardín Juarez**, which has a huge silvery kiosk designed by Gustave Eiffel, the same fellow who designed the Eiffel Tower and the ribbing of the Statue of Liberty, among other things.

Above: Cortés' palace in Cuernavaca. Right: The eagle and jaguar, symbols of the warrior caste in the main temple of Malinalco.

CUERNAVACA

Three blocks from the zócalo is the **Cathedral de la Asunción**, built in the mid-1500s with high walls and parapets. When side-chapels were removed in the 1960s, hidden Asian frescoes showing the persecution and martyrdom of Christian missionaries in Japan were discovered. It is believed that these were painted in the early 17th Century by a Japanese who had migrated, like many other ethnic groups, to Cuernavaca.

Nearby is the **Jardín Borda**, gardens laid out in the 18th century by Manuel de la Borda with pools and fountains to improve his ancestor's residence. It was here that José de la Borda, a wealthy predecessor of him, built an ostentatious mansion, where, in 1864, Maximilian and his wife, the empress Carlota, took up summer residence.

A short taxi ride south to the suburb of Acapantzingo, you may find Maximilian's second home in Cuernavaca, **La Casa del Olino**, a small dwelling where his mistress, Margarita Leguisamo Sedano, stayed when she visited the city. Today, it is the **Museo de la Herbolaria**, showing the traditional medicine of the area, mostly curative plants and preparations derived from them, that have been used to treat nervous diseases, colds, stomach ailments, and to assist in childbirth.

Ask for directions to the *taller* (workshop) and home of David Alfaro Siqueiros in **Colonia Jardínes**. There is a small shop, and if you are lucky, Carlos, one of the great muralist's students, will be on hand to take you on a guided tour. You may visit the home and the small bedroom where the master died. It is a simple but well-decorated home. In the garden is his postage-stamp-sized swimming pool where he cooled himself after long days working on the great murals for which he was famous. His tools are still laid out in his workshop. There are photos of him working. Some show him in prison, where he was locked up because of his socialist beliefs. He remained committed to the cause of the 1910 Revolution until his death at the age of 78, in

Above: Taxco – breathtakingly beautiful in its architecture and setting.

1974. In a courtyard one may see the towering steel walls where he worked until he was too ill to finish his last work.

Malinalco

The ruins at **Malinalco**, some 50 kilometers west of Cuernavaca, are famous for the **Temple of Initiation**, where eagle and tiger warriors of a small tribe of Nahua Indians practiced their rites of passage into the world of adult fighter. At the entrance to the temple is a broken figure of an eagle warrior sitting proudly with arms crossed below the head of Quetzalcóatl, the plumed serpent.

Xochicalco

A little-known site, only 35 kilometers southwest of Cuernavaca, **Xochicalco** is the most important and revealing archeological ruin in the state of Morelos. Known as the "House of Flowers", it was built on a hillside in approximately 800 AD as a fortress and ceremonial center (the latter already existed about 200 BC). The complex, with a ball court, underground passages – miraculous engineering feats – and an underground observatory show Toltec, Maya and Zapotec influence. The **Pyramid of Quetzalcóatl** shows the feathered serpent flying like a bird and squirming like a snake. The basreliefs are some of the finest in this region of Mexico.

TAXCO

Like a cluster of rubies set next to a polished piece of bright turquoise in a chunk of native silver, **Taxco** glitters in the sunshine like the jewelry for which it is famous. As you round the bend and gaze upon the spread town out over a mountainside, you must pull up at the road side and study it. The white stucco houses shimmer; the orange roofs glow; the sky is an unbelievable blue.

This is the view American architect William Spratling had in 1929 when he came upon this scene. He had been teaching at the Bellas Artes in Mexico City and had set out to discover a wilderness. Little did he realize when he left the city that he would find a place that would totally capture his heart and his imagination within 160 kilometers.

In an effort to find a way to stay here in this hillside town with its stone pathways up and down the hill, and meandering cobblestone streets, Spratling first wrote a book, *Little Mexico,* for which he received US$ 400 and then bought a house near the small zócalo across from the famed Santa Prisca Church.

Later, he learned the legend of Don José de la Borda, who by chance discovered a mother lode of silver in the hills nearby and who then built the church, with the motto "God gives to Borda, so Borda gives to God". Spratling went in search of a silversmith to work with the precious metal that was being mined here. With his talent and training as a designer, Spratling himself became a famous one. His reputation spread rapidly, and soon he was selling pieces through Nieman-Marcus in Dallas and the fashionable Tiffany's in New York. After it was suggested by U.S. Ambassador Dwight Morrow, he started to teach young Mexicans how to make jewelry.

Within a short while, Taxco became known as "the Silver Capital of the World". Not only did tourists pour into the town, shops in Paris and London clamored for the items the Spratling-trained youths made. When his students became so popular, they too opened places of business in Taxco, whereas Spratling moved several miles south of town to **Taxco Viejo**, where he continued to make "Spratling Silver".

After the master's death in 1967, a German friend, Alberto Ulrich, bought the *taller* (workshop), house and shop, which are still open today if Mr. Ulrich or his family are at home. He may even play the videotape of an ancient copy of a short-subject Warner Brothers film, *The Man from New Orleans,* based on a Readers' Digest article published in 1946, telling Spratling's amazing story.

Visitors may wander up and down the steep narrow streets of Taxco, which today is a town of about 120,000. On or near the main zócalo are a number of silver shops. Perhaps the most famous is **Los Hermaños Castillos** or The Castillo Brothers, who actually started their training under the tutelage of Spratling in the 1950s. While *La Mina de Plata,* or The Silver Mine, was being built, an 18th-century mining shaft was uncovered by workmen. It has been excavated and provides an interesting tour, showing tourists not only how the silver was originally mined but also how it was eventually fashioned into jewelry.

Behind the **Santa Prisca Church**, finished in 1759 and today still one of the religious showplaces of the country with its 12 altars and ornate gold altarpieces and paintings by Miguel Cabrera, you find the **Museo Guillermo Spratling**, where works of art, photos and exhibits from local life show off the life and times of Spratling the man and artist.

Beyond the zócalo, winding westward, is **Casa Borda**, the home of José de la Borda. Completed the same year as the church, it is a spacious, rambling home of five stories. Borda, who was of French and Spanish origin, lived in only half of the great house while priests from the church lived in the other half.

Nearby is **Casa Figueroa**, the home of one of Borda's friends, Count Cadena, who forced poor people, who could not pay their court-ordered fines, to do the construction work. The present name comes from the Mexican artist Fidel Figueroa, who restored the house in 1943. He used it as a studio and home, and today many of his most famous works hang on its walls.

Casa Humboldt was built by another of Borda's friends, Juan de Villanueva, in a Moorish style, and it was more recently renamed in honor of Baron Alexander von Humboldt (1769-1859), the famous German explorer and scientist who stayed here overnight in 1803.

Convento Bernardino was built in 1592 as a Franciscan monastery. 200 years later a fire destroyed the building, and it was rebuilt in neoclassical style in 1823. High atop a hill nearby is the **Monte Taxco Hotel**. One may drive up the winding road but it is far more spectacular to take a ride on the million-dollar Swiss-built cable car. It soars high above the city, and offers visitors a gorgeous view of the houses and the countryside far beyond. Above, you see bare mountains laced with waterfalls.

Above: Even the chefs of gourmet restaurants get their ingredients from the local markets. Right: Lapilla del Rosario – a perfect example of extravagant Baroque ornamentation.

Once at the Monte Taxco, tourists may hire horses, ride across the nature trails to the waterfalls, play tennis, golf or swim in the generously-sized pool. Every November there is a silver festival held in Taxco known as the *Feria Nacional de la Plata*, awarding the Spratling silver trophy to the silversmith who shows the most original and outstanding artistry.

PUEBLA

The fourth largest city in the country, **Puebla** is steeped in its rich Spanish history. It was settled early during the days of the Spanish conquest. They had landed at Veracruz and headed due west toward Mexico City, founding Puebla on the way. With some 99 churches in regular use, it often seems that there is a cathedral, convent, monastery or place of worship on every street corner. In this city of more than 1.2 million people, the streets are lined with small shops and the air is filled with the smell of candles on a hundred altars, blending with that of tortillas frying. Another of the unique aromas of Puebla is the pungent cooking of *mole poblano*, the dish which this city has made famous.

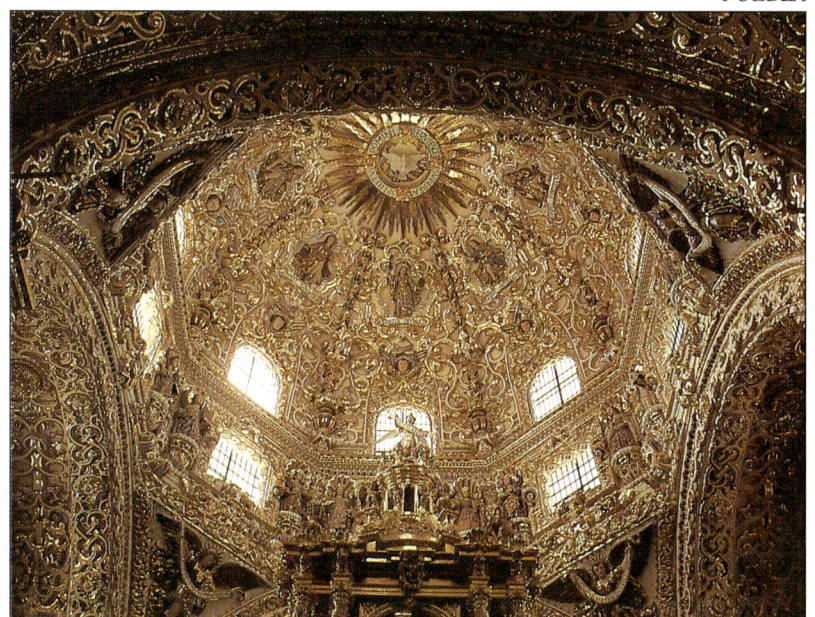

At the **Convent of Santa Rosa**, where the **Museum of Popular Arts** displays regional costumes, handtooled leather satchels, purses, toy soldiers and dancing girls, chinaware, and other objects of art made in the state of Puebla, you may visit the kitchen where the mother superior first put together the *mole* sauce. She concocted it to enhance the flavor of the festive dish she was preparing for a visiting bishop, Manuel Fernandez de Santa Cruz, who had built and furnished the convent. With the help of the other nuns, the mother superior baked the turkey and began working on a sauce that would be considered an adequate expression of gratitude toward the visiting dignitary. She mixed chili sauce, local spices, sesame seeds, ground in bits of chocolate and diced almonds. When finished, she poured the sauce over the turkey and served it. The bishop was very satisfied and the dish became a tradition. The food, today served in various styles, each claiming to be the original, is highlighted in almost every restaurant in the state.

The colorfully tiled ovens, which have been copied in other kitchens throughout Mexico, also baked the *chile poblano* or *chiles en nogada,* a second specialty from Puebla. This dish was created for General Agustín de Iturbide, who stopped in the town to celebrate his saint's day in August of 1821. The stuffed green pepper was covered with crushed walnuts, white cheese and pomegranate seeds. These colors represented the green, white and red of the Mexican flag, and it too has become a tradition, nowadays served presently during the celebrations of Independence Day in September.

While many people from other parts of the world believe all Mexico celebrates a military victory on May 5th – *Cinco de Mayo*, it is truly only the state of Puebla that holds a fiesta on that day.

In 1862, a force of 2000 Mexicans defeated a French force of 6000 soldiers.

PUEBLA

The Europeans, French, British and Spanish were in Mexico to try and "protect" their interests.

One of the most magnificent churches in this country of churches is the **Cathedral of the Immaculate Conception** on the main zócalo. The double-towered, tile-domed cathedral took almost 75 years to build. Begun in 1575 under the supervision of architect Juan de Herrera, it was not consecrated until 1649, with 14 uniquely designed chapels, each displaying religious paintings from different painters. The elaborate altar designed by Tolsa is built of onyx and marble dug from quarries in the state of Puebla. Carvings on the huge doors and the more delicate choir stalls on the periphery of the pulpit were done by Pedro Munoz, whose work here made him famous. One of the two organs is nearly 400 years old, and occasionally a total of 19 bells ring from the two towers. The way up into them is open between 11 am and noon, albeit the "way" consists of 164 steps. The view from up there is impressive, especially on a clear day. To the north are the two volcanoes, 5452-meter **Popocatépetl** (Smoking Mountain) and 5286-meter **Ixtaccíhuatl** (Sleeping Lady).

A block west of the southeast corner of the zócalo stands the **Museo Bello**, a gracious, golden-yellow building with exceptional stained-glass windows which houses the art collection of the late Puebla textile magnate José Luis Bello, and contains superb works of art from Europe and Asia.

Four years after Puebla was founded, **Iglesia de la Santo Domingo** was built as a convent in 1535. It is the most lavishly decorated church in the city, famous for its extravagant **Capilla del Rosario**, completed in 1690. This highly-decorated chapel, where 23-carat gold leaf was generously applied, is a masterpiece. Overhead are statues representing hope, faith and charity; on each side of the aisle to the altar are six pillars of local onyx, each representing an apostle.

The **Regional Museum** in Casa del Alfeñique presents a historical exhibition that chronicles the history of the city of Puebla: documents, colonial furniture, and paintings. The building is noted for its ornamented 18th-century Baroque exterior. The façade combines ornamentation with elaborate tile work and looks something like the frosting on a cake (*alfeñique* means "almond cake").

The **Church of San Francisco**, begun in 1550 and finished in 1575, is not as elaborate nor as ornate as Santo Domingo, but its ceiling is one of the highest in Puebla.

Puebla is also the home of the most successful make of car of all time – the German Volkswagen "Beetle", which in the 1960s was the great star of European roads. Over 15 years after production was closed down in Germany, the modern Puebla factory still turns out, under exclusive license, 450 of these sought-after "flat-fours" daily.

The Mexican car market has been expanding very fast in recent years: For example, in 1991, there were 27 percent more registrations than in 1990, and exports soared by 53 percent. Besides cars, trucks and buses are produced here, and Volkswagen has the largest share of the domestic market with 24 percent. The Volkswagen chiefs in Wolfsburg believe that thanks to Mexico their sales prospects in the USA have significantly improved. Starting in 1993, the "Beetle" will once again be allowed into the US, as it will meet the stringent emission controls in force there. In 1995 or 1996, a new VW series will roll off the Puebla production line, specially designed to take a large slice of the US-market.

Some respected forecasters claim that by the year 2000 there will be no motor

Right: Cholula – in its circumference the largest pyramid in the world, it now serves as a plinth for a church.

manufacturers left in the United States. Mexican taxi-drivers have long been devoted to the VW. They alter the suspension and remove the front passenger seat, so that their customers can get in the back more easily. In the rarified atmosphere of the high altitudes in Mexico, the VW, fitted with a special carburettor, is very reliable.

Perhaps the best way to end a trip to Puebla is to visit the tiny outlying village of **Cholula**, where the great pyramid, **Tenapana**, one of the largest in the world, dominates the flat countryside. This pyramid was sacred to the Olmecs, Zapotecs, Teotihuacános, Toltecs, Chichimecs and Cholultecs, an off-shoot tribe of the Aztecs.

It is surmounted by a catholic church, already built by the conquistadors. For a small fee, the visitor may climb through the underground passageways and enter the partially excavated site where the hillside has been carved away so that tourists can see the elaborate designs from the Classical period.

TOLUCA

Nestling in the center of a green valley about an hour's drive from Mexico City is **Toluca** (population 320,000), a town known for its colorful Indigena market. It derives its name from the Aztec *tollocan*, which means "those who bow their heads"; perhaps in shame, for the Toluca market is notorious for thieves and pickpockets. The invigorating, brisk weather is due to the 8760-foot altitude. **Nevada de Toluca**, an extinct, sometimes snow-covered 4583-meter volcano, and Mexico's fourth highest, towers over the city and the surrounding **Nevada de Toluca National Park**. The crater of the volcano holds the **Lake of the Sun**, filled with rainbow trout, and the **Lake of the Moon**. The crater is accessible by car and the views are spectacular; a funicular takes visitors into the crater.

Most visitors spend hours in the alfresco section of **Mercado Juárez** – a market which is located just south of the city close to the bus station. It is at its best

TOLUCA / INDIGENAS VILLAGES

on Fridays, when the Otomí and Matlatzinca locals flock in providing additional merchandise that overflows into the adjoining plaza.

Also worth a visit are the **State Museum of Popular Art** on Highway 15 at the eastern entrance to Toluca, which houses displays of modern as well as ancient folk art and artifacts, including beautiful textiles. The **Museum of Archeology and History** has a large, intricately carved *tlalpanhuehuetl*, a wooden war drum used by the Aztecs and discovered in Malinalco.

Also worth seeing is the **Museum of Fine Arts** downtown behind the **Governor's Palace**, and the nearby **Charro Museum**.

The town also has some interesting churches, particularly the **Parochial Church**, built soon after the conquest in 1521, but replaced in 1585. Just west of

Above: Toluca's "Tree of Life" is among Mexico's most beautiful works of folk-art.
Right: Small town life.

the city stands the **Church of Our Lady of Tecajic**, a popular Indian shrine with a much-venerated image, painted on cotton cloth.

Uetepec, a few miles south of Toluca, is a charming old town with buildings with the color of its fine pottery. Its market is held on Mondays. Also nearby are the Indian villages of **Metepec**, noted for its beautiful pottery. The work shows imagination, especially those with the *arbol de la vida*, or "tree of life", theme. This is a native interpretation of the tree in the Garden of Eden. All of the important figures –Adam, Eve, the serpent, the angels – are represented in a fantasy-like sculpture.

Also nearby are the Indian villages of **Tianguistengo**, famous for *sarapes*, typical, colorful woollen blankets; **Tenancingo**, where they make *rebozos* or shawls so fine that they can be drawn through a wedding-ring; and **Almoloya**, known for its finely decorated tablecloths. The village of **Xonocatlán** is now weaving tapestries, and the Otomí Indians of **Tamoaya** produce oriental-style rugs of their own design.

Five miles north of Toluca, off Highway 55, a dirt road leads to the **Calixtlahuaca Archeological Zone**, with an unusual round pyramid. Three periods are represented in the excavations, which include a three-tiered altar, a pyramid, and several temples. The museum at **Teotenango**, a fortress city dating back to the 7th century, 11 miles south of Toluca on Highway 55, displays a rich collection of archeological finds.

The **Desert of the Lions** is neither a desert, nor does it have any lions. Instead, it is a national park with a pleasant pine forest along Highway 15 on the way to Toluca from Mexico City. There are ruins of a 17th century **Carmelite convent** to be explored.

Ixtapan de la Sal, a popular spa and resort noted for its luxurious mineral baths, lies south of Toluca on Highway

55. The origin of the 105 mineral springs remains a mystery, but the Aztecs used to visit the sacred **Green Lagoon**, which villagers say was created by a volcanic eruption. The busiest season is winter, when tourists from colder climates flock here for relaxing sessions in the mineral baths. There are two towns: the old town, **Viejo Ixtapan**, purely Mexican, rustic, and bright with tropical vegetation and colorful houses; and **Nuevo Ixtapan**, a beautifully-landscaped village with a modern hotel, 9-hole golf course, and other accommodations.

West of Toluca on the road to Morelia is the turnoff to **San José Purua**, one of Mexico's most celebrated spas. The spa hotel at San José Purua perches on the edge of a canyon in a lush tropical setting of flowering trees, bubbling streams, waterfalls, and quiet ponds.

Valle de Bravo, a picturesque mountainous village, lies about 80 miles south of Toluca along Highway 134. Accessible through the village of Temascaltepec and then through the forest, the town slopes down to the shores of a lake constructed as part of the Cutzamala hydroelectric project. Wedged in between the slopes of the massifs of **Cruz de Misión** and **La Pena de Principe**, Valle de Bravo, at 1890 meters, has a mild, humid climate ideal for water sports. The placid 13-square-mile lake is excellent for water-skiing, swimming, sailing and rowing, as well as angling for whitefish and black bass. There are also trout in the river that flows into it. The **Bridal Veil Waterfall** is a favorite with visitors.

Nearby, at the base of the La Pena Principe, are archeological ruins, which have not yet been fully explored. They date back to when Valle de Bravo was known as **Temascaltepec**, or "the Village of the Baths", and was inhabited by the Mazahua. The town, with its cobblestone streets and colonial charm, is also an arts and crafts center, noted for its brightly-colored pottery and the delicate embroideries of the Mazahua Indians. On weekends, the town is crowded usually with tourists from Mexico City.

GUIDEPOST ENVIRONS OF MEXICO CITY

XOCHIMILCO
Sightseeing
The "Floating Gardens" **Jardines Florantes de Xochimilco**, ca. 25 km southeast of Mexico City, can easily be reached by public transport and are ideal for a weekend trip – best day for visiting is Sunday.

The *chinampas*, a labyrinth of canals, were the city's orchard and vegetable garden before the arrival of the Spaniards. If you travel by car take the Periférico Sur, exit Jardines del Sur. By underground: Line 2 to Taxqueña, the end of the line, then by bus or *colectivo* to Embarcadero. Or get off at the underground-station Pino Suárez (Line 1 and 2): *peseros* run from the Calle Izazaga to Xochimilco.

TEOTIHUACÁN
Arrival
By car via the Insurgentes Norte onto the D 85, then follow the sign Pirámides. By bus from the Terminal Central de Autobuses del Norte or from the underground station Indios Verdes (3) to the bus stop Pirámides Teotihuacán. Entrance to the ruins 8 am-5 pm, closing time 6 pm.
Accommodation / Restaurants
MODERATE: **Hotel Villa Arqueológica**, 10 minutes from the entrance to the ruins, Tel: 6-0750. Behind the Pyramid of the Sun is the small restaurant **La Gruta**.

TULA
Arrival
By bus to the *Zona Arqueológica* (open 8 am-5 pm): from the Central de Autobuses del Norte with Autotransportes Valle del Mezquital.
Accommodation
MODERATE: **Motel Lizbeth**, Ocampo 200, Tel: 2-0045.

TEPOTZOTLÁN
Arrival
By bus from the Terminal Autobuses México, Tlalnepantla, Cuautitlán y Anexas, Tel: 561-0282.
Accommodation
MODERATE: **Posada Familar**, Tel: 876-0520. *BUDGET:* **Hotel Virreyes** at the Zócalo.

CUERNAVACA
Accommodation
LUXURY: **Posada las Mañanitas**, Ricardo Linares 107, Tel: 12-4646.
MODERATE: **Hostería las Quintas**, Las Quintas 107, Tel: 12-8800. **Villa International de Tenis**, Chalma 702, Tel: 3-0829.

BUDGET: **Posada Cuernavaca**, Av. Paseo del Conquistador 57, Tel: 13-0800. **El Presidente Cuernavaca**, Narodo 58, Tel: 13-33993.
Posada San Angelo, Carrada de la Selva 100, Tel: 14-1325.
HACIENDA-LUXURY-HOTELS in the Federal State of Morelos, outside of Cuernavaca: **Hotel Hacienda Vista Hermosa**, Tequesquitengo, Tel: (734) 7-0492. Reservation in Mexico City, Tel: 535-0556 and 535-010.
Hacienda Cocoyoc, Cuautla, Tel: (735) 220-0006. Reservation in Mexico City, Tel: 550-7331/6480.
Restaurants
INTERNATIONAL: **Las Mañanitas**, Ricardo Linates 107, Tel: 12-4646. **Hacienda de Cortés**, Plaza Kennedy 90, Tel: 15-8844.
FRENCH: **Le Château René**, Atzingo 11, Tel: 17-2300.
MEXICAN: **India Bonita**, Morrow 6 B, Tel: 12-1266. **Palacio**, Morrow 204, Tel: 12-0553.
Festivals
A colorful flower festival is celebrated at the beginning of May.
Tourist Information
Morelos 802, Tel: 14-3920 and 14-3860.

TAXCO
Accommodation
LUXURY: **Hacienda del Solar**, Calle de Solar, 3 km outside of town, Tel: 2-0323. **Monte Taxco**, Frac. Lomas de Taxco, Tel: 2-1300. **Posada de la Misión**, Av. J. F. Kennedy 32, Tel: 2-0063.
MODERATE: **Hotel de la Borda**, Cerro de Pedregal 2, Tel: 2-0025.
BUDGET: **Agua Escondida**, Guillermo Spratling 4, at the Zócalo, Tel: 2-0726. **Posada de los Castillos**, Juan Ruiz de Alarcon 3, Tel: 2-1396.
Restaurants
INTERNATIONAL: **La Pagaduría del Rey**, Cerro de Bermeja, Tel: 2-3467.
MEXICAN: **Cielito Lindo**, Plaza Borda 14, Tel: 2-0603. **Señor Costilla**, Plaza Borda 1, Tel: 2-3215. **Arnoldo**, with a splendid panoramic view over the Zócalo, Plaza de los Gallos 2, Tel: 2-1272. Next door: **Bora Bora Pizza**.
Festivals
Fiesta de San Antonio Abad, January 17, blessing of the animals. *Fiesta de Santa Prisca*, January 18, folklore festival with fireworks.
Fiesta de la Candelaria (Candlemas), February 2 with candle procession.
Fiesta da la Vera Cruz, celebrated Thursday before Easter, procession with hooded men and flagellations. Numerous processions take place during Passion Week.

GUIDEPOST ENVIRONS OF MEXICO CITY

Fiesta de San Miguel Arcangel, September 29, with pilgrimages from the surrounding villages into the city.

Shopping
The "Silver Town" Taxco can boast more than 100 shops for silver jewellery, many around the Zócalo. Bargaining is absolutely essential!

Sightseeing
Grutas de Cacahuamilpa, ca. 30 km north of Taxco (Bus "Toluca"). Guided tours ca. 2 km through the fascinating labyrinth of the stalactite caverns, 10 am-5 pm.

Post / Telecommunication
Post Office: Juárez 6, Tel: 2-0501, Mon-Fri 8 am-7 pm, Sat 9 am-1 pm.
Telephone: for long-distance calls *Oficina de Teléfonos*, Calle de San Miguel. **Telegrams**: Veracruz 17, Tel: 2-0001, Mon-Fri 9 am-1 pm and 3-7 pm, Sat 9 am-1 pm.

Hospital / Police
Hospital: **Centro Médico** (emergency service): Calle de San Miguel / Av. Kennedy, Tel: 2-0112.
Police: Pajaritos 6, Tel: 8-0666.
Emergency Call: 2-3920 (24 hours).

Tourist Information
Plazuela de Benual 2, Tel: 2-1705.

PUEBLA
Accommodation
LUXURY: **Gran Hotel del Alba**, Avenida Hermanos Serdán 141, Tel: 48-6055 and 48-7344. **Aristos**, Avenida Reforma y 7 Sur, Tel: 32-0964 **El Mesón del Angel**, Avenida Hermanos Serdán 807, Tel: 48-2100.
MODERATE: **Misión de Puebla**, Calle 5 Poniente 2522, Tel: 48-9600. **Mesón del Molino**, Calzada del Bosque 10, Tel: 48-7060.
Hotel Panamericana, Avenida Reforma 2114, Tel: 48-5466. **Hotel Royalty**, Portal Hidalgo 8, Tel: 42-0204.
BUDGET: **Cuatro Caminos**, Hermanos Serdán 406, Tel: 48-6177. **Hotel Gilfer**, Oriente 11, Tel: 46-0611.

Restaurants
INTERNATIONAL and MEXICAN: **Charlie's China Poblano**, Avenida Juárez 1918, Tel: 46-3159/84. **Bodegas del Molino**, San José del Puente, Tel: 48-2262. **La Bola Roja**, rare Mexican specialities, 5 de Mayo 3510 (Plaza Dorada), Tel: 40-7582.
La Cabaña de Don Vill, Blv. Hermanos Serdán 646, Tel: 48-7007.
SEAFOOD: **El Puerto de Veracruz**, 33 Poniente 118, Tel: 40-8075.
The regional speciality is *mole*, a black, chocolate-based sauce that has been rounded off with about twenty different spices and is served preferably with chicken dishes.

Special Events
Día de la Batalla de Puebla, May 5, memorial celebration of the victory over the French, with military parades.

Sightseeing
Pyramids of Cholula, 8 km west of Puebla. The main pyramid Tepanapa is one of the largest in the world, open for visitors 10 am-5 pm.

Post / Telecommunication
Post Office: 16 de Septiembre / Av. 5 Ote., Tel: 42-2543, Mon-Fri 8 am-5 pm, Sat and Sun 9 am-12 noon. **Long-distance Calls**: *Caseta*, Calle 11 Sur/ Av. Pte., Mon-Sat 9 am-9 pm.
Telegrams: 16 Septiembre 504, Tel: 42-1779, Mon-Fri 8 am-midnight, Sat 9 am-9 pm, Sun 9 am-1 pm.

Tourist Information
Av. 5 / 3 Ote., Tel: 46-8781 and 46-1285.

TOLUCA
Accommodation
MODERATE: **Mansión de Milled**, Hidalgo Poniente 310. **Nuevo San Carlos**, Portal Francisco I. Madero 210.
BUDGET: **Hotel Colonial**, Avenida Hidalgo Oriente 11103, Tel: 5-9700.

Restaurants
Luigis, Lopez Mateos 142. **La Gamba**, Fabela Norte 105.

Market
Mercado Juárez at the bus terminal; best time for visiting the market is very early on Friday morning, when the Indigenas from the surrounding villages offer their wares.

Museums
Museo de Arte Popular, at the eastern town exit, known above all for the lovely ceramic masterpiece "Tree of Life" from the village of Metepec. Also on show are local arts and crafts such as pottery, weaving and glass, with sale of goods. Mon-Sat 9 am-12 noon and 4.30-7 pm.

Sightseeing
The Botanic Garden **Cosmo Vitral** is next to the **Palacio del Gobierno**, a former market hall, famous for its art-deco-style glass windows (125.000 separate pieces) by the artist Leopoldo Flores.

Shopping
In Toluca excellent products from the glass-blowing workshops are offered for sale. Local specialities are *Moscos*, fruity liqueurs made mainly from apricots.

Tourist Information
Palacio del Gobierno, Lerdo Pte. 300.

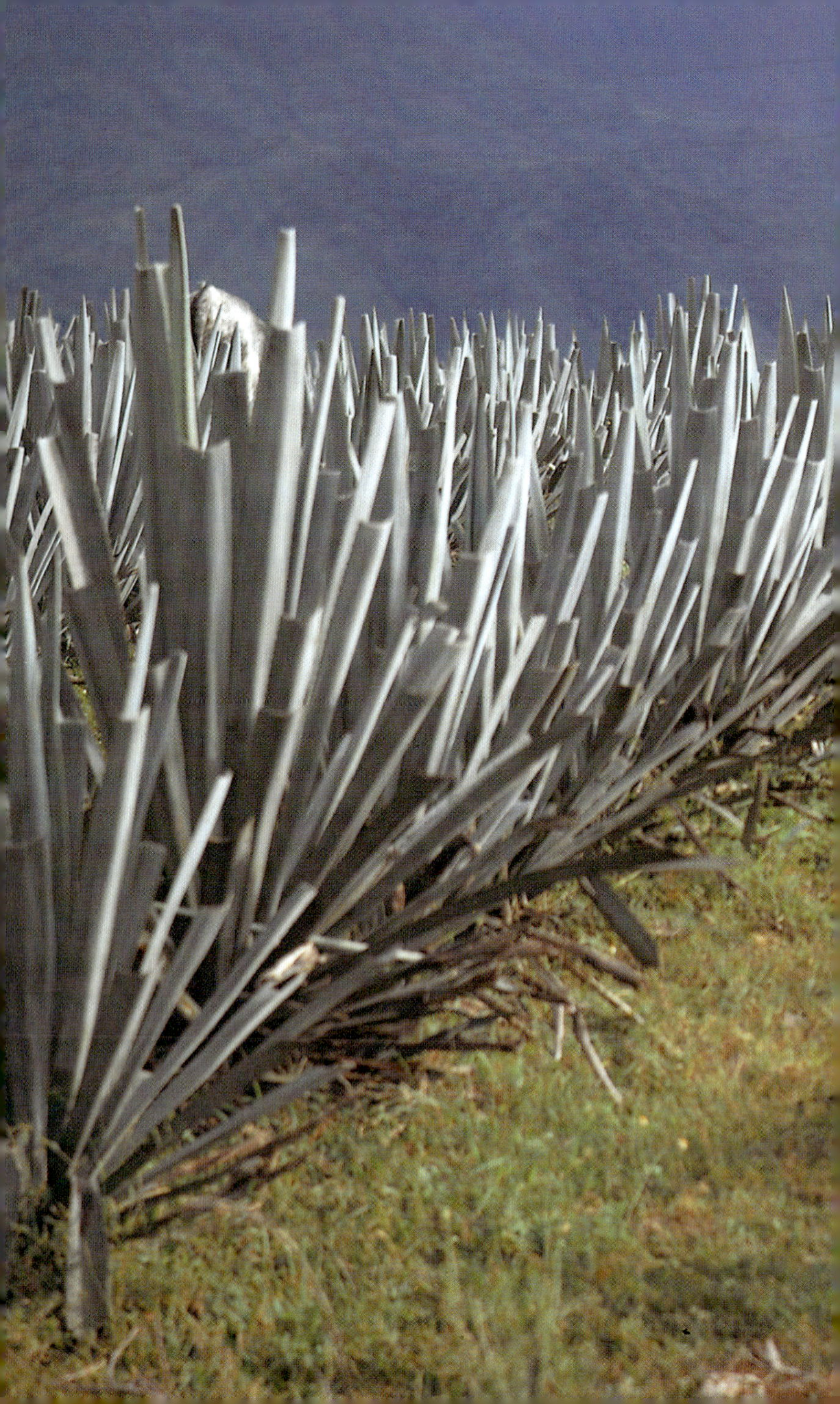

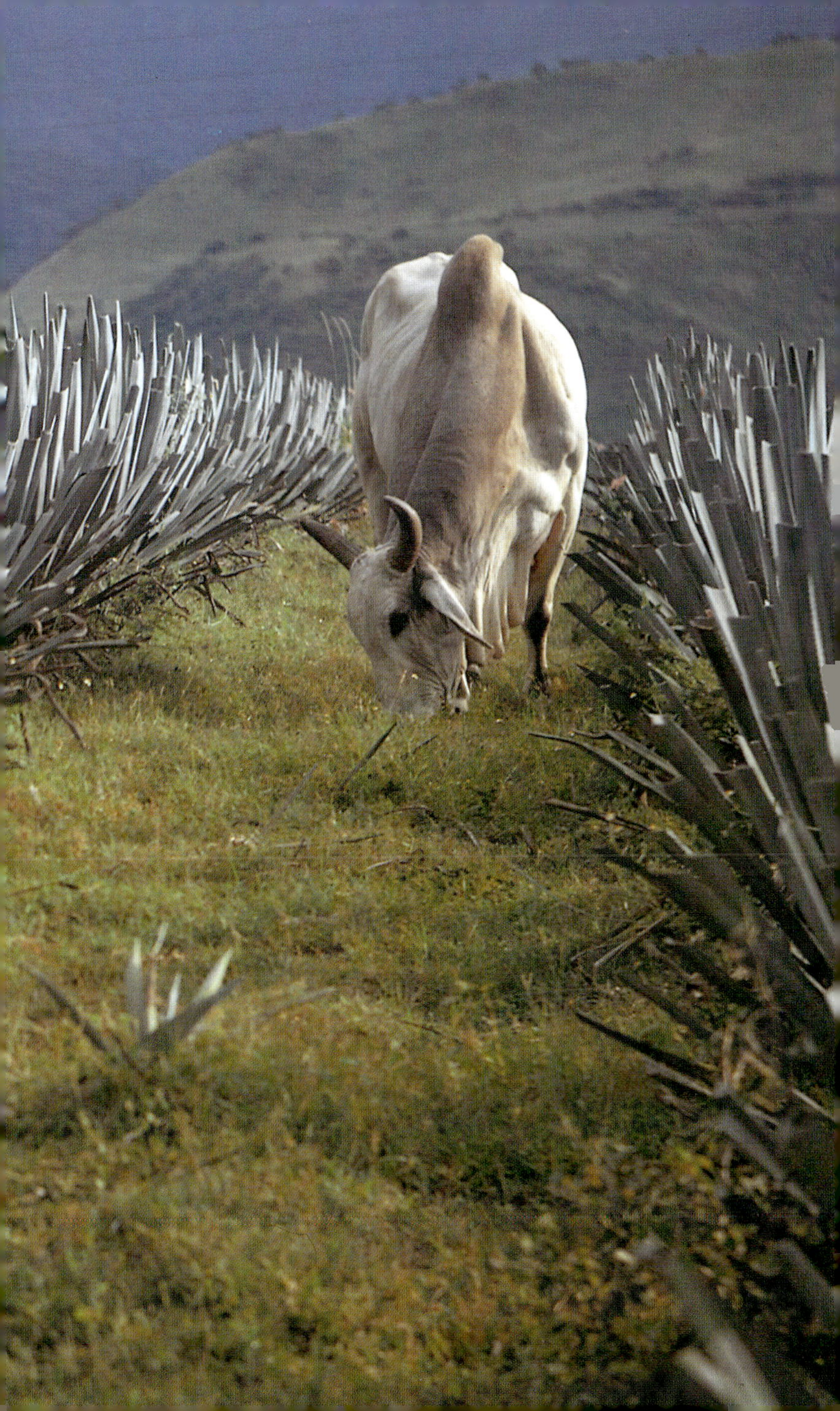

MORELIA

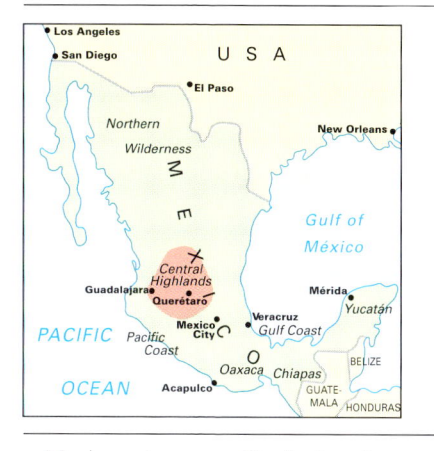

IN THE CENTRAL HIGHLANDS

MORELIA / QUERÉTARO
SAN MÌGUEL DE ALLENDE
GUANAJUATO
GUADALAJARA
LEÓN / AGUASCALIENTES
SAN LUIS POTOSÍ
ZACATECAS

Mexico enjoys a wealth of mineral resources. Many of them were already being worked into tools, weapons and jewelry by the Indigenas in pre-Columbian times. After the Conquest, the Spanish soldiers of fortune and merchants had a virtually unlimited reserve of slaves at their disposal for the exploitation of the gold, silver and other ores.

For 300 years, the minerals from the mines in San Luis Potosí, Zacatecas, Guanajuato, Querétaro, Michoacán and Hidalgo (as well as the so-called "Silver City", the present-day tourist-town of Taxco) were primarily exported to Spain. From the very beginning of this boom, (around 1700) a new geographical term came into being: the *bajío,* which denotes the heartland of Mexico, in particular the states of Querétaro, Michoacán, Guanajuato and Hidalgo. It wasn't long before this region distinguished itself for its economic dynamism. The Valenciana Mine in Guanajuato, for example, generated more than a million pesos from the sale of pure silver during the last quarter of the 18th century. Translated into modern currency, the total exports of all Mexican silver mines rose from $US 3 million in 1700 to more than $US 27 million in the year 1804! And along with the comfortable economy came progressive thought. Due to tensions between the exploiters and the enslaved mine and plantation workers, social conflicts naturally arose with the clergy. Long before the struggle for independence, the *bajío* was already ripe for revolutionary, social and political reforms.

Previous pages: A plantation of agaves.
Left: Jalisco is the home of the mariachis.

MORELIA

The city of **Morelia** bears a name of no small importance: that of the priest José Maria Morelos. Indeed, even the core of the city seems to be in the same condition it was when the Spaniards were driven out by Morelos' troops in the War of Independence. The entire center is well-preserved and has benefited from outstanding restoration; it is under protection as a historical monument. Hardly anywhere in Mexico can one find such a magnificent collection of huge Baroque palaces, churches and their adjoining cloisters in Renaissance and Baroque styles, proud mansions and stylish colonial townhouses.

The capital of the state of Michoacán has experienced rapid growth in recent years due to the industrial development on its edges. It now has a population of some 700,000 and is situated at an alti-

MEXICO'S HEARTLAND

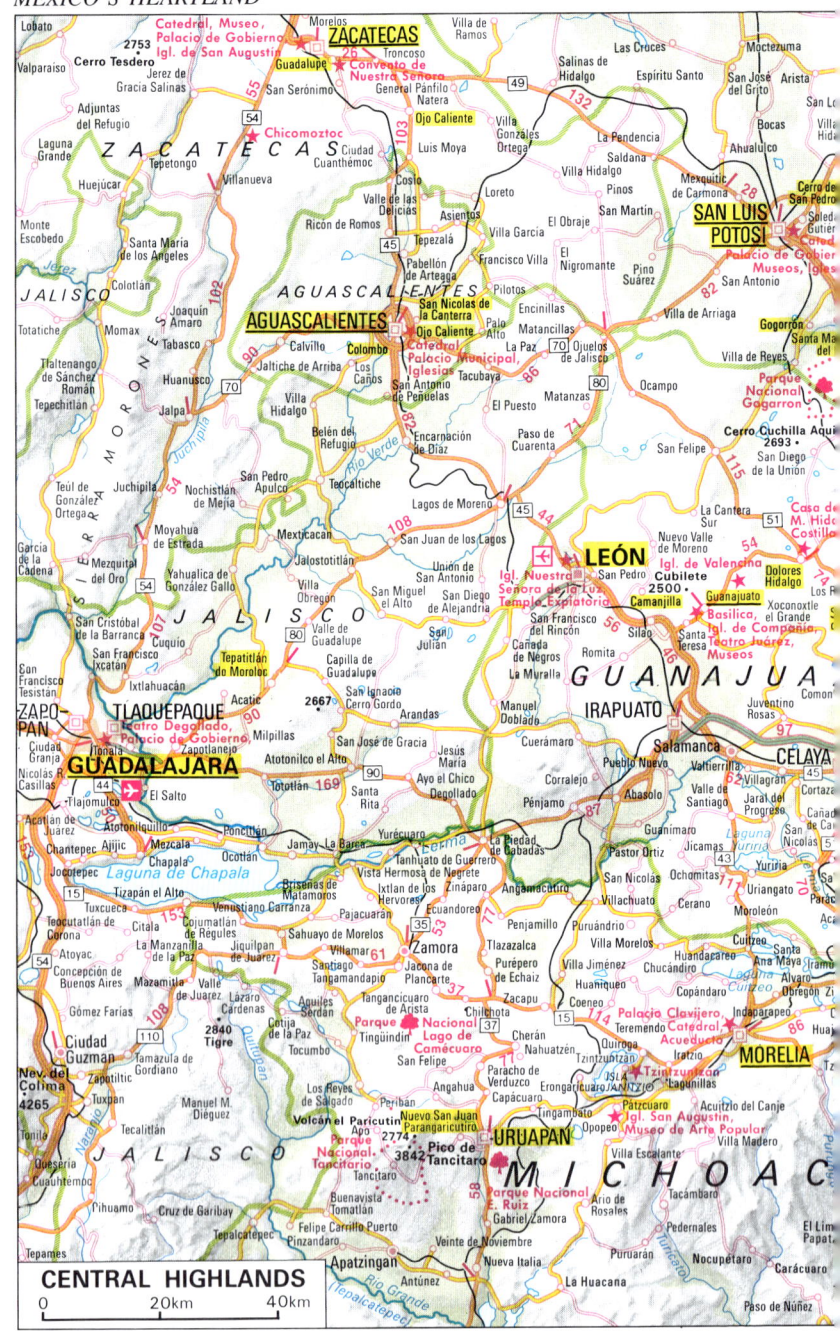

MEXICO'S HEARTLAND

MORELIA

tude of 1900 meters. It was founded by the Franciscans in 1531. The settlement received, as did so many others, the name of a Spanish city, Valladolid, from Viceroy Mendoza in 1541. It wasn't renamed Morelia until 1826, in memory of the valiant and indefatigable freedom-fighter José Maria Morelos, a native son of the city who was executed in 1815. Today Michoacán is among the Mexican states in which the percentage of Indigena population is substantially above the national average. As a result the descendants of the country's earlier owners can be seen in many villages and towns, (especially on Lake Pátzcuaro) although above all in the state's capital city.

Morelia is connected with Mexico City (which is 300 kilometers away) by a high-speed train service and brisk bus traffic in addition to a well-improved road (the *corta*) and can be reached comfortably in a trip of three to five hours. The road passes through a mountainous landscape dominated by spruce and pine forests occasionally interspersed with luxuriant groves of oak. Unfortunately, deforestation, one of civilization's symptoms, has brought about a significant decline in the groundwater level, with the result that one passes by numerous very shallow or even dried-out lakes on the surfaces of which algae and waterlilies have become established, creating a water problem for the local residents.

The local tourist information bureau is housed in the **Palacio Clavijero** (Avenida Nigromante 79), a magnificent 17th-century structure. The zócalo, the **Plaza de Armas**, is graced by laurel trees and a row of colonial buildings with beautiful arcades. It is even possible to spend the night in one of the palaces from the Spanish colonial period: the **Virrey de Mendoza** was built in 1744. It is located at the **Portal Matamoros**.

Dominating the plaza (since its belltower reaches a height of almost 70 meters) is the **cathedral**, which was constructed in 1640, although it did not achieve its current Baroque splendor until the 18th century. Its interior is a perfect example of the Mexican Churrigueresque style. The church is situated between the zócalo and another plaza (de los Mártires). On the other side of the Madero, a traffic-clogged main street, one finds the **Palacio de Gobierno**, completed in 1732. The numerous patios and arcades, galleries and staircases of the governmental building are examples of the finest in Mexican Baroque. Also give special attention to the murals on the first level, which were designed by the artist Alfredo Zalce from Pátzcuaro.

The **Museo de Michoacán**, a Baroque edifice from the 18th century, is also worth seeing (Allende 205, located diagonally across the plaza). It features archeological finds from the pre-Columbian epoch as well as a number of

Above: The aqueduct in Morelia. Right: Many Indigenas live only on what they can earn in the markets.

murals. Facing the museum is the 18th-century **Palacio de Justicia**, which didn't receive its profusely ornamented French façade until the 18th century.

Continuing further down the street one comes upon the **Palacio Municipal**, featuring the overwhelming Baroque ornamentation of the 18th century, where Morelos proclaimed his demand for the abolition of slavery. Only one block away from the Plaza de Armas (Corregidora 113) is the house where he was born, which has been converted into a small museum, as well as the former **Augustinian Convent** (Exconvento de San Agustín), constructed in the 16th century and extraordinarily well restored. The **Franciscan church and convent** on the Plaza Valladolid also date from the 16th century; their Renaissance style has been preserved. The **Casa de Artesanías**, as it is now called, is operated by the state and houses a sales exhibit of the finest of Michoacán handcraftsmanship.

An **aqueduct**, not constructed until 1789, conveys fresh springwater from the mountains into the city. Its 230 arches extend from the east toward the city center over 1.6 kilometers. It has been completely restored, and sometimes streets run through the *arcos*, which are up to nine meters high. The aqueduct ends at a fountain depicting three Tarascan women carrying a vessel laden with fruit and vegetables.

The Tarascans at Lake Pátzcuaro

The **Lago de Pátzcuaro**, with a surface area of 45 square kilometers, is located 60 kilometers to the southwest of Morelia. Coming by way of Quiroga one passes **Tzintzuntzan**. Even when you are still on the road, the gigantic pre-Columbian platform measuring some 400 by 250 meters is visible, as are five *yácatas,* 12 meter tall semicircular supports upon which there once stood a temple, probably of wood which would explain why it no longer exists.

Located on the lake's southeastern shore at an altitude of 2170 m, is the city

LAKE PÁTZCUARO

of **Pátzcuaro**. With its 50,000 inhabitants, it is the center of the Tarascan villages scattered along the lakeshore and around the vicinity. Its people survive by fishing and duck-hunting, agriculture and, most recently, from the production of handicrafts intended for the ever-growing tourist market.

Pátzcuaro is a gem of Spanish city planning, with a grid-type street layout featuring historical plazas, characteristic red-and-white houses, buildings of natural stone or unfired mud-brick construction as well as cobblestone alleyways. The entire town bears clear signs of the influence of the indigenous cultures. Standing on the **Plaza Gertrudis Bocanegra**, is the bronze statue of a woman who played a significant role in the independence movement of 1810 in Michoacán. The city's public library is housed in the former church of **San Agustín** (1576), located on the plaza. The entire rear wall is covered by a mural painted by Juan Gorman in 1942.

One should definitely not miss seeing the **Museo de Arte Popular** in the former *Colegio Don Vasco* (built in 1538); it features extraordinarily diverse exhibits of Tarascan handcraftsmanship, among them some very beautiful pieces from the pre-Columbian era and colonial period. A survey of contemporary handicrafts production can be made in the **Casa de los Once Patios**, a former Dominican monastery dating from 17th century, which today houses numerous artisans' workshops.

40 minutes' ride on a passenger ship brings one from the shore to **Janitzio Island**, which can be recognized from far away by its immense memorial to Morelos. On a stroll from the jetty to the monument, you will pass by countless restaurants, business, artisans' workshops and street-sellers' stands.

Above: The fishermen's nets on Lake Pátzcuaro look like butterflies' wings. Right: Janitzio Island, dominated by the huge memorial to Morelos.

Through Uruapan to Paricutín

Uruapan is situated roughly 60 kilometers to the southwest of Pátzcuaro. This colonial city, with a population of 280,000, boasts a number of beautiful buildings. Its impressive churches and former monasteries as well as the parks and markets make this city an inviting place to linger for a while. Its location at an altitude of 1600 meters gives it a mild, pleasing climate. The **Eduardo Ruiz National Park**, in the gorge of the Cupatitzio River, is a fantastic hiking area with numerous springs, brooks, waterfalls, bridges and sub-tropical vegetation. Uruapan, however, is by and large a stopping-off point on the way to the volcano **Paricutín** (2774 meters).

When it first erupted in 1943, reporters and tourists hurried in to view the natural spectacle. German writer Egon Erwin Kisch, who had obtained political asylum in Mexico, sent his reports on the eruption around the world. One year later, the town of **San Juan Parangaricútiro**, after beeing successfully evacuated in advance, was inundated by a river of lava and covered with cinders to a depth of up to 40 meters. Only the church tower still peers out from the hardened coating of lava. The volcano remained active for three years. It only became officially extinct in 1952. Its crater can be viewed during the dry season.

The Road of Independence

A series of colonial cities along a route leading northwest from Mexico City has been designated as being on the Road of Independence. We are speaking here of towns that played a particularly important role in the battles for independence between 1810 and 1821 (such as Dolores Hidalgo and Querétaro); and of cities from which notable fighters in the independence movement came (such as San Miguel de Allende). Finally, it applies to all of those in which the city's core or the entire town are especially well-preserved or restored and enjoy, to some degree, historical monument protection. A tour through the most significant cities is about 700 kilometers long and will ferry visitors to many of the country's colonial gems. The trip can be made quite easily by bus.

QUERÉTARO

Querétaro is located 220 kilometers to the northwest of Mexico City. It can be reached in two to three hours by way of a toll superhighway. A first class bus service also departs hourly from the capital. Situated on a plateau at an altitude of 1850 meters, this municipality of some 300,000 inhabitants is also capital of the (eponymous) state. Agriculture is one of the more productive means of subsistance in the surrounding vicinity, while on the city's edges there are a number of industrial operations which have brought it a certain affluence.

QUERÉTARO

Querétaro was founded in 1446 by the Otomí Indigenas, who were later subjugated by the Aztecs. Then, in 1531, the region fell under Spanish dominion. Nowadays the descendants of the Otomís work selling souvenirs on the plaza with the monument of the city's heroine.

The movement for independence from the Spanish began in 1810 in Querétaro, where the mayor (*El Corregidor*) and his wife Josefa Ortíz de Domínguez (*La Corregidora*) became participants in Pater Hidalgo's conspiracy. Since Doña Josefa found out in advance of the Spaniards' secret activities, she was able to inform Pater Hidalgo in nearby Dolores, thus triggering his immediate proclamation, the *Grito de Dolores,* and with it the beginning of the independence movement. Mexico's history knows many heroes. But for the first time in its savage history, it was a man of the cloth who advanced the cause of his nation and had to die a martyr for his deeds.

The city's charm lies in its many small plazas shaded by laurel trees, in its pedestrian areas with numerous magnificent historic buildings, some of which are constructed of pink sandstone, and in several very significant palaces, convents and churches that have had first-rate restoration work done on them and now house public institutions. The Rio Querétaro, a river flowing along the northwestern edge of the city, is crossed by numerous bridges.

One might begin a walking tour in the city center at the **Monumento de la Corregidora**. The imposing monument, with a statue of Doña Josefa holding the torch of liberty, four large eagles and a slave breaking free of his shackles, towers over a small square dotted with souvenir stands and open-air restaurants. The church of **San Francisco**, whose foundation walls date from 1540, didn't assume its present form until 1698. In 1817, the building became a hospital; 40 years later it became state property.

This house of God has again been serving its original function since its restoration in 1934. Today, the former convent next to the church houses the **Museo Regional** (Regional Museum). In addition to pre-Columbian finds from the city of Querétaro, one can also view documents from the independence movement and the brief period of French supported Habsburg rule. The entrance hall is embellished with one of Emperor Maximilian's elegant coaches.

Behind the convent, an alleyway in sandstone, graced with a profusion of flowers, leads up to the picturesque **Plaza de la Independencia**. This plaza is surrounded by a series of impressive, historically important buildings. One of the most significant and eye-catching edifices is the **Casa de los Condes de Ecala** (constructed in 1700) with an elaborate Baroque façade and finely ornamented balconies. On the southeastern corner the patio of a colonial-style hotel beckons the weary walker to take a break. To the north is the **Palacio del Estado** (1770), the former residence of the energetic *Corregidora* with its charming interior courtyard.

If one turns around and goes back through the alleyway, crossing the **Plaza de la Constitución**, where stands a statue of Venustiano Carranza, the father of the constitution of 1917, one then comes upon the **Palacio de Bellas Artes** (1804), today an arts academy and part of the University of Querétaro. Not far away from it, at the corner of the streets Pino Suárez/Allende, the **Church and Cloister of San Agustín** unfold their Baroque splendor. The cloister, completed in 1745, was occupied by Juárez' troops in 1867, then serving for a longer time as the *Palacio Federal,* or the seat of the state government, and is presently a tourist information office and museum. If you then continue a short way up Allende Street, the **Church of Santa Clara**, the interior of which is fashioned entirely in

Churrigueresque style, is found on a shady little plaza. Its priceless paintings and gilded altars are truly captivating. Also located in this neighborhood is the **Teatro de la República**, completed in 1845, and known for its stylish décor and elegant theater boxes. The new constitution was proclaimed here in 1917; the gilded monograms of the politicians who participated in this momentous event are a reminder of that memorable year. Fans of Baroque churches still come to visit **Santa Rosa de Viterbo**, founded by the Franciscans along with the adjoining cloister, built in 1752.

Of greater interest, however, are two pedestrian tours leading to destinations on opposite edges of the city. Located to the west is the **Cerro de las Campañas** with a monument commemorating Benito Juárez and a small memorial chapel, dedicated to Maximilian, which was erected by the Habsburgs on this spot in 1901 since it was on this very hill that Juárez had the Austrian prince and Emperor of Mexico executed. The hill itself has been transformed into a well-groomed park abounding in flowers, and from the top one can take in a beautiful view over the city and its surroundings.

Along the city's northeastern edge one first comes upon the **Convento de la Cruz**, located on the hill where the Spanish waged their decisive final battle against the Otomí. The gigantic cloister with its numerous patios, once the headquarters of Maximilian and later his prison, serves today as a cultural center. Soon afterwards, one arrives at the **Casa Mausoleo**, the *Corregidora*'s original burial place (the urn is now in the regional museum). From there, **Los Arcos**, a former colonial aqueduct completed in 1735, is already within sight. It is 1.5 km long and still bears 74 of its tall arches (up to 20 meters in height) in the Mudéjar style. Since its restoration, the aqueduct is intact once again, although it no longer carries water.

For a leisurely tour of the city an entire day ought to be allowed for in Querétaro, and due to the diversity of interesting

SAN MIGUEL DE ALLENDE

sights along the way the tour should definitely be made on foot. Economy and middle class hotels can be found in the city center, while about 10 kilometers outside of town is the **Hacienda Juríca**, which has been transformed into a very pleasant luxury hotel.

A good 70 kilometers to the northwest of Querétaro, a real gem of a town reposes picturesquely on a mountain slope (altitude 1900 meters) over the Rio Laja:

SAN MIGUEL DE ALLENDE

This city of 65,000 inhabitants was founded by the Spanish in 1542 on the site of a previously destroyed Chichimec settlement. In 1862, its residents added "de Allende" to their city's name in memory of its most celebrated son, the freedom fighter Ignacio de Allende. Born here in 1779, Allende was among the first

Above: Cities like Querétaro (left) and San Miguel de Allende are famous for their Mariachi music and colonial architecture.

(alongside with Pater Hidalgo) to revolt against the Spaniards in 1810.

The entire city is under historical protection, with the result that it has managed, by and large, to retain its colonial character. Steep, narrow alleyways paved with cobblestones, photogenic plazas with dense stands of trees and the nobility's splendid former townhouses, as well as Baroque churches and chapels, set the tone of this cityscape. Sheltered behind often quite modest façades are some truly beautiful inner courtyards and colonnades. New construction has been carefully designed to blend with the colonial character of the older buildings, while the latter have been elaborately and professionally restored. In the last few decades, the two art academies have been attracting an international clientele. The city has become the new home of many of their graduates.

The **Plaza Allende** is a meeting-place for both old and new residents as well as visitors to the city. Here the neo-Gothic **Parróquia de San Miguel** catches the

SAN MIGUEL DE ALLENDE / DOLORES HIDALGO

eye. Visible from quite a distance, the city's prime landmark is the highly individualistic creation of a Indigena architect named Ceferino Gutiérrez who erected it on the foundations of a destroyed 16th-century parish church, using the cathedrals of Europe as his prime model. It was completed in 1890. In the chapel next-door is a statue of Christ made of maize and orchid paste. Also dating from the 16th century, the chapel is a place of pilgrimage for the local indigenous population. Opposite the parish church is the house where Ignacio de Allende was born, featuring a memorable Baroque façade. It has been arranged into a small museum devoted to the independence movement and the national hero Allende. Visitors should definitely not miss taking a little stroll through the patio with its especially beautiful colonnades. Standing in front of the house is a monument to the Franciscan monk Juan de San Miguel, the city's founder. The former *Mercado Aldama* at the upper end of the plaza, constructed at the beginning of the century in Neo-Classical style, has been transformed into restaurants and the tourist information center. The prime eye-catcher on the west side is the former manor **Casa de Canal**; in the adjacent Umarán Street one comes upon the **Casa de los Perros**, so named for the carved stone dogs on one of its balconies. Continuing to the west along the Canal Street you will come upon the 18th-century **Convento de la Concepción** which features an enchanting patio and ornate colonnades. The former cloister now houses the **Nigromante Cultural Institute** and an art academy.

A brief stroll brings one to the **Plaza de San Francisco** with a church bearing the same name, completed in 1790, truly impressive with its florid Churrigueresque façade. Also, the church of the **Tercer Order** (1650) located next door has a particularly attractive collection of sacred art. The renowned art academy **Instituto Allende** is now housed in the **Casa de Solariega**, a count's former country residence, dating from 1735, on the city's southern edge. Visitors are quite welcome and can stroll along the extensive grounds with their wealth of flowers, cast a glimpse into the studios, buy handcrafted articles and then take a relaxing pause in its café. The municipal **Parque Benito Juárez** is situated next to the art academy.

The town of **Dolores Hidalgo**, some 40 kilometers to the northwest of San Miguel, played a special role in Mexico's independence movement. In the night of September 15, 1810, Pater Hidalgo declared the War of Independence from the Spanish from the parish church of this small city. To honor him, his name was appended to that of the town. Mexicans mainly visit the church for its political significance. Nonetheless, the building's early 18th-century Churrigueresque façade with its abundance of ornamentation is worth a visit in itself.

Another and equal pride of the town is the **Casa de Don Miguel Hidalgo y Costilla**, from 1804 to 1810 the residence of the national hero, today a small historical museum dedicated to him.

The route to Guanajuato takes one past the 2500-meter-high peak of **Cubilete**, which is said to be the geographical center of Mexico. The Christ figure standing at the summit is 20 meters tall and can be spotted from miles away. It can easily be climbed inside up to a platform that offers a breathtaking view over the country's silver-mining region.

GUANAJUATO

Without a doubt, **Guanajuato** is the most attractive of the cities along the Independence Route. This capital city (roughly 100,000 inhabitants) of the state by the same name is located 90 kilometers to the northwest of San Miguel de Allende and a distance of 375 kilometers from Mexico City. It nestles in a narrow valley at an altitude of some 2000 meters, and in spite of the most concerted of efforts, the colonial master-builders were unable to maintain a grid pattern in their layout of the city. The entire townscape is hilly, and in some places the streets turn into very narrow alleyways. Every now and then one comes upon secluded little plazas – oases of peace in this bustling city, which also suffers no shortage of tourists. The appearance of the city is characterized by cobblestone pavements, many colonial buildings (some of which are in Moorish style), elaborate town houses, Baroque churches and neoclassical architectural monuments.

Guanajuato is filled with the perfume of countless flowers which unfold their beauty in disused carts from the silver mines. A river that used to run through

Above: A reminder of San Miguel de Allende's pre-Columbian past. Right: Silver-mining was the source of Guanajuato's wealth in colonial times.

the city was drained and transformed into a street, which now in part runs beneath buildings and under a number of bridges. Branching off of it are mining shafts that have since been converted into pedestrian routes or connecting streets. Among the high-points of a tour through the city is a drive through this *subterránea*.

The Spanish had already conquered the mountain settlement of the Indigenas by 1529, founding a city soon afterward when its extensive gold and especially silver deposits were discovered. During the 18th century, silver mining reached its peak, after development had begun of the huge Valenciana Mine located to the north. The flow of wealth that resulted can still be seen in many places in the city, although there's no doubt that the greater portion of the precious metals were shipped to Spain. During the first year of the War of Independence, Pater Hidalgo and his troops had already succeeded in capturing the city, though not long afterwards it was again lost to the Spaniards. For a short period in 1858

Guanajuato was even the seat of the federal government under Benito Juárez. Around the turn of the century the dictator Porfirio Díaz furnished the city with a number of neoclassical buildings. Today Guanajuato is among the places protected and supported by UNESCO as a World Cultural Heritage site.

Before making a tour of the city one is well recommended to take a drive along the panoramic road (the *panorámica*) stretching along its southern edge. The vistas it offers are truly unique, and especially fine at the **Pípila Monument** where you can look out over the colorful city with its prominent church towers and mansions, while to the north it extends out to the Valenciana Mine. The monument itself is dedicated to a citizen of the city who risked and lost his life in the War of Independence in the storming of the Spanish fortress. On a closer look from up above at the **Teatro Juárez** on the triangular zócalo one can discover something that isn't visible from below: the theater's splendid façade is in fact a false front, disguising an otherwise rather mediocre building.

The city's center, the **Jardín de la Unión**, is shaded by dense Indian laurel trees. This triangular plaza is surrounded by numerous aristocratic residences, the theater, churches and several restaurants. This is also the location of the venerable **Santa Fé Hotel**, a magnificent structure completed in 1862. The neoclassical Teatro Juárez, commissioned in 1903 by Porfirio Díaz, can be toured during the day. The décor of the main hall, cloak room and bar as well as the foyer areas boast the finest in woodworking and elaborate metal fittings. Even the details are perfect, right down to the stylish cuspidors. Looming next to the theater is the **Templo Diego**, a Spanish church whose construction began in 1663 and lasted more than 100 years. The copious ornamentation of the Churrigueresque façade is particularly striking.

A brief stroll around the corner brings you to the **Plaza de la Paz** with the **Basilica Nuestra Señora de Guanajuato**,

GUANAJUATO

which was constructed in Baroque style during the 17th century. It shelters a statue of the Holy Virgin which was sent as a gift from Spain in 1557. Situated on a long, steep terrace just a few paces from the church is the **University of Guanajuato**, which was only constructed in 1955. With its mixture of neo-Baroque and colonial styles an effort was made to harmonize the seven-storied building's appearance with the rest of the city's architecture. Visible below the university is the 18th-century **Iglesia de Compañía**. The three Churrigueresque portals of this Jesuit church attract many art enthusiasts. If one then follows **Pocitos Street** in the other direction, one will find, on the right-hand side (Nr. 47), the house in which the great Mexican muralist Diego Rivera was born, now a museum. Continuing along the street you pass the neoclassical **Mercado Hidalgo**, a metallic structure completed in 1910, before finally arriving at the fortress **Alhóndiga de Granaditas**, a former granary dating from 1798 that was used by the Spaniards during the War of Independence as a prison for Mexican insurgents. For a brief period during 1810, the revolutionaries managed to take the building when the daring Pípila set an explosive charge to its gate. Soon thereafter the royalists reconquered the building, holding it until 1821. The heads of Hidalgo, Allende, Aldama and Jiménez, freedom fighters who had been executed in Chihuahua, were hung up in cages on its four corners. Today, this history-soaked building houses the **Museo del Estado** as well as serving as a memorial for heroes of the battle for liberation.

On the western city limits, beside the cemetery in the Calzada del Panteón, is the modern, but very macabre **Museo de las Momias**, in which more than one hundred well-preserved mummies await their visitors. Despite the rather gruesome atmosphere, there are always plenty of curiosity-seekers in its halls.

One should not miss the chance to pay a visit to the **Valenciana** silver mine located some 5 kilometers to the north on the road to Dolores Hidalgo. A church constructed especially for the silver miners (1780) can be seen from a considerable distance. It has an attractive rose hue and displays typical Baroque features. The wealth that once flowed from the silver is reflected in its Churrigueresque interior and the elaborate decoration of the cloister located next to it. Both the mine and church are surrounded by the *Barrio Valenciana*, a settlement used by workers during the mine's heyday.

GUADALAJARA

The capital of the state of Jalisco lies roughly 700 kilometers to the northwest of Mexico City at an altitude of 1550 meters. As a result, it has a pleasantly warm, dry climate almost year-round. With nearly 4.5 million inhabitants, **Guadalajara** is the second-largest city in Mexico. Its founding, by the conqueror Nuño de Guzmán, dates from 1542, when some 60 Spanish families settled here and laid out its first streets in the typical grid.

Today, Guadalajara is a modern industrial city that has nonetheless managed, by and large, to preserve its colonial tradition. Its wealth has enabled it to have a large number of its historical buildings skillfully renovated, and these are mostly used as public facilities. The local industries, of which there are quite a number, are located along the city's edges, while the center features zones of strictly controlled through-traffic, pedestrian streets and numerous parks. Although the main concentration of colonial plazas, palaces, townhouses and Baroque churches is, of course, in the city center, they can also be found in other sectors of this bustling city.

The most beautiful sightseeing walk that one can make through Guadalajara both modern and historic begins at the **cathedral**, and from there leads to the Hospicio Cabañas. Construction of the church started in 1571. It took so long to complete that the trained eye can identify six different decorative styles in its architecture. The renowned Murillo painting *The Ascension of the Virgin Mary* is on view in the vestry.

The cathedral is surrounded by four very beautiful plazas. The **Plaza de los Laureles** (Indian laurel trees) is situated across from its main portal, while the **Plaza de Armas** forms the city's historical center and is graced by a much-admired 19th-century bandstand. Opposite extends the **Rotonda de los Hombres Ilustres**, a small park with statues and busts of men who have served their city with particular merit. A succession of plazas and pedestrian zones begins behind the cathedral. It starts off with the **Plaza de la Liberación**, also known as the Plaza de los Tres Poderes (the three powers), since the buildings of the legislative assembly, government administration and the palace housing the judicial branch are located on it. The plaza, dominated by a monument to the revolutionary priest Hidalgo, is also decorated by two colonial fountains.

The **Palacio del Gobierno**, a magnificent building whose construction began in 1643, boasts on its imposing staircase a monumental mural portrait of Pater Hidalgo, done by the great mural painter Orozco. Also of interest is the parliamentary chamber with its murals depicting the origin of the Mexican constitution. The building with its impressive frontage is situated opposite the Plaza de Armas; and one of its sides is on the Plaza de la Liberación. If one follows along the latter, the sprawling building of the **Museo Regional** comes into view. This colonial structure, dating from 1758, displays not only archeological finds and documents from the independence movement but also paintings by Murillo and Orozco in its numerous exhibition halls, which are grouped around patios.

The far side of the plaza is occupied by the **Teatro Degollado**, a copiously orna-

GUADALAJARA

mented building in classical style commissioned by Emperor Maximilian in 1866. One should at least try to get a look at its interior (it's frequently closed) or see a performance by the *Grupo Folklórico* on Sunday mornings. The theater's dome is adorned with a scene from Dante's *Divine Comedy*. To the rear, the visitor will discover a scene, sculptured in bronze, depicting the founding of the city of Guadalajara. The way continues past alternating colonial and modern buildings, graced with a number of fountains and monuments as well. It ends at the **Plaza Tapatia**.

Rising up over this plaza is the unique splendor of the **Hospicio Cabañas**. Designed in 1805 by the architect Manuel Tolsá as an orphanage, today it is a popular cultural institute. As a result there's always quite a bit of activity in and around it. The interior of the spacious building leaves the visitor with some lasting impressions: More than 20 interior courtyards are connected with each other by passageways. In the chapel one can view the renowned ceiling fresco *Man in Flames* by the muralist José Clemente Orozco, painted in 1938. The numerous other rooms contain other works of him, contemporary art and a museum.

As you return to the Plaza Tapatia, the modern building of the **Mercado Libertad** comes into view. It is reputed to be the country's largest municipal market, which is easy to believe considering the enormous size of the individual departments. On the lower level there is also a gigantic hall devoted exclusively to leather goods, while on the first floor space is occupied by small restaurants.

The Legend of Tequila

All great things have a myth of creation. According to an ancient legend from the Guadalajara region, there was great commotion in heaven because the gods

Above: An oasis of peace in the center of busy Guadalajara. Right: Tequila is made from the juice of the agave.

were quarreling about who could "bless" humanity with a beverage both pleasurable and over-powering. The problem was solved by a bolt of lightning. It hit an agave plant, bringing its fruit to the boil. The juice that then flowed from it had an instantaneous effect on the people who came rushing up, curious to try ...

In reality, however, it was Cenobio Sauza, also known as the "Father of Tequila", who experimented with the fermentation of *piñas* in the rather run-down town of **Tequila** (population 30,000), located 52 kilometers to the northwest of the capital city of Guadalajara in the state of Jalisco. Among the 400 different varieties of the maguey plant, the most savory liquor turned out to be a distillate of the *mezcal azul*. Top-quality tequila is produced exclusively from this variety, by distilleries in Tequila and in **Tepatitlán** (cast of Guadalajara). The Mexicans call any sort of agave rotgut *mescal*. There is a popular saying heard throughout Mexico: *"Para todo mal mezcal, y para todo bien también"*. ("Drink *mescal* when things are bad, and also when things are good .").

The people of Mexico swallow their *mescal* as the Scots do their whisky and the Bavarians their beer. Most is produced in small distilleries for local consumption, but the *mezcal* of southern Mexico is famous far and wide.

On the other hand, tequila is a patented product and has also become synonymous with Mexico. For the record, the boom began in 1873, when the Exchequer registered the export of three barrels of mescal wine to New Mexico by way of El Paso. In those days, Tequila had 2,500 inhabitants and 16 distilleries. With the award of prizes for *mescal* brandy at the 1893 World Exposition in Chicago and in 1910 in San Antonio, Texas, for tequila wine the term tequila had become established abroad. Tequila experts at the University of Guadalajara (which even offers a course of study on this tasty subject!) have predicted a production volume of 100 million liters within the coming decade.

LEÓN

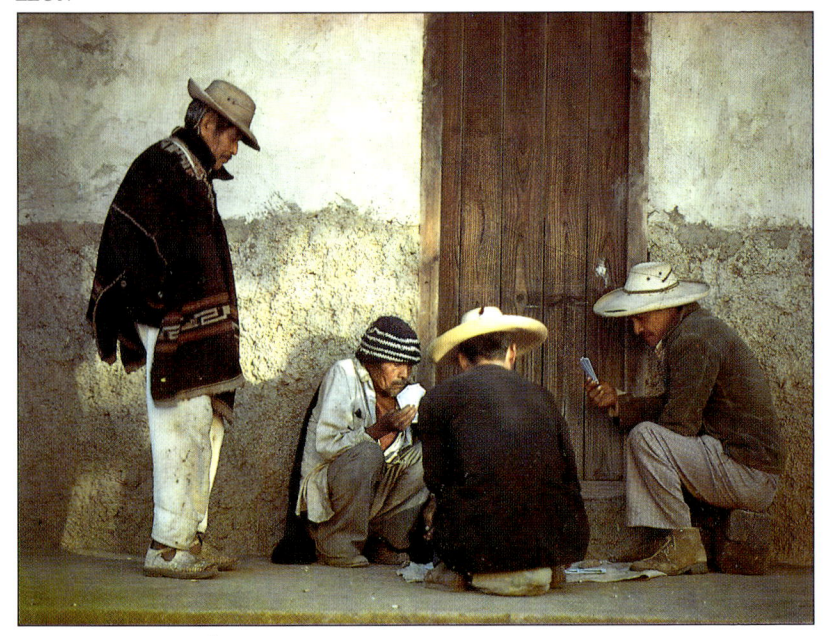

LEÓN

León (population 490,000), also known as León de los Aldamas, lies on the banks of the **Río Gómez** at an altitude of 1884 meters in a fertile valley with an equable climate. The largest city and main industrial center of the state of Guanajuato, it is Mexico's leading producer of shoes and saddles and other leather goods, as well as textiles, soap and steel products. The city is surrounded by a rich wheat-growing region.

The city didn't receive its municipal charter until 1836, although the Spaniards had established the first settlement in 1552. At that time, the area was inhabited by Tarascans and Aztecs and before that by Chichimecas. The words *de los Aldamas* were added to its name in honor of Juán Aldamas, one of the prominent figures in the Mexican fight for independence from the Spaniards.

Above: There is always time in León to gamble for a few pesos.

Although León is predominantly an industrial center, it has a number of handsome colonial buildings. The zócalo, surrounded by arcades, is flanked by the **Palacio Municipal** or Town Hall with a richly carved façade, and the Baroque church **Nuestra Señora de la Luz** (Our Lady of Light), built in 1746 by the Jesuits. Also of interest is the nearby **Templo Expiatorio**, a 20th-century church with catacombs beneath. They contain a series of altars, chapels, statues, and paintings. Bullfights are held regularly at the **Panteón Taurino**, and Leon's "Sport City" (Ciudad Sportiva) has an excellent reputation. 25 miles out of town is the sulphur springs spa of **Comanjilla**.

AGUASCALIENTES

Aguascalientes (population 460,000), was founded in 1575 by Jerónimo de Orozco and is the capital of the state of Aguascalientes (with a total population of 700,000). It is a pleasant colonial town with an agreeable climate situated at an altitude of 1889 meters and surrounded by orchards, vineyards and haciendas which breed *toros de lidia*, fighting bulls. Well-known for its attractive pottery, embroidery and textiles, it has become famous for its lively and colorful *Feria de San Marcos*, an annual spring fair (end of April to beginning of May with no fixed dates). The event has been held since 1604 in honor of the town's patron saint. It is alive with the excitement of bullfights, cockfights, *charreadas,* serenades and fireworks.

The town is also known as *Ciudad Perforada*, the "city riddled with holes", because of the labyrinth of passages under the town. These were originally catacombs hewn by Indians of unknown origin in the pre-Columbian days; however, they are not open to the public. After the Spanish had conquered the Indigenas, they established a town with the imposing name of *Nuestra Señora de la Asunción de las Aguas Calientes*, the last part of the name, "hot waters", referring to the numerous hot springs in the area. **San Nicolás de la Cantera**, **Ojo Caliente** (a modern *balneario*) and **Colombo** are all within a short ride.

For a long time, Aguascalientes was no more than a remote outpost providing defense against hostile Indigenas. In 1857, it was made the capital of the state of the same name. During the years of the Mexican Revolution, it served as a strategic railroad junction and passed repeatedly from one faction to another. On **Plaza Principal**, the zócalo, are the 17th-century **Palacio Municipal** and the 18th-century **Palacio de Gobierno**. The latter, formerly the feudal palace of the Marqués de Guadalupe, is a magnificent Baroque building, with murals by Osvaldo Barra – a pupil of Diego Rivera – in the inner courtyard.

Interesting religious buildings include the 18th-century **cathedral**, the **Iglesia de San Marcos**, with its picture *Adoration of the Kings* by José Alzibar, the **Iglesia El Encino**, with a Black Christ depicted by Andrés López, and the **Iglesia de San Antonio**, a neo-Byzantine church built in the 20th century. Both the **Convento de San Diego** and the **Museo de la Ciudad** are known for their exhibits of impressive paintings.

SAN LUIS POTOSÍ

The city of **San Luis Potosí** (population 730,000), is the capital of the state of the same name. Set on a steppe-like plateau, it is an important road junction and commercial center. Despite increasing modernization, the city has preserved much of its colonial history through its handsome old buildings and parks.

Originally settled by the Huachichili, it was later taken over by the Spaniards who were followed by Franciscan friars in 1585. During this period, considerable quantities of gold and silver were discovered and the town was called *Real de Minas de San Luis Potosí*. It took the latter part of its name from the Bolivian silver town of Potosí, meaning "place of great richness." During the French intervention, it was also the seat of Benito Juárez's government after it was expulsed from Mexico City in 1863 and again in 1867. It was here, in 1854, that Gonzalez Bocanegra wrote the Mexican national anthem. Also orginated here was the San Luis Plan, which started the Revolution of 1910. Overlooking **Plaza de Armas** with the adjoining **Jardín Hidalgo** are two of the city's landmarks. On the west side the **Palacio de Gobierno** is a massive neoclassical building dating from 1770. Opposite stands the Baroque **Catedral de la Expectación de la Virgin**, built between 1690 and 1737, which has a hexagonal porch with niches containing statues of the twelve apostles. It's interior has a welter of decoration in a mixture of styles. East of the cathedral, **Nuestra Señora del Carmen** (1749-64) graces a small *plazuela* named after it.

SAN LUIS POTOSÍ / ZACATECAS

The church has a magnificent Churrigueresque style façade and a dome coated in blue, yellow, green, and white tiles. The interior contains an elaborate high altar, an ornately carved pulpit, paintings by Vallejo, and the **Pordada de los Angeles**, a side doorway with a beautiful façade. The **Museo Regional** in the old **Convento de San Francisco** shows archeological finds from the region, including Huaxtec, Totonac, and Aztec artifacts. On the upper floor is the **Capilla a la Virgin de Aranzazú**, dating from the early 18th century and an outstanding example of the Churrigueresque style architecture of New Spain. The doors are of carved mesquite wood and there is a figure of Christ in the porch made from reeds coated with a resin mixture.

Both the **Iglesia de San Francisco** and **San Augustin** are worth seeing. The former is a 17th-century Baroque masterpiece with a blue-and-white-tile dome, while the latter, also from the 17th century, has a Baroque façade and a neoclassical interior. The **Museo Nacional de la Máscara** possesses a unique collection of about 1500 masks from pre-Hispanic to modern times. The **Museo Regional de Arte Popular y Casa de Artenanías** provide an insight into the history and culture of the city. A good selection of sarapes, basketwork, pottery and locally- made natural silk *rebozos* are for sale in the **Mercado Hidalgo**.

The attractive little town of **Santa María del Río** 45 kilometers south of San Luis Potosí, is noted for its *rebozos*, the best in the state for the lowest prices. Near here are also the spas of **Gogorrón**, **Agua de Lourdes** and **Ojo Caliente**. Also a place of interest is the ghost town of **Cerro de San Pedro**, where gold and silver were found in the late 17th century.

ZACATECAS

Another silver-mining center is the charming colonial town of **Zacatecas** (population 230,000), capital of the state of the same name. Situated in a narrow gorge dominated by the peaks of Cerro de la Bufa, Mala Noche and El Padre, it was for centuries an important silver-mining center. With its closely packed houses and steep stone steps that connect some of the cobbled lanes and streets, the city is a beautifull example of colonial architecture. The name Zacatecas means "land where *zacate* grass grows" in Náhuatl. Originally inhabited by kinsmen of the Chalchihuites and Quemada tribes, the city was founded in 1546 by conquistadors in search of silver.

La Catedral in the **Plaza Hidalgo** is one of the country's most lavish example of Mexican Baroque and was completed in 1752. The northern façade is Churrigueresque, the southern is European Baroque. The former has figures of Christ and the twelve apostles, and the

Above: Modern extraction methods have revived silver-mining. Right: Who could resist such a display?

four fathers of the church around the choir window. In the upper part is God the Father surrounded by eight angelic musicians. The interior is not as attractive. Most of the sumptuous furnishings were removed during the Revolution.

Next to the cathedral stands the **Palacio de Gobierno**, an 18th-century mansion with fine wrought-iron balconies. Painted in 1970 by the prominent artist Antonio Pintor Rodríguez, the mixed-media mural in the interior stairwell traces the history of Zacatecas from the days when the indigenous Caxanes lived here to the age of the industrial city. Built by the Jesuits in 1746, the **Templo de Santo Domingo** contains eight beautiful carved *retablos* – Baroque altars of gilded wood – and an 18th-century German organ. One of the most remarkable collections of modern art in Mexico is just next door in the **Museo de Pedro Coronel**. It includes works by Braque, Miró, Chagall, Picasso, and Goya.

Other sights in town are the **Iglesia de San Agustin**, now a museum, with the remains of a Plateresque doorway; the **Teatro Calderón** and the **Casa Moneda**, a 19th-century mint also called *tesoreria*, and the 2-kilometer-long late-18th century **aqueduct**. The five-minute cable car (*teleférico*) ride from Cerro del Grillo to Cerro de la Bufa over Zacatecas is a unique experience.

An underground visit of the **El Eden mine**, which produced unimaginable quantities of silver and gold, should not be left out. The **Convento de Nuestra Señora de Guadalupe**, founded by the Franciscans in 1707 and now a museum of art, is six kilometers east of town in the tiny village of **Guadalupe**. There is a library and a fine collection of paintings of the colonial period.

The **Chicomoztoc Ruins**, who are also called **Quemada Ruins**, are located in a peaceful valley about 50 kilometers south of Zacatecas. Although the ruins are only partially restored, they show the narrow streets and sturdy foundations of the homes and temples of an unknown ancient people.

GUIDEPOST CENTRAL HIGHLANDS

MORELIA
Accommodation
LUXURY: **Villa Montaña**, Santa Maria, situated 3 km to the south, Tel: 4-0179.
Calinda Morelia Quality Inn, Avenida de las Camelias 3466, Tel: 4-5669.
MODERATE: **Hotel Catedral**, Zaragoza 37, Tel: 3-0783. **Alameda**, Av. Madero/Guillermo Prieto, Tel: 2-2023. **Posada de la Soledad**, Zaragoza 90, Tel: 2-1888.
BUDGET: **Casino**, Portal Hidalgo 229, Tel: 3-1003. **Virrey de Mendozo**, at the Zócalo, Tel: 2-0633.
Restaurants
The restaurant of the **Posada de la Soledad** (see above) serves an excellent Mexican buffet. **Las Morelianas**, El Ratajo 90, Tel: 4-0891. **El Solar de Villagran**, Rincon de las Comadres 7, Tel: 4-5647. **La Huacana**, Garcia Obeso 15, Tel: 2-5312, popular, local cuisine.
Shopping
Casa de las Artesanías, Plaza Valladolid, arts and crafts from Michoacán.
Special Events
Procession in Santa María de Guido on August 15. *Arts and Crafts Fair*, May 1-12.
Market Thursdays and Sundays.
Tourist Information
Palacio Clavijero, Nigromante 79, Tel: 3-2654, 9 am-8 pm, weekends until 7 pm.

QUERÉTARO
Accommodation
LUXURY: **Real de Minas**, Constituyentes 124 Pte., Tel: 6-0444. **Mesón de Santa Rosa**, Pasteur 17, Plaza de Armas, Tel: 4-5781.
MODERATE: **Mirabel**, Constituyentes 2 Ote. **El Senorial**, Guerrero Nte. 10 A, Tel: 4-3700.
BUDGET: **Plaza**, Juárez Nte. 23, Tel: 2-1138. **Gran Hotel**, Sexta Oriente/Madero, Tel: 2-0124.
HACIENDA-LUXURY-HOTELS out of town: **La Mansión Galindo**, San Juan del Río, Tel: (467) 2-0050, reservation in Mexico City, Tel: 533-3550/53. **La Estancia de San Juan**, Tel: (467) 2-0120, reservation in Mexico City, Tel: 514-5711. **Hacienda Jurica**, Tel: (463) 8-0022.
Restaurants
Fonda San Antonio, Mexican and international cuisine, Corregodar Norte 44, Tel: 2-0299. **Comedor Natura**, vegetarian, Vergara Sur 7, Tel: 4-1088. **La Flor de Querétaro**, Mexican food, Juárez Norte 5, Tel: 2-0199.
Tourist Information
Palacio Municipal, near the Plaza Independencia, Tel: 22-2802, Mon-Fri 9 am-2 pm and 5-8 pm, weekends 9 am-2 pm.

SAN MIGUEL DE ALLENDE
Accommodation
LUXURY: **Casa Sierra Nevada**, Hospicio 25, Tel: 2-0415. **Villa Jacaranda**, Aldama 53, Tel: 2-1015. **Hacienda de las Flores**, Hospicio 16, Tel: 2-1808. *MODERATE*: **Aristos**, Calle Ancha de San Antonio 30, Tel: 2-0149. **Casa de Lujo Inn**, Pila Seca 35, Tel: 2-0951. **Posada San Francisco**, Plaza Principal 2, Tel: 2-0072.
BUDGET: **Quinta Loretto**, Callejón de Loreto 15, Tel: 2-0042. **Mesón de San Antonio**, Mesones 80 (near the Zócalo), Tel: 2-0580.
Restaurants
Villa Jacaranda, Aldama 53, Tel: 2-0415. **Sierra Nevada**, Hospicio 35, Tel: 2-0415. **Mesón Bugambilias**, Hidalgo 42, near the Zócalo, regional food, Tel: 2-0127.
Special Events
Fiesta de San Miguel, September 29–October 4, with fireworks and bullfights.
Tourist Information
At the **Zócalo**, Tel: 2-1747, Mon-Fri 10 am-2.45 pm and 5-7 pm, weekends 10 am-12 noon.

LEÓN
Accommodation
LUXURY: **La Estancia**, Blvd. **López Mateos** 1311 Ote., Tel: 6-3939. **Hotel Real de Minas**, Blvd. López Mateos, Tel. 4-3677.
MODERATE: **Condessa**, Portal Bravo, Tel: 3-1120. **León**, Madero 113 at the Zócalo, Tel: 4-1050. *BUDGET:* **San Diego**, Jardín de la Unión, Tel: 2-1300.

AGUASCALIENTES
Accommodation
MODERATE / BUDGET: **Río Grande**, José Chavez 101, Tel: 6-1666. **Las Trojes**, Blv. Campestre, Tel: 4-0468.
Restaurants
El Quijote, José María Chavez 701, Tel: 5-5406. **Villa Jardín**, regional food, López Mateos 511 Pte., Tel: 8-1791.
Tourist Information
Plaza Patria 141 Pte., Tel: 5-1155.

SAN LUIS POTOSÍ
Accommodation
MODERATE / BUDGET: **Panorama**, Av. Venustiano Carranza 315, Tel: 2-1777. **Real Plaza**, Av. Venustiano Carranza 890, Tel: 4-6969. **María Cristina**, Juan Sarabia 110, Tel: 2-9408.
Restaurants
Veda Mariscos, seafood, Bravos 510, Tel: 4-8033. **La Parroquia Potosina**, Carranza 301, Tel: 2-6681.

GUIDEPOST CENTRAL HIGHLANDS

Tourist Information
Jardín Hidalgo 20, Tel: 9-1481 and 4-2994, Mon-Fri 9 am-9 pm, Sat 9 am-2 pm.

ZACATECAS
Accommodation
MODERATE / BUDGET: **Aristos**, Loma de la Soledad, Tel: 2-1788. **Hotel Gallery**, Blvd. López Mateos, Tel: 2-3311. **Plaza Zacatecas**, Blvd. Zacatecas Guadalupe, Tel: 2-8511.

Restaurants
Mesón La Mina, Mexican food, Juárez 15, Tel: 2-2773. **Los Faroles**, reasonable prices, Mexican food, Tacuba 1179.

Tourist Information
Hidalgo/Callejón de Santero, Tel: 2-6683, Mon-Fri 8 am-3.30 pm and 6-8 pm.

DOLORES HIDALGO
Accommodation
MODERATE / BUDGET: **Hotel Hidalgo**, Veracruz 5, Tel: 2-0862. **Posada Cocomacán**, Plaza Principal (Zócalo), Tel: 2-0018. **Caudillo**, Qerétaro 8, Tel: 2-0198.

Restaurants
El Delfín, Guerrero/Veracruz, Tel: 2-0022. **Aladino's**, Plaza Principal 8 (no phone).

Post / Police
Post Office: Puebla 22, Tel: 2-0807, Mon-Fri 9 am-1 pm. **Police**: Tel: 2-1442.

Tourist Information
Plaza Principal, daily 9 am-3 pm and 5-8 pm.

GUANAJUATO
Accommodation
LUXURY: **Castillo Santa Cecilia**, ca. 2 km in the direction of Dolores Hidalgo, Tel: 2-0485. **El Presidente**, ca. 1,5 km out of town at the Marfil Highway, Tel: 2-3980. **Parador San Javier**, Aldama 92, ca. 2 km in the direction of Dolores Hidalgo, Tel: 2-06626.
MODERATE: **Villa de la Plata**, ca. 3 km in the direction of Dolores Hidalgo, Tel: 2-5200. **Posada Santa Fe**, Jardin de la Unión 12, Tel: 2-0084. **Del Frayle** (in a 17th century house), Sopena 3, Tel: 2-1179.
BUDGET: **El Insurgente**, Av. Juárez 226, Tel: 2-2294 and 2-3192. **Hacienda de Cobos**, Padre Hidalgo 3, Tel: 2-0350.

Restaurants
The good restaurants (international and Mexican) are situated outside the town center in the better class hotels. **Restaurant-Bar 4 Ranas**, Jardín de la Union 1, Tel: 2-4257. **Venta Vieja**, Javier 1, Tel: 2-0626. **Las Palomas**, Ayuntamiento 19 (town hall), Tel: 2-4936.

Shopping
Mercado Hidalgo, Av. Juárez, with a wide variety of stalls, arts and crafts, open daily.

Museums
Museo Diego Rivera, birthplace of the famous painter, Calle Pocitos 47, closed Mondays.

Special Events
Festival Cervantino, September–October, Mexico's most important international cultural event.

Post / Telephone / Police
Post Office: Ayuntamiento 25 (town hall), no phone, Mon-Fri 8 am-8 pm, Sat and Sun 9 am-1 pm. **Telephone** (long distance): *Caseta* in the bus terminal, 7.30 am-9.30 pm. **Telegrams**: Sopeña 1, Tel: 2-00429, Mon-Sat 9 am-8.30 pm, Sun 9 am-12 noon. **Police**: Tel: 2-0266.

Tourist Information
Juárez / 5 de Mayo, Tel: 2-0086, Mon-Fri 8.30 am-7.30 pm, Sat and Sun 10 am-2.30 pm.

GUADALAJARA
Accommodation
LUXURY: **Camino Real**, Av. Vallarta 5005, Tel: 21-7217. **Fiesta Americana**, Aureio Aceves 225, Tel: 25-3434. **El Tapatío Resort and Raquet Club**, ca. 6 km south of the center, Blvd. Aeropuerto 4275, Tel: 35-6050. **Guadalajara Sheraton**, Av. 16 de Septiembre / Niños Héroes, Tel: 14-7272. *MODERATE*: **Hotel Malibu**, Av. Vallarta, Tel: 21-7676. **Hotel Diana**, Av. Circ. Agustín Yañez 2760, Tel: 15-5510. **Calinda Romana**, Juárez 170, Tel: 14-8650.
BUDGET: **Francés**, oldest hotel in town, Maestranza 35, Tel: 13-1190. **Fénix** (Best Western), Corona 160, Tel: 14-5714.

Restaurants
Guadalajara has a broad spectrum of first-class restaurants. **Albatros**, seafood, Av. de la Plaza 1840, Tel: 25-9996. **Brazz Campestre**, regional food, López Mateos Sur 2260, Tel: 31-1367. **Brazz Jardín**, great steaks, López Mateos Sur 6022, Tel: 31-5725. **Sin Nombre**, Mexican food of the 19th century, Madero 80, in Tlaquepaque, Tel: 35-4520.

Post / Telecommunication
Post Office: Carranza between Jaun Manuel-Calle Independencia Sur, Mon-Fri 9 am-6 pm, Sat 9 am-1 pm. **Telephone** (long distance): Guerra between Moreno-Juárez, daily 7 am-8.20 pm. **Telegrams**: Palacio Federal, Alcalde/Juan Alvarez, Tel: 14-2632, at the bus terminal, Tel: 19-4133 and at the airport.

Tourist Information
Morelos 102, Tel: 14-8686, Plaza de la Liberación, open Monday-Friday 9 am-9 pm, Saturday 9 am-1 pm and 3-7 pm.

117

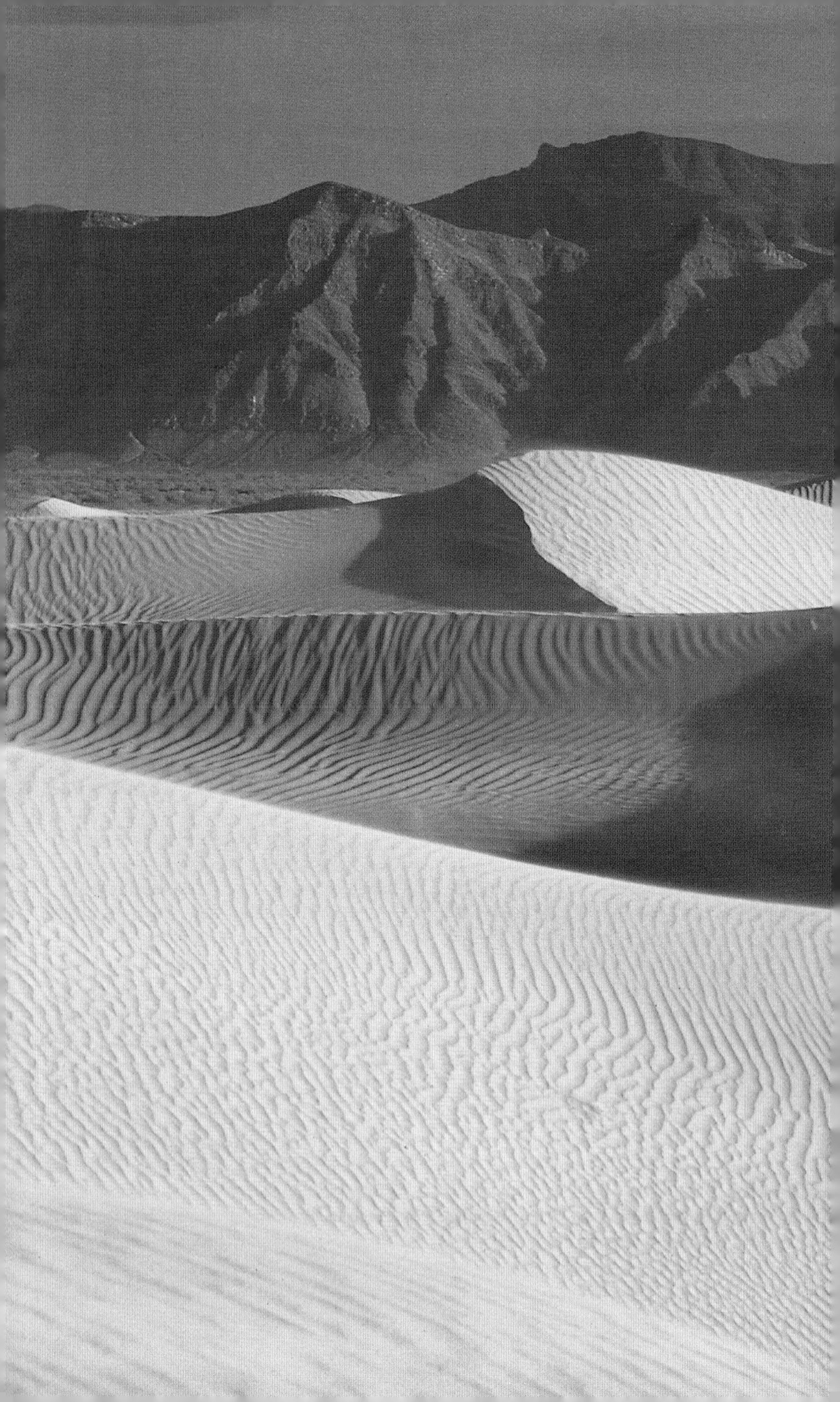

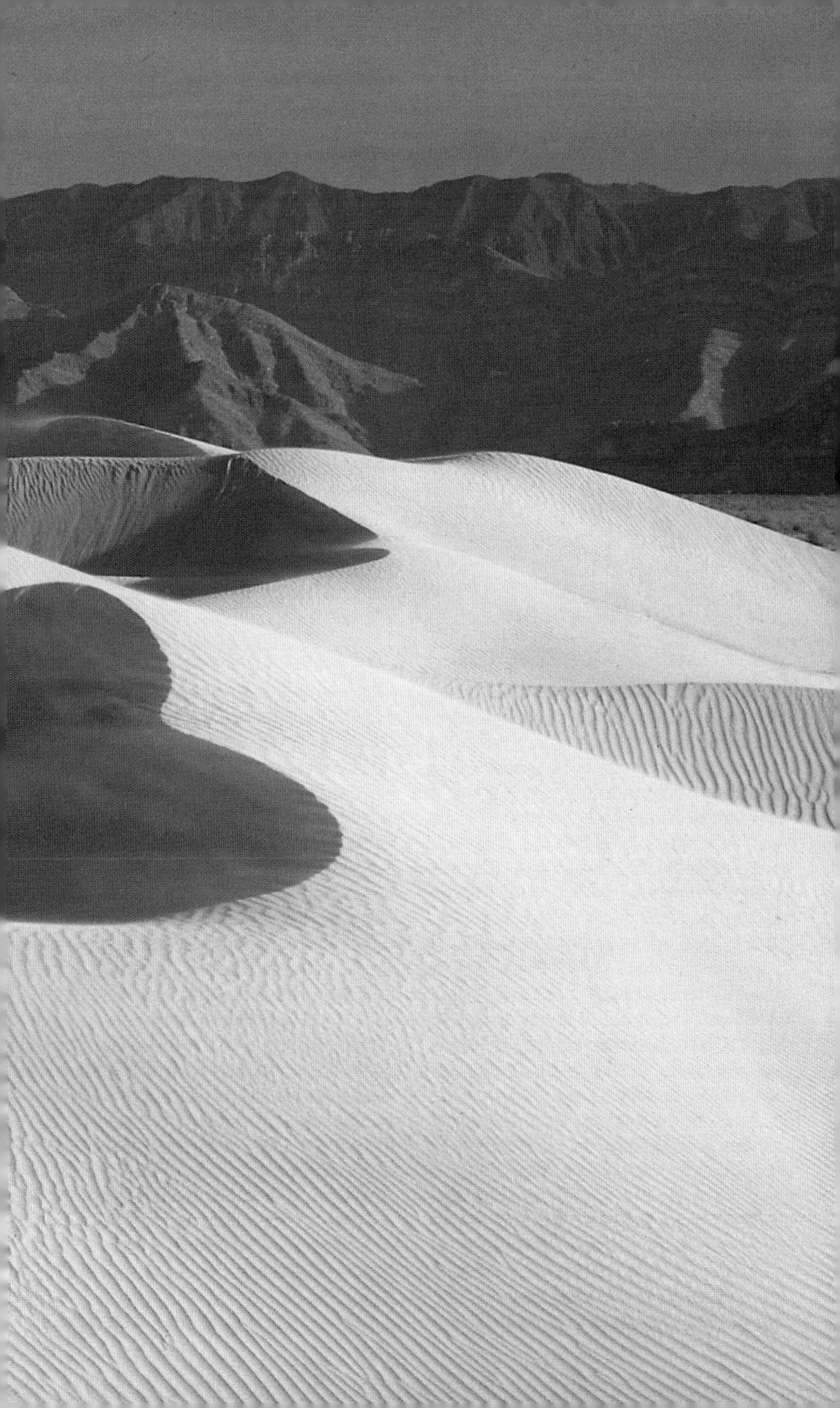

MEXICO'S WILD NORTH

MONTERREY
THE BORDER STATES
BARRANCA DEL COBRE
BAJA CALIFORNIA

The north of Mexico, a rough and inhospitable mountainous desert, has always been wild and rebellious. It is the land of the Huastecs, a tribe whom the Aztecs scorned for their shameful lack of morals. The Huaxtecs are spread over the states of Tamaupilas, Nuevo León and Veracruz, but unlike other tribes they have not left spectacular sites to be admired by tourists. Throughout modern history the "wild north" has been a notorious cradle of revolutionary ideas, and a bone of contention for a period of more than 100 years. The famous outlaw Francisco "Pancho" Villa made himself quite at home in this region.

MONTERREY

Monterrey's troubles in the "Wild North" began as soon as the colonial outpost was founded in 1579. A natural crossroads between north and south, the small settlement with a population of 258 in 1775 stood in the path of whatever was occurring at the time, whether it be hostile tribesmen moving from one place to the next, heavy floods, alternate Spanish and Mexican troops during the Mexican War of Independence or US troops invading during the Mexican-American War.

Monterrey, surrounded on three sides by the craggy peaks of the Sierra Oriente mountains, was a small settlement of little importance until a railroad connection to Laredo in 1882 opened up great new opportunities, in the shape of United States-financed smelting and other heavy industry. Today Monterrey, capital of the state of Nuevo León, is Mexico's third largest city. With a population of more than 1.8 million, it is an industrial center, involved principally in forging steel and brewing beer.

Monterrey considers itself quite different from the rest of Mexico: a modern city with few colonial buildings, proud of its industrialization, its connections with and resemblance to its northern neighbor. Even the food is special – particularly the mesquite-grilled beef, the *cabrito* and the Mexican beer.

Monterrey is not a tourist town, but there are several things of interest. Impressive is the city's **Grand Square** (Gran Plaza), 100 acres of urban renewal created in 1984. Its center is marked by a tall, slender monument raised to the "gods of commerce". The long green plaza, well-landscaped, with sparkling fountains, and an underground shopping mall, is bounded on the south by the

Previous pages: The Sonora Desert – Mexico's driest region.

SONORA / NOGALES / HERMOSILLO

Palacio Municipal (New City Hall) and on the north by the **Palacio Federal** (Old City Hall) with a beautiful 16th-century courtyard; the view from the upper floors is excellent. Just south of the latter is the **Palacio del Gobierno** (Government Palace), built in 1908, with a historical exhibit featuring the guns used to execute Emperor Maximilian in 1867.

The **Cathedral**, on the edge of the Gran Plaza, was begun in 1600 but it took some 250 years to complete. Notable are its richly carved Baroque façade and the Catalonian bell tower as well as the interior murals. The **El Obispado** (Bishop's Palace), built in 1788, is the only landmark from the colonial era. During the Mexican-American War it was turned into a fort, now it contains the Regional Museum of Nuevo León. Another attraction is the **Alfa Cultural Center** (Centro Cultural Alpha), a fine museum of science and technology with an unusual shape: It has been compared to a giant tin can set into the ground at an angle. The original building of the Cuauhtémoc Brewery houses the **Museum of Monterrey**, where paintings by Rufino Tamayo, David Siqueiros and José Orozco are displayed.

THE BORDER STATES

The border states of Mexico consist at their northern edge of a flat and inhospitable desert rising southwards up into the craggy peaks of the Sierra Madre mountains. The rocky desert is barely redeemed on the east coast by the irrigated farmlands of Tamaulipas sloping down to the Gulf of Mexico, and on the west coast by the descent to Sonora's desolate **Desierto Altar** (Altar Desert) along the **Sea of Cortés**, a fishermen's paradise. Across this vast northern expanse only five major roads bisect the harsh land, one for each of the five border states. From the cities of Nogales, in Sonora; Ciudad Juárez, in Chihuahua; Piedras Negras, in Coahuila; Matamoros, in Tamaulipas; and Nuevo Laredo (where the highway crosses a narrow strip of Tamaulipas to enter the state of Nuevo León) all lead south to Mexico City. This is very rough terrain. Cactus and mesquite are what meets the eye as the roads climb toward the great peaks of the Sierra Madre Oriental or the Sierra Madre Occidental. The cities are miles apart and the rural areas are punctuated only by small settlements.

Sonora, which borders the state of Arizona in the northwesternmost corner of Mexico, has tamed some of the desert with mighty dams, but much of the area is still as stark as ever, with ancient volcanic lava beds.

A fence separates **Nogales**, Mexico, from it's neighbor Nogales, Arizona, and there is little of interest for the tourist in this center of ranching, dairy and irrigation farming. 275 kilometers south, the modern and wealthy state capital **Hermosillo** (population 350,000) is also not really a tourist town. It owes its prosperity to the **La Presa Rodríguez** (Rodrigues Dam), built to harness the Río Sonora and make irrigation possible. The local cathedral in the **Plaza Zaragoza** is attractive only for those who wish to pray, whilst the **Museo Regional de Historia** (Regional Historical Museum) contains a fine collection of Indigena artefacts. In the immediate area around Hermosillo hunting is popular, with deer, coyote and rabbits as game. **Guaymas**, west on the Sea of Cortés, is a seaport and shrimping center, surrounded by craggy sun-baked mountains and neighbor to **San Carlos**, a resort filled with hotels and condominiums, with the interest to the tourist being blue-water fishing.

The state of **Chihuahua** bordering Sonora on the east and the states of New Mexico and Texas on the north, has 375 kilometers of flat desert plains with cactus and mesquite until the highway reaches the mountains around Chihuahua

121

CIUDAD JUÁREZ / SALTILLO

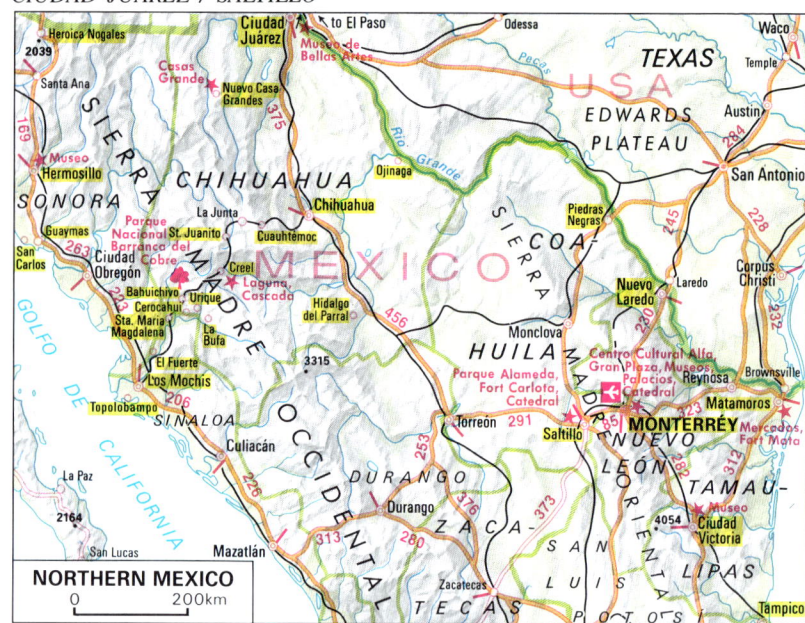

and **Barranca del Cobre** (Copper Canyon). The border city of **Ciudad Juárez**, with a population of 850,000, Mexico's fifth largest city, lies across the Rio Grande (for Mexicans *Río Bravo del Norte*) opposite from El Paso. The two towns are connected by two downtown bridges and a third to the east. Wide boulevards, the **Museo de Arte e Historia** (Museum of Art and History), an **Arts and Crafts Center** (both in Centro Cultural Juárez), and a shrine to Mexico's patron saint, the **Misión de Nuestra Señora de Guadalupe** (Mission of our Lady of Guadalupe) are worth visiting. The mission, an adobe building, dates back to the year 1658.

Between Ciudad Juárez and Chihuahua there is an archeological excavation site of interest 7 kilometers southwest of Nuevo Casas Grandes on a side road off main Route 45. The ruins of **Casas Grandes** resemble the dwellings of the pueblo inhabitants of Arizona and New Mexico and were probably inhabited until the 16th century.

Approximately 320 kilometers south of Chihuahua, the old mining town of **Hidalgo del Parral** is notorious as the site of the assassination of Francisco "Pancho" Villa. **Coahuila**, adjoining Chihuahua on the east, shares its northern border with Texas at the town of **Piedras Nigras** (Eagle Pass in Texas), a town of about 35,000 inhabitants with shops full of handcrafted items at bargain prices. There are restaurants, night clubs and bullfights at intervals during the summer months. The state is known principally for the town of **Saltillo** (population 415,000), state capital at an altitude of 1550 meters in the Sierra Madre Oriental. Here manufacturing plants produce pottery, silver articles and jewelry, and in particular, leather goods and Saltillo's famous *sarapes*, which visitors can watch being created from raw wool to finished product. The **Cathedral of Santiago** (1746-1801) overlooks the **Plaza**

Right: Bigger than the Grand Canyon – Mexico's Barranca del Cobre.

de Armas and is considered to be one of the finest examples of Churrigueresque architecture in North America. The **Alameda**, a park west of the Plaza de Armas, contains a pond in the shape of Mexico, and the **Fortress of Carlota** in the old section of the town is dedicated to Charlotte of Belgium, Emperor Maximilian's wife, who was plagued by madness even before her husband was captured and shot by Mexican nationalists.

Tamaupilas's capital is **Ciudad Victoria** (population 100,000) on the old Pan American Highway. It's a sportsman's town, thanks to **Lake Vincente Guerrero**, a few kilometers north of the city. The lake was created in 1970 and is surrounded by a great number of fishing camps. The city itself doesn't offer much. There is only a small **Casa del Arte Tamaualipeco** (Museum of Art), the **Palacio del Gobierno** (Government Palace) and a nice zócalo.

312 kilometers to the north, the Highway 101 ends up in **Matamoros**. Here, across from Brownsville, shopping is a high priority for tourists, with the **Mercado Pazaje Juárez**, the **Mercado Juárez de Artensanías** and the **Arts and Crafts Center** in the first place. The historical heart of the town is the old **Fort Mata** with the **Casa Mata Museum**.

The twin city to Laredo, Texas, is 400-year-old **Nuevo Laredo**. (population 350,000) on the plains of Mexico's northeastern frontier. Until the 1839 Declaration of Independence both from Mexico und the United States they were one.

The State of Tamaupilas has 427 kilometers of coast as it drops south along the Gulf of Mexico to **Tampico**, an industrial port with tropical climate.

BARRANCA DEL COBRE

The Sierra Madre Occidental is among the most trackless regions of our planet. By and large, the main laws in force here are those of nature. All is lost for those who fail to adapt. Even the conquistadors have capitulated in the face of the rugged mountain landscape of northern Mexico, bandits and rebels have taken flight into its canyons, and the Tarahumara Indigenas managed to evade christianization there. As settlement increased, the *sierra* also became an area of retreat for endangered species. Technology has only conquered a narrow strip of the region, several hundred kilometers long, in the form of a railroad track passing through desolate highlands, fissured mountain ranges, deep chasms and drilling its way right through immense precipices. Rolling on its rails between Los Mochis on the Pacific and Chihuahua in the highlands are the diesel-powered trains of the *Ferrocarriles Chihuahua al Pacífico*, passing by a colossal labyrinth of *cañons*: The **Barranca del Cobre**, consisting of four canyon systems (only one of which is visible from the train), is four times larger than the Grand Canyon of the Colorado River. The "Copper Canyon" is an unforgettable experience that thousands of travelers enjoy each year. This train route is among the most exciting and beautiful in the world.

Let's set off on this adventure in **Los Mochis**, located 20 kilometers from the harbor city of **Topolobambo**. In the dialect of the Mayo Indigenas, Los Mochis means "Place of the Tortoise". That may sound romantic, however, this city of 130,000 inhabitants is the very antithesis of the tourist's notion of Mexico. There are no Baroque colonial facades, no *mariachi* musicians. The large number of *zapaterías* shoe-shops featuring cowboy boots betray the fact that the major cattle ranches aren't far away. Nonetheless, Los Mochis is packed with tourists who flood into its hotels the night before their crack-of-dawn *ferrocarril* departure for the journey of their dreams. Five dark-blue railroad cars and a dining car, pulled by two diesel locomotives, head off to the northwest at 6:00 a.m. on-the-dot with 653 single-track kilometers ahead of it before arriving at Chihuahua, the state's capital city.

Starting from **Ojinaga**, there are 920 kilometers of track leading to the Texas border. The route of the Kansas City, Mexico & Oriental Railroad Co. reached its completion there in 1914. Construction on the Mexican side began in 1902, but the Revolution delayed the continuation to Chihuahua. Legend has it that Francisco "Pancho" Villa, one-time bandit, later revolutionary and today a national hero, is supposed to have swung the pick-axe, *not* a gun, along this track in those days. In 1918, Ojinaga was finally connected with Chihuahua (at kilometer 268), and by 1930 it was possible to travel through to Creel.

The railroad's history is and reads like a chronicle of bankruptcies, a novel featuring utopian dreamers, desperate private investors and dare-devil engineers as its chief protagonists. Everyone agreed that the Sierra Madre Occidental couldn't be overcome, with its average altitude of 2300 meters and a maze of canyons reaching depths of up to 1700 meters. On November 23rd, 1961, when the completed line was opened by President Alfonso López Mateos, the railroad's construction had taken 90 years and swallowed (at least) $US 90 million. The Mexican "Orient Express" runs through 86 tunnels, clatters over 37 bridges and puffs its way up to 2461 meters above sea-level, the highest point on its course. Altogether, the *ferrocarril* passes through 17.2 kilommeters of tunnels and ventures over 3.6 kilometers of bridges.

At **El Fuerte**, a former missionary outpost established in 1564, later a fortress and silver-mining center, and today the center of a gigantic fruit and vegetable plantation (the "Garden of Los Mochis"), the train crosses the **Rio Fuerte** on a 538-meter-long bridge, the route's longest. Another 26 kilometers down the line

Right: The railway plunges through deep cuttings and ravines on its way from Los Mochis to Chihuahua.

complete darkness prevails for almost 2 kilometers. This shaft through the mountain has been named the "Tunnel of Thieves" after the shady characters who probably travel the stretch rather frequently. And the train has scarcely wound its way out of tunnel number 83 when an abyss opens up before the travelers' eyes: One is suspended at a height of several hundred meters above the **Rio Chinipas**. A pedestrian bridge crossing it at the narrowest point is visible down below. After this, your nerves have a chance to settle a bit, with one tunnel after another, railroad encampments and the Jesuit mission **Santa Maria Magdalena**.

La Perla is the name of the next engineering masterpiece, a 1000-meter-long tunnel. The landscape to the right before entering the horse-shoe shaped tunnel appears to the left afterwards. A couple of minutes later one can catch a glimpse of three winding stretches of track at different levels all at the same time. At the **Bahuichivo** station travelers should make the first break in their journey. In a 45-minute ride, an ancient bus shakes and jolts the passenger to the Hotel Misión in **Cerocahui**, where the Italian Jesuit priest Salvatierra first sounded the church bell in 1681 to announce to Huehueteotl, the "old god" of the Tarahumara, that Christian competition had arrived. Indeed, the roughly 40,000 Rarámuri ("runners", as they call themselves) have integrated Christ into their system of religious beliefs, but otherwise they have quite deliberately turned their back on civilization. To this day they live beneath cliffs and in caves, scattered around in small clans. From Cerocahui one can proceed via a logging road to the edge of the magnificent **Urique Cañon**. From one ledge, the view sweeps across a vast, wild panorama of rugged mountains. Glinting in the valley bottom is the silvery ribbon of the Urique River. In the shimmering heat an abandoned silver mine bears mute witness to bygone days. Once there was bustling activity in the midst of a pitiless and thoroughly inhospitable landscape where pumas, ocelots and other rare species still have a chance to survive. Thereafter, at kilometer 585, comes **La Lazo**, a "loop" inside a mountain. As you leave it you can see the tunnel entrance above you – an engineering masterpiece indeed!

The Copper Canyon Express does *not* travel according to the motto *mañana* (tomorrow). The longest stopover, all of 20 minutes, is at the **Divisadero** railway station, where two familiar postcard motifs await the traveler: Indigena women selling handcrafted items and piping-hot snacks, as well as the most spectacular view into the canyons found anywhere along the entire route. The Hotel Posada Barrancas, just a stone's throw from the station, is bounded on one side by a yawning chasm over which the vultures make their lazy circles. It's just a short walk from the station to an observation point over the **Urique Cañon**, through which the Rio Urique threads its way, at this point some 1200 meters below. The short hike is certainly a rewarding one – the view here is really fantastic. By the way, at the hotel it is possible to rent horses. The riding excursions over passable trails into the land of the Tarahumara (as well as longer treks descending into the canyons) are led by native guides.

The station that follows, **Creel**, is an equally popular overnight stop. In recent years, this town has developed into a little "Wild West Dorado". Hotels, several restaurants, souvenir shops, a bookstore and even a bank draw on the constantly growing number of Mexicans and foreigners on mini-adventures. In Creel it is also possible to hire horses and make bookings for local bus tours and those going further afield, for example, to **Laguna Araceco** (a small artificial lake) for a refreshing swim; to the **Cusárare Waterfalls** or even to the legendary gold- and silver-mining town of **La Buffa**. The remaining train route to Chihuahua leads

Above: This little Tarahumara girl is proud of her hat. Right: In the scorching heat of the north the candelabra-cactus provides welcome shade for man and beast.

through **Ciudad Cuauhtémoc**, a German-founded Mennonite colony that has become renowned for its cheese. Along the last 100 kilometers, via **St. Juanito** to the capital of the state of Chihuahua, the signs of civilization become increasingly frequent: herds of cattle and goats, shabby little huts, a lot of litter and an *autopista* (motorway) accompanying the railroad tracks.

After a travel time of at least twelve hours the train pulls into **Chihuahua** with un-Mexican punctuality. The biggest attraction here is a cathedral in Churrigueresque style. In the Tarahumara language the city's name means "dry place".

BAJA CALIFORNIA

The **Baja Peninsula** is a world apart. Running 1700 km from Mexico's border with Southern California, it is a land of desert and semi-desert separating the Pacific Ocean from the Gulf of California (also known as the Sea of Cortés). Both the Pacific and the Sea of Cortés are dotted with islands, including Todos Santos, Isla Cedros, and Isla Santa Margarita in the Pacific, and Isla Espiritu Santo in the Gulf.

For centuries, small groups of Indigenas lived here in isolation, visiting each other by foot along the shore or by boat. Jesuit missionaries built the first missions and taught the Indians to farm, plant vineyards, olive trees and date palms. Until 1973, its secrets were safe with the few adventurers who were willing to risk the severity of the terrain for the pleasure of hunting, fishing, rock and fossil collecting, bird watching and surfing in an almost pure natural environment. Then the 1700 km Transpeninsular Highway, called the Benito Juárez Highway, opened. It links Tijuana and Cabo San Lucas, passing through all the major towns en route – Ensenada, San Quintin, Guerrero Negro, San Ignacio, Santa Rosalia, Mulege, Loreto, and La Paz.

With a 1400 kilometers coastline on the Pacific and the Gulf of California, the Baja is a paradise for anglers, swimmers

BAJA CALIFORNIA

and surfers. Its beaches are rich in crabs and oysters and the emerald-green waters of the gulf and the deep-blue Pacific Ocean support an incredible variety of big-game fish. California gray whales mate and calve every winter along the west coast. As the highway penetrates the Baja, the dry landscape is occasionally relieved by oases of green, while the coasts are dotted with fishing villages. With the highway came hotels and resorts and villages became towns overnight.

Baja California is divided into two states: Baja California Norte (BCN) and Baja California Sur (BCS). **Baja Norte** comprises the area from the U.S. border south to the 28th parallel, about midway down the peninsula. **Baja Sur** begins there and stretches to Cabo San Lucas at the tip. Baja Norte has a population of over two million, while Baja Sur has only half a million. The climate of the northern state is mild and dry in summer, and cool, with a little rain, in winter. Southern Baja is warm and humid in summer and temperate and dry in winter.

Mexicali, with a population of over one million, is the capital city of Baja Norte. It is an agricultural center situated in a fertile valley. La Paz is the capital of Baja Sur and is situated on the Gulf. At its widest point, the peninsula measures about 186 kilometers; at its narrowest point only 45 kilometers. Along the length of the Baja run two major mountain chains – the **Sierra San Pedro Martir** in Baja Norte and the **Sierra de la Giganta** in Baja Sur. The highest crest of these, the **Cerro de la Encantada**, rises to more than 3000 meters and there are good trout to be caught in the streams. While there are a few spots of total desert in the Baja, much of it is semi-desert.

Tijuana, with over 40 million border crossings per year, has the highest transient population of any border town in the world. It is a prosperous city of about one million people, with the highest per capita income in Mexico. Since Baja California is a duty-free zone, the shops of this city are its main attraction. For fun, there are dog races five nights a week, horse races on Saturday and Sunday afternoons, bullfights every Sunday afternoon. Nighttime action centers around the many discos. Unfortunately, Tijuana is also one of the most unattractive cities in Mexico.

Ensenada, a charming town on Todos Santos Bay, lies just south of Tijuana. Known for its sport and commercial fishing, it is a popular place for eating seafood. This town of 130,000 is mild in winter and cool in summer. Its *malecón* is a pleasant promenade. On the southern outskirts of town is **La Bufadora**, a big, hollow, cave-like rock through which the ocean penetrates to make a blowhole, roaring and spouting water high into the air. Lobster is the specialty of most restaurants here, but *tacos* are also popular.

Above: Thousands of casual workers help with the fruit and vegetable harvest in the irrigated oases of Baja California.

There's a varied and active nightlife, also, including discos and nightclubs. Below Ensenada is **San Quintín**, a small agricultural town in a fertile valley. The highway parallels the ocean and many small side roads lead to the beach.

Guerrero Negro, known for whale watching, is below San Quintín and the village of **Rosario**. The whales can be seen in Scammon's Lagoon, in Sebastian Vizcaino Bay, from the last week in December to the first week of April. Besides Scammon's Lagoon, the whales take refuge in the adjoining Guerrero Negro Lagoon and the nearby San Ignacio Lagoon.

San Ignacio, an oasis 128 kilometers across a sun-baked desert from Guerrero Negro, is shaded by date palms. Like many other towns in Baja, San Ignacio began as a Jesuit mission, established in 1716. The mission at the heart of town is well preserved and faces a little plaza shaded by huge trees.

The Baja Highway passes the volcano of **Las Virgenes** (1996 meters), believed to be the most recently active on the peninsula. Here, the ground is covered with solidified lava. Below San Ignacio is **Santa Rosalia**, a unique mining town that resembles a town in the Old West. Its most interesting sight is the **Mission Church of Santa Rosalia**, originally built by Gustave Eiffel, a galvanized structure transported section by section from Europe. The beaches north and south of town are also beautiful.

Several miles south of Santa Rosalia, a side road leads to the **caves of San Borjita**, site of the oldest cave paintings found in Baja. The Misión de Santa Rosalia, founded by the Jesuits, is actually located in **Mulegé**, a lush green town at the mouth of the Santa Rosalia River. **Loreto** is the first of the "new" Baja resorts. The original Misión de Nuestra Señora de Loreto, in the heart of town, was severely damaged by earthquakes

Above: A forest of cacti in Baja California.
Right: Cabo San Lucas has become the El Dorado of deep-sea fishing.

and has been almost completely rebuilt. The **Museo de las Misiónes Californias**, next to the mission, was organized by the Mexico City Museum of Anthropology and History and offers a fine exhibit of artifacts and manuscripts relating to old mission days. Boat excursions can be made to **Isla Coronado**, in the Sea of Cortés, which is inhabited by a large colony of sea lions.

La Paz, the capital of Baja Sur, with a population of 157,000, is located on a deep inlet in the La Paz Bay on the Sea of Cortés. It is protected from the bay by a long sand bar called *El Mogote*. For over 400 years, La Paz has been known for the black and pink pearls that have been discovered there. However, today, the city survives more from commercial and sport fishing. Founded in 1720 by the Jesuits, who built the mission Nuestra Señora de la Paz, the town is a quiet and peaceful place. The Sea of Cortés can be seen from every point in town, and at sunset, it often appears red, hence its other name, the Vermilion Sea. The *male-cón* or promenade is a superb place for strolling and enjoying the views. Above it on a hill is the main plaza and a cathedral built in 1861. The Government Palace, a modern building, stands nearby. Like other resorts along the northern Pacific coast, La Paz is known for the myriads of game fish in its waters. Charters can be arranged through any of the leading hotels. One of the city's greatest attractions is shopping. As with other Baja towns, La Paz is a duty-free port and all varieties of imported goods are available.

Below La Paz, on the way to the tip of the peninsula, is the semitropical town of **San José del Cabo**, population 10,000, an agricultural and cattle-raising community surrounded by fields of mango, avocado, and orange trees. The town's **House of Culture** has a museum and library, and the old church next to the plaza stands on the site previously occupied by the mission. The **Paseo Mijarés**, with its stone arches and white cottages full of flowers, is a lovely place to stroll. The Baja's deluxe resorts are found in **Cabo**

CABO SAN LUCAS / COSTA AZUL

San Lucas, a town of 14,000 at the tip of the peninsula. Take a boat ride to **El Arco**, the arch where the Sea of Cortés and the Pacific waters merge in a swirling spectacle. The **Playa del Amor**, next to the arch, is one of the best here. The **Cabo Falso** is an old lighthouse standing on the giant rock formations all the way at the very tip of the peninsula.

Unlike other Mexican beach resorts, the nightlife here is practically non-existent. Fishing is the main sport here, although there is good scuba diving to see the coral beds, underwater caves and the largest coral reef on the west coast of the Americas. Surfing is good at the **Playa Costa Azul**, halfway between San José del Cabo and Cabo San Lucas. There are also horseback tours on the beaches. Because of its remoteness, visitors should bring plenty of cash or traveler's checks with them, because credit cards are often not accepted here.

Above: Cabo San Lucas, the southernmost point of the Baja California peninsula.

MONTERREY
Accommodation
LUXURY: **Ambassador**, Hidalgo 310, Tel: 42-2040. **Gran Hotel Ancira**, Plaza Hidalgo, Tel: 43-2060. **Hotel Crowne Plaza**, Av. Constituyentes 300 Ote., Tel: 44-9300.
MODERATE: **El Paso Autel**, Zaragoza 130 Nte., Tel: 40-0690. **Jandal**, Cuauhtémoc 825 Nte., Tel: 72-3636. *BUDGET*: **Hotel Jolet**, Padre Mier 201 Pte., Tel: 40-5500. **Colonial**, Hidalgo 475 Ote., Tel: 43-6791/96.
Restaurants
Luisiana, Hidalgo 530 Ote., Tel: 43-1561. **Regio**, Plaza Hidalgo, Tel: 43-6250. **El Tío**, Av. Eugenio Garza Sada Sur 3069, Tel: 58-8877.
Shopping
Mercado, Bolivar Nte., souvenirs. **Cerámica Miguel**, Pte. Calle Sur 419, suburb Garza García, best selection of ceramics. **Kristalux**, José Vigil 400 (by taxi), lead chrystal.
Museums
Museo de Monterrey, Av. Universidad 2202, Tue-Fri 9.3 am-5 pm, Sat, Sun 10.30 am-6 pm.
Post / Telephone / Police
Post Office: Zaragoza/Washington, Tel: 42-4003, Mon-Fri 8 am-8 pm, Sat, Sun 9 am-1 pm. **Telephone** (long distance): 5 de Mayo, daily 9 am-8 pm. **Police**: Tel: 42-4546 and 43-4315.
Tourist Information
Zaragoza/Matamoros, Tel: 45-0870 and 45-0902.

HERMOSILLO
Accommodation
LUXURY: **Holiday Inn Hermosillo**, Blvd. 369, Tel: 5-1112. *MODERATE*: **San Alberto**, Rosales/Serdán, Tel: 2-1800. **Bugambilia**, Blvd. Kino 712, Tel: 4-5050. **Calinda**, Rosales/Morelia, Tel: 3-8960.
BUDGET: **America Colonial**, Juárez between Serdán/Chihuahua, Tel: 2-2448.
Tourist Information
Comonfort, in the Palacio Administrativo, Tel: 7-2964, Mon-Fri 8 am-2 pm and 5-7 pm.

NOGALES
Accommodation
MODERATE / BUDGET: **Hotel Granada**, Av. Jópez Mateos/González, Tel: 2-2911. **Hotel Villa Alegre**, Torres 128, Tel: 2-5552. **Hotel Olivia**, Av. Obregón, Tel: 2-2200.

CIUDAD JUÁREZ
Accommodation
LUXURY: **Lucerna**, Paseo Triunfo de la República 3976, Tel: 13-3232. *MODERATE*: **Calinda**

GUIDEPOST THE NORTH / BAJA CALIFORNIA

Juárez, Escobar 35515, Tel: 16-3421. **Hotel del Prado**, Calle López Mateos, in the Centro Comercial, Tel: 16-8800. *BUDGET*: **Embajador**, Francisco Villa 102, Tel: 15-1406. **Puesta del Sol**, Río Conchos 1135, Tel: 16-3460.

Tourist Information
Malecón betw. Lerdo/Juárez, Tel: 4-0123, Mon-Fri 8 am-3.30 pm and 4-7 pm, Sat 8 am-2 pm.

STATE TAMAULIPAS
Accommodation
Accommodation facilities near the border crossing points at Nuevo Laredo, Reynosa and Matamoros are mostly motels of the moderate category at the arterial roads.

CHIHUAHUA
Accommodation
LUXURY: **Castel Sicomoro**, Blvd. Ortíz Mena, Tel: 13-5445. **Exelaris Hyatt**, Av. Independencia 500, Tel: 16-6000. *MODERATE:* **San Francisco**, Victoria 409, Tel: 34-9631. **Rancho La Estancia**, Carranza 507, 12-2282. **El Presidente**, Libertad 8, Tel: 16-0606. **Victoria**, Av. Juárez/Colón, Tel: 12-8893.
BUDGET: **El Dorado**, Calle 14/Julán, Tel: 12-5770. **El Campanario**, Blvd. Díaz Ordaz/Libertad, Tel: 15-4545.

Museums
Museo de la Revolución, Calle 10 Nr. 3017, Tue-Sun 9 am-1 pm and 3-7 pm.
Museo Regional, Av. Bolivar/Calle 3, Tue-Sun 9 am-1 pm and 3-7 pm.

Post / Telegrams / Police
Post Office: Juárez between Guerrero/Carranza, Mon-Fri 8 am-7 pm, Sat 9 am-1 pm. **Telegrams** (as above), Mon-Fri 8-11.30 am, Sat 8-10 am, Sun 9 am-1 pm. **Police:** Tel: 12-5007.

Tourist Information
Calle Cuauhtémoc 1800, Tel: 1-6000, open Mon-Fri 9 am-1 pm and 3-5 pm.

LOS MOCHIS
Accommodation
Santa Anita, with a travel agency for the train journey and hotel bookings, Leyva/Hidalgo, Tel: 2-0046. **El Dorado Motel**, Leyva/Valdez, Tel: 5-1111. **Motel Plaza Inn**, Leyva/Cárdenas, Tel: 2-0075.

Excursions
An unforgettable experience is the train journey Los Mochis–Chihuahua through the gorges of the *Barranca del Cobre*. Trains run daily in both directions, accommodation alongside the track, i.e. **Cabañas Divisadero-Barrancas**, Tel: 12-3362, with spectacular views over the gorges.

BAJA CALIFORNIA MEXICALI
Accommodation
LUXURY: **Holiday Inn**, Blvd. Benito Juárez, Tel: 66-1300. **Hotel Lucerna**, Blvd. Benito Juárez 2151, Tel: 64-1000.
MODERATE: **Castel Calafia**, Calz. Justo Sierra 1495, Tel: 64-0222.

TIJUANA
Accommodation
Hotel El Conquistador, Blvd. Agua Caliente, Tel: 86-4801. **Fiesta Americana**, Blvd. Agua Caliente 4558, Tel: 81-7000. **Palacio Azteca**, Av. 16 de Septiembre 213, Tel: 86-5301. **Hotel Lucerna**, Paseo de los Héroes, Tel: 84-1000.

Tourist Information
Av. Revolución/Calle 1, Tel: 84-0537.

ENSENADA
Accommodation
San Nicolas Resort, Av. López Mateos/-Guadalupe, 6-1901. **El Cid**, López Mateos 993, Tel: 8-222401.
Casa del Sol, Blancarte 122, Tel: 8-1570. **Bahia**, López Mateos/Riveroll, Tel: 8-211101. **Motel Ensenada Travel Lodge**, Blancarte 130, Tel: 8-1601/5.

Tourist Information
Av. López Mateos/Floreta, Tel: 6-5010.

LOS CABOS: SAN JOSE DEL CABO / CABO SAN LUCAS
Accommodation
LUXURY: **Calinda Aquamarina**, Av. Malecón, Tel: 2-0101. **Calinda Cabo Quality Inn**, at the Transpeninsular at km 4.5, Tel: 2-0007. **El Presidente**, Tel: 2-0211. **Solmar**, Tel: 3-0022.

LA PAZ
Accommodation
LUXURY / MODERATE: **Grand Hotel Baja** (**Ramada**), Calle Rangel, Tel: 2-3900. **Los Arcos**, Av. Avaro Obregón 498, Tel: 2-2744. **La Perla**, Av. Alvaro Obregón 1570, Tel: 2-0777. **Gardenias**, Aquiles Serdán Nte. 407, Tel: 2-3088. *BUDGET*: **La Posada**, Reforma/Plaza Sur, Tel: 2-0663.

From the Gulf to Central Mexico
Flights: To Guadalajara, Mazatlán, Mexico City, Los Mochis, Mérida. **Ship:** Ferries daily to Mazatlán and twice weekly to Los Mochis. Booking: Ejido/Jamírez, Tel: 2-0109.

Tourist Information
Obregón/16 de Septiembre, Tel: 2-7975, open Mon-Fri 8 am-7 pm, Sun 9 am-1 pm.

ACAPULCO

SUN, SAND, SEA

ACAPULCO
IXTAPA-ZIHUATANEJO
MANZANILLO
PUERTO VALLARTA
MAZATLÁN

ACAPULCO

The Bay of Acapulco was discovered by Francisco Chico on December 13, 1521 and named Santa Lucia. The Spaniards chose it as their main port for trade with the Orient, and in 1532, it was officially named Ciudad de los Reyes, or City of the Kings. A fort was built, but it was destroyed by an earthquake in 1776. Its replacement, the **Fuerte de San Diego** (housing a museum of the city with displays emphasizing the epoque of Acapulco's trade with the Orient), dates from 1799 and overlooks the bay from its hill above the dock area and cruise-ship pier. Though pirates came occasionally to plunder its shores, the place was booming. As early as 1579, during the reign of King Philip II, the town had around 12,000 inhabitants.

Acapulco, in Náhuatl "place of the thick reeds", was described by the German explorer Alexander von Humboldt as "wild, lonely and romantic". It remained a forgotten fishing village until a road was built from Mexico City in 1928, but even then it took ten years for it to get its start as a beach resort. Acapulco began to attract the Hollywood crowd and really came into its own in the 1950s when it began to be known as "The Riviera of the West".

The resort, now with a population of more than 500,000, is divided into two sections, Old Acapulco and New Acapulco. The center of the original area, also known as *Acapulco Tradicional*, is the fountain-filled zócalo, or **Plaza San Juan Alvarez**, facing the sport-fishing piers. At the foot of the square is the mosque-like blue-and-gold **Catedral de Nuestra Señora de la Soledad**, built in the 1940s. The neighborhood around the zócalo retains the atmosphere of "Old Mexico". New Acapulco consists of a multitude of highrise hotels stretching for ten kilometers along the beach from town, and is a heaven for hedonists from all over the world.

23 beaches are strung out along Acapulco Bay. Balmy breezes keep the temperature moderate most of the year. From mid-December to Easter – the high season – you can count on blue skies and plenty of sun. Even in the so-called rainy season – May to October – showers are short and mostly in the afternoon.

In the resort's early days, beach lovers would head for **Playa Caleta** in the morning, on the peninsular spit of "Old Aca", and facing from there the island of

Left: Acapulco has always been Mexico's beach resort par excellence, especially for Mexicans.

ACAPULCO

La Roqueta. In the afternoon, they would lie on **Playa Los Hornos** (The Ovens). But nowadays action has moved from Los Hornos, or the "afternoon beach," to **Playa Condesa** and **Playa Paraíso**, both punctuated by highrise hotels. This strip, along the eleven-kilometer *costera*, offers everything for *la dulce vida* under palm-thatched seaside bistros. All hotels have dining service, bars and snack bars both on the beach and at poolside.

Along the *Carretera Escénica*, the scenic road to the airport, is the exclusive world of **Las Brisas**, Acapulco's Shangri-La-hotel. **Puerto Marqués**, an almost untouched fishing village further beyond the hills, has one of the prettiest tropical beaches and a calm bay for water skiing and sailing. **Playa Revolcadero** is highlighted by the Aztec pyramid-shaped **Acapulco Princess** and elegant **Pierre Marqués** hotels with their championship 18-hole golf course. Horseback riding along this beach early in the morning is a favorite activity.

It seems as if Acapulco never sleeps. Most shops open at 10 a.m., when most jet-setters are sleeping off the night before. Hotels cater to late risers and many serve breakfast until noon. After a morning on the beach, many people stroll along the **Avenida Costera Miguel Alemán** with sidewalks that absorb the heat and make barefoot walking bearable. This boulevard is packed with numerous shops, restaurants and discos. It passes under the 50-acre **Parque Papagayo** by way of the longest underpass in Latin America. Another amusement park with trained dolphins and seals, **CiCi**, fronts the *costera* near the Naval Base.

Acapulco is a sportsman's delight, with two championship 18-hole golf courses, a 9-hole course in town and numerous tennis courts, many lighted for night play. Angling, particularly for sail fish, is exceptional. Water sports of every

Right: The famous cliff divers of Quebrada defy death by leaping from a dizzy height into a narrow inlet of the sea.

variety are catered for by all beach hotels. A popular event are Sunday water skiing tournaments at Coyuca Lagoon, located behind **Playa Pie de la Cuesta**. Surfing is not permitted on the beaches along the strip, but is at Playa Revolcadero. To hire a one- or two-person motorboat, ask for a *bronco*, and parasailing has long become everybody's kick.

Acapulco, thanks to the crowd it attracts, is equally famous for its nightlife. This is the best time to take a ride in a balloon-festooned *calendria*, or horse and carriage. Dining, dancing, spectacular shows, all offer a romantic escape. This town has some of the best discos in the world – **Aca Tiki, Bocaccio, Fantasy**, **The News**, **Baby-O**, **Magic**, to name a few. **Centro Acapulco**, a vast convention complex, features Mexican Fiesta Nights in its Plaza Mexicana. A Mexican Folkloric Ballet performs in the Centro's **Teatro Netzahuacóyotl**, and performing arts events are often held in the **Teatro Juan Ruiz Alarcón** in the same complex.

Not to be missed are the cliff divers of **La Quebrada**. Holding flaming torches (after sunset), they plunge from a 45-meter cliff into a shallow inlet. Performing midday and three shows a night, they can be seen from the **El Mirador** hotel's **La Perla** nightclub. Another attraction is the flight of the *voladores*, a performance based on an ancient religious ritual.

Before that, many people head out to **Playa Pie de la Cuesta** to take in the *hora de la puesta del sol* (sunset hour) – a riot of deep orange, yellow and vermilion red, changing slowly to black velvet. West of the city proper, once the exclusive turf of "Acapulco regulars", is the best place to watch the sunset while cuddled up in a hammock and sipping a *coco loco*. Just beyond lies **Coyuca Lagoon**, a freshwater lagoon and bird sanctuary bordered by coconut palms.

Besides being (by many accounts) Mexico's most glamorous resort, the area near the port still remains the commercial center. The municipal market, the **Mercado Municipal**, is one of the country's

IXTAPA-ZIHUATANEJO

biggest. A five-minute walk from the zócalo one comes to **El Mercado de Artesanías** with products strictly for foreign consumption, shamelessly inauthentic. One block north of the *Avenida Costera Miguel Alemàn,* behind the Baby-O disco, is **Artesanías Finas de Acapulco** (**AFA**), also with a vast selection of handicrafts from all over Mexico; the downtown **Bazar del Arte Mexicano** and many other shops belong in the same "souvenirs for dollars" category.

IXTAPA-ZIHUATANEJO

230 kilometers northwest of Acapulco the twin resorts of **Ixtapa-Zihuatanejo** have depeloped into a booming tourist destination. Whilst Zihuatanejo is one of the oldest settlements on the coast, Ixtapa is the country's second "blueprint resort" (after Cancún), designed by Mexico's National Trust Fund for Tourism (**FONATUR**). With a total of 15,000 hotel bedrooms, Ixtapa-Zihuatanejo is hoping for a great future; the population meanwhile has risen to 40,000 from only 15,000 ten years ago.

Meaning "Land of Women" in the language of the Aztecs, the litte fishing village of **Zihuatanejo** is situated 7 kilometers southeast of Ixtapa on Bahía de Zihuatanejo. Adjoining the zócalo, is the usually crowded **Playa Municipal**. From its pier taxi-boats cross the bay to **Playa las Gatas**. The quiet beach is lined with

mar. All in all, there are 30 kilometers of palm-lined white beaches and coves, namely **Playa Mahava**, **Playa Hermosa**, **Playa Casa Blanca**, **Playa las Cuatas**, and at the far western end **Playa Quieta**. Opposite the hotels are the 18-hole **Palma Real Golf Club** course (open to the public) and Ixtapa's shopping district. The shopping area contains a maze of fashionable malls and is probably the biggest of its kind in Mexico.

MANZANILLO

Surrounded by tropical fruit plantations and deserted beaches, **Manzanillo** (with a population of 80,000) on Mexico's famed "Gold Coast" offers visitors sophisticated comfort in a setting of natural beauty. The weather is excellent, since Manzanillo is on the same latitude as Hawaii, with January, February and March the months of lowest humidity.

The city of Manzanillo rests on a peninsula at the southern end of **Bahía de Santiago** and **Bahía de Manzanillo**. An important seaport even before the Spanish conquest, it claims 700 years of commerce with Asia and ranks as Mexico's most important west coast port. Except for a lively zócalo, the downtown section is lacking in interest. Nightlife and shopping, too, can be summed up in a few words – there isn't much of either. What little nightlife there is centers around the hotels and a few restaurants. Mexican Fiesta Nights are staged at two of the largest hotels. Shopping is concentrated in several small plazas, and typical souvenirs can be bargained for at the **Mercado Municipal** on **Avenida Cinco de Mayo**.

Manzanillo's main attraction are its fine beaches stretching many kilometers in both directions and around the **Santiago Peninsular**. Here, an oasis of luxury and rendezvous for international jet-setters opened in 1974: **Las Hadas**. This super deluxe resort village with 206 villas

restaurants (fresh oysters!) but is not very good for swimming due to its rocky bottom. There is an offshore coral reef that is great for diving and snorkeling. Equipment can be hired on the spot. East of town is **Playa Maderas**, a favorite for campers. Following the curve of the bay (or by car over a hill), **Playa la Ropa**, with its luxurious hideway hotel **Villa del Sol**, compares favorably with the country's best small beaches. Both **Isla Ixtapa** (or **Isla Grande**) and **Morro de los Pericos** are wildlife reserves and can be reached from the pier by charter boats.

Ixtapa has an International Airport (20 minutes by bus) and a line of luxury hotels along the beach between **Playa del Palmar** and landscaped **Paseo del Pal-**

PUERTO VALLARTA

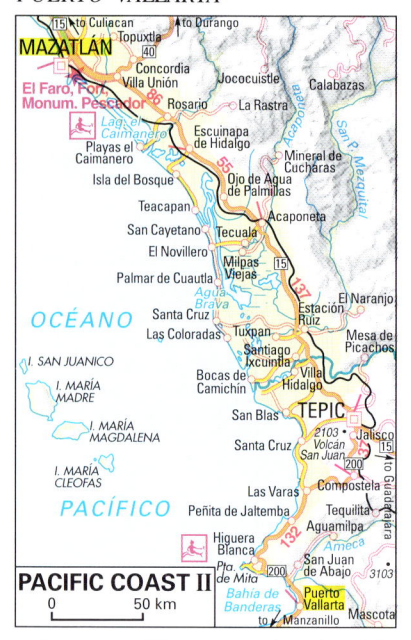

and rooms, golf course, and yacht club-cum- marina is the result of a dream of multimillionaire Ateñor Patiño, known as the Bolivian Tin King. At the tip of the peninsula one of the best beaches for sunning and swimming, **Playa de Audienca**, nestles in a protective inlet within the bay. The waves are gentler here than elsewhere. Because of this, it is a favorite destination for excursion boats. Leaving the downtown section along the Bay of Manzanillo, **Playa Azul** offers minimal to moderate surfing. The better beaches are out of town further to the north in the Bay of Santiago: the secluded beach known as **Playa de Oro** and the dark sand of **Playa Santiago**, **Playa Olas Atlas**, which is good for body surfing, and **Playa Miramar**, the top surfing spot in the area.

Just south of **Melaque** about 55 kilometers from Manzanillo, lies the picturesque fishing village of **Barra de Navidad**. It is a quiet beach resort of about 3500 inhabitants with excellent rustic beachside seafood restaurants, terrific fishing and a bohemian atmosphere. On the same road, **Costa Careyes** offers tranquil secluded coves. To the south, **Playa de Campos de Coco** and **Playa de Venta** are the more popular ones. Considered one of the best deep-sea fishing spots in the world, the waters of Manzanillo are teeming with sailfish, snapper, sea bass and yellowtail.

PUERTO VALLARTA

Once a remote and forgotten fishing village, **Puerto Vallarta** has blossomed into one of Mexico's most popular resorts, combining the slow paced ambiance of yesterday with the sophisticated facilities of today. Tucked in beside the beautiful **Bahía de Banderas** amidst lush tropical foliage and rugged coastal mountains, this fast growing town of now approximately 200,000 inhabitants still maintains the the charm and authenticity of old Mexico. It is a city with rustic cobblestone streets, red tile roofs, whitewashed buildings, exquisite restaurants and a fairly active nightlife.

Back in the 1950s, Puerto Vallarta was known to travelers only as Mexico's "Little Acapulco". Today tourists fill 7500 hotel rooms. Puerto Vallarta's fame began in 1964 with the filming of *Night of the Iguana* starring Elizabeth Taylor, Richard Burton and Ava Gardner. Since then, many filmmakers have used the area for their locations.

One area overlooking the **Cuale River** – nicknamed "Gringo Gulch" because so many vacation homes have been built there by foreigners – is the town's main attraction. But much of the action is along the *malecón*, the waterfront drive that leads to the town's main beach, **Playa del Sol**, also known as *Los Muertos*, are only one mile south.

Right: The rapid growth of tourism on the southern Pacific coast has meant a new source of income for the fishermen.

Here are fruit carts, boys selling fish on a stick, and a great variety of peddlers of souvenirs, chewing-gum and postcards. There are palm-roofed restaurants, cocktail bars, musical combos and dancing in the afternoon. It's beaches are legendary, with mile after mile of soft sand. Swimming is safe year round and the best beaches are found south of town. **Playa las Estacas**, **Playa Palo Maria** and **Playa Mismaloya** (the setting for *Night of the Iguana)* are three of the best.

The greatest concentration of hotels and two marinas lie north of town along **Playa de Oro** toward the airport. Major shops and restaurants as well as a few small hotels are downtown.

The heart of Puerto Vallarta is **Cuale River Island**, where the city market is located, and where fishermen sell red snapper in the streets each morning.

The town's most distinctive landmark is the **Church of Guadalupe**, built only 30 years ago on the main plaza, with a crown on top of its steeple. Cobbled streets can be treacherous to those without rubber-soled shoes and the kerbstones are unusually high. A popular excursion from Puerto Vallarta is to the village of **Yelapa**, set on a picturesque cove surrounded by mountains. Along the beach are several small rustic retaurants serving fresh seafood. Nearby is a quaint Indigena village and a spectacular 50-meter waterfall. For a more light-hearted trip, take the three-hour *Sombrero* cruise around the bay.

As with other Mexican Pacific resorts, Puerto Vallarta offers a full range of sports. There's the challenging 18-hole par 72 golf course, **Los Flamingos**, north of town and two excellent tennis clubs – **Club de Tenis**, near Playa de Oro, and **Racket Puerto Vallarta** off **Playa Gloria**, both floodlit at night.

The usual parasailing, windsurfing, snorkeling, scuba diving and waterskiing is available at most beaches, and surfside horseback riding is also very popular. Angling for mackerel, bonito, tuna and red snapper has always been a favorite, with a fleet of boats available for charter.

MAZATLÁN

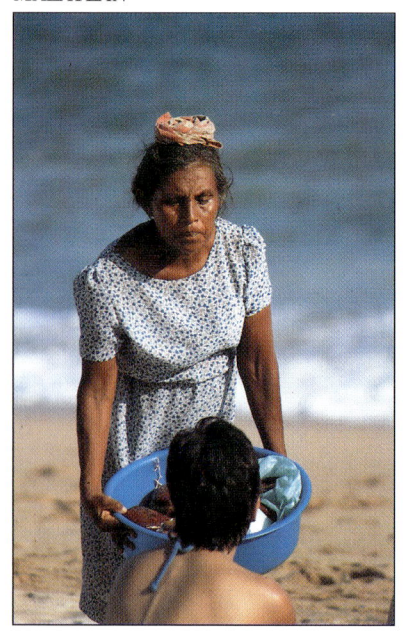

Unlike Acapulco and Ixtapa, Puerto Vallarta is much quieter in the evening. There are several discos – **Capriccio**, **City Dump** and **Jungla** are among the best – and Mexican Fiesta Nights are held on Saturdays at several larger hotels. *Charreadas,* or rodeos, are held on Sundays during the winter.

MAZATLÁN

Chibachas Indigenas were the first settlers of **Mazatlán**, which means "place of the deer" in the Náhuatl tongue. In 1531, the bay was chosen as the departure point for Spanish galleons loaded with gold from mines in the Sierra Madre Oriental. Mazatlán itself was first mentioned as a settlement near the old site of Villa Unión in 1602. It became an important city in the early 17th century, attracting pirates like Drake and Cavendish to prey upon the galleons bound for Spain with their treasures. The town was not incorporated until 1806 and had no municipal government until 1837. Today the city of Mazatlán (population 420,000) is a bustling commercial port and harbors Mexico's largest shrimp fleet – more than 800 boats. About 20 million kilos of shrimp are processed each year and shipped off, mostly to the USA. From near the docks ferry boats run across the Sea of Cortés (Gulf of California) to La Paz, Baja California's largest southern city. Over the last decade Mazatlán has earned the reputation as one of Mexico's most popular and active beach resorts. In February it is also the scene of one of the best *carnavales* in the country. The best stop for a panoramic view is **El Faro**, the old lighthouse at the very tip of the peninsular. This massive landmark is 154 meters-high, ranking as the second highest lighthouse in the world after the one in Gibraltar. Another excellent view is from **Icebox Hill** (Cerro de la Neveria), a former military observation point.

El Centro, the downtown area, has a small yet charming zócalo and a cathedral with brightly colored yellow and blue mosaic towers. The **Acuario** has more than 50 fish-tanks with some 250 species of fish from all over the world. After the **Fishermen's Monument**, the city's most famous landmark, and the **Old Spanish Fort** you have done all the sightseeing there is. Most of the action centers on the **Zona Dorada**, or Golden Zone, stretching from **Punta Camarón** north to the **Costa de Oro**. Mazatlán's finest asset is its 16-kilometer beach front: **Playa Olas Atlas** for surf; **Playa Norte** for fun and entertainment, popular with the local residents; **Playa Las Gaviotas** is crowded and **Playa Sábalo** is a sheltered, quiet and fashionable beach – but a long way from town. Mazatlán is the deep-sea fishing capital of the mainland and the waters are filled with tuna, marlin, black marlin, sailfish, dorado, bonita, yellowtail and sea bass.

Above: Even lying around and sunbathing can give you an appetite.

ACAPULCO
Accommodation
LUXURY: **Las Brisas**, Carret. Escéncia 5255, Tel: 4-1650. **Acapulco Princess**, Playa Revolcadero, Tel: 4-3100. **Pierre Marqués**, Playa Revolcadero, Tel: 4-2000. **Excelaris Hyatt Regency**, Costera Miguel Alemán 1, Tel: 4-2888.
MODERATE: **Calinda Acapulco**, Costera Miguel Alemán 1260. Tel: 4-0410. **Acapulco Malibu**, Costera Miguel Alemán 20, Tel: 4-1070. **Hyatt Continental**, Costera Miguel Alemán, Tel: 4-0909. **Acapulco Plaza**, Costera Miguel Alemán 123, Tel: 5-8050.
BUDGET: **Copacabana**, Tabachines 2, Tel: 4-3260. **El Mirador**, Plazoleta de la Quebrada 74, Tel: 3-1625.
Restaurants
The food in larger hotels is always good, but predominantly international. The hotel zone along the Costera Miguel Alemán is dotted with good-quality restaurants, for typical Mexican cuisine try the old part of Acapulco.
Nightlife
Nightly entertainment is one of the trademarks of Acapulco, almost every hotel has its own disco with hot music and dancing. **Superdiscos**: **Baby O**, Costera Miguel Alemán, 10 pm-4 am. **Boccaccio**, Costera Miguel Alemán.
Special Events
Carnaval (Mardi Gras) is celebrated in early spring, no fixed date.
Post / Telecommunication
Post Office: Costera 125, Tel: 2-2083, Mon-Fri 8 am-8 pm, Sat 9 am-8 pm, Sun 9 am-1 pm. **Telephone**: La Paz/Zócalo, Mon-Sat 9 am-8 pm. **Telegrams**: Costera near the Zócalo, Mon-Fri 8 am-midnight, Sat 8 am-8 pm, Sun 9 am-1 pm.
Tourist Information
Costera, M. Alemán 187, Tel: 5-1178. Costera at the Centro, Tel: 4-7050, daily 9 am-9 pm.

IXTAPA-ZIHUATANEJO
Accommodation
LUXURY: **Villa del Sol**, exquisite, romantic bungalow-complex at the beach, Playa la Ropa/Zihuatanejo, Tel: 4-2239. Along the "hotel row" in Ixtapa all major hotel chains are present. Small hotels in the old town of Zihuatanejo.
Restaurants
Good restaurants serving Mexican and international cuisine can be found in the old town.
Excursions
To the nature- and wildlife reserve **Isla Ixtapa**. **Swimming** and sunbathing next to the hotel-beaches; a boat runs from the harbor to the lovely beach **Playa las Gatas** (15 minutes).

Tourist Information
Paseo del Pescador 20, Tel: 4-2207.

MANZANILLO
Accommodation
LUXURY: **Las Hadas**, Av. Audiencia, Tel: 3-0081. **Club Méditerranée Playa Blanca**, Costa de Carreyes, reservation in Mexico City, Tel: 533-4800. **Club Santiago**, Santiago Bay, Tel: 3-0412. *MODERATE*: **Posada**, Lázaro Cárdenas 201, Tel: 22-2494. **Playa Sol Las Hadas**, Peninsular de Santiago, Tel: 3-0080.
BUDGET: **Colonial,** Av. México 100, Tel: 2-1080. **Las Brisas**, Av. Cardenas, Tel: 2-1951.
Restaurants
Le Récif, seafood, Vida del Mar, Tel: 3-0624. **Oasis**, in the Club Santiago, Mexican food, Santiago Bay, Tel: 3-0937. **El Vaquero**, Crucero Las Brisas, Tel: 2-2727.
Tourist Information
Av. Juárez 244, 4th floor, Tel: 2-2090.

PUERTO VALLARTA
Accommodation
LUXURY: **Camino Real**, Playa las Estacas, Tel: 2-0002. **Bugambilias Sheraton**, Carretera Aeropuerto, Tel: 2-3000. **Fiesta Americana**, Playa los Tules, Tel: 2-2010.
MODERATE: **Buenaventura**, Av. Mexixo 1301, Tel: 2-3737. **Plaza Vallarta**, Paseo de las Glorias, Tel: 2-4360. *BUDGET*: **Oro Verde**, Rudolfo Gómez 111, Tel: 2-3050.
Restaurants
La Cebolla Roja, Mexican food, Díaz Ordaz 822, Tel: 2-1087. **La Cabaña**, steaks, seafood, Venustiano Carranza 232, Tel: 2-1066.
La Iguana, Mexican and Chinese dishes, Lázaro Cárdenas 167, Tel: 2-0105.
Tourist Information
Calle Juárez, Palacio Municipal, Tel: 2-0142.

MAZATLÁN
Accommodation
LUXURY: **El Cid Resort**, Calz. Camarón Sábalo, Tel: 3-3333. **Los Sabalos Resort**, Rudolfo T. Loaiza 100, Tel: 3-5409.
MODERATE: **Hotel de Cima**, Av. del Mar, Tel: 2-7855. Aristos Mazatlán, Camarón Sábalo 51, Tel: 3-4611.
BUDGET: **Posada Don Pelayo**, Avenida del Mar, Tel: 3-1977.
Special Events
Carnaval (Mardi Gras), end of February/beginning of March, Mexico's most famous carnival.
Tourist Information
Paseo Olas Atlas 1300, 2nd floor, Tel: 1-4210.

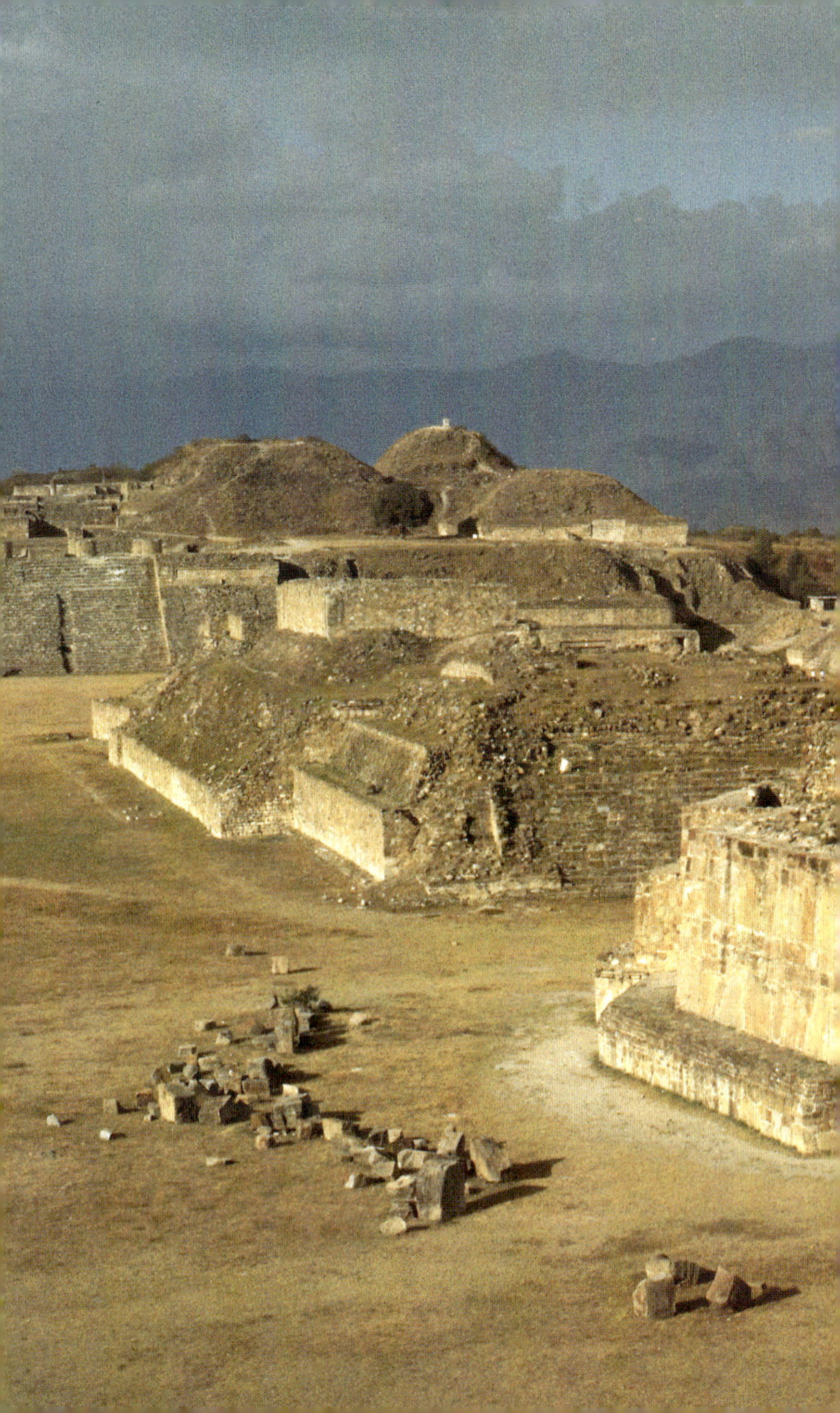

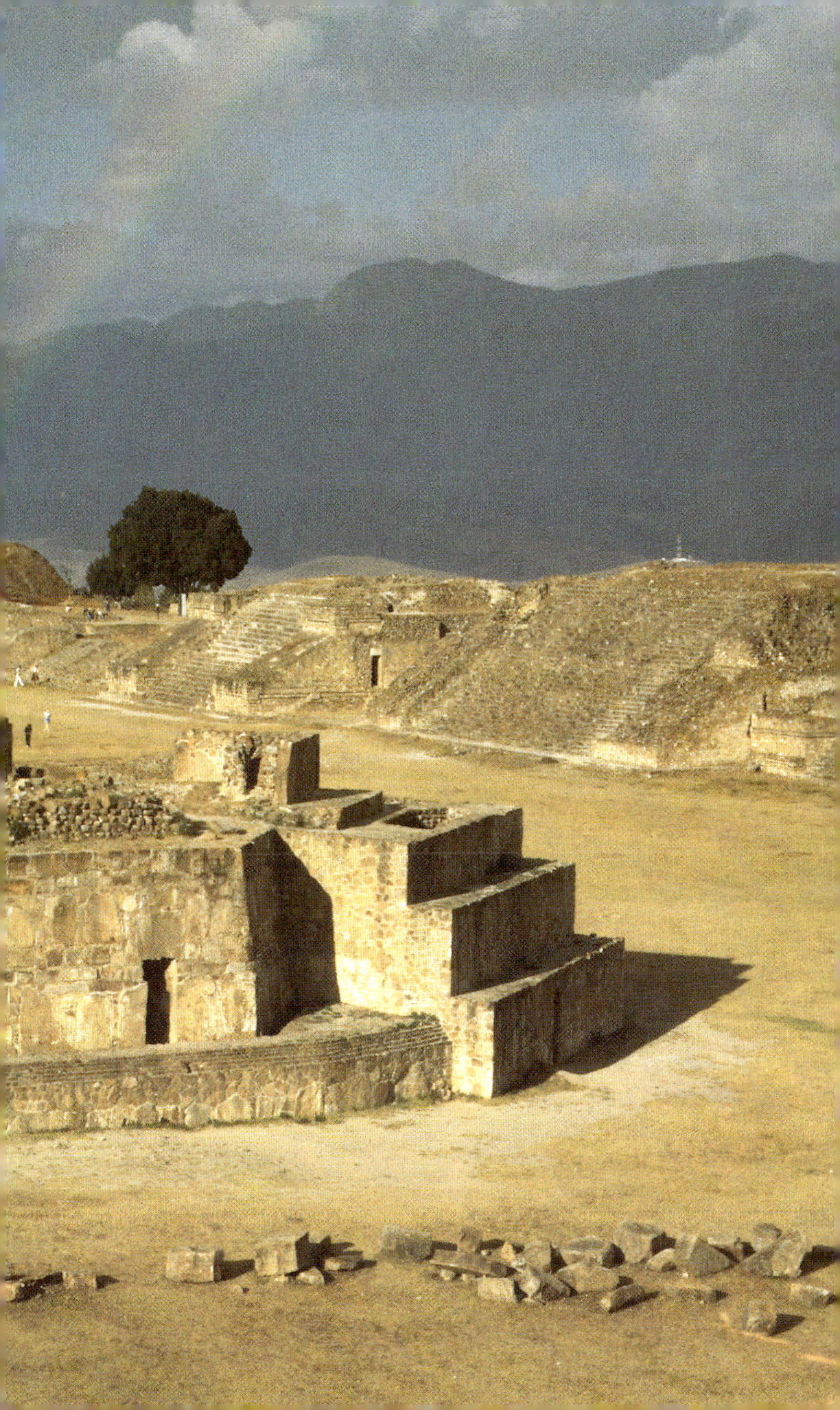

OAXACA

INDIGENAS AND TOURISTS

OAXACA
CHIAPAS

OAXACA

The state of Oaxaca, located roughly 500 kilometers to the southeast of Mexico City, is the most scenically attractive part of the country, with its impressive landscape of mighty mountain ranges and secluded bathing beaches on the Pacific and its hinterlands with their strong Indigena influence (in Oaxaca 20 percent of the population are Indigenas; the national average is 10 percent) as well as a multitude of pre-Columbian sites. It is all too easy, in view of Oaxaca's beauty, to forget that this state is among the poorest in the country. In this predominantly mountainous, arid landscape the people are hard put to make a living from farming and livestock breeding. The state authorities have begun to realize only too slowly that a reforestation program must be urgently implemented to slow down the progressive erosion caused by the destruction of the region's forests. However, Oaxaca does not have the resources to undertake this project on its own. The Indigenas, descendants of the Mixtecs

Previous pages: 400 meters above the valley, the temple and necropolis of Monte Albán was built on a mountain top. Left: The ultimate in colonial Baroque – St Domingo in Oaxaca.

and Zapotecs, live in small villages of simple shanties, often surviving hand-to-mouth. Many of them are migrating to the state's capital city, also named Oaxaca, where their situation often fails to improve.

Situated in a pleasant valley at an altitude of 1600 meters surrounded by the outer spurs of the Sierra Madre del Sur, the city of **Oaxaca** enjoys an agreeable, temperate climate. While the sun shines most of the time during the day, it can get quite cool in the evening. This former Aztec military stronghold enjoyed a magnificent expansion during Spanish rule. Its splendid Baroque churches, one and two-storied patio-houses with wrought-iron ornamentation, spacious, copiously decorated plazas and broad cobblestone avenues recall Oaxaca's heyday as an episcopal see. Today the city is, of course, still the center of trade for the surrounding villages, although when seen in relation to the whole national economy, it is only of secondary importance. On Saturdays, Indigena women spread out blankets at the market, upon which they display shawls, cloth puppets, wooden combs and woven bags. The heart of the city is formed by the arcade-fringed zócalo (free of automobile traffic) with its many small cafés and restaurants. Every night there are musical performances

OAXACA

OAXACA / CHIAPAS
0   50   100 km

here, although the *marimba* bands that appear on Saturday and Sunday are especially popular. By the way, visitors to Oaxaca should definitely not miss the **Guelaguetza**, the festival *Lunes del Cerro,* held on the Monday after July 18, where Indigenas dance in gorgeous, multicolored costumes to traditional melodies.

Rising up to the north of the zócalo is the **cathedral**, which suffered damage in a 1727 earthquake, though it has since been reconstructed, albeit in a different style than the original.

It is possible to get good insight into the Indigenas' living and working conditions in the ethnographic department of the **Museo Regional de Oaxaca**, which is housed in the former Cloister of Santo Domingo. Its unassuming architecture is a perfect backdrop, bringing out the best in the exhibits, most valuable among them being the burial gifts of gold, silver and precious stones that were found in grave number 7 at Monte Albán.

Located right next-door to the museum is the 16th-century **Church of Santo Domingo**, one of the most famous in the entire country. The church's gold-encrusted interior is sheltered behind a massive façade. Above the main entrance is a plaster relief with the coat-of-arms (portraying a grapevine) of Domingo de Guzmán, the patron saint of the Dominican Order. The ultimate eyecatcher here, however, is the particularly richly ornamented Rococo high altar, embellished

MONTE ALBÁN

concoctions, which are thoroughly delectable and inexpensive. New cafés and restaurants open up almost daily in Oaxaca, while new hotels are being established in its colonial buildings. The best recommendation for an overnight stay continues to be the **Hotel El Presidente**, housed in the former **Santa Catalina Cloister**, which dates to the second half of the 16th century. The lodgings consist of rooms with meter-thick walls, some with open fireplaces and furnishings from Mexico's colonial days.

Isolated Indigena villages in the vicinity of Oaxaca, nestling in attractive landscape, spur many travelers into some often rather adventurous outings. Quite often you will travel over unpaved roads in ancient buses loaded to the bursting point with entire families of Indigenas and their live chickens.

Monte Albán

Monte Albán, the phenomenal mountain city of the Zapotecs and one of the most famous of the country's (and indeed Latin America's) pre-Columbian complexes, is only a short drive away from Oaxaca. The air up here is a good deal fresher than in the valley, of course, an additional incentive for an excursion. There are bus connections up to the ancient city several times daily from the hotel Mesón del Angel. Travelers who climb aboard the bus in springtime and see the mountain covered in trees with white blossoms will quickly know how Monte Albán, the "White Mountain" got its name.

Presumably it was the Olmecs who leveled the mountain's crest, laid out terraces and constructed retaining walls in order to build an impregnable temple-city on a 200 by 300 meter plateau high above Oaxaca. It is still a mystery how the Olmec people ever managed to achieve such a remarkable feat. Building continued, lives were lived and the dead

with gold leaf. It is also possible to enter the **Capilla del Rosario** (rosary chapel) and view its elaborately-painted dome, a later addition to the church.

A **museum** dedicated to and named after one of the city's most well-known sons, the Zapotec Benito Juárez (later to become president of Mexico) is housed in his former residence. A monument to him stands at the **Cerro del Fortin**. From this high-placed platform, one can take in an outstanding panorama of Oaxaca.

A lively hurly-burly prevails in the roofed-over **Benito Juárez Market** in the neighborhood of the zócalo. Almost every imaginable article used in everyday life is available here. In the eatery there are local specialties and exotic fruit-juice

MONTE ALBÁN

MONTE ALBÁN

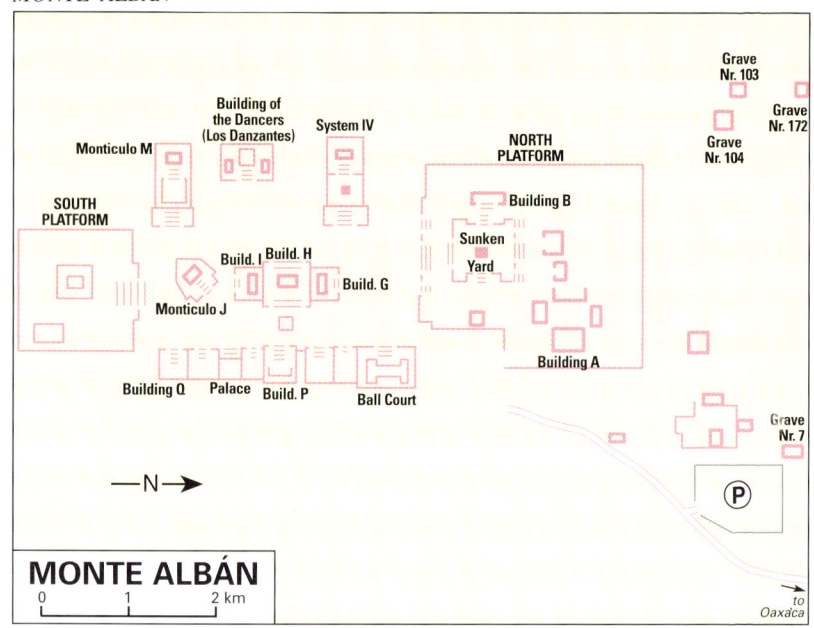

were buried on Monte Albán for nearly 2000 years. After the Olmecs (800-300 BC), the Zapotecs made their appearance (until 1250 AD). They built over the older structures and erected new pyramids. Around 900 AD, they began with the construction of burial facilities, which were later emptied by the Mixtecs and used for their own dead.

The cultic center consists of some two dozen edifices. The oldest of the buildings is believed to be the **House of the Dancers**, named after *Los danzantes*, the renowned stone tablets found here. These depict human figures with Olmec characteristics in peculiar bodily positions. Scientists are still speculating about their significance. It is wondered, for example, why several of the figures are portrayed as wearing beards, even though the pre-Columbian peoples were beardless. In places, written characters appear next to the figures. Perhaps this and many other questions could be answered if only the glyphs could be deciphered.

The internationally renowned Mexican archeologist Alfonso Caso has excavated more than 175 graves in Monte Albán. Since the majority of them had already been plundered, the discovery of **grave number 7** was a sensation. Experts spoke of it as the largest and most precious treasure of gold that had been found in Mexico to date. Grave number 104 is also of interest for the colorful murals adorning its walls. These convey an impression of the once gorgeous appearance of the entire complex.

At the **ball court** (about 5th century), a plaza in the shape of a flattened H, 41 meters long and 26 meters wide, located directly to the left of the entrance, altogether three layers of construction have been found. The tourist guides point out a special feature: At the base of the slanted walls is a beveled lower molding, an element which was later adopted by the Zapotecs in other structures.

Right: Priceless burial gift from Grave No. 7 in Monte Albán. Far right: These stone mosaics decorate the temples of Mitla.

Another building, the **Monticulo J**, is puzzling due to the fact that its geographic orientation is completely at odds with all the others in the complex. Its ground-plan is reminiscent of a ship's bow. Could it actually be an observatory? What is the function of the reinforced underground passageway running through the building? These are among the truly great riddles of early Meso-American history yet to be deciphered.

The geometric mosaics in **Mitla**, lying 44 kilometers to the east of Oaxaca, are particularly beautiful. Situated here in the valley of the river Mitla are five groups of buildings, all of which were oriented toward the south by their builders. The Mixtec stonecutters who worked on these buildings were masters of their craft: With great skill and patience, they hewed countless small stone "bricks" in such a manner that after they were assembled they would create the impression of a mosaic. The zenith of this art can be seen in the **Palace of Columns** (Grupo de las Columnas). In one interior courtyard, the **Patio de las Grecas**, and the adjacent rooms, rhombic and meander patterns have been ingeniously combined. The tropical sun awakens this stony ornamentation to new life. According to estimates, more than 100,000 pieces went into the building of the palace. Its main hall is distinguished by its remarkable size, measuring 40 by 7.5 meters. Six round columns more than four meters in height once supported a flat roof, lending the palace its name.

On the return route to Oaxaca, one should pay a visit to **Santa Maria El Tule**. The chief landmark of the small village, a gigantic Sabino cypress, is famous far and wide. It is 40 meters high and has circumference of 42 meters! Experts assess the tree's age at over 2000 years; if true, it would be the oldest on the American continent, and indeed one of the oldest in the world. During the church festival which takes place from the 5th to the 11th of August, the cypress is adorned with garlands and flowers. There are other local ceremonies that are held in the

PUERTO ANGEL

Above: Family activities on the beach at Puerto Angel.

parish church situated right next to it. The Indigenas-operated handicrafts shop located opposite the church is also worth a visit.

Along the Coast

Long one of Mexico's poorest states, Oaxaca is ripe for touristic development beyond its famed capital city of Oaxaca. For years, backpackers and budget travelers have been drawn to the fishing village of **Puerto Angel**. During the sixties dropouts drifted down to the tropical settlement on the bay, some to get close to nature; others to meditate and sleep in hammocks near the beach. Sometimes they hung around fishing boats picking up Spanish by osmosis. *Palapas* along the town's protected harbor beach sold freshly-cooked fish at incredibly cheap prices. Coffee and beans once were shipped out of the port (hence the large concrete pier), but when the road north over the Sierra Madre del Sur to Oaxaca became passable year-round, Puerto Angel became a sleepy backwater – and to the delight of many, remains so today. True, there is an incongruous hilltop hotel, Angel del Mar, with a superb view of the great bay, but it was constructed when many assumed this town would be selected for tourist development; to bring in foreign exchange and to provide employment in an impoverished area where farming and fishing were the principal occupations. Fortunately the harvesting of sea turtles, prevalent along this coast, has been sharply curtailed.

Besides the town beach, several nearby beaches also provide swimming and sunning. Four kilometers from Puerto Angel is a beach called **Zipolete** where one can relax, rent a hammock or *cabaña* (little hut) for the night, eat inexpensively at seaside restaurants covered with *palapas* (sun shelters), and even swim *au naturel* in a remote rock-protected beach – a rare thing in Mexico.

PUERTO ESCONDIDO / HUATULCO / TUXTLA GUTIÉRREZ

To the west, the fishing settlement **Puerto Escondido** ("hidden port"), seemed better suited to development, for the coastal roads from Acapulco ran through the town. Today surfers, swimmers and fishing enthusiasts outnumber the locals, thanks to an airport that replaced a tiny local landing strip. The town's rutty dirt streets were paved, hotels sprang up, and the word traveled all the way to California and beyond: "Surf up!" There is a safe protected beach right in town, not to mention several small nearby beaches easily accessible by car and boat. But the big waves surfers should head for **Playa Zicatela**, which stretches southeast of the town.

When Cancún became too expensive for residents of Mexico City to spend weekends and holidays, they turned to Puerto Escondido, a mere 40 minute flight from the capital. On this tropical coast, where mid-afternoon temperatures can hover just below 40°C, they found a tranquility that no longer existed in either Cancún or Acapulco.

Both of these coastal resorts are connected by tortuous mountain roads to the state capital. Oaxaca buses run back and forth, often via the dusty inland town of **Pochutla** where the Highways 175 (north and south) and 200 (the coastal road) intersect. The town has little interest except as a transfer point: *colectivo* taxis leave here to wind down a curving road to Puerto Angel and the Pacific.

It's to the east of Puerto Angel that a huge tourist development is underway. The **Bays of Huatulco** (with an international airport of the same name) offer a challenge: to create a resort around nine separate coastal bays, each with own beaches. And eventually to link the bays by land and water routes. So far a commendable start has been made on the 30 kilometers of coastline. First to open was a 500-room Club Med, the largest in the hemisphere, followed by the 346-room Huatulco Sheraton Resort. Then, next to it, an equally large Royal Meava, an all-inclusive resort. Hotels are limited in hight. Thus low-rise rather than sun-blocking hotels will prevail as this resort nears completion in the next century. Incidentally, by law all ocean beaches in Mexico are open to the public even in Acapulco. However, in Huatulco you have to stay in a hotel in order to have access to the beach.

CHIAPAS

Being the southernmost state, bordering to the south with Guatemala and the Pacific Ocean, **Chiapas** may also be the most diverse and complex of Mexico's 30 states. It belonged to Guatemala until a treaty was signed making it a part of Mexico in the latter half of the 19th century. Chiapas changes from the modern, loud traffic of its capital **Tuxtla Gutiérrez** (approximately population 100,000) to the most primitive lifestyle imaginable among the Indigenas still living deep within the Lacandon Rain Forest.

Just north of the industrial hub of Tuxtla, a gray mountain opens to reveal a spectacular canyon cut by eons of winds and rain, leaving high multi-colored walls jutting straight upward to heights of 1100 meters above the **Rio Grijalva**, a river that has been dammed to provide hydroelectric power to the region. Tourists may rent boats at the tiny Spanish-built town of **Chiapa de Corzo**, with its red and white colonial church and open-air riverside restaurants. As the walls of the **Sumidero Canyon** rise higher and higher, hundreds of birds may be seen along the river bank – flocks of buzzards and hawks – and the guide tells of an eagle that swooped down once with a wing-span wider than his arms. Halfway through the four-hour boat ride, water gushes from above. Even if the waterfall is not in full flow, there is enough mist to form a rainbow when the morning finds its way into the canyon.

153

SAN CRISTOBAL DE LAS CASAS

As one begins to climb up into the mountains toward **San Cristobal de las Casas**, the road zigzags back and forth through a sombre pine forest. The town seems to be filled with churches. Between the hill overlooking the town on the southwest corner, where the **Templo de San Cristóbal** stands white and glorious at the top of more than 100 steep steps, where locals warn visitors never to walk alone because it is frequented by pickpockets, to the more sedate and solid **Templo de Santo Domingo** on the northern end of town, there are at least a dozen churches worth visiting. Santo Domingo, however, is especially interesting for being much more rigorously devout than most Mexican churches. The paintings of Juan Correa and Miguel Cabrera show Christ and the Virgin Mary in a much more down-to-earth way than one expects in the traditional Baroque churches.

Above: At festivals – like the one here in Zinacantán – and at other times, the highland Indigenas wear their colorful costumes.

Behind the church is the building that once housed the **Convento de Santo Domingo**. Now the visitor may visit a small regional museum and **San Jolobil** (House of Weaving), where the work of a cooperative of Tzotzil and Tzeltal tribes (modern day Mayas) is for sale. This colorful material and the garments cost more here than along the walkway outside, where dozens of Indigena women spread their goods on blankets to sell to passers-by. Locals will tell you that the Tzotzil and Tzeltal handiwork is far superior to that of the free-lance sellers along the sidewalk.

About a half-mile to the northwest of Santo Domingo, you will find the home of the late archeologist-explorer Frans Blom. **Na-Bolom** is now a museum and a tribute to Blom's work, and it is also the home of his widow, Gertrude Blom, who is famous in her own right as a fighter for the preservation of the rain forest and the ways of the Lacandon Indigenas. Since her husband's death in 1963, she has allowed students to stay in her home when

SAN JUAN CHAMULA / ZINACANTÁN

they prove to her that they are serious about their archeological or anthropological studies.

Open the large wooden door marked Na-Bolom and step into the sheltered patio where Indian artifacts decorate the washed yellow walls and green-leafed plants grow abundantly. For a small fee you may take the tours (Tuesday - Sunday), seeing Professor Blom's bedroom, visiting his study with its many books on the Indigenas and the region, and looking at the hundreds of photographs taken by Gertrude Blom during her innumerable hikes into the forest. At a small shop at the end of the tour you may purchase postcards, souvenirs and maps of the Lacandon Forest.

It is also possible to arrange guided trips to nearby Mayan villages from the students who work and live at Na-Bolom. From them, you may also plan visits to the ruins of Chiapas, some of which can only be flown or reached by boat during the severest part of the rain season.

Two of the Mayan tribes near San Cristobal live on their own land, are controlled by their own laws, and are ruled by their own elected or appointed politicians. At **San Juan Chamula**, the Chamulan men wear white or black wool *sarapes* fastened around their waist by leather belts. Some of these men wear short pants. The leaders of the village wear dark wide-brim hats with pointed crowns and colorful blue ribbons. The women often braid their black hair down their backs, working similar blue ribbons into the hair to show off their beauty and their marital status.

At fiesta time, especially on January 18th or 19th, at the time of celebration to San Sebastian, red, blue, green, yellow and purple banners are hung from the front spires of the white church that sits at the edge of a huge flat square zócalo. On its southern side is a well-marked Indigena tourist office where outsiders may be sold passes to the church and to the festival. Only after you have paid your fee should you enter. *And never take photographs!* The Chamulans hate cameras. It is against their religious beliefs. Several years ago a tourist had her camera snatched from her hands and smashed against a concrete post. She was ordered to leave the area immediately.

Within the church, healing ceremonies are often held by Catholic priests from San Cristobal. But as the sun nears dusk, the priests leave San Juan Chamula, because they are not allowed to stay after nightfall. During their stay in San Juan, however, they pray over the sick while families burn candles and chant their Indigena prayers. Here most of the statues portray the saints naked. They are clothed only when money or crops were sufficient to pay to cover their bodies.

In the zócalo, during fiesta, Chamulan men drink *poosh*, fermented sugar cane juice, from soft drink bottles, stagger about, dance to the music of trumpets, drum, guitars and makeshift banjos, or any other instrument they might have. The council of elders sits in straight-backed chairs and presides over the ceremonies, often weaving back and forth between swigs from the bottles, and sometimes falling from the chairs and lying upon the ground until they awaken and get in their chairs again.

Over a hill and a few miles away is the smaller village of **Zinacantán**, where the Indigenas wear bright pink *sarapes*. Both sexes wear wide-brim straw hats from which red and purple ribbons hang. Next to the small town that looks like a street from a spaghetti western stands a white church with little adornment other than the Mayan cross. Across a field near the main road is a small chapel. It is in this field next to the chapel that the colorfully clad Zinacantáns celebrate San Sebastian's birthday in January. They too drink *poosh*, ride horseback and joust drunkenly. During the fiesta, men dressed as monkeys with short loin-cloths, climb

PALENQUE

Above: Dense jungle surrounds the Mayan temple city of Palenque.

a tree that has been skinned of all bark. They dangle in the limbs, chattering obscenities and showing their genitals, until the more powerful jaguar man, wearing the mask of a tiger, climbs into the tree and chases them away. Then he, the jaguar, rules the tree. According to local lore, each of their festival activities are based upon traditional Mayan ceremonies that have been performed among the Indians in Chiapas for hundreds of years.

About a half-hour from San Cristóbal to the northeast are the magnificent ruins of **Palenque** in the lower hills of the Altos de Chiapas. Set amid an emerald tropical forest, the temples, ball court and pyramids look like a perfect Indigenas paradise. This "place of the sun's daily death" was built for Pacal, a Mayan king who ruled from the time he was a boy until his death, allegedly aged 68.

To your right as you enter the grounds is one of the most impressive sights in all of Mexico. High on a pyramid sits the **Temple of Inscriptions**. You may choose to climb the steep stone steps to the front or you may follow a path up a gradual incline to the rear, passing over a babbling brook, then working your way inside, where you will find the narrow passage down into the floor that archeologist Alberto Ruz Lhuillier discovered in 1949 hidden beneath the stone. You may climb down the slippery stairs and peer through an opening into the crypt where Ruz found a five-ton sarcophagus with a perfectly inscribed lid which has been studied and translated by numerous scholars. The king buried here wore a jade and gold death mask. With Pacal was a huge cache of jade and pearl jewelry, gold and other precious metals.

Following the trail out behind the Temple of Inscriptions you wind your way up another hill to the **Temple of the Jaguars**. In an inner chamber are the faded remains of a wall painting difficult to decipher here but reworked completely in the small museum at the edge of the

YAXCHILÁN / BONAMPAK

ruins. It shows life at Palenque, including the palace next to the ball court, where Mayan priests cavorted in pools fed by running water.

To visit the more remote ruins in Chiapas, the tourist would need to make guided tour arrangements at San Cristóbal or in the town of Palenque.

During the dry season, the sights of Bonampak and **Yaxchilán** may be reached by four-wheel-drive vehicle. The fastest and most expensive way is by plane. Both on the banks of the Usumacinta River, Yaxchilan is a Mayan ceremonial center growing almost straight up the hillside within the thick growth of vines and 60-meter-high mahogany trees. During the Golden Age of the Maya rule of these jungles, Yaxchilan became an art center as well as political capital. Jaguar Shield moved here and obviously had sculptors carve stelae in his honor over a number of the buildings. Next to a ball court on the side of the hill is a huge stela of a jaguar crouched and ready to leap next to a life-sized crocodile. At Yaxchilán, the visitor may climb so high that he is looking out onto the top of the highest trees. Here the view is not only spectacular, but one may see and hear dozens of scarlet macaws singing their songs and hosts of howling monkeys jumping and jabbering around in the foliage.

Some miles down-river is **Bonampak**, or the City of Painted Walls. In one of the buildings you can see great murals telling the story of Mayas conquering a foreign city, returning with captive slaves and putting them to death. The colors have faded but they are still impressive. Once again you are taken back in your imagination to the time when only the Mayas lived here.

Now and then, in this rain forest a tourist may glimpse a strange dark face with a prominent wide nose and deep-set black eyes. It is sobering to know that several hundred Lacandons still live in the jungle and look exactly like the images of their ancestors carved in the stone stelae.

OAXACA
Accommodation
LUXURY: **El Presidente**, 5 de Mayo 300, Tel: 6-0611. **Misión de los Angeles**, Calzada Porfirio Díaz 102, Tel: 5-1500. **San Felipe Misión**, Jalisco 15, Tel: 5-0100. **Victoria**, Carret. Panamericana at km 545, Tel: 5-2633.

MODERATE: **Margarita**, Calzada Madero 1254, Tel: 6-4100. **Monte Albán**, Alameda de León 1, Tel: 6-2777. **Señorial**, Portal de Flores 6, Tel: 6-3933. **Villa de León**, Reforma 405, Tel: 6-1977.

BUDGET: **Méson del Rey**, Trujano 212, Tel: 6-0033. **Principal**, 5 de Mayo 208, Tel: 6-2535.

Restaurants
El Asador Vasco, at the Zócalo, typical regional food, *mole*-dishes, Tel: 6-9719. **El Biche Pobre**, largest selection of *mole*-dishes in town, Mártires de Tacubaya/Abasolo, no phone. **Salsa Gourmet**, international, Dalias 1006, Tel: 5-6690. **Mi Casita**, regional food, Hidalgo 616, near the Zócalo, Tel: 6-9256. **Fonda del Rincón**, Mexican food, Emilio Carranza 1201, Tel: 5-4564. **La Morsa**, seafood, Calzada Porifirio Díaz 240, Tel: 5-2213.

Museums
Museo Regional, in the monastery next to the church Santo Domingo, famous Mixtecs-treasure, precious grave furnishings, Calle Alcalá, Tue-Fri 10 am-6 pm.

Museo Rufino Tamayo, prespanish artefacts, Av. Morelos 503, Mon, Wed, Sat 10 am-2 pm and 4-7 pm, Sun 10 am-3 pm.

Casa de Juárez, former house of Benito Juárez, García Vigil 609, Tue-Sun 9 am-7 pm.

Shopping
Oaxaca is famous for arts and crafts of the Indigenas, mainly pottery and weaving. The most beautiful ceramics are made in Atzompa and Coyotepec, lovely woven items are produced in Teotitlán del Valle.

Mercado Sabado (Central de Abastos), this weekend-market is frequented by many locals from the region. **Mercado de Artesanías** (arts and crafts), García/Zaragoza. **Mercado Benito Juárez** (covered market). Pretty souvenirs are *rebozos* (colorful shawls), *serapes* (capes) and *huipils* (blouses/shirts).

Fiesta
Virgen de la Soledad (December 16-18), colorful fiesta in honor of the town's patron saint with corso and folklore.

Sightseeing
Ruins of Mitla, 44 km east of Oaxaca at Ruta 190, open to visitors from 8 am-5 pm. Zapotec-village **Teotitlán del Valle**, for woven materials.

Ruins of Monte Albán, open to visitors from 8 am-5 pm, 9,5 km west of Oaxaca. *Colectivos* run four times daily from the hotel Mesón del Angel.

Post / Telecommunication
Post Office: Alameda de León, Tel: 6-2661, Mon-Fri 8 am-7 pm, Sat 9 am-1 pm.

Telephone: Long distance calls from the Farmacia Hidalgo, 20 de Noviembre/Hidalgo, Mon-Sat 9 am-9.30 pm, Sun 10 am-1.30 pm.

Telegrams: Independencia/ 20 de Noviembre, Tel: 6-4255, Mon-Sat 8 am-11 pm.

Tourist Information
Palacio Municipal, Independencia 607, Tel: 6-3810.

HUATULCO
FONATUR is building a large new holiday resort in Huatulco. 9000 hotel rooms are planned for the year 2000. At the moment, the complex at the *Bahías de Huatulco* is still in the first building phase.

Accommodation
LUXURY: **Club Med**, Bahía de Tangolunda, Tel: 1-0033. **Sheraton**, Bahía de Tangolunda, Tel: 1-0055.

MODERATE: **Posada Binniguenda**, Bahía de Santa Cruz, Tel: 4-0080. **Fiesta Americana**, Bahía de Tangolunda.

BUDGET: **Royal Maeve**, Bahías de Huatulco, Tel: 1-1000.

Restaurants
Good food is served only in the hotel restaurants; simple dishes and snacks can be obtained at the marina.

PUERTO ANGEL
Accommodation
Puerto Angel has a few telephones only. Best acommodation is the **Hotel Angel del Mar**, Playa del Panteón, Tel: 6. Almost all accommodation is very basic (small hotels, guest houses). *Cabañas* with hammocks can be rented at the beach Playa Zipolete.

La Buena Vista, Calle de la Buena Compañía. **Casa de Huéspedes el Capi**, from the harbor in the direction of Playa del Panteón. **Las Cabañas**, at the Playa del Panteón. **Posada Rincon Sabrosa**, near the bus terminal. **La Posada Cañon Devata**, Playa del Panteón. **Casa de Huéspedes Gundi y Tomás**, Playa del Panteón.

Restaurants
A fair amount of unpretentious street cafés and no-frills restaurants are in the harbor area and along the Playa del Panteón. The delicious seafood – including lobster – is a real treat in almost every eatery.

Brico's y Cornelia. El Capi. Restaurant Susy. Beto's. El Tiburon, at the bus terminal.
Beaches
There is a town beach, and among several beaches nearby the **Playa Zipolete** is the most popular; 45 minutes on foot, accommodation in *cabañas* only (hammocks), basic *palapa*-restaurants serve fresh fish.

PUERTO ESCONDIDO
Accommodation
MODERATE: **Posada Real**, Blvd. Benito Juárez, Tel: 2-0133. **Castel Puerto Escondido**, Benito Juárez, Tel: 2-0428. **Hotel Santa Fe**, Del Morro 10, Tel: 2-1070. **Villa Sol**, Fracc. Bacocho, Tel: 2-0382. **Paraíso Escondido**, Calle Unión 10, Tel: 2-0444.
BUDGET: **Las Gaviotas**, 2 A Nte., Tel: 2-0254. **Nayar**, Av. Pérez Gasga 407, Tel: 2-0113. **Aldea Bacocho**, Av. Monte Albán 5, Tel: 2-0335.
Restaurants
The **Fat Lobster**, Av. Pérez Gasga. **Las Mariposas**, international cuisine, side-alley off Juárez, Tel: 2-0197. **Santa Fe**, in the Hotel Santa Fe, seafood and Mexican dishes, Playa Marinero, Tel: 2-0170. **Da Ugo**, Italian, Av. Pérez Gasga. **Los Crotos**, seafood, Av. Pérez Gasga.
Post / Telecommunication
Post Office (also for telegrams): Av. Oaxaca, Tel: 2-0335, Mon-Fri 9 am-2 pm and 4-7 pm, Sat 9 am-2 pm. **Telephone** (long distance): Pérez Gasga, Tel: 2-0000.
Tourist Information
Pérez Gasga, Tel: 2-0175.

TUXTLA GUTIÉRREZ
Accommodation
MODERATE: **Flamboyant**, Blvd. Belisario Domínguez 1081, Tel: 2-2959 and 2-9311. **Real de Tuxla**, Carretera Panamericana 1088, Tel: 2-5958. **Bonampak**, Blvd. Domínguez 180, Tel: 3-2050. **Gran Hotel Umberto**, Av. Central Poniente 180, Tel: 2-2044 and 2-2080.
BUDGET: **Posada de Rey**, Primera Calle Ote. 310, Tel: 2-2871. **Hotel Avenida**, Central/1 Poniente., Tel: 2-0807. **Hotel María Teresa**, Calle 2 / 259 B Nte., Tel: 3-0102. **Esponda**, Primera Calle Nte. 142, Tel: 2-0080.
Restaurants
London, seafood, Segunda Nte./ Cuarta Poniente, Tel: 3-1979. **Las Pichanchas**, Av. Central Ote. 837, Tel: 2-5351. **El Pollo Loco**, chicken specialities, Av. Central/ 10 Pte., Tel: 2-0677. **Restaurant Tuxtla**, regional food, Calle Central 262 Nte., Tel: 2-0648. **Chung Chang Shan**, Chinese, 1 A Nte./Pte. 217, Tel: 2-2823.

Post / Telecommunication
Post Office: at the Zócalo, Tel: 2-0416, Mon-Fri 8 am-7 pm, Sat-Sun 9 am-12 noon.
Telephone: long distance calls from phone-boxes possible.
Telegrams: next to the post office, Tel: 8-0144, Mon-Fri 8 am-midnight, Sat 8 am-9 pm, Sun 9 am-1 pm.
Tourist Information
14 de Septiembre 1498, 14 blocks west of the Zócalo, Tel: 2-4535 and 2-5509, Mon-Fri 8 am-8 pm.

SAN CRISTÓBAL DE LAS CASAS
Accommodation
MODERATE / BUDGET: **Posade Diego de Mazariegos**, 5 de Febrero, Tel: 8-1825. **Hotel Santa Clara**, Plaza Central, Tel: 8-1140. **Hotel Bonampak**, Calzada Mexico 5, Tel: 8-1621. **Ciudad Real**, Plaza 31 de Marzo, Tel: 8-0187. **Hotel Mansión del Valle**, Diego de Mazariegos 39, Tel: 8-2581.
Restaurants
Rafaello's, regional and international cuisine, Madero 9, Tel: 8-2238. **Plaza**, Hidalgo 1, Tel: 8-0887. **Toluca**, popular Mexican restaurant, Insurgentes 5, Tel: 8-2090. **Unicornio**, Insurgentes 33, Tel: 8-0732. **Los Arcos**, Madero 6, Tel: 8-0457.
Festival
The *Carnaval* in the nearby village of San Juan Chamula begins one week before Ash Wednesday. Thousands of Indigenas take part in this fiesta, one of the most exotic of the region.
Post / Telecommunication
Post Office: Cuauhtémoc/Crescencio Rosas, Tel: 2-0427, open Mon-Fri from 8 am-7 pm, Sat and Sun from 9 am-1 pm.
Telephone: Some *casetas*, a telephone is in the Perfumería la Popular, at the Zócalo.
Telegrams: Diego de Mazariegos, Tel: 2-0051, Mon-Fri 8 am-midnight, Sat 9 am-9pm, Sun 9 am-12 noon.
Tourist Information
At the Zócalo (Palacio Municipal), Tel: 8-0414, Mon-Fri 8 am-8 pm, Sat 8 am-1 pm and 3-8 pm, Sun 9 am-2 pm.

PALENQUE
Accommodation
MODERATE: **Misión Palenque**, Rancho San Martin de Porres, Tel: 5-0300 and 5-0241. **Chan-Kah**, Carretera a Las Ruinas at km 31, Tel: 5-0018.
BUDGET: **Casa de Pakal**, Juárez 10, no phone. **Hotel Palenque**, 5 de Mayo, Tel: 5-0300. **Tulipanes**, Cañada 6, no phone.

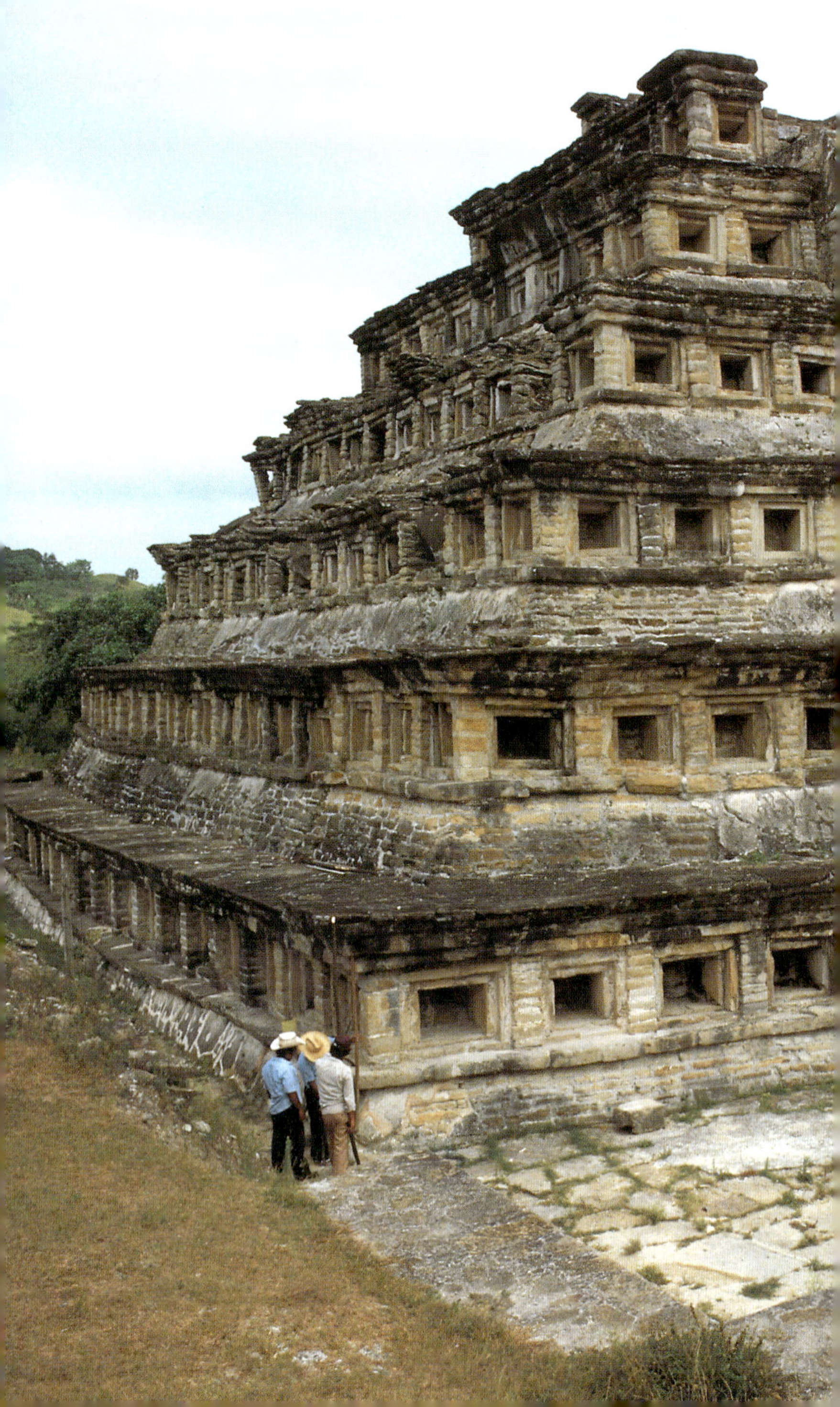

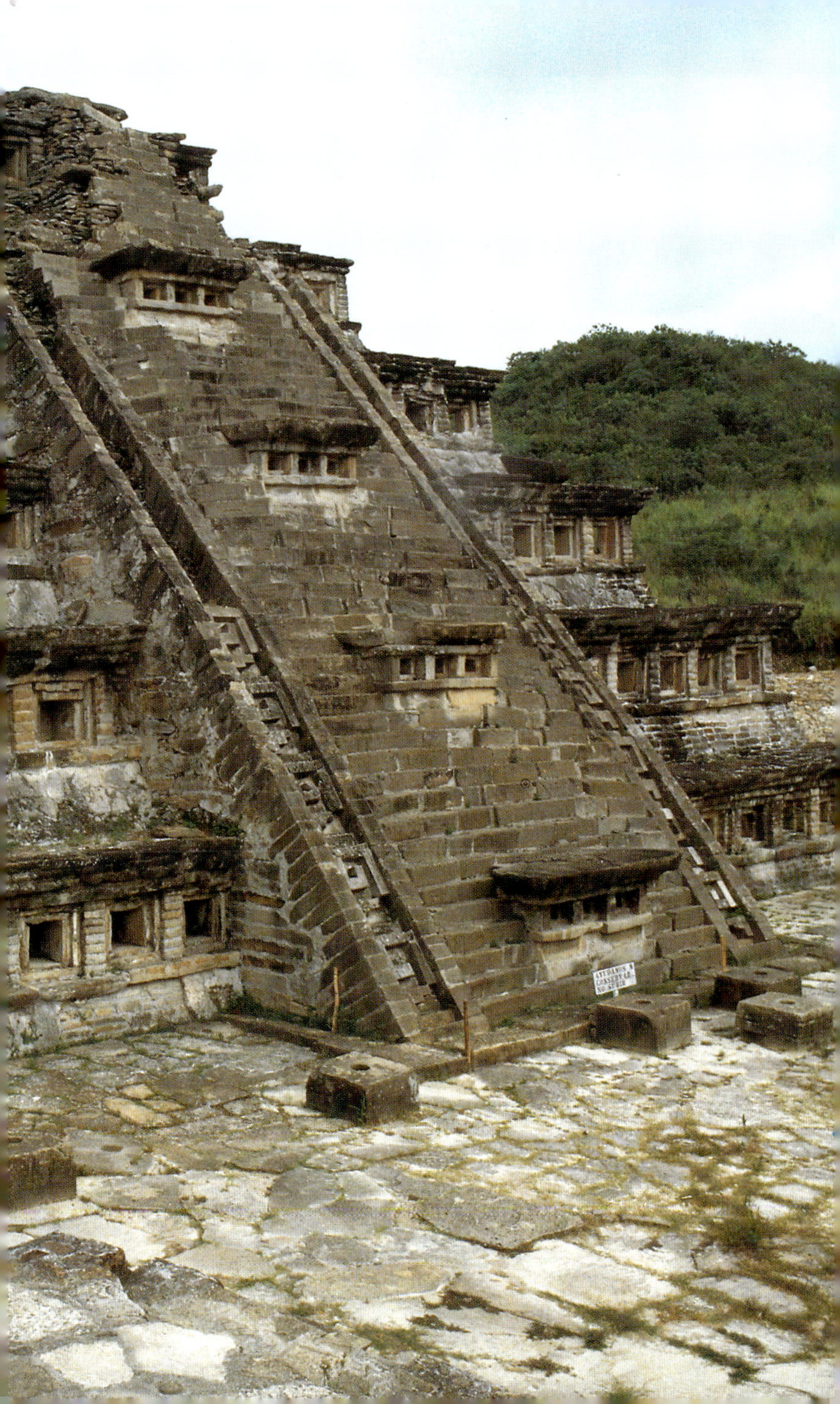

ALONG THE GULF OF MEXICO

VERACRUZ
TABASCO
CAMPECHE

VERACRUZ

Veracruz is one of Mexico's most populous states. Stretched along much of Mexico's Gulf coast and bounded by seven other states, its landscape is full of variety. Between the rugged Sierra Madre Oriental and the long beaches of the Gulf of Mexico, coffee plantations alternate with vast fields of maize and vanilla, industrial towns and menacing oil fields with primeval tropical forest.

Originally the homeland of the Olmecs, who established the New World's first civilization around 1000 BC, the state is now populated mainly by *mestizos*, along with descendants of African slaves and Totonac Indians.

Tampico, which numbers well over a half million inhabitants, is the most important port on the Gulf of Mexico after Veracruz. It is often called the "New Orleans of Mexico", because its downtown port area on the Rio Panuco has the quaint, rundown, balcony-trimmed look of that American city's French Quarter.

Tampico's grandiose and palm-graced **Plaza de Armas**, or zócalo, is full of vitality and is the center of activity of the entire city. Here, also, are the **cathedral**

Previous pages: The famous Pyramid of Niches at El Tajin.

and the **Palacio Municipal** or Town Hall. There's also the colorful **Plaza de la Libertad**, which looks down on the steaming portside **Mercado Hidalgo**, a chattering market full of produce and cantinas.

This city is full of color and spice with a gawdy riverfront district featuring restaurants serving some of the best seafood in the country. The centerpiece of this district is the white-brick Victorian **Aduana Maritimo** (Customs House), constructed in 1889 along the docks.

7 kilometers north of the city is the **Huaxtec Museum**, located in the satellite town of Ciudad Madero. Displays include stone sculptures, terracotta figurines, pottery, various and sundry ornaments, jewelry made of gold, silver and copper, weapons and costumes produced by the Huaxtec people.

Playa Miramar is Tampico's most popular beach. To the north it blends with solitary **Playa Altamira**.

The ancient Huaxtecan ceremonial center of **El Tamuin** is only 30 kilometers away. Though this trip can be rough and involves a ferry crossing, it is worth seeing the site from the bluff above the Tamuin River.

Ciudad Valles, a town of 75,000 people at an important railroad junction in the neighboring state of San Luis Potosí, is in the region called Huasteca, which comes from the name given to the Maya's distant cousins who lived there. This is the jumping off point for **Tamazunchale**, a village accessible through jungles of bamboo and banana trees. This is the site of one of the region's best Sunday Indigena markets. The area around the town is good for bird watching and is also noted for its butterflies, mounted varieties of which can be found in many of the village shops.

About some 150 kilometers south of Tampico lies the industrial city of **Poza Rica** (population 250,000), meaning "rich well", where the first big oil gusher was struck in 1930. It was transformed almost overnight into a modern city with wide boulevards and beautiful buildings. Oil derricks, refineries and storage tanks dot the landscape. This region is the largest producer of oil in the country.

Nearby is the archeological site of **Castillo de Teayo**, not really a castle but a pyramid, which was built by the Toltecs, then taken over by later groups. 23 kilometers further south through dense jungle is the town of **Papantla**, whose name means "place of the birds" in the native Totonac language. Once this region was the center of Totonac culture and today 143 communities of Totonacs still live in the surrounding orchid jungles cultivating vanilla.

Papantla (population 90,000), some 200 kilometers from Veracruz, is an attractive town in a hilly region of dense tropical forests and is surrounded by the largest vanilla plantations in North America. Papantla is known as the home of the Totonac *voladores*, the Indigena fliers who dress as red birds and spin from a tall pole by a rope attached to their feet. The ancient ritual, once a rain dance, involves four fliers, each representing one of the four points of the compass, and a fifth musician who represents the center of the world sitting on top of the pole playing while the others hurl themselves head first off the top. This ceremony is performed on weekends in the **Plazoleta del Volador** in front of the cathedral and at the entrance to the nearby ruins of El Tajin.

El Tajin

El Tajin, just 16 kilometers northwest of Papantla and 17 kilometers south of Poza Rica, is one of the most important pre-Columbian sites in Mexico. It marked the height of the Totonac culture around 800 AD. Covering an area of four square miles, only a small part of which has been excavated, it is remarkably well preserved. Unknown invaders from the north sacked it about 1200 AD. The sculptural decorations are typical of the Veracruzan civilization of the classical period, with interlocking scrolls and the "stepped fret", the dominant motifs. Among the ruins one can make out ten overgrown ball courts, and it is believed that El Tajin was the center of the ball game, which originated on the Gulf coast. At the ends of the impressive south ball court are panels of bas-reliefs, lying between horizontal friezes of stylized serpent motifs. There are four principal scenes – the dedication of a young warrior; a ball-player being held on a sacrificial altar by one priest while another plunges an obsidian knife through his heart; two players conversing with one another being watched by gods; and the dedication of a ball-player to *Tlachtli*, the god of the ball game.

On the west side of the main plaza is the main structure, the unique **Pyramid of the Niches**. With a height of 25 meters on a base 35 meters square, the pyramid, built between the 6th and 7th centuries, has seven stories, including the temple. Around the sides are 365 shallow niches symbolizing the days of the year. The exterior was originally faced with colored stucco, and the niches were painted in bright red and blue. The steep staircase on the east side was added later and fea-

EL TAJIN / JALAPA

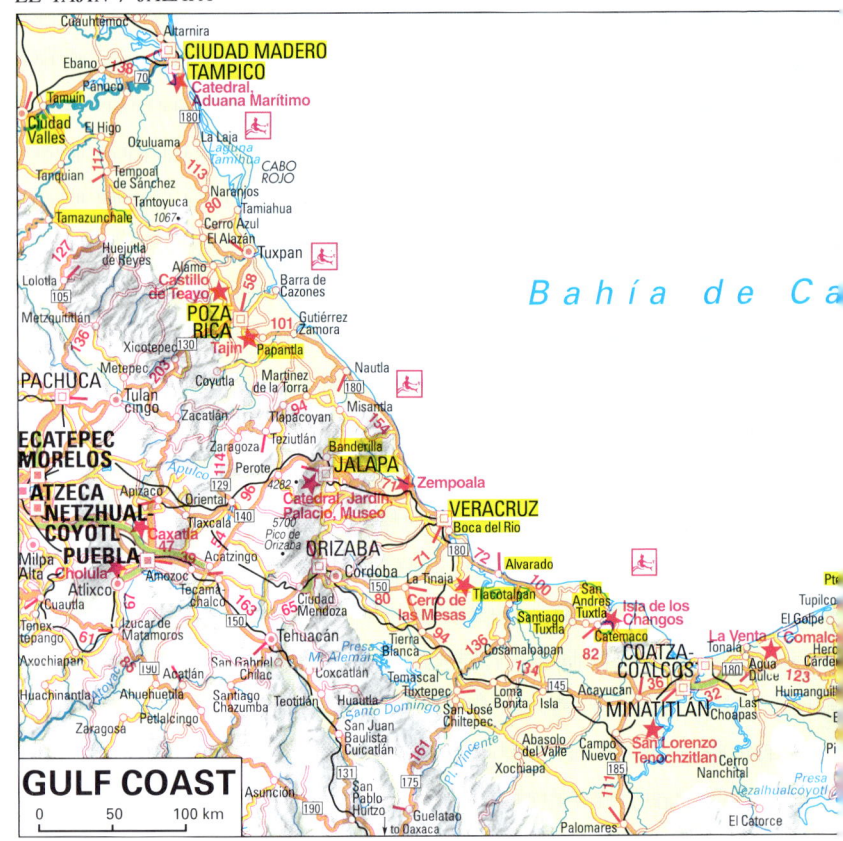

tures four rows of three niches. The entire structure was built on a previous one, as was the custom of the time.

To the rear of the site is the **Plaza El Tajin Chico** or Little Tajin. The finest structure in this area is the **Edificio de las Columnas** (Building of the Columns), which covers an area of 35,000 square yards. Standing on a small mound, it reaches a height of 45 meters and also features niches and a grand staircase, although it is believed that the stairs were not used for climbing but just for decoration. Huge columns forming a gallery decorated the façade of the building. These were decorated with bas-reliefs depicting scenes involving warriors and priests, human sacrifices and hiero-glyphs. Nearby is the **Edificio de los Tuneles** (Tunnel Building), from which two underground passages lead to a large courtyard. Up to now, only 16 structures have been excavated.

Jalapa (population 380,000), 112 kilometers north of Veracruz, is the capital of the state of Veracruz, and is built on a number of hills in a garden-like region at the foot of the **Cerro de Macuiltepec**. It is surrounded by other high mountains, including the **Cofre de Perote**, or Nauhcampatepetl, and the **Pico de Orizaba**, or Citlaltcpctl, (a pre-Columbian name meaning Star Mountain), Mexico's highest at 5700 meters. Thus, the area receives abundant rainfall and is often clouded over, promoting a luxuriant ve-

JALAPA / VERACRUZ CITY

light-stoned colonial-style **Government Palace**, containing interesting frescoes and faced by ornate fountains. The adjacent **Jardín Morelos** offers a fine view of the city. Other attractive parks are the Parque Hidalgo and Parque de los Berros.

However, the main attraction in Jalapa is the magnificent **Museum of Anthropology**, designed by Edward Durrell Stone, and a part of the University of Veracruz. This museum contains an impressive collection of Olmec heads, Aztec and Huaxtec stone sculptures, as well as a large selection of stelae and cult objects, pottery vessels and figures and articles made from semi-precious stones. It brings together for the first time collections of artifacts that were formerly stored around the state. The museum's landscaped atriums show giant Olmec heads in natural settings, and an 18-level orientation hall explains exhibits and puts it all in context. The cultures shown in this museum influenced future cultures throughout Meso-America.

The **Jardín Lecuona**, a botanical garden with more than 200 species of orchids, is located nearby in the garden city of **Banderilla**, located four and a half miles northwest of town.

The City of Veracruz

It is said that there are *chilangos* (as the inhabitants of Mexico City are called) who get into their car on Saturday mornings, invite a few friends along, and set out on a five-to-seven hour drive over winding roads, involving a tremendous difference in altitude, and then – later Sunday afternoon – put themselves through the same strain on the return trip purely for the sake of spending one long night in **Veracruz**. For many enthusiasts, this port city on the Gulf of Mexico is synonymous with *joie de vivre* – the joy of life. Particularly during the carnival season, Veracruz turns into one big festival arena. The colorful parades with fan-

getation. The locals call the rain *chipi-chipi*. The town itself is often called the "Flower Garden of Mexico" due to the profusion of flowers and fruits in its parks and gardens.

Once a former stronghold of the Spaniards and a stagecoach stop, Jalapa's old town is a maze of narrow streets and lanes lined with colorful houses and lush gardens, left over from the Spanish colonial period. This is in striking contrast to the broad boulevards and modern buildings in the newer sections of town.

One notable building of the colonial period is the massive late-18th-century **cathedral**, which has been restored. This stands near the attractive **Parque Juárez**, on the other side of which is the long

VERACRUZ CITY

tastically decorated floats begin nine days before Ash Wednesday. There is music and dancing everywhere you look, including popular rhythms for everyone to dance to, as well as folklore presentations. Children have their own parade, sporting competitions are held, and the evening sky is illuminated by fireworks.

Even on "normal" days, the atmosphere in this tropical city – where the heat of high summer is toned down a bit by a constant seabreeze – is relaxed and cheerful. The city's exuberant inhabitants, called *jarochos*, are of predominantly Spanish descent. They have their own traditional way of dancing: the *son jarocho* which has many variations. The stamping rhythms of the dancers contrast with the rather monotonous accompanying music played by a band *(conjunto jarocho),* consisting of a harp, tenor and bass guitars and sometimes violins). The men wear white trousers and shirts with a

Right: The zócalo of Veracruz throbs with life by day and night.

166

red neckerchief and a straw hat. The women ornament their white, frilly dresses with an embroidered black apron. *La bamba* is a vivacious, rhythmic dance-song which has become internationally famous. Its lyrics inevitably claim that all one needs to dance, is a bit of gracefulness, although it sometimes takes dexterity as well: In one dance, to a stamping rhythm, the men tie knots in ribbons the women have laid at their feet.

The zócalo, the **Plaza de Armas**, is filled with music every evening. Players with virtuoso command of the *marimba,* a xylophone-like instrument, gather together at the regional competitions. *Mariachis* and *trios norteños,* musical groups from the north, also participate in these volume contests, which might not be exactly to everyone's taste. In unison with the "concert" are the happy shrieks of children, church bells and the twittering of the countless birds that have made their home in the palms around the attractive plaza with its splashing fountains. Tourists and locals lounge in front of the cafés and bars, beneath the colonnades of beautiful colonial buildings. Shoe-shine boys hurry from table to table, street peddlers sell tortoise-shell combs, made of sea-shells or gigantic carved wooden ships. Beggars also hope to get a few pesos or some leftovers from people who have had better luck than they.

Otherwise, there really isn't so much for a sightseeing tour in Veracruz. The façade of the **Palacio Municipal** on the zócalo is beautiful, while the churches and the **cathedral**, also on the zócalo, are rather plain, as is the city's oldest church, the 16th-century **San Cristo del Buen Viaje** on the Plaza Gutiérrez Zamora. Imposing works of architecture in neo-Classical style dominate the **Plaza de la Reforma**, which is located directly on the harbor. A little way out to sea, connected with the mainland by an embankment, is the fortress **San Juan de Ulúa**, which was once supposed to protect the city from pirates and was used as a prison during the 19th century.

There are also a couple of small museums that should be mentioned: In the lighthouse **Faro Carranza** there are furniture and documents to commemorate one of Mexico's revolutionary heros, Venustiano Carranza, who drew up the Mexican Constitution here in 1914/15. The **Museo de la Ciudad** houses the city's historical and archeological collections, though the display hardly does them justice. The regional museum **Baluarte de Santiago**, housed in the only remaining section of the former city wall, features a collection of armaments. For more than 200 years, Veracruz was Mexico's only trading port and long afterward remained its most important connection to the Old World, besides being a port of entry for invaders and settlers, traders and exiles, slaves and rulers. On Good Friday of the year 1519, the "Day of the True Cross" *(Día de la Vera Cruz)*, Hernán Cortés landed opposite the Isla de San Juan Ulúa and named the place *Villa Rica de la Vera Cruz.* To his astonishment, he was received by emissaries of Aztec emperor Moctezuma and showered with gifts because he was believed to be their returning god Quetzalcóatl. The treasures aroused Cortés' venal curiosity. However, before he set off on a march to Tenochtitlán, he founded the first Spanish settlement on Mexican soil several kilometers further to the north. This town, the present-day **La Antigua**, was later relocated to the mouth of the Río Huitzilapan. The city of Veracruz wasn't established until 1589 under the protection of the island fortress San Juan de Ulúa. Veracruz developed into a lively trading port which soon attracted British, French and Dutch pirates, whose raids didn't end until the construction of a fortified city wall in 1746.

During the 19th century, Veracruz was the center of political events: In 1825, the last Spaniards entrenched on the fortress island were driven out of the now-independent Mexico. In 1847, the city was seized by US troops during the Mexican-American War. The French invasion began in 1862, after Mexico had failed to pay its foreign debts; two years later Maximilian of Habsburg landed in Veracruz as the Emperor of Mexico. In 1914, American troops landed in Veracruz once again, this time to stop Victoriano Huerta, who was forced by revolutionary leader Venustiano Carranza to resign in the same year.

Veracruz still bears the hallmarks of an international city. Merchant seamen congregate in the neighborhood around the harbor, where the navy is also stationed and parades in public every evening. On the harbor promenade, the *malecón,* there are a number of quiet hotels and a market for (rather corny) arts and crafts as well as a gigantic customs building. To the south of the promenade the beaches begin, the most beautiful of them being the **Costa de Oro** and **Mocambo**.

The best of the city's fish dishes, including *huachinango veracruzana*, are to be found in the suburb of **Boca del Río,** a popular destination for weekend outings, not least for the family-oriented prices. By the way, no fish is served on the zócalo! Here, at the most popular meetingplace in the city, the traditional dish is the *torta*, a large roll with a generous filling and an abundance of garnishings, customarily washed down with a good cup of Mexican coffee. The best place for this culinary experience is in the **Gran Café de la Parroquia**, although it is often necessary to queue for a seat.

In southern Veracruz, Federal Highway 180 cuts through vast fruit plantations. Fruit and freshly-squeezed juices are sold from streetstands, including mango in the summer months and pineapple and banana throughout the year. Tobacco, vanilla and sugar cane are also cultivated on this tropical plain; in fact, Veracruz is the largest sugar producer in

Above: Many festivals in and around Veracruz clearly show Spanish influence. Right: A hidden wonder of nature – the Falls of Testapan, near Catemaco.

Mexico. Nonetheless, the nearby petroleum industry yields far more income than agriculture. Many *campesinos* have therefore left the orchards and fields in the hope of finding a job with PEMEX, the state-run oil company.

Gems to the East of Veracruz

There are several true gems remaining to be explored: On the narrow spit of land that separates the Lagoon of Alvarado from the Gulf of Mexico, the fishing town of **Alvarado** straddles both banks of the Río Papaloapan where it flows into the Gulf. A couple of kilometers further inland on the road to Tuxtepec, **Tlacotalpan** is also worth a side-trip. Agustín Lara (1900-78), probably Mexico's most famous composer and lyricist of romantic love-songs, has designated this enchanting little city on the Río Papaloapan, which translates as "Butterfly River", as his place of birth. Whether this is true is not known by his biographers, but the town fits the composer's image:

The zócalo, framed by whitewashed houses with colorful balconies and arcade passages, looks like the backdrop of some romantic film.

The best interpreters of the *sones veracruzanos*, as the dances and songs (particularly *huapangos*, and *sones jarochos*) of the region are called, come from Tlacotalpan. On the occasion of the four-day-long *Fiesta de la Candelaria* (around February 2), when the statue of the Virgin of Candelaria is taken for a cruise on a specially decorated boat, musicians and dancers take part in a competition, usually being cheered on by a rather noisy audience.

The hinterland of Veracruz, which even today is still quite inaccessible, was once the home of the Olmecs, the "mother culture" of Central America, of whose existence nothing was known until 1925. **Tres Zapotes** and **San Lorenzo** are the most important sites for archeological finds in the state of Veracruz.

Of course, the treasures of the Olmecs, including huge heads of carved basalt, jaguar sculptures and tiny jade figures, are no longer where they were discovered; they can now be admired in museums. The most magnificent specimens are in the possession of Mexico City, Jalapa and Villahermosa. The state of Veracruz displays its most beautiful side in the **Sierra de los Tuxtlas**, a mountainous region rising to altitudes of 1800 meters with (extinct) volcanoes, forests, lakes and waterfalls.

Santiago Tuxtla, the main plaza of which is ornamented by a colossal Olmec head (a small museum displays additional specimens excavated in Tres Zapotes), and **San Andrés Tuxtla** are a couple of attractive colonial towns. **Catemaco**, on the lake which shares its name, is nestled in a storybook landscape. It has become a popular vacation spot for devout Mexicans who believe in miracles. They make pilgrimages to the *Virgen del Carmen,* or come in search of

Above: Only the easily satisfied Zebus can be breeded in the Gulf coast region.

the services of miracle healers *(curanderos)* and sorcerers *(brujos).* Boat trips lure the visitor to take a cruise around the 16-kilometer-long lake, which is surrounded by tropical vegetation.

The lake's prime attraction is the **Isla de los Changos** (Monkey Island). Its inhabitants, who derive their main sustenance from fish, were purposely settled here by the University of Veracruz for research purposes.

One should breathe deeply in the "Switzerland of Veracruz" (so-named by Alexander von Humboldt), because located at the feet of the Sierras are the most important cities of the Mexican petroleum industry, **Minantitlán** and **Coatzacoalcos,** with their eerie drilling and refinery towers spewing out poisonous fumes and clouds of smoke.

A superhighway runs over the **Coatzacoalco Bridge**, an engineering masterpiece. The PEMEX oil fields extend far into the neighboring state of Tabasco, which begins on the other side of the Tonalá River.

STATE OF VERACRUZ
TAMPICO
Accommodation
LUXURY: **Camino Real**, Av. Hidalgo 2000, Tel: 13-8811. **Posada de Tampico**, Av. Hidalgo 2200, Tel: 13-3050. *MODERATE*: **Colonial**, Madero Ote. 210, Tel: 12-7676. **Inglaterra**, Salvador Díaz Mirón 116 Ote., Tel: 12-5678.
BUDGET: **Imperial**, Cesar López de Lara/Carranza 101 Sur, Tel: 14-1363.
Restaurants
As good restaurants are scarce in Tampico, it is advisable to dine in the larger hotels. **Gran Muralle**, Mexican food. **López de Lara**, Tel: 12-4789. **Muralto**, Aduana/ Héroes Canoners Tampico, seafood, Tel: 13-6305.
Post Office
Madero 309/Plaza de la Libertad, Tel: 2-1917, Mon-Fri 8 am-7 pm and Sat 9 am-1 pm.
Tourist Information
Olmos 101, at the Zócalo, Tel: 12-0007, Mon-Fri 8 am-7 pm.

PAPANTLA
Accommodation
MODERATE: **El Tajin**, Calle Jesús Núñez/Domíngues, Tel: 2-1062. **Totonocapan**, Olivio /20 de Noviembre, Tel: 2-1220. **Hotel Papantla**, at the Zócalo, Tel: 2-0080. **Hotel Pulido**, Enríquez 205, near the Zócalo, Tel: 2-0036.
Restaurants
Basic mexican food is served in the hotels **El Tajin** and **Pulido**, at the **Terraza Grill**, 20 de Noviembre (at the Zócalo) and at some stalls in the covered market.
Sightseeing
Ruins of El Tajin, ca. 16 km north of the town. Buses run several times daily from the bus terminal of the *Transportes de Papantla*, 20 de Noviembre, Tel: 2-0015.
Festivals / Special Events
Festival de Papantla, one-week festival starting on Corpus Christi Day. **Feria**, agricultural fair with fiesta, bull- and cockfights. Special attraction: Performance of the *voladores* ("flying men") on the Plaza in front of the church. The performances at the Ruins of El Tajin have been cancelled because of restauration work.

JALAPA (XALAPA)
Accommodation
MODERATE: **Hotel Xalapa**, Victoria/Bustamante, Tel: 8-2222. *BUDGET*: **El Mirador**, Av. Xalapa 366, Tel: 5-1099. **Hotel Ensueño**, Av. Murillo 16, Tel: 8-2199. **Hotel Palacio**, Av. Avila Camacho 1179, Tel: 5-4600.

Museums
Museo de Antropología, Avenida Acueducto/Rayon, open Tue-Sun from 10 am-5 pm, this is Mexico's second best anthropological museum after the one in Mexico City.
Tourist Information
Palacio Municipal, Zócalo, Tel: 2-0177.

VERACRUZ / TOWN
Accommodation
LUXURY: **Mocambo**, ca. 8 km south at the Malecón, Tel: 37-1400. **Torremar**, Blvd. Ruiz Cortines 4300, Tel: 35-2100.
MODERATE: **Emporio Veracruz**, Paseo del Malecón, Tel: 32-0020. **Posada del Sol**, Blvd. Ruiz Cortines 444, Tel: 37-4716. **Gran Hotel Diligencias**, Av. Independencia 1115, Tel: 32-2967. *BUDGET*: **Hotel Impala**, Calle Orizaba 650, Tel: 37-0169. **Hotel Cristóbal Colón**, Blvd. Camacho 681, Tel: 32-3844.
Restaurants
Garcli's, seafood, Blvd. Avila Camacho, Tel: 35-1034. **Hostería Suiza**, European cuisine, Manuel Suárez/España, Tel: 37-9493. **Prendes**, seafood, Plaza de Armas, Tel: 32-0153.
La Bamba, international cuisine, Avila Camacho, Tel: 32-5355. **La Parroquía**, Plaza de Armas, Tel: 32-2584. **Los Cedros**, Libanese, Calzada Mocambo, Tel: 37-7670. **La Paella**, Spanish cuisine, Zamora 138, Tel: 32-0322.
Special Events
Carnaval, February 3-7, one of the largest and best known festivals in Mexico.
Sightseeing
El Castillo de San Juan de Ulúa, mighty harbor-fort, Tue-Sat 9 am-5 pm.
Baluarte de Santiago, Avenida 16 de Septiembre/Rayon, daily 9 am-6 pm, closed Tue.
Excursions
La Antigua, ca. 25 km north of Veracruz, first Spanish port. Worth a visit in town is the **Casa de Cortés** (former house of Cortés) and the – allegedly – first church in Mexico. **Zempoala**, ca. 45 km north of Veracruz via Ruta 180. Ruins of the former Totonac capital.
Post / Telecommunication
Post Office: Plaza de la República 213, Tel: 32-2038, Mon-Fri 8 am-5 pm, Sat 8 am-1 pm.. **Telephone** (long distance) from the *caseta* on the Independencia between Juárez and Emparan, Mon-Sat 7.30 am-9.30 pm. **Telegrams**: Plaza de la República, Tel: 32-4434, Mon-Fri 8 am-2 pm, Sat 8 am-8 pm, Sun 9 am-1 pm.
Tourist Information
Palacio Municipal, at the Zócalo, Tel: 32-9942, 9 am-9 pm.

TABASCO

It can be seen clearly from the air: Broad sections of Tabasco to the north and east of Villahermosa are swampland, an endless sweep of green laced with the tributaries of the Grijalva and Usumacinta Rivers, which flow into the Gulf of Mexico between Frontera and Campechito on the border of Campeche, forming dozens of lakes and lagoons.

La Venta, the third of the Olmec culture's significant archeological sites, is located to the west in a humid region of tropical swamplands along the Tonalá River. The capital city of the "people from rubber country", whose influence extended through central Mexico, Oaxaca and into the Mayan Empire, was settled between 1200 and 600 BC. However, this complex, which features the oldest pyramids of the Americas has suffered extensive destruction since the hunt for black gold began at the end of the thirties. Unfortunately, La Venta is situated in the midst of the oilfields.

Comalcalco is better preserved and quite unique indeed: Due to a shortage of stones, sun-dried earthen bricks and mortar of clay, sand and oyster-shells were used in its construction. The ceremonial center of the Maya Chontales, the Mayan tribe that advanced furthest to the west, was established during their classical period (600-900 AD).

It bears a resemblance to the Palenque complex. The temple, the palace on the great acropolis, and a burial chamber have plaster reliefs and masks, some of which have been well preserved.

It was the Maya Chontales who were forced by Hernán Cortés to retreat from Tabasco in 1519, although not without presenting him with a "gift" of 20 slaves, among them La Malinche, who became Cortés' interpretess and lover. The coastal region wasn't subjugated until 1540, by Francisco de Montejo.

The inhabitants of Tabasco, who were not involved in Mexico's battles for independence from Spain, managed to resist the French invasion of 1863, and fought fiercely in the revolutionary wars between 1910 and 1920. Afterward, Governor Tomás Garrido attempted to introduce an "ideal socialism" in the state. He had schools built, ordered all churches to be destroyed, organized workers and farmers, and banished the clergy.

50 years ago, Mexico's southeastern reaches were still considered hostile to habitation: Heat, humidity and malaria-carrying mosquitoes made the area a living hell. The modernization and cultivation of the region began with the construction of the railroad during the 1950's. When oil was discovered in the Gulf of Mexico and the swamplands (in the vicinity of the industrial city of Cárdenas), Tabasco, the eighth-smallest of Mexico's 30 states, experienced a tremendous upswing, but the destruction of nature was its price.

Be this as it may, along the coast there are still appealing little beach-towns set in picturesque lagoon landscapes with such promising names as **El Paraíso, El Límon,** and **Puerto Ceiba**, which are not (yet) affected by the pollution. The lagoons and rivers have an abundance of fish, and the coastal flood-plains are very fertile. Bananas, oranges, pineapples and mangos grow here; chillis, tomatoes, cocoa beans, tobacco and sugar cane are also cultivated.

To the south, the plain gives way to hill country with forests, caves (**Grutas de Coconá**) and waterfalls at **Teapa**. Visitors can admire a cultural attraction in the midst of the jungle: The **Laboratorio de Teatro Campesino e Indígena** (Farmers' and Indigenas' Theater Workshop) in **Oxolotán** is attempting to preserve the traditions of the old cultures in modern theatrical forms.

Right: In the rainy season, the low-lying plains of Tabasco become a huge lake-land.

Tenosique and **Emiliano Zapata** are located in virtually untouched tropical surroundings. The latter features the **Zapata Museum**, which, in addition to the revolutionary hero, also commemorates the Tabasco-born poet Carlos Pellicer. In the **Parqueológico**, sculptures and stelae of the Mayan and Olmec cultures are exhibited amid plants and animals of the region.

Villahermosa, the state capital of Tabasco, is a modern and wealthy city, though it isn't – as its name would have us believe – a "beautiful city". Its affluence is a product of the oil boom of the seventies. Broad, tree-lined boulevards cut through and encircle this city of some 500,000 residents. There is a monument commemorating heroes of the past every couple of kilometers. Villahermosa has set it sights on the future with the **Tabasco 2000**, a governmental and convention center. This futuristic project has been modeled on buildings in the USA.

The old center of this city, founded in 1598 on the west bank of the Grijalva River, was restored and renamed the **Zona Luz** (District of Lights). It is a clean, bustling pedestrian zone with dozens of shops and snack-booths. On the other hand, there is hardly an appealing street-café to be found. Nor does the zócalo (in Mexico's southern regions usually called *parque,* in this case *Parque Benito Juárez)* which is not exactly inviting for an afternoon stroll.

To compensate, there are attractive, spacious public parks such as the **Parque Tomás Garrido Canabal**. Adjacent to it is one of the things that make Villahermosa worth visiting: The **Parque Museo de La Venta** is a unique museum. The Olmec monumental heads (the largest of which is said to weigh 24 tons) have found a perfect setting on the **Lagoon of Illusions**. The 31 huge sculptures, which depict jaguars, heads and humans with negroid facial features, as well as many altars and stelae, originate from the La Venta archeological zone. This museum-park (indeed a piece of jungle in the middle of the city) was created in the fif-

VILLAHERMOSA / CIUDAD DEL CARMEN

ties by poet, anthropologist and collector Carlos Pellicer (1897-1977). He also laid the groundwork for the **Museo Regional de Antropología** in the CICOM complex. This museum has a rich collection with special emphasis on the arts of the Olmec and Mayan cultures. If you do not have enough time to see all its extensive exhibits, which provide an interesting overview of all of Mexico's cultures, you should concentrate on the regional section on the first level. Its displays trace the influence of the Olmecs on other cultures; the buildings of La Venta are also documented. The sophisticated arts of the Mayas, who are considered the "Greeks of the Americas" are represented by some extraordinarily beautiful specimens.

Among the most outstanding of these are figures from the island of Jaina (Campeche), miniature copies of paintings from Bonampak and a reconstruction of the burial tablets of Palenque in book format. The Mayas, who left a particularly notable legacy of gigantic burial urns, are given special emphasis.

CAMPECHE

The Yucatán Peninsula is divided into three federal states, the borders of which roughly describe a "Y". The western portion, with an area of about 50,000 square kilometers belongs to Campeche. The state possesses everything it needs to lure tourists, including an adventure-filled history, archeological sites and a capital city with plenty of atmosphere. Only the beaches along the Gulf of Mexico are, despite their many palm trees (the processing of copra and coconut oil are important branches of the local economy) not quite as inviting as those on the Caribbean side.

Travelers driving on the coastal road from Villahermosa must take a little ferry over to the **Isla del Carmen**, crossing the **Laguna de Términos** (a fresh-water lake open to the sea) at **Zacatal**. **Ciudad del Carmen**, on the southwest side of the narrow 40-kilometer-long island, has developed into a boom-town since oil was discovered off the coast in 1977. This industrial city, which is also an important fishing harbor (particularly for the export of jumbo prawns), is taking pains to acquire a cosmopolitan character with cultural presentations and sports activities. On the main plaza, the **cathedral** is of interest for its multicolored stained glass, as are several picturesque colonial buildings. When it comes to eating, the specialties of Ciudad del Carmen and the coastal region are cocktails of prawns, fish, mussels or oysters seasoned with lemon and chili peppers.

For 150 years, between 1558 and 1717, the island was the stronghold of pirates, who made the Gulf of Mexico a dangerous place. The chief target of their attacks were the ships sailing for Europe from Campeche loaded with treasure.

Above: A colonial idyll in Campeche. Right: A typical Mayan building in Edzná.

Nor was the city itself spared from their onslaughts. Campeche was plundered over and over again until a massacre of its population in 1685, after which the construction of a city wall was begun (completed 1704).

Campeche, founded by the Spaniards in 1531 on the location of the Mayan city Ah Kim Pech, was for centuries the richest city on the peninsula. The most important export products were exotic hardwoods, *palo de tinte*, a tree of the primeval forest from whose trunk a deep red dye-stuff was made for the textile industry, and chicle, a resin used in the production of chewing gum. Splendid mansions from this prosperous period still give the town its charm today. Certainly, for many years they had been neglected. Not until quite recently was restoration work begun on the buildings of the old city center, which covers an arca four blocks wide by about ten in length. The **Mansión Caravajal** (near the zócalo) with Moorish arches and elaborate wrought-iron balustrades is a model example of the progress being made. Many of the sites of Campeche are based on bastions of the former fortifications of the town: Today a botanical garden surrounds the Baluarte de Santiago, and in the Baluarte de la Soledad there is a museum with Maya stelae. The Baluarte San Carlos houses a crafts center, and finally the town's historical museum can be found in the Baluarte San Pedro.

Campeche's most exciting museum is the **Museo Arqueológico**, in a palace that once served as residence for the Spanish viceroy. On its upper floor the history of Campeche is documented from the conquest until it became independent in 1863. Among its precious archeological finds are figures from the burial-island of Jaina, jade jewelry and a mosaic mask that was found in a grave in **Calakmul**. This Mayan city, difficult to reach because it is in the rainforest, is still being researched.

Becán, **Chicanná** and **Xpuhil** have been partially excavated. These ruin complexes have been classified in the so-

Above: Well-earned rest at the end of a hard day in the hot Campeche climate.

called Río Bec style because of their looming towers and facades with copious mask ornamentation.

The **Río Bec** archeological zone is located only a few kilometers further on, already in the neighboring state of Quintana Roo, though beyond (and therefore only accessible during the dry season) the well-improved Federal Route 186 which, when coming from Villahermosa, continues further on to Francisco Escarcéga at Chetumal.

Located to the north of this junction is **Champotón**, a hospitable little fishing town and starting point for high-seas fishing excursions and hunting trips in the region's dense forests.

Edzná is Campeche's chief archeological showpiece, about 50 kilometers from the port city. The **Edificio de los Cinco Pisos** (Building of Five Stories) towers over the site. An open-air staircase divides the rather sombre façade of this well-preserved terraced structure, whose floor plan becomes smaller with each higher level. Four floors apparently served as residential quarters for the priests, while the fifth was a temple featuring a roof-crest six meters in height, decorated with stucco figures. At the base of one of the small temples to the south, gigantic masks displaying fascinatingly expressive faces and finely modeled features were unearthed during the most recent excavations.

Edzná was once a major city and ceremonial center (200 - 900 AD) on the edge of the "Chenes" region, which gets its name from the numerous natural wells (*chenes*). An architectural style of façades copiously adorned with masks also has this name. Edzná is of particular significance to archeologists due to its ingenious system of canals and water conduits which were built both for irrigation and drainage.

On Yucatán's limestone plateau, into which water runs off very rapidly, the residents are still dependent on underground springs, or *cenotes*, created by natural breaches (sinkholes) in the limestone, or man-made cisterns, called *chaltunes*. There are seven *cenotes* sheltered in the interior of the grottos (*grutas*) of **Xtacumbilxunan**, which in the year 1842 aroused the American archeologist John L. Stephens to an enthusiastic description following an adventurous descent to a depth of 150 meters. Today, a paved, illuminated path leads to the entrance; but only experienced spelunkers should go further.

The drive to Uxmal passes through typical Mayan villages and pretty little colonial towns. **Hecelchakan** has a majestic parish church and an archeological museum with discoveries from the island of Jaina. There is a 16th-century monastery in **Chalkini**. In the underground workshops of **Becal**, *jipis*-hats are made from palm fronds; they must be woven when damp to retain their shape.

VILLAHERMOSA
Accommodation
LUXURY: **Holiday Inn**, Paseo Tabasco, Tel: 3-4400. **Exelaris Hyatt Villahermosa**, Av. Benito Juárez 106, Tel: 3-4444.
MODERATE: **Hotel Villahermosa Viva**, Blvd. Ruiz Cortines/Paseo Tabasco, Tel: 5-0000. **Hotel Cencali**, Juárez/Paseo Tabasco, Tel: 2-6000. **Hotel Manzur**, Madero 418, Tel: 2-2499. **Hotel Hostal del Sureste**, Bastar Zozaya 626, Tel: 2-5742.
BUDGET: **Hotel Miraflores**, Reforma 303, Tel: 2-0024. **Maya Tabasco**, Blvd. Ruiz Cortines 907, Tel: 2-1111. **Hotel Guayacan**, Bastar Zozaya 207, Tel: 2-7603.

Restaurants
This region is a delight for lovers of seafood: Here one can try a broad palette of fresh, delicious seafood prepared in many different ways. In the vicinity of the coast, especially in Paraíso, a multitude of charming little restaurants tempt the passing visitors.
Chon Chupon, seafood, Parque la Choca, Tel: 3-3593. **Cheje**, regional cuisine, Madero 7732, Tel: 4-1600. **Gemenis**, regional food, Madero 712, Tel: 2-8149. **El Mesón de Castilla**, international and Spanish cuisine, José Pages Lergo 125, Tel: 2-56621. **Chez Monett**, French, Av. Gregorio Méndez 1515, Tel: 2-9021. **Restaurant-Boot Capitán Beulo** on the river Grijalva, departure Lerdo de Tejada/docks, Tue-Sun three times daily at noon, Tel: 3-5762.

Museums
Parque de la Venta, open-air museum with Olmec colossal heads, Paseo Ruiz Cortines, open Tue, Thur and Fri 8 am-5 pm, Mon, Wed and Sun 8.30 am-5 pm.
Museo Regional de Antropología (also known as **Museo Carlos Pellicer Camara**), Av. Carlos Pellicer 511, Tel: 2-1803, open daily 9 am-8 pm.

Sightseeing
Archaeological Zone of **Comalcalco**, situated ca. 55 km to the northwest, by bus in the direction of Paraíso.
Agua Azul, the most beautiful waterfall-cascades in Mexico, Ruta 186 in the direction of Palenque.
Ruins of Palenque, 145 km on Ruta 186, 9 km outside Palenque town.

Post / Telecommunication
Post Office: Saent 131/Lerdo de Tejada, Tel: 2-1040, Mon-Fri 8 am-7 pm, Sat 9 am-1 pm.
Telephone (long distance) from the *caseta* in the Café la Barra, Lerdo 608, Mon-Sat 9 am-2 pm and 3-9 pm. **Telegrams**: Lerdo 601, Tel: 2-2494, Mon-Fri 8 am-midnight, Sat 9 am-1 pm.

Tourist Information
Paseo Tabasco, opposite the Palacio Municipal, Tel: 5-0694, open Mon-Fri 9 am-3 pm and 6-9 pm, Sat 9 am-1.30 pm.

CAMPECHE
Accommodation
LUXURY: **El Presidente**, Av. Ruiz Cortines 51, Tel: 6-2233. **Baluartes**, Av. Ruiz Cortines 61, Tel: 6-3911. **Ramada Inn**, Av. Ruiz Cortines 51, Tel: 6-2233 and 6-4611.
MODERATE / BUDGET: **Alhambra**, Av. Resurgimiento 85, Tel: 6-6822. **Hotel América**, Calle 10 Nr. 252, Tel: 6-4588. **Hotel Colonial**, Calle 14 Nr. 122, Tel: 6-2222. **Hotel López**, Calle 12 Nr. 189, Tel: 6-3344.

Restaurants
The restaurants in Campeche prepare extremely tasty seafood, especially prawns.
La Parroquia, seafood, Calle 55, Tel: 6-0240. **Del Parque**, Calle 57 Nr. 8, Tel: 6-0240. Next door in house Nr. 2 is the restaurant **Campeche**, good regional food. **Miramar**, Calle 8/Calle 61, Tel: 6-2883. **El Refugio de Lorencillo**, Las Palmas 49.

Sightseeing
Numerous *baluartes* (fortifications) are open to the public: **Baluarte de la Soledad** (town center), **Baluarte de Santiago** in the Jardín Botánico (north of the town center, Calle 8). In the immediater vicinity is the fortress **Baluarte San Carlos** with an arts and crafts center.

Museums
Museo Regional de Campeche, Calle 59 between Calle 14 and 16, open Tue-Sat 8 am-8 pm, Sun 8 am-1 pm.
Museo de Estelas Maya (in the **Baluarte de la Soledad**), open daily 8 am-8 pm.

Excursions
To the **Ruins of Edzná**, ca. 50 km in the direction of Mérida, Ruta 180, turn right after 20 km, turn right again after further 13 km. Open 8 am-5 pm. By bus: Viajes Programados, Prolongación 57, Tel: 6-8333. If you continue in the direction of Mérida via Uxmal, you will pass the **Grutas Xtacumbilxunán** at Ruta 261, open 9 am-5 pm.

Post / Telecommunication
Post Office: 16 de Septiembre/Calle 53, Tel: 6-4390, Mon-Fri 8 am-7 pm, Sat 9 am-1 pm.
Telephone (long distance) from the *caseta* El Atravieso, Gobernadores 519, Mon-Sat 8 am-5.30 pm. **Telegrams**: In the post office, Mon-Fri 8 am-midnight, Sat 9 am-8 pm.

Tourist Information
Plaza Moch Couch, Tel: 6-6068 and 6-6767, Mon-Fri 8 am-9 pm, Sat, Sun 9 am-2 pm.

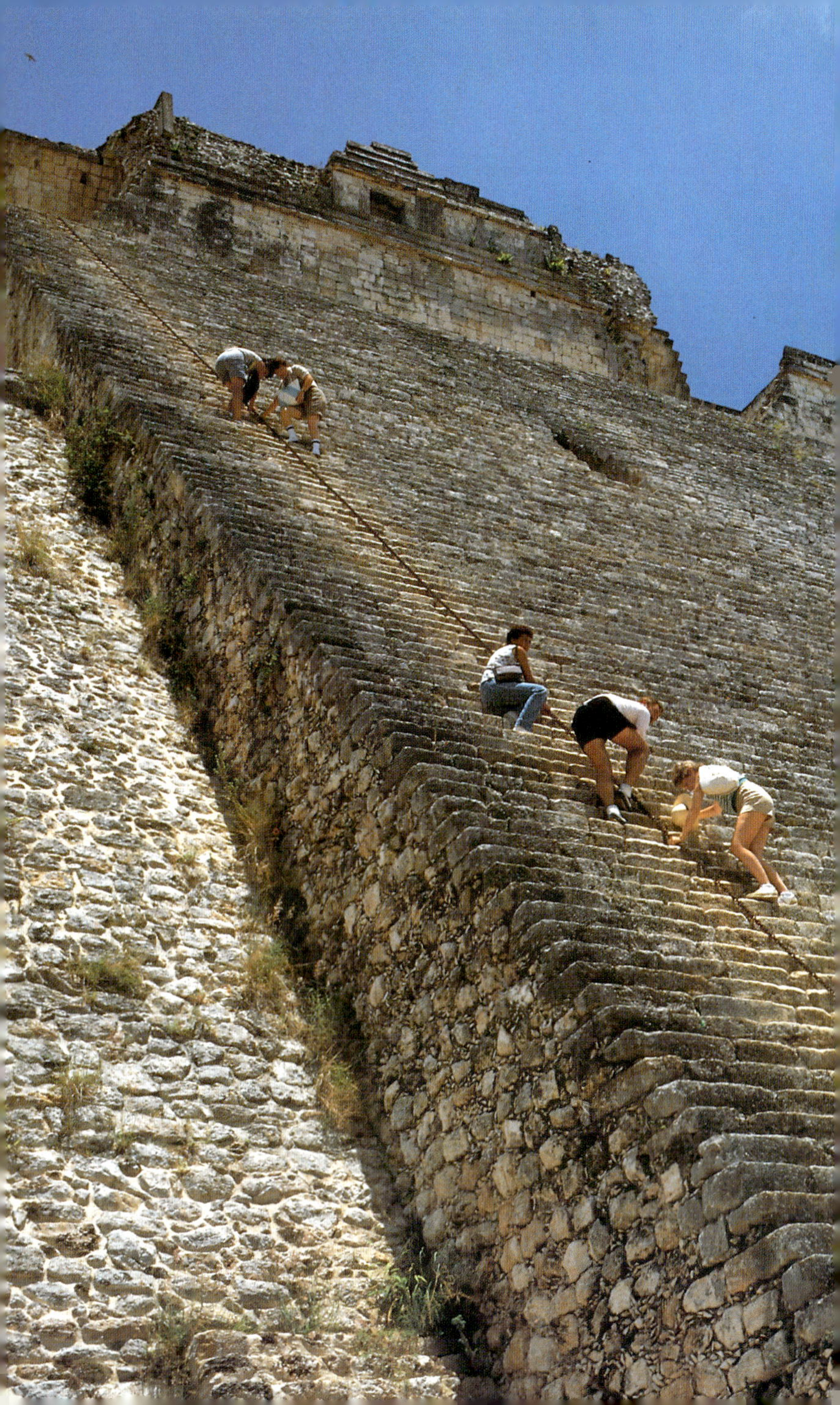

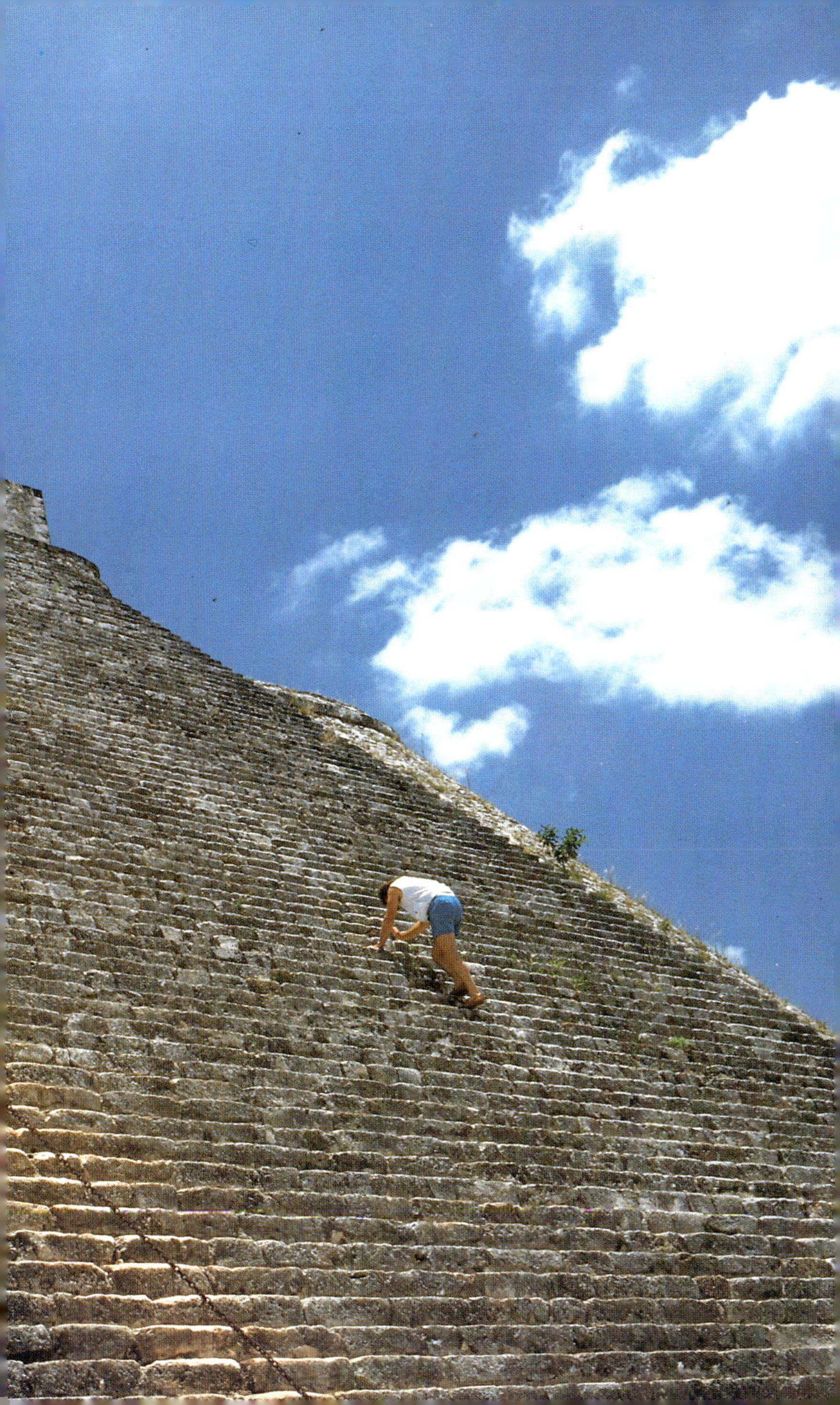

YUCATÁN

THE MAYAN RUINS AND BEACHES OF YUCATÁN

**MÉRIDA
CHICHÉN ITZÁ
UXMAL
CANCÚN / COZUMEL
COAST OF QUINTANA ROO**

Peninsula of Ruins and Beaches

Yucatán is first and foremost a geographical term denoting a peninsula, which contains the three Mexican states of Campeche, Yucatán and Quintana Roo as well as Belize and northern Guatemala. It is characterized by a hot, humid climate, bush and low jungle, vegetation with here and there tropical rain forests and swamps. There are few rivers since the rain seeps into the limestone subsoil and forms subterranean watercourses called *cenotes* in Spanish.

For a long period this region was of little interest to the Spanish conquistadors. The peninsula's subjugation was not even reported to the Spanish Crown until the founding of Mérida in 1542. Even then the inaccessible territory remained largely isolated from the center of the viceroy's realm; nor was it given much attention. It was abandoned by the Spaniards after the end of the War of Independence in 1821. Their white descendants, the Creoles, governed it with an iron hand. Without political rights or access to education, the region's Mayan

Previous pages: Uxmal – the way to the gods is steep. Left: Sisal-harvesting has long since given way to tourism as the main source of revenue.

population became increasingly disillusioned at the powers-that-be. Their attempts at rebellion, however, were mercilessly crushed. The rulers sought union with the United States. *Henequén*, a variety of the sisal plant that made its plantation owners into millionaires, was cultivated in Yucatán. For this reason, the port city of Progreso used to be called Sisal. It was the region's only gateway to the USA, Europe and the world. People wishing to travel from Mexico City to Mérida in those days had to take a ship from Veracruz to Sisal. That remained the case until the construction of the first covered road to Mérida in the early 1950s. Yucatán was considered Mexico's impoverished backyard, and residents of the capital city still look down upon its inhabitants, the *yucatecos*.

But the situation in Yucatán today has changed: The expansion of the road network (now one of the best in the country) combined with the construction of seven national or international airports, as well as a number of smaller local ones for light aircraft, have opened the way for tourism on the peninsula. The chief assets of Yucatán and of Quintana Roo (a federal state in its own right since 1974) are their beaches and cultural monuments. The unemployed *yucatecos* from the former *henequén* haciendas now work in the

181

MÉRIDA

tourism industry, which is booming here as in no other region of the country.

MÉRIDA

There is a special charm in the air of **Mérida** that makes it different from the more typical of Mexico's cities, the brashly modern or the old colonial ones. Though surrounded by the flat and steamy Yucatán jungle, a certain southern graciousness pervades the air of the town, whose clean streets and white-clad inhabitants led many years ago to its being known as "the White City". Founded in 1542 at the northern end of the Yucatán Peninsula by one of Cortés' captains, Don Franciso de Montejo, the city is on a porous limestone plain, ideal for the cultivation of the cactus-like *henequén* plants from which sisal hemp fibers are made. This has assured the city's prosperity. Today stronger synthetic fibers may have replaced sisal in the manufacture of rope, but the cultivation of *henequén* is still a major industry. It is used for hammocks, shoes, baskets and tablemats as well as twine and rugs. A Cordemex plant north of Mérida weaves the fibre into carpets, and there are factory tours.

Today, a metropolis of more than 550,000 inhabitants, Mérida was built on the ruins of the ancient Mayan city *Tihó*; and the Mayas have left their mark in the people, the language and the dress. Indigena women still wear the *huipil*, a straight white shift embroidered at the neck and hem, and men often wear the *guayabera*, a self-tailored short-sleeved jacket-shirt with vertical tucks, worn outside the trousers. The Mayas are a friendly, pleasant, honest people, proud of their ancient heritage still evident in the surrounding archeological ruins of Chichén Itzá, Uxmal, Dzibiltchaltún, Labná and other sites.

Like most of Mexico, Mérida has had its share of turbulence. To secure their territory in 1542, the Spaniards beat off tens of thousands of Mayas who laid siege to the fledgling colony. The Mayas lost, becoming virtual slaves until an act of parliament in 1930 restored to them some of their ancestral lands. During 1840, in the War of the Castes, Indigenas armed by their masters during the Mexican-American War, turned against their masters. It was not until 1855 that the Spanish Mexicans could regain control, forcing many of the Mayas to retreat to southern Yucatán, the present state of Quintana Roo.

Thanks to the sisal boom, Mérida became one of the richest towns in the whole of Mexico. The small French community is responsible for the city's version of the Champs-Elysées, the **Paseo**

MÉRIDA

Montejo. With all its wide, tree-lined boulevards, plazas and parks shaded by handsome trees, the ambience of Mérida is a very special one. Many travelers use the town as a base for viewing the surrounding archeological ruins, and indeed it's the perfect place for this. But the city itself has much of interest to offer the tourist, too. The wealthy *henequén* plantation owners built beautiful 18th-century European-style mansions in the city as well as functional dwellings in the country. Today, *calesas*, horse-drawn carriages, travel the length of Paseo de Montejo to view these mansions.

Rather than street names, Yucatán's capital has a simple system of street numbers: All north-south streets have even numbers; all east-west streets have odd numbers. Addresses are written like mathematical equations: calle 63 x 64 means the place is on calle 63 near the intersection of calle 64.

The central zócalo is the **Plaza de la Independencia**, also called **Plaza Principal**, a lovely shady square with *confidenciales* (S-shaped love seats) surrounded by government buildings and the **cathedral**, a large twin-towered edifice resembling a fortress.

It was begun in 1561 and completed by 1598. The coat-of-arms of Spain is above the entrance and inside is a statue called *Christ of the Blisters*, carved from wood that is said to have miraculously survived two major fires.

MÉRIDA

On the south side of the zócalo is **Casa Montejo**, the founding family's palace. Originally covering an entire block, only one section remains but it is still impressive. The large rooms, built around two patios, are filled with imported European furniture. Particularly striking is the Montejo coat-of-arms carved above the entrance. On each side, the figure of a Spanish conquistador stands with his foot on the head of a Maya Indian. (Now a bank, the building may be visited during banking hours.)

The **Palacio del Gobierno** (Governor's Palace) on the north side of the zócalo contains walls lined with murals depicting the history of Yucatán, executed by the painter Fernando Castro Pacheco. Another attraction is the **Teatro Peón Conteras** (theater), designed by Italian architects and named after a Yucatán poet. A marble staircase, a fresco-decorated dome, and three enormous entrance doors make this a handsome opera house. Concerts and other events take place there frequently. (calle 60 x 57)

La Pinacoteca, the state art gallery, has a permanent exhibition of 16th- and 17th-century paintings by both Yucatán and European artists. (calle 63 x 64) The **Museo Nacional de Arte Popular** is a treasure-house for those interested in the traditional ethnic skills and customs of the region. There are permanent displays of handcrafted jewelry, wood, traditional Maya clothing and the famous Panama hat (*jipi*), made not in Panama but in Becal, a small town in Campeche. (calle 59 x 48) **Palacio Cantón**, housing the **Museo de Antropología e Historia** is an impressive 19th-century building, once the home of a Yucatán governor. The building, inspired by European architecture, was recently restored. Archeological finds illustrate the Indígena history of the peninsula. (Paseo de Montejo x 43.)

La Ermita de Santa Isabel, a small church whose gardens contain Maya statuary, was built in 1742 outside the city

Right: The plantation-owners built themselves magnificent palaces in Mérida.

walls. Now barely four blocks from the zócalo, people would pray there for a safe journey. (calle 64 x 66)

Mérida is a lively town, and cultural events are staged free of charge every night of the week in many of the city's gardens and parks. In the **Jardín de los Compositores** directly behind the Palacio Municipal, at calle 62 x 61, folk dancers perform every Monday night and on Saturday nights there is live theater. On other evenings at **Parques Santiago** (calle 72 x 59), **Iglesia de Santa Ana** (calle 60 x 42), **Iglesia de Santa Lucía** (calle 60 x 55) and Ermita de Santa Isabel (calle 64 x 66) there are various programs of dance music, operettas and opera arias, guitar groups and works by Yucatán composers. On Saturday at **Parque Santa Lucia** there's an **Antique Bazaar** where coins, crafts, books, ceramic, furniture – and food – are sold. Sunday is celebrated with a street fair on calle 60, blocked off then from traffic between calle 59 and Avenida Itzás. Starting at 11 a.m., there are folk music groups and other entertainment for the entire family. And at **Parque Hidalgo**, near the zócalo, there are *marimba* concerts every Sunday.

Mérida's main shopping street is along Calle 60 to Calle 65. Hammocks and other sisal products as well as Panama hats are a good buy and less fine straw hats are sold at bargain prices. The **Mercado García Rejon** is another place for local handicrafts and souvenirs, and there are stalls selling hammocks, *huipils* and *guayaberas* under the arcades of the **Palacio Municipal** on the zócalo, a building dating from the Montejo era but reconstructed in 1928. Other shopping opportunities abound at the **Casa de las Artesanías**, a government-operated store offering regional clothing, fine gold and silver jewelry, wood carvings, articles made of sea shells and tortoise shell and a variety of other Mexican handicrafts.

Puerto Progreso

Puerto Progreso, 33 km north of Mérida on a highway (Route 261), serves as

PUERTO PROGRESO

the "White City's" beach resort. Buses run from Mérida every 15 minutes from 5 a.m. to 9 p.m., a 30 to 45-minute ride. The town of almost 40,000 is surrounded by a deep marshy swamp, redeemed by a pleasant *malecón* (waterfront), a palm-lined beach and an interesting choice of accommodation – from beachcomber's digs to luxury ones. Although a very quiet town, Progreso is an active port, since 1871 the chief port of entry to the Yucatán Peninsula, in particular serving the prosperous *henequén* industry. The two-kilometer *muelle* (pier) is being extended to provide better cargo handling service, as well as to accommodate cruise ships, which was not previously possible, and at five kilometers, it will be one of the longest piers in the world.

The main reason for coming to Progreso (many Mérida residents have summer homes here) is the beach scene. The ocean is calm, and smooth white sand slopes gently into the water, barely covering the shoulders even half-kilometer from shore. **Playa Progreso** is lined with palms and backed by a good number of restaurants serving fresh seafood. Fishing, motorboating, snorkeling, sailing and swimming are the water activities; on land, bicycles and mopeds can be hired to explore the waterfront. Except during the *temporada* (the busy season of July-August) the beaches are fairly deserted.

From Progreso take Route 261 further west to the fishing village **Yucalpetén** with restrooms, showers and picnic areas at the *balneario popular*, then on to the pleasant beaches of **Chelém** and further via Sisal to **Celestún** at **Punta Nimún**. To the east **Puerto Chicxulub** and **Dzilam de Bravo** are popular, the latter supposedly the last resting place of the pirate Jean LaFitte.

The coast on both sides of Progreso, with its salt marshes bordering the sea, is a bird-watchers' paradise with rare species, especially the pink flamingo.

Above: The evening sun bathes Chichén Itzá in golden light. Right: Chac Mool figures represent the Toltec epoch in Chichén Itzá.

CHICHÉN ITZÁ

Chichén Itzá is the largest and most renowned of the Yucatán's pyramid complexes. The site, which has been included on UNESCO's World Cultural Heritage list, is extraordinarily well-preserved, making a visit to it a rare pleasure. Chichén Itzá was originally a Mayan site, founded around 400 AD. For nearly 600 years, the settlement experienced an economic and cultural Golden Age. Then, suddenly, strangers ended its long-lasting prosperity. Their leader, the Toltec Emperor Quetzalcóatl (named *Kukulcán* in the Mayan language) took possession of Chichén Itzá.

The origins of the people who named themselves *Itzá* is quite puzzling. Bishop Diego de Landa reported: "The Indians are of the opinion that the Itzá who established themselves in Chichén were ruled by a great lord named Kukulcán ...and they say that he came from the West. They hold varying opinions as to whether he came after the Itzá, or with them."

Researchers are still puzzling over the question of whether Kukulcán and the tall, bearded Toltec Emperor Quetzalcóatl ("Plumed Serpent") from Tula, a wise and just ruler, were one and the same person. Favoring this conclusion is the fact that a Quetzalcóatl did happen to leave Tula around 1000 AD, probably going to Yucatán. On the other hand, it seems difficult to understand why *this* particular Quetzalcóatl, who had forbidden the barbaric blood-sacrifice of human beings, would have reintroduced it in Yucatán.

Around 1250, Chichén Itzá was abandoned by its inhabitants, after which tropical vegetation gradually took possession of the site in the following centuries. The overgrown area was discovered by archeologists in 1841, and 14 years later it was acquired privately by an American consul, who began excavations and research on his own.

The most famous building of Chichén Itzá is the **Temple of Kukulcán**, also known as **El Castillo**. This nine-story py-

CHICHÉN ITZÁ

ramid, with a height of 24 meters and a base measuring 55 meters, vividly illustrates the Mayan culture's understanding of calendar-based time reckoning. 91 steps on each of the structure's faces lead up to the temple. This total of 364 steps, added together with the step before the temple entrance yields the number of days in a year. The 52 slabs fitted to the sides represent the 52 weeks of the year. Speculation continued for a long time on the significance of the serpent heads mounted on the lower end of the stairs. Only twice in the year, namely in the afternoons of March 21st and September 23rd, is the key to this sublime mystery revealed: A shadow is thrown that conveys to onlookers the impression that the serpents are leaving the temple and creeping down the pyramid.

Yet another secret awaits visitors inside the pyramid. When archeologists discovered the beginning of another staircase at the pyramid's base they proceeded rapidly with its excavation. They came upon a second temple which had been built over. Their delight was great when they realized that the contents of the Mayan building hadn't been plundered. In the entrance area, visitors can view a **Chac Mool**, one of the stone sculptures of Toltec origin, that have been found at quite a number of historical sites. It consists of a life-size male figure, reclining with his knees pulled up to his chest and erect torso supported by the elbows. The head is turned to the left and covered by a cylindrical helmet. On his belly the figure holds a stone platter. Archeologists believe that this vessel is intended for the blood and heart of human sacrificial victims. Standing in the inner sanctuary is a stone "jaguar-throne", painted red and covered with bits of jade (corresponding to the markings of the beast's pelt). It's thought probable that Kukulcán resided in this older temple and accepted the sacrificial offerings brought to him while sitting on the throne.

Above: The famous Wall of Death's Heads at the complex of Chichén Itzá.

CHICHÉN ITZÁ

The **ball court** located to the northwest of the Kukulcán pyramid is the largest of its kind in all of Mexico. The playing field, measuring 85 by 35 meters, has walls seven meters high at each end in the center of which are large stone rings, or goals. The players would shoot the rubber ball through the ring – a difficult undertaking in which neither hand nor foot could be employed, but only the elbows, hips and knees. Look closely at the reliefs on the spectators' benches below the wall, which depict the ballgame's bloody conclusion. In the middle of the frieze two groups of seven people in festive uniforms face each other. One person in the left-hand row (the winning team) holds a knife and a human head in his hands. Kneeling across from him is the beheaded man from the opposing team, with blood spurting from his neck in the form of seven snakes.

Rising up to the east of the ball court is the **Temple of Jaguars** with a frieze depicting these animals. The fragments of the wall paintings found inside the temple presumably depict the Toltec's conquest of Chichén Itzá. Fascinating ornamentation also decorates the **Platform of the Jaguars** (*tigres*) **and Eagles** (*aguilas*), once a stage for ritual events: The jaguars and eagles grasp human hearts in their talons.

A rectangular platform also reminds the viewer of the Toltecs' gruesome rites; its name corresponds closely to its function: *tzompantli*, **Wall of the Death's Heads.** The Toltecs skewered the heads of the people sacrificed to the gods on its spikes.

The **Templo de los Guerreros** (Temple of Warriors) is also of interest. The shrine is perched atop a pyramid 40 meters wide and 12 meters in height. There are numerous extant pillars in its hall of columns. On their four sides are reliefs of Toltec warriors carrying their javelins (*atl-atl*) and barring unwelcome visitors from the temple. The **Grupo de las Mil Columnas** (Hall of the Thousand Columns) in the warriors' temple is so called because of the great number of pillars that once carried the roof structure of an immense hall.

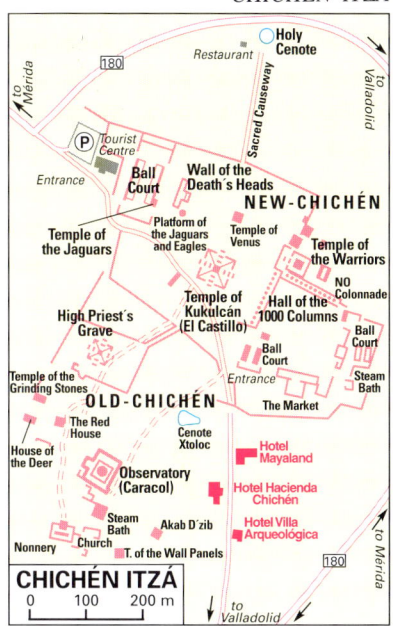

The Toltecs also performed their sacrificial rituals at the **Holy Cenote** (on a roadway that had previously been paved by the Mayas). Tradition has it that the natural spring, which was 60 meters wide and lay 25 meters below the earth, was a destination for pilgrims. During excavation work done in the 1960's, archeologists brought to light not only skeletons, but also sacrificial offerings of gold, copper and jade.

On the path from the main plaza to the southern grouping one passes the **High Priest's Grave.** In the floor of the temple, which stands on a small pyramid, the archeologists discovered a secret passage leading to the interior. There they found seven graves, apparently the burial place of high dignitaries.

The **Observatory** is not only the most famous building of the southern group, it

189

UXMAL

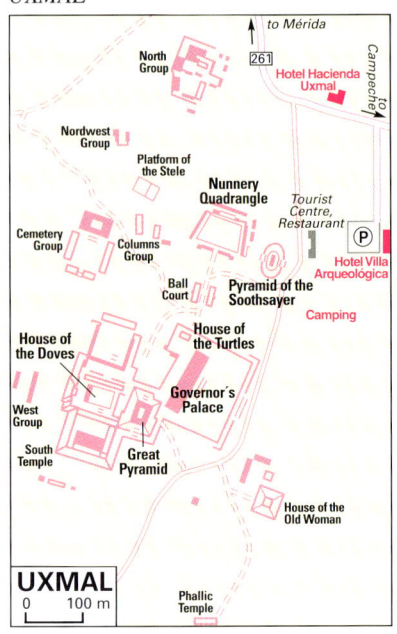

is also the most unusual building at Chichén Itzá. The Spaniards dubbed it *Caracol*, the "Snail". By way of a staircase one proceeds to two rectangular platforms, where a rounded tower stands. A spiral staircase in its interior leads to the upper level. In a small chamber, openings resembling shooting-ports point in all directions. The observatory bears witness to the great astronomical expertise of its creators. Their scholars were able precisely to determine the moment of the summer solstice.

UXMAL

There is another Mayan religious center that numbers also among Mexico's most important historical sites. **Uxmal** means "three-times-built" in the Mayan language, a clear reference to the common practice among the region's ancient cultures of building on top of existing

Right: Morning calm at Uxmal before visitors by the hundreds swarm over the Maya ruins.

structures. In fact, researchers have been able to identify several periods during which its construction took place. This complex, founded and expanded during the classical epoch (between 600 and 950 AD), was built in the Puuc style, based mainly on geometric forms. A typical characteristic is the elaborate and beautiful ornamentation of the stucco façades. On the other hand, many hallmarks of the Mayan classical period, including stelae and hieroglyphic characters, are absent.

The 38-meter-high **Pyramid of the Soothsayer** (Templo del Enano) consists of five temples, built over a period of 300 years. The oldest of these has been partially unearthed at the base of the oval pyramid's west side. It dates from the year 569; the sculpture found at its entrance, a serpent with a human head protruding from its gaping maw, can now be seen at Mexico City's Museum of Anthropology. **Temple II** is located inside the pyramid and can be entered through an opening on the upper section of the eastern staircase. Behind its rear wall are the shrine and ante-room of **Temple III**, which, not being visible from the outside, is located on the interior or west side. **Temple IV** has also been exposed, its cubic form being visible on the west side below **Temple V**, which rises up on the point of the pyramid. The temple's façade, in the Chenes style, represents an immense Chac mask through whose jaws the temple is entered – an indication of the initiation rituals that once took place here. Only those who died in the throat of the god could hope for reincarnation. The uppermost temple contains three chambers and a latticework decorative motif on its façade. Its design is reminiscent of the governor's palace. This final structure dates from the end of the ninth century. Standing to the west of the pyramid is the **Quadrangulo de las Monjas** (Nunnery Quadrangle), a complex consisting of four buildings arranged around a patio, featuring a large number of small, cell-like rooms. To this day, nothing is known about the function of these chambers. The northern building, reached from the interior courtyard by a 30-meter- wide staircase, is of particular interest. Impressive representational reliefs are mounted above the entrances of its 13 rooms. The architectural high-point of the site, however, is the **Palacio del Gobernador** (Governor's Palace), which archeologists refer to as the most beautiful and spectacular building of the pre-Columbian Americas. Situated on a plateau, the almost 100-meter-long palace, with its eleven entranceways, is rendered impressive by its three-meter-high frieze, which decorates its entire façade and is composed of more than 20,000 stones. Its striking ornamentation includes some 150 Chac masks. This rain-god has horns above its ears, a trunk-like nose and menacing fangs and wears a demonic grin. The meander patterns symbolize the serpent of the Mayan pantheon.

The **Casa de las Tortugas** (House of Turtles) is also located on the same platform. Its façade is likewise decorated with sculpted eaves, in this case with the turtle as the recurrent motif. Researchers are still speculating over the function of this graceful structure. The only thing that is more or less definite is, that the ornamentation holds the key to the puzzle. Several investigators are convinced that the turtle was a personification of the solstice and that the building was used for astronomical purposes. Another hypothesis is that the turtle quite simply symbolizes water, the elixir of life.

The **Great Pyramid**, which to date has only been restored on one side, stands behind the palace to the south, as does the **La Casa de las Palomas** (House of Pigeons) which is also only partially restored, with a triangular superstructure as its chief distinguishing feature.

Approximately 20 kilometers to the south of Uxmal lies its daughter-city **Kabáh**. The causeway laid out by the Mayas between the two sites was presumably used for religious processions and the transport of sacrificial offerings.

Unfortunately, restoration efforts are still at a very early stage. They are differentiated into east, central and west groupings, of which only the first has been excavated. The complex's most famous structure is the **Palace of Masks** (eastern section). Almost the entire façade of the palace, which is 45 meters in length with a height of six meters, is covered with some 300 masks of the rain-god Chac. The impression it creates is overwhelming, even though most of the protruding, trunk-like noses are broken off. This *palacio* is also one of the very few Mayan buildings in which two different construction styles are found: The lower section of the façade is also copiously decorated, a characteristic of the Chenes style. Also typical of this style is a rather Baroque looking ornamentation. On the other hand the stylization of the Chac masks bears the hallmark of the Puuc style. The building's three-meter high roof comb has disintegrated almost completely. A short distance from the Palace of Masks one comes upon the **Palace of Justice**, sometimes referred to as the *teocalli* (sanctuary), the façade of which is decorated with clusters of engaged columns. Beyond the road a partially intact *sacbé* (ceremonial way) leads to the **Kabáh Archway**, a free-standing structure raised on a platform, where the 15-kilometer-long procession route to Uxmal begins.

The Archway in Labná

The majority of visitors to **Labná**, a smaller Mayan temple site 13 kilometers from Kabáh, make the journey to see its famous **archway**. However, one first passes the **palacio**, a group of buildings in the Puuc style set on a large terrace. The frieze on the east wing with clustered columns, geometric ornamentation and a gaping serpent's maw with human head (*la cabeza*) are all in good condition. A 170-meter-long paved ceremonial causeway (*sacbé*) leads from this point southward to the archway, a most successful example of the "false arch". The principal is quite simple: By cantilevering the stones of two facing walls a little closer as the construction proceeds upward, the point is reached where finally one single stone at the peak is all that is needed to hold it together as an arch. However, the builders must have known how much strain they could safely put on the structure without it collapsing. A typical distinguishing feature of the Mayan corbelled vault is a ledge that extends out from the arch. The archway rests on this ledge, from which a frieze extends to the adjacent masonry on the left and right sides. The structure's eastern façade, which is intricately decorated with spiralled meanders, is also worthy of some attention. Standing on the roof are the scanty remains of a collapsed roof comb. The building's wealth of decorative ele-

Above: The city gate at Labná. Right: In Sayil, some of Yucatán's young Maya girls.

ments includes a trellis and, above the entrances to two of the interior chambers, two stylized Maya dwellings in high relief. The processional road to Kabáh began at the archway. Standing next to it is the **observation tower** (*el mirador*), a pyramid surmounted by a temple; to date it has been only partially restored.

Following this sightseeing tour, an excursion (about 20 kilometers to the northwest) to the **Caves** (*grutas*) **of Loltún** is recommended. These stalactite caverns, which hadn't been explored and mapped until two Americans did so in 1959, were apparently used as human dwellings as early as 2000 BC. Ceramics, rock-paintings and childrens' skeletons have been found in them. There are three tours daily, the last beginning at 1:30 pm.

Mayan Palace in Sayil

The main purpose of a visit to the former Mayan center of **Sayil** (roughly ten kilometers from Kabáh) is a visit to its **palace**. This building, constructed on a tremendous scale (80 by 40 meters), consists of three levels, each higher one being slightly recessed from the one below it, thus creating a terrace for each floor. The western wing is quite impressive, when the afternoon sunlight sets off the decoration of its helically fluted columns. The frieze that extends above them features masks of Chac, though they are unfortunately not in good condition. From the upper story one gets an outstanding view over a large cistern and its surroundings. There are hundreds of stones lying on the terraces and around the palace's periphery; all of them will be used in the future restoration work on the structure.

Sites of the "Descending Gods"

"The Great Cairo!", was the astonished cry of Francisco Hernandez de Córdoba's crew when, on March 3, 1517, they first caught sight of a fortress-like settlement from their ship. Throned high on a cliff above the turquoise-blue sea opposite the

TULÚM

Caribbean island of Cozumel, **Tulúm** must have made a lasting impression on the Spaniards. To this day visitors continue to wax poetic over this perfect synthesis of tropical landscape with grey-and-white temple architecture. The town was originally called *Zama,* or "City of the Dawn".

Tulúm was once a Mayan fortified city, built starting around 1000 AD; on its landward side it is surrounded by a defensive wall 650 meters in length, three meters thick and four in height. From 1200 AD on, Tulúm became an important religious center. Starting from the city, pilgrims crossed over to the island of Cozumel, a place of worship for the goddess Ix Chel. The Mayas set off from their pilgrimages from Chichén Itzá and Cobá, passing through Tulúm on their way to Cozumel, as is suggested by the remains of a pre-Columbian road.

Above: The magic of Tulúm lies in its position on the Caribbean. Right: Only few of Cobá's ruins have been uncovered.

Five gates consisting of corbelled vaults, of which one is still intact, cut through the fortification wall and led to the center, an extensive palace and temple complex in relatively good condition. From an architectural point of view, however, the structures are of rather secondary importance. The temples and palaces are not constructed on top of pyramids, standing instead on low mounds. In addition, several of the walls lean outward slightly. Whether the builders did their work imprecisely or if the skewed construction was planned remains a matter of conjecture.

The most significant building here is the **Castillo**, which rises up over the sea on a rock ledge. A broad staircase leads up to the temple. Two serpent-pillars divide the entry. And here one sees, in the central niche above the doorway, the enigmatic "Descending God", a winged figure, hanging upside down, with a little crown on its head. Researchers surmise that this peculiar fellow either symbolizes the sunset or represents a bee-deity.

Immediately to the north of the Castillo is the **Templo del Dios Descendente** (Temple of Descending Gods). In the center of the complex, the **Temple of Frescoes** is quite well-preserved. In this building one comes yet again upon the nose-diving deity. The glistening blue-green wall-paintings in the temple's interior depicting gods, animals and plant life are also worth a look.

Town of Wind-Ruffled Water

The ruins of **Cobá** are hidden in a protected area of dense jungle. The beauty of this complex shines best during the rainy season, in other words, during the summer months, when the trees and bushes wear their deepest green and the innumerable species of birds engage in singing competitions. The site's buildings are widely scattered, grouped around two large and three small dolina (or sinkhole) lakes created by fissures in the limestone surface of the Yucatán flatlands. Nearly 40,000 people are believed to have once lived here, attracted by the area's rare abundance of water. A large number of causeways (*sacbé*, plural *sacbeob*) connected Cobá with other settlements. These boulevards, paved with gravel and uten consolidated with a mortar of crushed limestone, were as much as ten meters wide, running dead straight and forming a dense network with branches running in every direction. One 100-kilometer-long "highway" connected Cobá with a ceremonial site to the west. Commerce flourished. There was a brisk trade in cocoa beans and honey, both highly coveted luxury goods among the Mayas. Cobá, the "Town of Wind-ruffled Water" was not only a commercial hub, but a significant religious cult-center as well, whose Golden Age lasted from 600 to 950 AD (during the Mayan classical period). Cobá was inhabited into the 17th century, in other words, well into the period of the Spanish occupation (the Spaniards had not discovered its existence). It was rediscovered in 1891 by the Austrian researcher Teobald Maler, a Mayan specialist who was the first to write a description of the complex.

Archeology fans could easily spend many weeks in Cobá, since to date more than 10,000 structures have been identified, scattered over an area of 70 square kilometers, the majority of them still hidden under dense vegetation. The most significant edifice is a 24-meter-high pyramid, named **La Iglesia** (The Church). An immense staircase leads up to a small temple, which is in poor condition.

If one carries on past the Cobá's group for another 1.5 kilometers or so, the highest pyramid in Yucatán suddenly towers up out of the dense greenery. It is the chief landmark of the **Nohoch Mul Group**. If you did not climb up the "Church" you should take the opportunity to ascend these 128 steps. From a height of 42 meters one can fully apprehend the tremendous extent of this archeological site.

CANCÚN

CANCÚN

The early Mayas believed **Cancún** to be a pot of gold at the end of the rainbow; the modern Mexicans know it is. The unpolluted waters are warm, sparkling clear and multi-hued, the light tan beaches as soft and senuous as talcum powder, the air untainted by smog. It seems made only for the benefit of pale Northeners and stressed out city dwellers.

Once a tiny and sleepy fishing village, the world's first computer-designed resort has developed since 1975 into a boom town of over 250,000, with facilities unmatched by any equal other resort in Mexico. No two building designs or pool and beach layouts are the same. In addition, no building rises higher than nine stories, guaranteeing a human sense of proportion and an agreeable view.

Cancún is really three destinations in one: First, colorful hospitable Mexico, with a great deal of English spoken; second, a base from which archeological trips can be taken to the Yucatán's most noted sites; and finally, the exotic Caribbean, since Cancún is associated more with the West Indies than with the rich tradition of old Mexico.

The sun shines 240 days a year, the average temperature is 27°C, and the rains fall in the afternoons and evenings during July and mid-October. Days in summer and autumn can be partially overcast but never stifling.

The resort is divided into two parts: a long, narrow island lined with beachfront hotels, known as the **Zona Turística**, and the downtown mainland, known as **Cancún City**, where most of the shops and handicraft markets are located. The two sections are linked by a causeway that makes travel between them fast and easy by bus, bicycle, taxi, or rented car.

Left: Exceptionally fine beaches have turned Cancún, Cozumel and Isla Mujeres (picture) into a mecca for holidaymakers.

In fact, public transportation is so good here that it is not necessary to rent a car unless it is needed to drive to and from beaches down the coast. The bus is inexpensive and a flat fare takes you anywhere. Taxis are also quite cheap and the bicycle paths around the resort are all flat and easy to negotiate.

The island on which the resort is located has two shores – east and north. The east shore faces the Caribbean, with good surf, turquoise-blue water and sandy beaches. On the north shore, the beaches face a bay or one of two lagoons – Nichupte and Bojorquez – and the water is calmer and shallower. Most of the deluxe hotels, many in a Mayan style and set in flamboyant tropical gardens, are located along the Caribbean side.

Each of the 40 or more hotels is situated in large grounds so that a good distance is kept between each one. Because of the planned nature of the resort, only a limited number of hotels will be allowed, in the hope that Cancún will not suffer from the overcrowding that mars other Mexican resort areas.

Paseo Kukulcán, a scenic boulevard with pink brick sidewalks, bicycle route, and a central strip of garden decorated with topiaries of tropical birds and animals, connects all hotels with the new town of Cancún City. The highway runs east until it comes to **Punta Cancún** (Cancún Point), the "elbow" of the island, where it turns south. The "elbow" is the center of the island's activity. The stretch of Cancún island west of Cancún Point was the first to be developed. Today, many of the most popular hotels, restaurants, and shopping plazas are located along this stretch as well as the **Centro de Convenciones**. This large circular building, one of the first built here, has a soaring sculpture and a mall, **El Parian**, where a colorful folkloric ballet is performed nearly every night. Adjacent to the Convention Center is a small but comprehensive archeological museum with exhibits of ancient Mayan relics excavated in the area. One of the unusual, courious displays is a Maya footprint dicovered in a temple at Yamil Lu'um – dating back 400 to 700 years.

The **Cancún Golf Club** is on the lagoon side on one of the arms of land that separates the two lagoons. This 18-hole course, designed by Robert Trent Jones, winds around Mayan ruins.

Next to the **Cancún Sheraton Hotel** there is a site with a temple/observatory which is illuminated at night. This post-classical Mayan observatory not only served an important religious function but also as a navigational lookout.

Nearby are the **El Rey ruins**. The legendary harem of Maya emperors is claimed to have existed here. Accessible by boat, the ruins consist of small pyramids, altars and some building and temple bases dating back to a 1200 AD

Above: In only a few years the hotel city of Cancún has grown up into a big resort beside the Caribbean sands.

It is the only resort in Mexico where the water can safely be drunk from the tap, since all water supplies come from deep inland wells or from the ocean through desalinating plants. An advanced sewage treatment system ensures that the water supply will remain unpolluted in the future.

Thanks to the winds blowing off the Caribbean, there is no smog, but during the winter months it can get very gusty, making it diffult to follow the ball on a tennis court.

Unlike other resorts in Mexico, Cancún does not have a crime problem. Unemployment is practically non-existent, thanks to tourism, which coopts crime and makes it safe to walk the city's well-lit streets at any hour.

Fortunately for the visitor, Cancún's restaurants compete to serve the best food. Caribbean lobster, fish, shellfish and Yucatecan dishes enliven the menus. Since the majority of visitors are from the USA, Canada and the U.K., restaurants also specialize in excellent steaks and roast beef. Cuisines range from gourmet French to local Mexican, with fast foods – pizzas, hamburgers, pasta and sandwiches – thrown in. Cancún is informal and very few places require formal clothes for dinner, though shorts are discouraged.

Evening entertainment, beginning at sunset, is centered around the resort hotels, where numerous *mariachi* and *marimba* bands play in cocktail lounges and lobby bars to tune in the evening.

For the later hours, Cancún sports its own super-sophisticated discos – **Christine's**, **Daddy O**, **Extasis**, **La Boom** – all offering state-of-the-art entertainment.

The Cancún Convention Center not only provides a venue for meetings, but offers entertainment as well. Usually on Sunday evenings, there is a Mexican Fiesta Night, complete with chilled *margaritas,* a delicious dinner and a colorful folklore show. The Convention Center is also the place for film festivals, cultural events, art shows and the world-famous national *Ballet Folklorico,* presented four times a week from October to May.

As with other Mexican beach resorts, Cancún is a haven for watersports enthusiasts. A snorkel mask is needed almost as much as a bathing suit. Besides snorkeling, there is waterskiing, deep-sea fishing, jet-skiing, scuba diving, parasailing, windsurfing, Hobie Cats and even kayaking. Bookings can be made at a number of marinas and all the larger hotels. Deep-sea fishing boats can be chartered at any marina. Mackerel and sailfish are caught from March to July, bluefin tuna in May, blue and white marlin in April and May, and wahoo and kingfish from May to September.

Cancún also has a **bullring**, but there is no exact schedule for the *corridas*. When there is a bullfight, a leading matador is usually featured.

Along Cancún's 20 kilometers of sandy shores there are three distinct beach zones: the protected **Mujeres Bay**, the open-sea Caribbean side, and the lagoon side.

A dozen pearly beaches edge the windward side. The first four – the **Playas Las Perlas**, **Langosta**, **Tortugas**, and **Caracol** – lie on the gentle Bay of Mujeres. **Playa Chac Mool** and **Playa del Rey** lie on the Caribbean side, which has some dangerous currents. Narrow beaches with hotels line the glassy inner lagoons.

Of all the beaches here, Playa Las Perlas is one of the most natural. ChacMool, known as the public beach (although all are public), sports most of the action. Much of it was washed away by Hurricane Gilbert but is being put back slowly by man and nature. A good restaurant overlooks the beach. Playa del Rey, the southernmost beach on the island is bordered with jungle and remains much as it was.

Beside watersports and miles of modern shopping malls, Cancún offers the largest selection of archeological sites of any resort in Mexico. Easiest to reach by tour or taxi is **Tulúm**, a breathtaking walled Mayan ceremonial center overlooking the Caribbean 110 kilometers south of Cancún. 39 kilometers inland is **Cobá**, a remote jungle-covered city with the feeling of an Indiana Jones adventure. Both are described above.

Another popular excursion is to **Xel-há National Park**, usually included in tours from Cancún. Here a lagoon is set aside for observation only with no diving. For those who wish to snorkel and see the fish first hand, a special area has been conveniently set aside.

Cancún has also been designated as a bird and wildlife sanctuary by the Mexican government. Usually seen on the beaches and in the lagoons are several species of herons, as well as hawksbill, loggerhead turtles and green turtles, which nest on the open beaches. Racoons, grey fox, and small wildcats are just a few of the animals lurking in the mangrove jungles.

ISLA MUJÉRES

One of several all-day excursions from Cancún is to Isla Mujeres, an island north of the resort.

Isla Mujéres

Isla Mujéres, eight kilometers long, is a relatively undeveloped island accessible by ferry from Punta Sam or Puerto Juárez. It is a laid-back sort of place where about the only thing to do is enjoy the sun and sand. It was named after statues of temple goddesses first seen by the Spaniards in 1517. Its transparent waters and coral reefs are ideal for snorkeling and scuba diving. Small game fishing is good as is waterskiing and an island specialty – riding giant sea turtles. The island can best be explored on motorbikes, which are available for rent at the ferry dock in town.

The island's only town is more like a fishing village with a few small hotels,

Above: Beach idyll on the Isla Mujéres
Right: Cozumel beckons.

and nighttime entertainment consists of watching a basketball game in the plaza.

The remainder of the island is hilly with scrubby vegetation. About two-thirds of the way down the island from town are the ruins of an old **hacienda**, supposedly built by a pirate named Mundaca to woo a local beauty called la Triguena, who later jilted him and eloped with a penniless lover. The entrance path is across from **Playa Lancheros**, on the southwestern side of the island, where there are turtles to ride. **Playa Indios**, the next beach to the north, is good for swimming, while those on the eastern side of the island are not.

Playa Los Cocos, Isla Mujeres' most beautiful beach, is a continuation of the village beach that begins near the docks and curves around a point. Unfortunately, it lacks shade, which in these latitudes can be quite tedious.

El Garrafón, a national underwater park at the southern end of the island, visited by tour boats, is a 20-minute ride from town and offers a fine coral reef, great for snorkeling, and a restaurant. A short hike away is a Mayan lighthouse and a crumbling temple where women worshipped the goddess of fertility.

North of Isla Mujeres lies uninhabited **Isla Contoy**, a national park and bird sanctuary where people go to picnic, snorkel, explore and sun on the beach. Tranportation can be arranged in town.

COZUMEL

Centuries ago, **Cozumel** was a holy place to which Mayan women were expected to make a pilgrimage at least once in their lifetime.

Today, it is a place where scuba divers make a pilgrimage of a different sort. **Palancar Reef**, discovered by Jacques Cousteau in the early 1960s, is the second largest reef in the world and ranked among the world's top five dive sites.

But Palancar isn't the only reef here. The entire southwestern quarter of the island is surrounded by excellent reefs and visibility often exceeds 200 feet. It is also well-prepared for visitors: There is a reef for every level of expertise, making Cozumel the ultimate diving resort. There are over 20 dive shops, and lessons can be arranged, as well as rentals of underwater video cameras. The best months for diving are from May through August.

Isolated from the rest of the world until recently, Cozumel underwent a dramatic change after the opening of Cancún. However, the Mayan culture is stronger here than elsewhere and many residents still speak the Mayan language and the women still wear *huipiles*, the traditional embroidered blouse. The Mayas have inhabited Cozumel since 300 AD, when the island was used for religious festivals. Total isolation was broken during World War II, when the United States built a naval base here.

San Miguel de Cozumel, the island's only town, has also changed. Once a sleepy fishing village, it has developed into a duty-free shopping center of over 6000 people. Most of the shops, diving suppliers, and restaurants are located north of the **Plaza del Sol** along a 12-block waterfront, the *malecón*. Near the south end of the *malecón*, an aquarium presents close-up exhibits of tropical marine life in these waters.

With increasing competition from Cancún, new hotels were built and old ones upgraded. Most are concentrated in the northwest corner of the island. The coastal road links these hotels with others to the south near **Chankanab Lagoon National Park**. Chankanab Lagoon, meaning "small sea" in Mayan tongue, offers excellent swimming and snorkeling in crystalline waters, and is worth every peso of the admission charge. It has fantastic underwater caves, tropical fish and some sunken ships, but little coral. Snorkel equipment can be rented on the beach, and a restaurant serves light lunches and drinks. Amateur botanists like the clear labeling of over 2000 species of plants in the **botanical garden**, with its replica of a Mayan house.

Nearby lies **Playa San Francisco**. This is actually two beaches in one. The northern one is the one most used by bathers, while the southern one, the larger of the two, is less visited and offers more shade. Inner tubes and snorkel equipment can be rented on the beach. A beachside restaurant at the northern one serves good lunches either on the sand under a *palapa* or off the beach nearby.

But the most beautiful beach on Cozumel's eastern shore, perhaps on the entire island, is **Punta Chiquero**, a primitive paradise of sheltered coves and open sea. Cages holding parakeets dangle from the eaves of a quaint thatched-roof restaurant.

One thing should never be forgotten: There are strong, unpredictable currents all around the island. It is best to inquire about them before diving and snorkeling.

Right: The pelicans have got used to posing for tourist cameras.

Deep-sea fishing is good here, also, from March to mid-July. The waters are filled with sailfish, wahoo, bonita, dolphin, and kings. Barracuda, red snapper, and grouper are also plentiful. Yachts are moored at **Caleta Inlet**, while glass bottom boat cruises depart from the Sol Caribe Beach. This is a very pleasant way of "visiting" the underwater paradise.

One of the must-do excursions on Cozumel is a Robinson Crusoe Cruise, which takes passengers to a deserted beach on **Passion Island**, at the northern end of Cozumel. On the way, the crew scours the sea bottom for conchs and lobsters, from which lunch is prepared.

A paved road encircles the southern half of the island. A dirt road turns off to the Mayan "Tomb of the Snail", dating from 1200 AD, which is interesting for those who haven't seen Chichén Itzá. Further along the same road is **Punta Celerain** and an antique lighthouse at land's end.

COAST OF QUINTANA ROO

South of Cancún lie over 150 kilometers of gorgeous, unspoiled beaches, with dozens of hidden coves. The farther south, the wilder they get. All are within two hours of the resort and well worth an excursion. In addition, ancient historic sites dot the beach-bordered highway all the way to Chetumal, about 480 kilometers to the south.

Playa Akumal, meaning "place of the turtles," a mile-long crescent of sand located on a tranquil bay 72 kilometers south of Cancún, offers the best scuba diving and snorkeling, as well as a yacht club and accommodation. A small museum, sponsored by CEDAM, Mexico's elite underwater exploration society, houses relics taken from 15th and 16th century shipwrecked galleons in the waters nearby. Scuba divers can also explore an unusual underwater museum where anchors and guns encrusted with coral and thick coats of rust lie among the rocks much the way they were found. Scuba and snorkel gear is easily available for rental just in case you would like to try your luck at finding a similar relic yourself.

Playa Chemuyil, quite possibly the most beautiful beach in Mexico, is a small horseshoe-shaped cove, protected by a reef.

Further south lies **Playa del Carmen**, an area with miles of uncrowded beach, good restaurants, comfortable hotels, and a peaceful setting. Cruise ships dock here and a pedestrian ferry departs for Cozumel several times a day.

It's hard to imagine a more exotic place than **Chetumal**, capital of Quintana Roo, set between Mexico's border with Belize and the Bay of San José on the Caribbean. Though by no means as comfortable or luxurious as the resorts farther north, it has the atmosphere of a Hollywood movie of the 1940s. It is a free port town, where a wide variety of imported goods is sold. Formerly a smugglers' haven, Chetumal is now the setting for hardwood and chicle exporting businesses. Its beautiful bayside Plaza Civica and Parque Central have some prettily colored fountains.

Due east of town, about 32 kilometers offshore, lies **Banco Chinchorro**, a notorious shoal of reefs every experienced diver dreams of exploring. About 40 kilometers northwest of Chetumal is **Bacalar Lagoon**, also called "the Lagoon of Seven Colors". Here, according to Mayan legend, is where the rainbow was born, and this theory is not surprising when looking at the lagoon: It's placid turquoise waters reflect many colors and, like other places along the coast, is ideal for snorkeling.

West of Chetumal via a side road off the main highway that tunnels through the jungle, lie the remote ruins of **Kohunlich**. Here, most of the structures are still covered with thick vegetation, but deep in the palm forest stands a pyramid that served as a tomb, carved with huge but finely detailed masks of Mayan gods.

GUIDEPOST YUCATÁN

MÉRIDA
Accommodation
LUXURY: **Holiday Inn**, Avenida Colón 498, Tel: 25-6877. **Casa del Balám**, Calle 60 Nr. 488, Tel: 24-8844. **El Castellano**, Calle 57 Nr. 513, Tel: 23-0100. **Montejo Palace**, Paseo Montejo 483, Tel: 24-7644.
MODERATE: **Mérida Misión**, Calle 60 Nr. 491, Tel: 23-9500. **El Conquistador**, Paseo Montejo 458/Calle 35, Tel: 26-2155. **Colonial**, Calle 62 Nr. 476, Tel: 23-644.
BUDGET: **Caribe**, Calle 59 Nr. 500, near the Zócalo, Tel: 21-9232. **Hotel del Parque**, Calle 60 Nr. 497, Tel: 21-7840.

Restaurants
Pórtico del Peregrino, Yucatecan cuisine, Calle 57/60, Tel: 21-6844. **Los Palomas**, Calle 56/55, Tel: 32-1545. **Alberto's Continental Patio**, Libanese cuisine, Calle 64 Nr. 482, Tel: 21-2298. **La Casona**, seafood and steaks, Calle 60/47, Tel: 23-8348. **Los Almendros**, Mexican food, Calle 50 A, Tel: 21-2854.

Markets
Mercado Municipal, Calle 56/67, Méridas largest market.

Shopping
Casa de las Artesanías, Calle 63 Nr. 513, popular souvenirs are *hamacas* (hammocks), *jipis* (superior quality panama hats), *guayaberas* (embroidered Mexican gents' shirts*)* and *huipiles* (dresses with colorful embroidery).

Museums
Museo de Antropología e Historia, in the **Palacio Cantón**, Paseo Montejo 43, open Tue-Sat 8 am-8 pm, Sun 8 am-2 pm.
Museo Nacional de Arte Popular, Calle 59, between Calle 50 and 48, open Tue-Sat 8 am-8 pm, Sun 8 am-1 pm.

Folklore
From October to April, folklore-evenings take place at the **Teatro Peón Contreras**, opposite the university near the Zócalo.

Special Events
Carnaval, in February, with its climax on Shrove Tuesday; Yucatán's largest festival with processions, fireworks and folklore.

Sightseeing
Ruins of Dzibilchaltún, ca. 20 km from Mérida, open to the public 8 am-5 pm.
The numerous *cenotes*, natural, sometimes subterranean water-reservoirs in the limestone, make for an unusual and interesting excursion. Locals will show you the way.
Day trips to the **Ruins of Chichén Itzá**, **Uxmal**, **Labná**, **Sayil** and **Kabáh** can be booked at the hotel receptions.

Rental Cars
Avis: Tel: 21-6025 (at the airport) and Tel: 32-7849 (Paseo Montejo).
Budget: Tel: 27-8755 (airport) and Tel: 24-9891 (Calle 60). Additional small rental firms have their offices at the airport.

Post / Telecommunication
Post Office: Calle 65, between Calle 56 and 56 A, Mno-Fri 8 am-7 pm, Sat 9 am-12 noon.
Telephone (long distance): *Caseta* in the Edificio Condesa, Calle 59/Calle 62, daily 8 am-9 pm.
Telegrams: In the post office, Tel: 21-3703, Mon-Fri 8 am-midnight, Sun 9 am-8 pm.

Tourist Information
Calle 59 between Calle 62 and 64, Tel: 24-8013, Mon-Fri 8 am-8 pm, Sat 8 am-2 pm.

CHICHÉN ITZÁ
Accommodation
All accommodations are situated in the vicinity of the ruins.
LUXURY: **Hacienda Chichén**, Tel: 24-8722. **Mayaland**, Tel: 24-8722. **Misión Inn Chichén Itzá**, Tel: 32-9607.
MODERATE: **Villas Arqueológicas**, Tel: 6-2830. **Pirámide Inn**, Tel: 24-0542 from Mérida.
BUDGET: **Dolores Alba**, at km 122, Tel: 21-3745 from Mérida.

UXMAL
Accommodation
LUXURY: **Hacienda Uxmal**, Carret. Mérida-Campeche at km 78, Tel: 24-7142.
MODERATE: **Villas Arqueológicas Uxmal**, next to the ruins, Tel: 24-7053.
Misión Uxmal, situated ca. 3 km from the ruins, Tel: 24-7308.

CANCÚN
Accommodation
At the moment, one can pick and choose between 65 hotels – most of them in the luxury class – in the hotel zone at the lagoon. In Downtown-Cancún are ca. 20 more hotels in the moderate and budget category. The following list of hotels can only comprise a small selection.
LUXURY: All listed hotels are on the "Hotel Row" *Zona Hotelera* on Blvd. Kukulcán.
Aston Flamingo, Tel: 3-1544. **Beach Club Cancún**, Tel: 3-1177. **Calinda Quality Inn**, Tel: 3-1600. **Cancún Palace**, Tel: 5-0533.
Cancún Sheraton, Tel: 3-1988. **Carrousel**, Tel: 3-0513. **Fiesta Americana Plaza Cancún**, Tel: 3-1022. **Fiesta Americana Coral Beach**, Tel: 5-1080. **Holiday Inn Crowne Plaza**, Tel: 5-1022. **Hyatt Regency**, Tel: 3-0960.

Ramada Renaissance, Tel: 5-0100. **Marriott Cancún**, Tel: 5-2000.
BUDGET: In Cancún City: **América**, Avenida Tulum/Brisa, Tel: 4-7500. **Antillano**, Tulum/Claveles, Tel: 4-1532. **El Batab**, Av. Chichén Itzá 52, Tel: 4-3822. **Carrillo's**, Claveles 2, Tel: 4-1227. **Parador**, Av. Tulum 26, Tel: 4-19922.

Restaurants
All hotels along the "Hotel-Row" have their own, excellent restaurants; the following list gives a selection of recommendable restaurants in downtown Cancún only.
Los Alemandros, Yucatecan cuisine, Av. Bonampak/Sayil, Tel: 4-0807. **La Dolce Vita**, seafood, Cobá 87, Tel: 4-1384. **Augustus Caesar**, seafood, Clayeles 13, Tel: 4-1261. **Soberanes**, seafood and Yucatecan cuisine, Av. Tulum/Cobá, Tel: 4-1125.

Nightlife
Nightly entertainment is an important factor in Cancún, almost every hotel has its own disco; popular and recommendable are the discos **Christine**, in the Hotel Krystal, **Aquarius**, in the Camino Real, **La Boom**, **Dady'O**, **Extasis** and **Magic**, all on Av. Kukulcán.
Additional discos: **Friday López, Fiesta Americana, Carlo's 'n Charlie's, Marina, Bum Bum, El Presidente.**

Shopping
The shopping centers **El Parían**, **Mayfair Plaza**, **Plaza Caracol**, **Plaza Flamingo**, **Plaza Lagunas**, **Plaza Nautilus** and **Plaza Terramar** offer a wide selection of goods.

Leisure
Bullfights take place every Wednesday at 3.30 pm in the Arena Bonampak/Sayíl.
Golf: There is an 18-hole golf-course in the hotel zone, Tel: 3-0871.

Boat Tours
Boat tours to the Isla Mujeres, some of them with drinks and food inclusive, can be booked from **Aqua II**, Tel: 3-1909 and **Treasure Island**, Tel: 3-1488.
Boat tours with snorkeling: **Fantasy**, Tel: 7-4643 and **La Bamba**, Tel: 3-3011. **Nautibus** arranges boat tours to the coral reefs, Tel: 3-3552.

Transportation
Ferry connections from Cancún (Punta Sam) to the Isla Mujeres, seven times daily.
Flights from Cancún to Cozumel nine times daily with Aerocozumel, Av. Tulum 29, Tel: 4-2000.

Post / Telecommunication
Post Office: Sun Yax Chén, Tel: 4-1519, Mon-Fri 9 am-6 pm, also for telegrams.
Telephone (long distance): Best connections from the hotels, but very expensive. A *caseta* for long-distance calls is at Mercado 28, behind the post office, 8 am-10 pm.

Tourist Information
Palacio del Gobierno, Av. Tulum, Tel: 3-0094, Mon-Fri 9 am-3 pm.

COZUMEL
Accommodation
LUXURY: **Club Cozumel Caribe**, Playa de San Juan, Tel: 2-0110. **Fiesta Americana Sol Caribe**, Playa Paraíso, Tel: 2-0466. **Mayan Plaza**, Playa Santa Pilar, Tel: 2-0411. **Stouffer Presidente**, 5 km south of San Miguel, Tel: 2-0332. **La Ceiba**, Paradise Point, Tel: 2-0379.
MODERATE: **Plaza Azul**, Playa de San Juan, Tel: 2-0033. **Baracuda**, Avenida Melgar Sur, Tel: 2-0002.

Restaurants
El Acuario, seafood, Malecón in San Miguel. **Morgan's**, seafood, delicious lobster, Placa Central, Tel: 2-0584. **Pepe's Grill**, seafood, Av. Rafael Melgar, Tel: 2-0213.

Sightseeing
Interesting excursions lead to the archaeological areas **Aguada Grande**, **Buena Vista**, **El Cedral**, **Santa Rita** and **San Gervasio** – the latter is the most important of all and within easy reach from Cozumel.

Diving
The best reefs for phantastic diving are **San Francisco**, **Palancar**, **Santa Rosa**, **Yacab**, **Colombia**, **La Ceiba** and **Maracaibo**.

Transportation
Ferry connections to Cozumel from the beach Playa del Carmen (Quintana Roo). Ferries run ten times daily. **Transportation**: Local buses don't keep to a regular schedule. As distances are relatively short, it's worth taking a taxi or renting a moped; however, some parts of the island can only be reached by jeep.

ISLA MUJÉRES
Accommodation
MODERATE: **El Presidente Caribe**, at the northern tip of the island, Tel: 2-0002. **Rocamar**, Nicolás Bravo, Tel: 2-0101.
BUDGET: **Hotel Cabañas María del Mar**, Av. Carlos Lazo, Tel: 2-0179.

Restaurants
Gomar, seafood, Hidalgo/Madero, Tel: 2-0142. **Ciro's Lobster House**, Matamoros 11, Tel: 2-0102. **Sergio's**, Guerrero at the Zócalo.

Tourist Information
Avenida Guerrero 8, Tel: 2-0173 and 2-0188, Mon-Sat 8 am-2 pm and 5-7 pm.

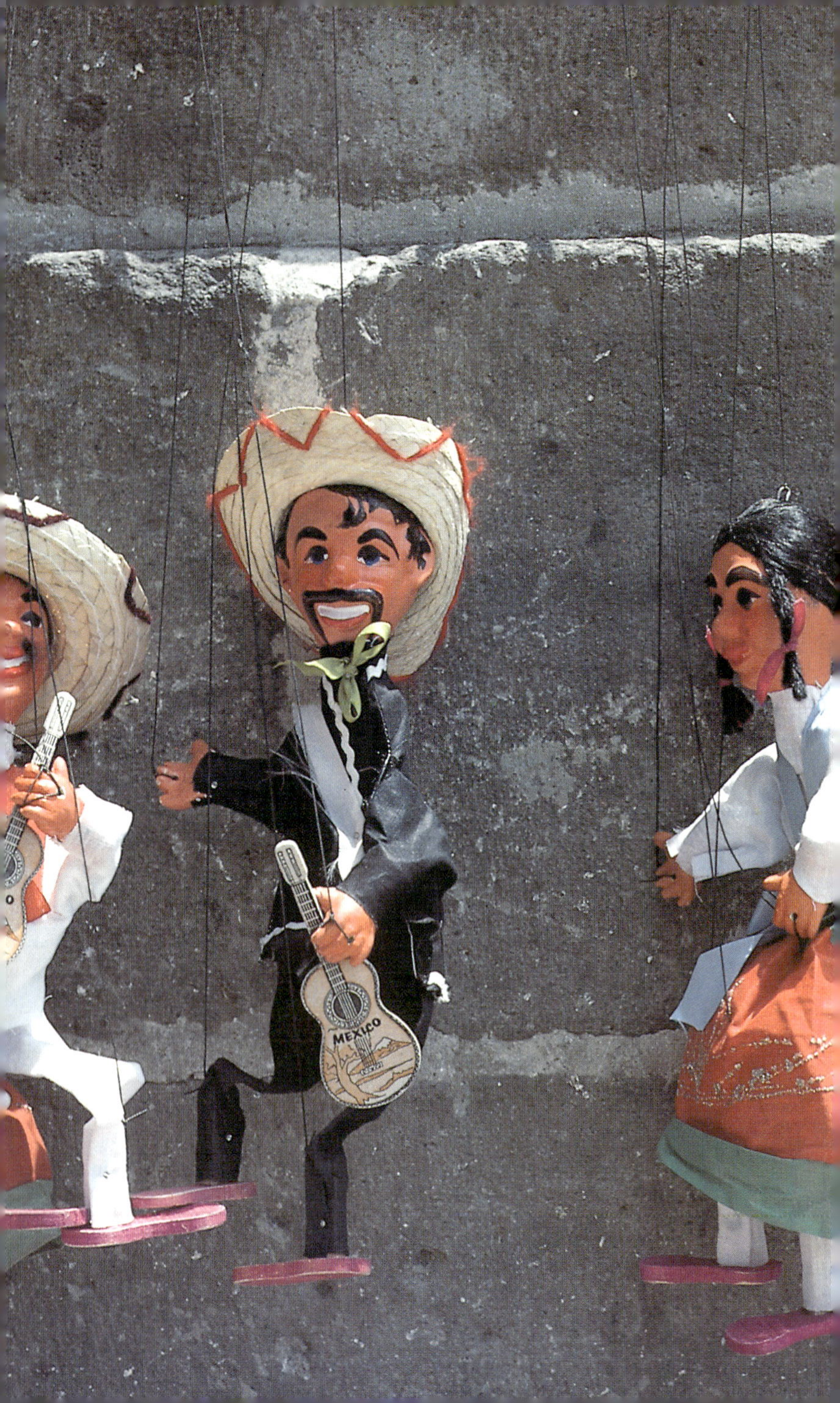
MEXICO

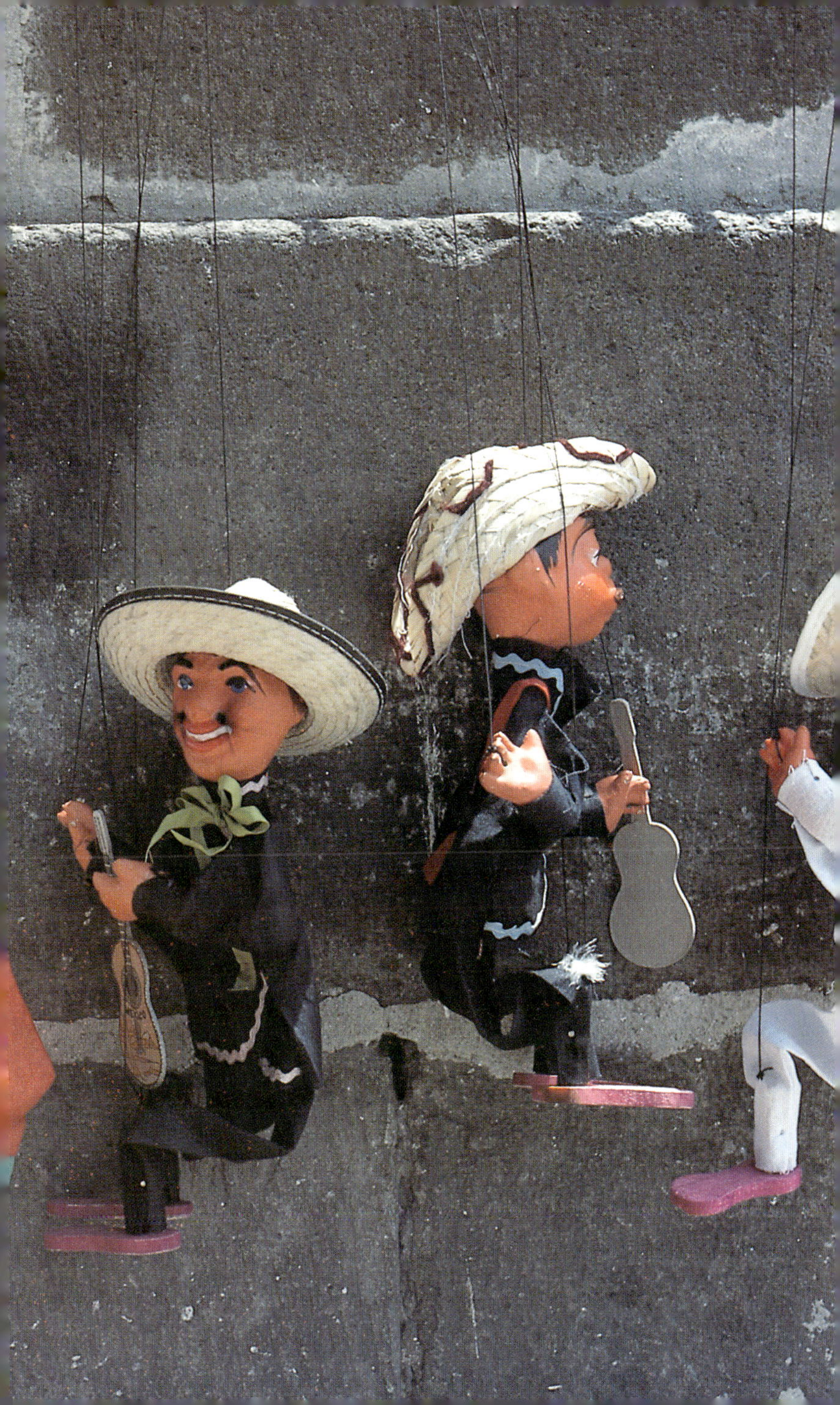

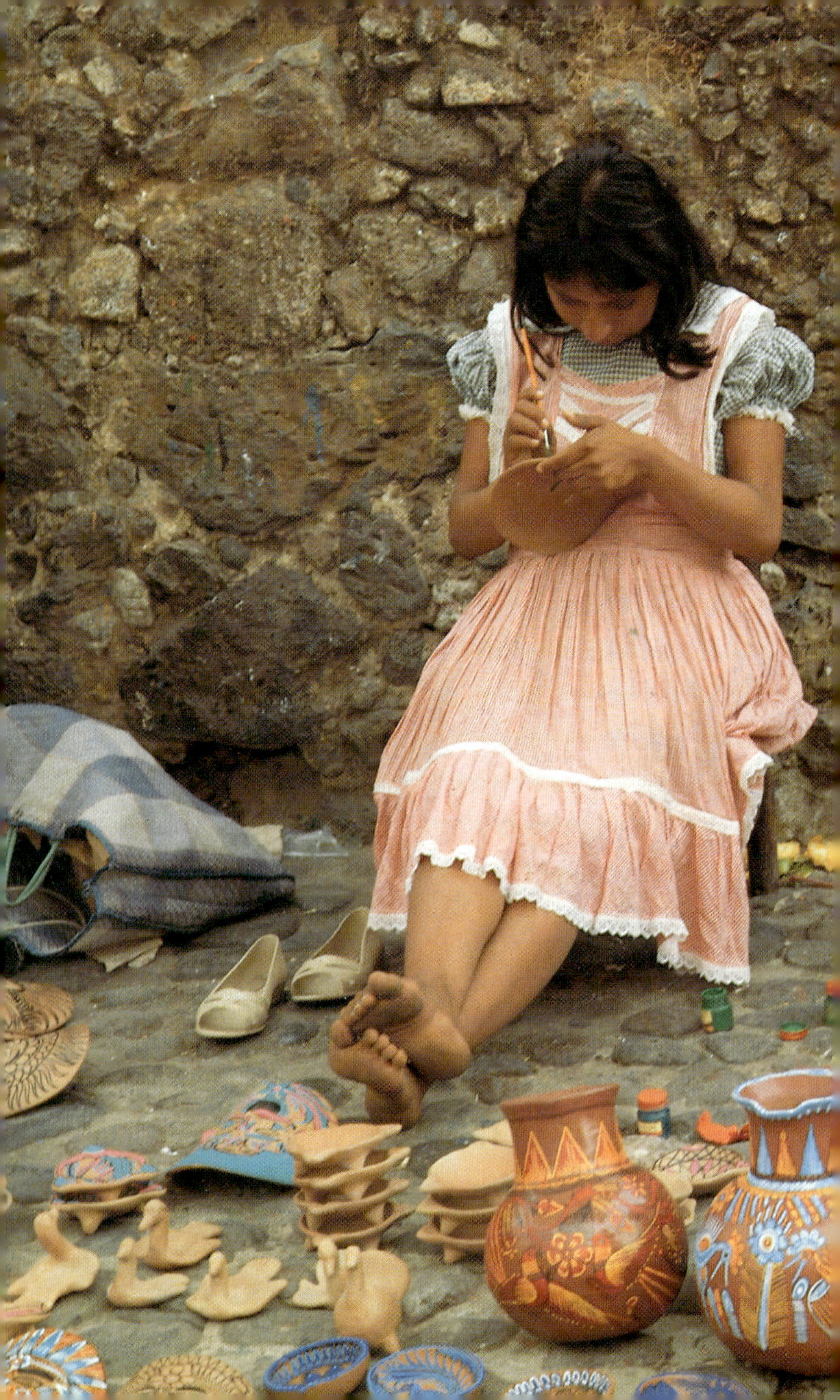

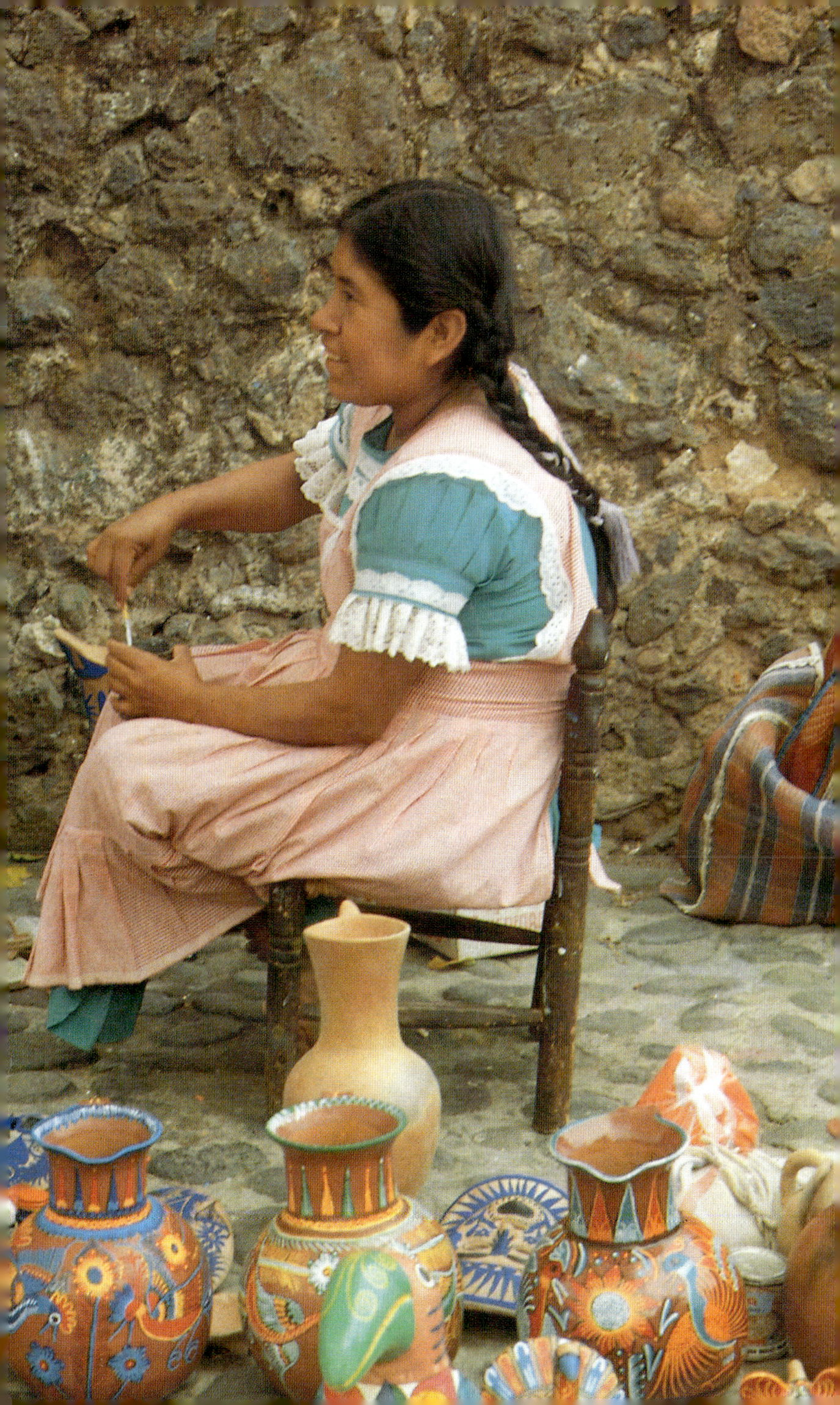

MEXICAN CUISINE

Mexican food begins with the Aztec, Mayan and Zapotec cultures. Some of their staples have not only remained Mexican mainstays, but have also spread around the world. They cultivated maize (generally referred to as corn), the raw material for the ubiquitous *tortilla*, a flat, unleavened dough baked in a pan (formerly on flat stones) and functioning like bread. They ate a red fruit that Europeans feared as it belonged to the nightshade family. The Nahuátl word for it was *tomatl*. They drank a muddy, blackish brew that the Dutch later refined using milk and sugar. It was called *chocoatl* and became chocolate.

Mexican cuisine is extremely varied, even if the menus throughout the country seem to offer the same dish frequently. In fact, that same dish comes in myriad variations depending where it is eaten. There are, of course, certain basic forms of food, just as there are world-wide certain basic architectural laws that apply to the igloo as well as the cathedral of Chartres. The plain tortilla can be transformed into various dishes that themselves come in different forms. There is, for example, the *burrito,* the *taco* and the *enchilada,* a filling of sorts wrapped in a soft or crispy torilla either covered in cheese, drowned in sauce or both. The *tamale* is something like a pancake that gets filled. The *tostada* is a crispy tortilla eaten with meat, cheese salad and beans. *Guacamole* is a very tasty topping made of crushed avocados and garlic.

The famous chili (as the *gringos* call it), like curry in India and "goulash" in Hungary, cannot be standardized. Furthermore, it is somewhat of a misnomer, a convenience for foreigners. Ask for chili in Mexico and you are likely to harvest a blank stare, for chili is a blanket term itself meaning pepper. Every region has its own specialties, of course, and not only in chili dishes.

In Puebla, the *mole* sauce has survived from the pre-Columbian days. The name is supposed to be derived from the Nahuátl word *mulli*, meaning "the sauce made of ground chili peppers". The ancestor of the *mole* was in fact created by the nun Andrea de la Asunción, who combined the *mulli* with some Old World spices. Since then, the "tribe" has grown to well over 300 variations. One of them is the *pipian* sauce that includes ground and roasted pumpkin seeds.

By the way, *chiles en nogada* (chilis with a creamy walnut sauce) is also a Pueblan specialty that was created for Emperor Iturbide and is eaten to celebrate the end of the War of Independence. *Chile poblano,* plain old Pueblan chili if you will, is conjured in the following fashion: A green chili is filled with a stuffing of ground meat, fruits, pine nuts, cloves and cinammon, all baked together, smothered in a creamy walnut sauce and garnished with pomagranate seeds.

Mérida, which is hot, refreshes its residents and visitors alike with a drink called *pozol*. Tortillas here come served with a combination of sweet ground meat and Dutch cheese, strips of chicken (*salbutes*) and *papadzules* of ground and roasted pumpkin seeds with *epazote*. All of this is served with *kol* sauce.

In Quintana Roo, in the ancient Mayan settlements of Chichén Itzá, Uxmal and Tulúm, fish is the mainstay of the local cuisine. Sea bass, saw fish and sea snails are prepared with a strong red onion, bitter orange, salt, radishes and, at times, *cilantro*. Another local specialty is suckling pig, roasted and flavored with anis.

Oaxaca is particularly rich in regional dishes. There is a panoply of *tamales* and *chile chipotles*; find the stringy cheese that is formed into an oblong shape, for it

Previous pages: Mariachis in full swing. Tourism has revived the ancient crafts of Mexico. Right: An open-air tortilla bakery. Far right: In a birrieria (beer saloon).

MEXICAN CUISINE

can only be tasted here. Oaxacan are also: *molotes*, chicken soup, roasted lamb, *lima* beans baked in a crock, cactus fruit paddies fried in their own juice, *quelites*, *tlayudas*, which are giant tortillas spiced up with a mixture of tomatoes, chili peppers and garlic.

The cooking of Tabasco is also very particular to the region owing to the fact that a lot of the ingredients can only be found in that state. Mayan and Olmec culture meet up here, and many of the local recipes have been handed down through the generations and changed as well. A look at the market in Villahermosa reveals some of the delights produced by the local farmers, mounds of garlic, *achiotes* wrapped in banana leaves, heaps of melons and every kind of exotic fruit imaginable, and of course the famous Tabasco pepper: Indeed, the name Tabasco is usually associated with the egregiously hot sauce made from the pepper, but food in Tabasco, the curious visitor will find, does not burn its way straight through people. Breakfast consists of strong coffee, a slice of *guanabana* or *tamalillos* in their juice, green bananas, *torrejas de yuca* or crunchy *totopostes*. *Tamales* are prepared with turkey or pork meat, spiced up with *epazote* or *achiote*, and served on a *herbia santa* leaf. The *tamales de hoja de chipilin* is another dish that is similar. The Tabasco sauce is generally optional.

Among the popular dishes in Tabasco is also turtle *poychitoque*, *hicotea* and *quao*. The animal is stewed with *momo*, chili peppers and *chiplin*. The *piquas*, giant craw fish that can only be found in Tabasco, are roasted in a garlic sauce.

Guerrero, a state on Mexico's western coast, has an interesting tradition. An old connection with China has given the local cuisine a distinctively Asian touch where spices are concerned. Like Quintana Roo, however, Guerrero is known for its great variety of fish. Definitely worth trying are the fresh shrimps with *chiles quajillos* (prepared with tomato sauce), or *pescado a la talla*, charcoal-grilled fish with a sauce. The *chilapitas*

MEXICAN CUISINE

are an excellent snack consisting of small maize tortillas (tortillas can also be made of wheat) with beans or strips of chicken. And if you are in the state on a Thursday, watch out for *pozole verde,* a special soup served only on that day and made of pumpkin seeds, *cacahuazintle,* sea food or pork. Finally, to close off a fine, spicy meal, there are the *iguana tamales,* sweets made of tamarind or coconut.

There is no better place to explore Mexico gastronomically than its markets, colorful, aromatic, sensuous affairs that seem to run year round. Among the most exciting ones are those in Veracruz where the specialty is fish and other gifts of the sea. The area is known for vanilla which adds a penetratingly sweet smell to the air. The food peddlers on the market sell some of Mexico's most flavorful "fast" foods: *tamales rancheros,* a corn pancake stuffed with chicken, tomatoes, olives and a slice of *chile serano* (ham), all wrapped up in a banana leaf or *hierba santa; molotes* or *barbacoa de becerro* filled with cheese or *chorizo sausage.*

The stalls offer pumpkin seeds, black beans, piles of different peppers, radishes, tomatoes and an endless selection of fresh fruit: pineapple, papayas, mangos, oranges, limes, grapes, *guanabanas*, watermelons, bananas, etc. The *licuado* stands offer cooled fruit juices mixed with water or milk, but the untrained stomach should remember that these not only refresh, but have a tendency of over-promoting digestion.

Among the Veracruz specialties are two with amusing names. First there is *vuelve a la vida,* "back to life!", a cocktail of shrimps, oysters, *ceviche de pescado* (raw fish in lime juice), sea snails, tomato sauce, Tabasco sauce, oil, whereby the fish is always from the catch of the day. The second dish is called *ropa vieja,* literally "old clothes", and it consists of a *chile poblano* or chicken and potatos with tomato sauce, onions and oregano.

Above and right: Whether fish or meat is being served, Mexican food is famous for its many delicious side-dishes.

MEXICAN CUISINE

Mexicans drink. They have to owing to the heat. They have wonderful fruit juices available on every market, they have bottled water, they even have fine beers and wines thanks to their warm climate. The nuns at the Convent of Santa Clara in Puebla concocted a drink closely resembling eggnog and referred to as *rompope*. Sometimes, when further mixed, it comes under the heading *pasitas*.

The agave plant has also the basis for a number of drinks, notably *pulque,* whereby the juice of the plant is fermented. Sometimes other fruit juices, mango, pineapple, guava, celery, are added to it for taste. *Pulque,* which is generally consumed in the central part of the country, has been found to be very rich in vitamins.

The agave plant also serves the purpose of making *tequila,* a spirit first distilled (and still primarily distilled) in the town of Tequila. At one time it must have been difficult to swallow, but over the decades its popularity became national, then international, and its taste improved, especially with the process of aging in oak barrels that have to be imported from Europe.

Tequila is traditionally drunk over a pinch of salt and washed down qith a squirt of lime. Two of the most famous cocktails with tequila are the *Tequila Sunrise* and the *Margarita.* Tequila is strong and, combined with the tropical sun and drilling heat, can cause the drinker to become uncomfortably drunk and make a fool of him- or herself.

As a final note on food, and a gentle warning, Mexican food has a reputation for being sharp, and it is. The combination of spicy peppers, beans, fried foods and fresh fruit, can cause havoc with the untrained intestines. A mild antacid will help counteract the effects of the food until you get used to it. Remember too, that when eating very "hot" food, the best way to put out the flames is not to douse them with liquids, but to bite into something neutral, like a bit of un-chilied tortilla, tamale, or the like.

So come and taste Mexican cuisine!

MEXICAN MUSIC

MEXICAN MUSIC

Music in Mexiko is an essential part of life. Be it for fiesta or for a simple meal, some band, choir, even individual, will inevitably show up to provide the musical background. When it is performed, it is on a wide variety of instruments. Furthermore, one could hardly say Mexican music is homogenous, for it is an expression of, and perhaps even the reconciliation of the clash between the European and Indigena cultures.

In the state of Chiapas in the southern highlands, Zinacatáns and Chanmuláns, the last survivors of the pre-Columbian Mayas, perform their ancient rituals by blowing a shrill hand-hewn whistle to imitate the sound of a bird's call, while youths dressed only in a loin-cloth tap their toes and beat their heels against the ground. "It is the ancient music of the bird and the dance of the holy jaguar,"

Above: It was the Spanish who introduced the trumpet to Mexico.

explained a chieftain at the annual January 19th fiesta of San Sebastian.

Many say, the vocal tradition began with Netzahualcóyotl, the ancient king of Texcoco. Not only did he sing ballads praising his own brilliance, he became the patron of many court musicians who put his poetry to song. He also designated the "House of Song" or *cuicacalli*, where all children were taught the art of music.

Mayan music was only performed in religious rituals and ceremonies. Instruments as such were considered divine. The first missionaries found that music helped in the converting process. In fact, by 1523 the first music school had been founded by Pedro de Gante, a Franciscan priest. A guitarist, Juan Ortiz, who had come along with Cortés, also introduced the thrills of secular music to the Indigenas. This led to the only truly harmonious encounter between the two cultures. In the 16th century, a Spanish friar, Bernadino de Sahagún, researched and wrote down the music of the Indigenas. Their music was accompanied by percus-

MEXICAN MUSIC

sion instruments, the drum or *huehetl*, a hollow log which was beaten by sticks. This style is still found in the towns of Dolores Hidalgo, Tabasco and Veracruz. In many small villages of Sonora, Coahuila, Chihuahua and Nuevo León, the Aztec wind instruments of reed and clay flutes, jugs with whistles, are used by the local musicians at fiesta times to play the music of their ancestors. Along the shore in Sinola, Nayarit and Jalisco, the mournful tones of a musician blowing a conch shell are heard at many funerals. In the northern state of Chihuahua, musicians play an archaic type of violin brought over by Spanish conquistadors.

From this, blended with the bass fiddle and the addition of trumpet and guitar, came the *mariachi* bands that stroll round nearly every town. *Mariachi* groups were formed during the 18th Century in the state of Jalisco and throughout Central Mexico. At first, only the string instruments were played, then trumpets were added nearly 100 years later. From the well-knwon birthday song *La Mañanitas* to ballads of a man facing his own execution, the songs are as much a part of the history of Mexico as the Indigenas' bird calls. The most sophisticated of the *mariachis* play in Mexico City's famed Plaza Garibaldi, where the troupes in their spangled, tight-fitting trousers and wide-brimmed sombreros serenade through the night. The music of the *mariachis* is by and large folk music influenced by the Spanish heritage. At first it was religious, then, during the 19th century, it fell under the sphere of influence from Italy.

A far more individual sound began developing at the opening of the 20th century. Arguably, the influence was still European, but the means of expression, the individual style and the increasing use of native instruments, primitive rhythms and melodies do suggest something one could call a "Mexican School".

There was Manuel M. Ponce (1866-1948), influenced by the Impressionists. His most famous works include his triptych *Chapultepec*, *Ferial* and *Estrellita*. Ponce incorporated the guitar into the repertoire of 20th-century music. Julián Carrillo (1875-1965) was the great experimenter with music, having shaped his own system of microtones. Another important Mexican composer was Silvestre Revueltas (1899-1940). A spontaneous genius, he was sensitive to pre-Columbian as well as contemporary Mexico, and wrote symphonies with titles such as *Cuauhnáhuac*, *Sensemaya*, and *Magueyes*. Carlos Chávez (1889-1978), who looked to the folk song for his inspiration, is perhaps the best-known Mexican composer, because he toured as a conductor and lecturer, and wrote several books on music. His 1940 *Xochipilli Macuilxochitl* is a fascinating symphonic work using Indigena percussion instruments.

The Ballet Folklórico

After the War of Independence in the mid-19th century, the waltz became popular, the musicians of Jalisco, Oaxaca and Michoacán giving it a distinctive traditional flavor with lilting phrases and melodic undertones. Ethnic music has gained popularity throughout the nation in recent years with the *Ballet Folklorico*, performed at the Palacio de Bellas Artes in Mexico City. Beginning with the most basic Indigena music, it moves through the history to the Mexican bolero, to the heroic ballads singing the praises of "Pancho" Villa and Emiliano Zapata, and the marching songs that developed into dance tunes, such as *La Cucaracha*. In perhaps its most sophisticated form, the traditional music of Mexico flows out from one of the country's most dramatic fiestas, the bullfight or *la fiesta brava*. The event itself becomes the background for the music. When the killing of the bull is done with perfection, the trumpets blare, the drums roll, and the entire show becomes a celebration.

FOLK ART

Your first contact with the fantastic world of Mexican folk-art will probably be in one of the state-operated FONART shops in Mexico City or on a Saturday at the Bazar Sábado in the romantic quarter of San Angel. Even the most sober traveling businessman can fall victim to buying fever when faced by the diversity of color and form in which almost any imaginable material is transformed into a piece of *arte popular*. Many of the articles in the enormous selection are genuine folk-art; in other words, not purely decorative, but fulfilling a function in the society from which it came. For example, if you could trace an embroidered blouse back to the hands that made it, you would discover that a blouse of this sort is part of a traditional costume. Or that one of the bulging clay pots sold at the markets also appear in a smoke-blackened village kitchen boiling up *frijoles*, the Mexican brown beans.

Wooden masks are still worn for the old dances as well. The folk artists' imagination know no bounds, and now and then utility ceases to matter. It branches out into man-high "trees of life" made of clay, it mocks death and the Devil with skulls made of sugar or with grotesque or even downright obscene clay devils, who are named *ocumichus* after their place of origin.

Indigenous or Spanish?

An element of Mexican craftsmanship is rooted in indigenous traditions: The ancient Mexicans had a superb command of the stone-cutter's art, fashioning objects of onyx, jade and obsidian. To this day the Indigenas' woven belts are still made on the pre-Spanish *telar de cintura*, a

Right: Paintings on bark-paper make easily portable souvenirs. Far right: An Indigena woman with her hip-mounted loom.

kind of loom which is tied around the workers' hips. Other crafts are based on imports from the conquerors. Spanish potters brought along the potters' wheel and a faience technique from Talavera de la Reina which is used in Puebla for the production of tiles and dishes. The missionaries founded schools in which the native population were not only preached to on the benefits of the Bible, they were also taught European artisan techniques.

Then, when Mexico served as an entrepôt during the colonial period for Spanish trading ships going to and from the Philippines, Mexican handicrafts even took on Far Eastern influences. One of the clearest examples of this is the delicate lacquer-work with gold inlays from the state of Michoacán.

A third type of craftsmanship combines old traditions with new ideas in a sophisticated way. One example is the *papel amaté* seen at so many markets and now being exported the world over. This tree-bark paper, on which the Aztecs recorded their picture-stories, is still handmade sheet-by-sheet in remote mountain villages. Covered with magical figures, they are still used there in healing ceremonies. In the 1960s, a dealer from the capital city came up with the idea of having the sheets painted by potters from a village several hundred kilometers away who graced their earthenware with highly original designs. This turned out to be the birth of a new decorative folk-art and a best-seller as well. There is scarcely another product perceived as so "typically Mexican", not to mention that as a souvenir, a rolled-up bark-paper painting fits into a suitcase rather more neatly than a fragile clay pot.

In the handicrafts markets of the capital, such as the Bazar Sábado, the Mercado Ciudadela or the Mercado de San Juan one can find practically anything that the *artesanos* throughout the entire country produce. Naturally these included silver jewelry, copper plates, leather bags and belts, facsimiles of archeological discoveries and figures of paper-maché. This is a very convenient solution for those visitors who haven't the chance to purchase their souvenirs right where they're produced.

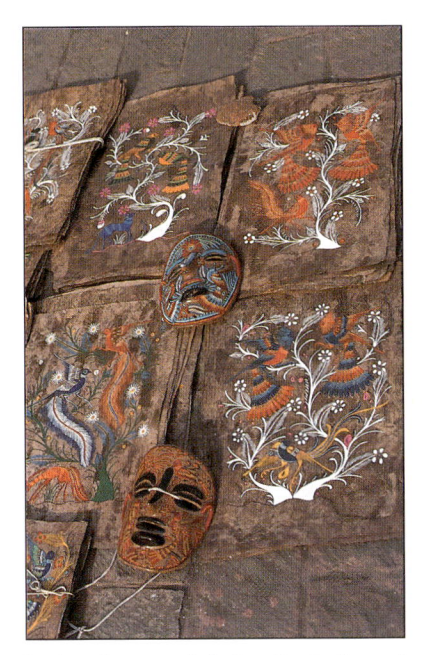

Regional Specialties

Visitors interested in watching as wooden plaques and boxes are elaborately decorated with the scratch-and-paint technique in Olinalá must certainly allow for some fatigue and inconvenience to reach their goal.

The village is located in the mountains of Guerrero, and the roads to it are frequently impassable. In earlier days, Olinalá mainly produced chests of an aromatic wood decorated with lacquered patterns; they were used for storing the dowries. This craft might have died out if tourism had not created a new demand for this type of lacquer-work. It has now become an important trade for a number of families in Olinalá.

The "Silver City" of Taxco is also located in Guerrero. A side-excursion en route to Acapulco is very worthwhile. In its narrow alleyways there are countless silversmiths with their imaginative displays. The impetus for Taxco's renaissance in the silversmith's art (the city used to derive its existence from its silver mines) came from an outsider. The American William Spratling, named "Don Guillermo" by native residents, came to Taxco in 1929, opening a silversmith shop in which he had jewelry fashioned using the motifs of ancient Mexico. His success helped the craft to a phenomenal new revival.

Every one of Mexico's regions has its own specialties. In Oaxaca, the selection of woven rugs (chiefly produced on the looms of Teotitlán del Valle) is simply overwhelming. Their traditional patterns are as old as the stone mosaics on the Palace of Mitla, although the pastel hues have been adjusted to meet popular demand. Some rather cheeky weavers have even used a painting by Juan Miró

FOLK ART

as a pattern. Black ceramics are also typical of Oaxaca. The pitchers, whistles and bells are not, in fact, artificially glazed. Their shimmering metallic color comes about during the firing process, when a smoky fire in the earthen kilns deposits soot on the clay surface. One area with an exceedingly rich tradition of craftsmanship is the region around Lake Pátzcuaro in the state of Michoacán. Almost every one of the fishing and farming villages of the Tarascan and Purépecha Indigenas surrounding the lake have specialized in a particular craft. The skilled artisanry of the Purépechas, already legendary in pre-Columbian times, was promoted by the Dominican Vasco de Quiroga, who, as Bishop of Michoacán (from 1539) became this people's benefactor. To this day memory of *tata Vasco* ("Papa Vasco") is still held in high regard by the Purépechas. At the Museo de Arte Popular in Pátzcuaro one can examine a cross-section of the region's tremendous diversity of handcrafted products, many of which can be purchased at the Casa de los Once Patios (House of Eleven Patios). Carved furniture and musical instruments are created out of woods from this region's thriving forests. In addition there are pottery and basket-wares, copper and lacquered products as well as woven and embroidered textiles.

Another rewarding expedition might be undertaken to Santa Clara del Cobre, which even has the word copper in its name. The metal gleams from under the shadows of the town's arcades, where the merchants sell copper vessels and jewelry. There is hammering and forging going on behind many of the town's doors. The history of copper-working here can be traced in its museum. Once again an American, Jim Metcalf, played a significant role in vitalising this craft. He trained young people as decorative metalsmiths in his huge workshop. In the neighboring state of Jalisco, its multi-

Above: This sombrero is a real feast for the eye. Right: A lot of souvenir shops offer all kinds of kitsch.

FOLK ART

faceted *artesania* (artisanry) is also a tourist magnet. There are hundreds of shops and workshops to be discovered in the vicinity of Guadalajara, the state capital, especially in the towns of Tlaquepaque and Tonalá. At the twice-weekly pottery market in Tonalá one can still find the traditional ceramics that are molded with traditional skill in small family workshops, painted with earthen hues and then finely polished before being fired (*loza brunida*). But the Tonalán potters' glazing technique is also being used now by manufacturers producing stoneware with modern designs. Of course, the old traditional plaster sculptures are still being made in Tlaquepaque, but meanwhile the competition has stiffened from other workshops, both large and small, in which articles of paper-maché, leather goods, glassware and brass are created.

Kitsch and Curios

In this world of commercialized handicrafts it may well be that the only genuine folk-art remaining is at the Museo Regional de la Cerámica. On the other hand, the genre of "Mexican Curios" is *well* represented.

Souvenirs are fabricated especially for the tourist market, most of which are actually nothing more than knick-knacks. Throughout the country they look as if they have come from the same factory, and probably have! They make use of motifs reflecting stereotypes of Mexico, the so-called "Aztec calendar" being especially prominent among them. The original, a stone weighing many tons in the National Museum of Anthropology, is copied in a thousand different ways, appearing on silver ashtrays, leather bags and onyx brooches.

Another "typical" item is the sombrero-sporting Mexican who is leaning against a cactus and taking his siesta and useful as a bookend into the bargain! But who can really blame the Mexicans for adapting to the international demand for collecting dust-collectors, when the result is the creation of jobs and income, especially in the rural areas? In some places, often far removed from the tourist centers, the brakes have been put on migration to the large cities (especially the capital). This is a still an important reason for state support through FONART, the *Fondo Nacional de Fomento de las Artesanías*, which maintains a chain of well-organized shops, particularly in Mexico City. Nonetheless, the lion's share of Mexican handcrafted products are marketed by private dealers, who profit nicely, while the artisans themselves only rarely achieve any affluence. The Mexican *artesanos* have an unending wealth of inspiration. You really have to take off your hat – no, your sombrero – to their remarkable creativity. They know how to conjure up a work of art from the most miserable junk, and they can even – if the customer so wishes – transform a Mexican leaning against a cactus, into a Fakir ...

MURAL ART

Above: Many artists like J.C. Orozco used murals to express their social commitment. Right: D. Rivera announced a return to the values of Mexico's pre-Hispanic culture.

MURAL ART

The tradition of mural painting in Mexico goes back hundreds of years. The first wall paintings were done by an early Mayan civilisation in caves in southern Mexico, where the artists attempted to portray the gods of the moon, sun, stars, and the netherworld. The Lacandon tribe of southern Chiapas still venerate the ancient murals on the walls of the Templo de las Pinturas at Bonampak which in the language of the Maya people means "Place of the Painted Walls".

The birth of the Mexican Mural Movement in 1922 resulted from the Mexican Revolution of 1910-1920. From the great social upheaval that engulfed the Mexican artists of the revolutionary period, the youngest of the "Big Three", David Alfaro Siqueiros, led the formation of a mural movement in which the artists of that period could best serve government aims with their art. By their very nature, murals were a public art-form and thus were an effective way of addressing the people, especially when large numbers were illiterate.

Mexico's finest muralist's work on the wall of the lobby of the grand Del Prado Hotel in Mexico City drew harsh criticism in the years following World War II because of its alleged socialist message, so it was covered with a large piece of plywood and drapery. Years later, when the criticism of Diego Rivera's (1886-1957) *A Dream of a Sunday Afternoon in Alameda Park* had abated and, indeed, it was praised as a profound and lasting work, it was uncovered and shown to the public.

This story alone shows the reverence with which the government of Mexico, even when faced with popular criticism, views its mural art. Indeed, if the government had destroyed the painting, those same people who were criticizing the

MURAL ART

message would have raised their voice – if not their fists – in protest.

Rivera painted his first mural, *The Creation*, in 1922. From that moment he never put down his brushes and soon developed the style for which he became celebrated. He progressed from flat to modeled painting, worked on the characters, and emerged with a powerful political message. *The Market* shows the masses as working people, bringing their hard-earned crops to sell, a humble and proud people. Later he experimented more and became more complex, using the same rethorical style but adding an element of grimly realistic humour in, for example, *The Day of the Dead*.

Also in the 1920s, José Clemente Orozco (1883-1949) developed mural art at the Preparatory School in Mexico City. Showing youth at play in the barren fields of his homeland, Orozco caught the eye of the art critics of his time. These early walls were more simplistic than the richness and complexity that he showed in his work at the University, Governor's Palace and the Chamber of Deputies at Guadalajara.

In his home city, he created a dark, foreboding series of panels where the viewer is shocked by the agony of destitution. Here his imagery becomes the poetry of the brush. His *First Battle of the Revolution* is torn between victory and death, the horror of a lonely scream against the background of a huge hand holding a drawn sword.

A third master mural artist is David Alfaro Siqueiros (1896-1974), who moved from the conventional Indigena faces to a more symbolic approach of figures wearing gas-masks, repetitions of faceless men and women, a study of society struggling with the industrial revolution and space-age modernism. He saw strength in size, finally creating his elongated images of missile-like jets of red and yellow and bright green on massive sheets of steel to be hung in public places. When he died in 1974 in Cuernavaca, he was at work on these. Many of his imaginative works can be seen on the walls of class buildings at the University of Mexico, showing streamlined bomb-like objects soaring through a fiery inferno. There is little that is reassuring in Siqueiros' work.

Modern Mexican mural painters, such as Rufino Tamayo, Gonzalez Camarena, Carlos Orozco Romero, Fermin Revueltas, Carlos Merida (his *Mexican Legend* is 2000 square meters in size), Juan O' Gorman (his *Allegory of Mexico,* a mosaic of natural stones and colored glass, measures 3900 square meters!), and others, have moved even beyond Siqueiros in endowing this dramatic country with a strong and visually exciting symbolism.

Today, the Mexican Government recognizes the great heritage of mural treasures left behind by its painters of genius and has under the law for Protection of National Monuments, established a department for the protection and restoration of murals.

LITERATURE

"It is not possible to understand Mexico without having read *The Labyrinth of Solitude* (1950)", claimed the commentary upon the award of the 1990 Nobel Prize for Literature to poet and essayist Octavio Paz. The book is a multi-layered social analysis with an eye constantly fixed on the rift between its two pasts and its contradiction-laden present. In his search for a *mexicanidad*, the identity of a people which takes delight in festivals just as seriously as it takes death lightly, Paz treats matters ranging from the downfall of the Aztec culture to the predominant influence of its neighbor to the north. Mexican literature, it could almost be said, was born of a woman, and in a revolutionary fold. It is a questioning, provocative literature, serious and funny at the same time, obsessed with death, life and, not infrequently a magic world.

Above: "Literature" of a very different kind – a newsvendor in Mexico City.

A woman's isolation in a pre-feminist society forms the core of *Las trampas de la fe (The Traps of Faith,* 1982). In this essay, Octavio Paz (born 1914) describes Sister Juana, a 17th-century nun and poetess, as well as the first intellectual to fall foul of the orthodox-religious dogmen of the Counter-Reformation. Sister Juana Inéz de la Cruz (1648-1694) chose the cloister as the only place where women could acquire knowledge. In its seclusion she wrote frankly erotic lyric poetry, comedies and devotional plays which were performed outside the convent's walls. However, the fact that she went further, posing critical questions and publically declaring womens' right to receive an education, was too much for the Bishop. She died a penitent. The "Tenth Muse of Mexico" is seen as the founder of a Mexican literature. In the view of Octavio Paz, when considering the contribution of Latin-American peoples to the body of world literature, this would mean the literature of the second half of the 20th century "which examines our reality and our languages". The proportion of women among successful authors is considerable: Rosario Castellanos (1925-74) described life on a hacienda in Chiapas during the thirties from a child's viewpoint in *Balún Canán* (*The Nine Watchmen, 1957).*

Mexican Tango is the English title of Angeles Mastrettas' very successful debut novel *Arrancame la vida* (1949), the story of love and emancipation of a young woman at the side of a politically powerful man. It is set in Puebla, also in the thirties.

Elena Poniatowska (born 1933), committed journalist and author, recounts in *Hasta no verte Jesus mío* (1969) the life of Jesus, who is as old as this century. In her volume of essays *Fuerte es el silencio (Strong is the Silence*) she grapples with the student movement of 1968.

History, the present and the search for a national identity are also the core questions addressed by the novelist Carlos Fuentes (born 1928). With poetic force and a delight in the fabulous, his novels and stories provide gripping insights into the Mexican character: in the semi-autobiographical *La región mas transparente (Landscape in a Clear Light),* the literary thriller *La cabeza de la hidra* (*The Hydra*'s *Head),* the Revolution novel *Gringo viejo* (*The Old Gringo*) and the volumes of short-stories *Chac Mool* and *Agua quemada* (*Burnt Water*).

Juan Rulfo (1918-1986) has laid a milestone in modern literature with only two works. The volume of stories titled *El llano en llamas* (*The Burning Plain*, 1953) and the short novel *Pedro Páramo* offer insightful, sparingly poetic sketches of rural Mexico.

A flavor of the Mexican everyday life also lurks in its crime thrillers. The moloch of Mexico City is the territory of Paco Ignacio Taibo II (born 1949), while provincial Mexico is the backdrop for the novels of Jorge Ibargüengoitia (1928-1984).

Of course, this sort of short overview can hardly be comprehensive, though a very brief sketch of Mexico's literary historical development should be made: The literature of the pre-Columbian high cultures, recording the deeds of its rulers and matters of everyday existence in hieroglyphic form (the *codices)* were destroyed by the Spaniards as "heathen" in origin. Bishop Diego de Landa did a thorough job in Yucatán. Only three *codices* escaped the "book-burning" of 1562; they are now housed in European museums. A historical irony: With his *Re-Relación de las cosas de Yucatán (Report on the Affairs of Yucatán)* a few years later, the bishop became a painstaking chronicler of Mayan customs, even attempting to decipher the hieroglyphs and calendar symbols. The Mayan books *Popol Vuh* and *Chilam Balam* are recordings of text from their oral tradition.

Bernardino de Sahagún created a unique chronicle, which he had illustrated by Aztec artists: *Historia general de las cosas de Nueva España* (*General History of the Events of New Spain*). Sahagún also collected the Aztec's epic songs and translated works of the poet-king Netzahualcóyotl (1402-1472) and his son Netzahualpilli (1484-1515).

Afterward, the Spanish motherland dictated what could or could not be published in the colony for some 300 years. A multitude of realist novels were written following Mexico's independence; then at the end of the last century authors oriented themselves toward fashionable French sources. This was followed by *Modernismo*, which attracted attention with its cosmopolitan themes and the search for new linguistic forms. The Revolution was a critical turning-point: Mariano Azuela, with the socio-critical novel *Los de abajo* (*Those from below*), and Martín Luis Guzmán with *La Sombra del Caudillo* (*The Shadow of the Caudillo*) stood at the threshold of a modern national literature.

FIESTAS

Before they were conquered by the Spaniards, the Indigenas lived in a polytheistic society: They worshipped a multitude of deities, to which they made human sacrifices. Catholicism was forced upon them by the missionaries, but from a distance, there did not seem to be such a great difference between the two systems. The Mayas took the saints to be the white mens' gods. Furthermore, the crucifixion of Jesus, also a "human sacrifice", required no particular new understanding. The pomp of the Catholic church also corresponded to the colorful religious ritual of the high priests and deities. Thus, the acceptance of the new beliefs and a transference onto their traditional "pagan" customs evolved into a symbiosis of the two traditions. The fiestas are based on both Indigena customs and the holidays of the Spaniards.

Above: Colorful scene from a quetzales ceremony in the Sierra de Pueblas.

The festivals of the pre-Columbian era are often thought of as gruesome cults (with the heart-ripping ritual), but they later became more humane and merry. Today they bear, almost without exception, the stamp of Catholicism; only the costumes occasionally hearken back to heathen days. The Spaniards introduced the more entertaining and pleasurable elements: The bullfight or *corrida de toros*, and the *charreadas*, mounted sports similar to the American rodeo. In his novel *Labyrinth of Solitude*, Octavio Paz wrote: "For us, the fiesta is a kind of explosion, an outburst of death and life, jubilation and despair...the solitary Mexican loves them...".

The Ministry of Tourism vaguely indicates the number of festivals at "between five and six thousand", of which 556 are organized regionally and chronologically (see *Fiestas in Mexico*, Editiones Lara). Each town venerates its own saints. There are 27 major festivals celebrated throughout the country, in addition to six national holidays. But that's not enough:

carnaval, *ferias* and a variety of neighborhood celebrations round out the world's most extensive festival calendar.

Only a few of the Indigena tribes living in remote regions, such as the Coras, Huichols, Yaquis, Tzotzils and Tarahumaras in the forbidding Sierra Madre Occidental, have managed to retain a significant degree of authentic (pre-Columbian) originality in their dances, festivals, religious customs and celebrations.

The Tarahumaras' Dance of the Turkey-cock, the *deturburi*, is performed at both their traditional native and Christian festival alike. In Michoacán the *viejito* or Old Man, performed with wooden masks, has survived. The ancient origins of some festivals and dances have been verified by the few codices still in existence, as can the *quetzales*-ceremony in the Sierra de Pueblas (this most extraordinarily colorful of festivals revolves around a brightly decorated wheel 1.5 meters in diameter representing the cosmos, or the *acatlaxqui*, the Otomi Indigenas' "Dance of the Thatchers"). In the state of Guerrero, the Nahua still celebrate the *tlacoloreros* fertility festival.

Other pre-Hispanic festivals have merged into one-another, such as the *Día de los Muertos* of the Aztecs, who revered their dead during the month of *quecholli* (October 20 to November 8). The Tzeltales of Chiapas also venerate the spirits of their departed. In the state of Veracruz, the Dance of the Voladores has retained its original form. The term *voladores* is, of course, Spanish; the Totonacs call it *tocotines*, as they did before the Christians' arrival. Their largest festival, in Papantla, falls on the Catholic holiday of Corpus Christi. The *judea* festival, the Easter Passion play of the Cora Indigenas in Nayarit, was introduced by Jesuit missionaries.

The following chronological festival calendar is supplemented by the travel information boxes at the end of each regions' respective chapter.

January 1st: *Año Nuevo* (New Year's Day), fireworks and lots of music, parades and folk dances; **January 6th**: *Día de Santos Reyes* (Epiphany), Christmas presents are exchanged; **January 18th**: *Fiesta de Santa Prisca* in Taxco, blessing of animals, pilgrimage marches; **February 3rd-7th**: *Carnaval* in La Paz, Veracruz and Mazatlán; **February 5th**: *Aniversario de la Constitución* (Constitution Day); March/April: *Semana Santa* (Easter Week), nationwide processions, candle-light procession in Taxco, Palm Sunday procession in Uruapan, Passion-plays in Ixtapalapa; **from April 17th**: (about 2 weeks) *Feria de San Marcos* in Aguascalientes; **May 5th**: *Día de la Batalla de Puebla* (Day of the Battle of Puebla), parades; **end of May/beginning of June**: *Corpus Christi;* **July 16th**: V*irgen del Carmen* (Holy Virgin), nationwide, flower festival in the Mexico City district of San Angel; **last two Mondays in July**: *Guelaguetza,* dance festival from pre-Columbian days in Oaxaca, sacrificial ceremonies to honor the gods of fertility; **September 15th/16th**: *Día de la Independencia* (Independence Day) with military parades; **end of September** (the Saturday after the *Día de San Miguel*: *Festival de San Miguel Arcangél* in San Miguel de Allende, largest festival of the region with fireworks, fair and bullfights; **October 12th**: *Día de la Raza* (Day of the Races, known as Columbus Day), the Mexicans celebrate the assimilation of Indigenas and Europeans; **November 1st and 2nd**: *Todos los Santos* (All Saints'Day) and *Día de los Muertos* (All Souls' Day); **November 20th**: *Aniversario de la Revolución*; **December 12th**: *Día de Nuestra Señora de Guadalupe* (Virgin of Guadalupe), in Mexico a high ecclesiastical holiday; **from December 16th on**: Family celebrations with *posadas* (processions) and *piñatas* (smashing open paper figures filled with sweets); **Christmas**: *Noche Buena* (December 24th) and *Navidad* (December 25th).

BULLFIGHTS AND MOUNTED GAMES

The Spaniards call it the *fiesta brava*, the bullfight, which was already being held as long ago as 2000 BC on the island of Crete, although without bloodshed at the time. The Mexicans call this gruesome spectacle, which was probably imported to Spain by the Moors, alternately *seda, sangre y sol* (silk, blood and sun), *sombra y sol* (shadows and sun), *lidia de toros* (bullfight) or simply *corrida de toros* (chasing the bull).

It is no sport. Not, at any rate, for the half-ton *toro bravo*, who is selected from among some 50,000 of his species which are raised on more than 150 *ganaderias* (cattle ranches) according to strict standards for death in the arena. For the performers, the *corrida* is a risk-laden ritual, for the majority of the audience an entertaining spectacle and certain death for the bull, with very few exceptions. If he fights particularly "bravely" he can be come an *indultado*. He is allowed to spend the sunset of his life on the pastures, and is used for breeding purposes. Normally, however, his corpse is sold to a butcher shortly after the "fight". Still, compared to the brief and cruel, hormone-filled life bed by most domestic animals, raised in few years to become sausage, steak and hamburgers, the life of a *toro bravo* is not all that bad.

The first bullfight in Mexico took place in 1526. Cortés had returned from an expedition to Honduras and one of his officers tried his hand as a *torero*. In the summer of 1529, a bullfight was held, this time as an organized spectacle, to celebrate the Spaniards' 1521 conquest of the Aztec capital. The first paid bullfighters appeared in 1769, and after the construction of the first arena in Mexico City (1877) many of them became genuine

Right: Taking the bull by the horns at a charreada, the Mexican version of a rodeo.

national heroes. Over the course of time, these *corridas* have been alternately banned and then permitted again. Today, this bloody business in its truest sense attracts millions of spectators annually, among them many tourists, into some 220 arenas (Plaza de Toros in Mexico City holds an audience of 50,000, the largest n the world) and several hundred improvised fighting rings.

As a rule, the show begins at 4:00 pm on the dot, when the *presidente* of the *corrida* gives the awaited signal from his loge. After the *desfile*, or opening parade, six bulls (as a rule) meet their deaths in six fights of each divided into three acts (the *tercios*).

First *tercio*: The *peones*, assistant *matadors,* excite the bulls with a reddish-yellow cloth, the *capa*. In the process, the *torero* observes the animal's behavior to get a grasp of its peculiarities and how dangerous it is. After that, two *picadores* ride in, both of them stabbing the bull twice in the neck with their lances.

2nd *tercio*: The *banderillos* and/or the *matador (=torero)* himself set three pairs of barbed *banderillas* in the bull's neck. The beast has already begun to bleed and is thoroughly excited.

The 3rd *tercio* is the so-called *hora de la verdad,* the moment of truth. The *presidente* signals permission for a kill, after which the bull must be killed within 16 minutes. Now begins the phase of the *pases*, daredevil manoeuvres which must be performed with as much elegance, harmony and perfection as the *torero* can muster. The killing is a ritual and bullfighting aficionados are well aware of the strict rules involved. So it's either honor or shame for the arena-macho, who usually dedicates the death-blow to a woman. The bull is not, as a matter of fact, excited by the red color of the *capa*, but rather by the matador's movements; he's colorblind, in fact. Once the beast has become so weakened that it begins to hang its head, the *suerte de matar* can't be kept in its sheath much longer. The ceremonial killing is done with a sword: A stab between the shoulder blades, perhaps with an added coup de grâce from the *picador's* dagger. The jury rewards the *matador* for his efforts with the ear of the victim, sometimes with both and even the tail as well. There have been fights where the hero also received a severed hoof amid the wild jubilation of his fans.

Ernest Hemingway, a bullfighting enthusiast, wrote in his book *Death in the Afternoon* that there are two kinds of spectator: those who identify with the bull and others with the *matador*. The former take no pleasure in a bullfight. Worldwide appeals for a boycott have remained unsuccessful, however.

On the other hand, Mexican equestrian games are a feast for anyone's eyes. The high art of riding is called *charreada*, a piece of tradition from the days when the major landowners possessing vast herds of livestock were still the country's rulers. The men on horseback are called *charros*, superior riders who have developed the everyday handling of the horse and lasso into an art. It would be an insult to call them cowboys, and thus rodeos are also quite different from *charreadas*. The *charros* were an elite cadre among the cattle-drovers, and in their free time they honed their skill at horse-training, lasso tricks and handling a branding iron. They formed the core of the cavalry during Mexico's wars, but after the Revolution many of the cattle ranchers' holdings were expropriated. The cattlemen then took their "redundant" art and turned it into a lucrative business: They went to the city and entertained the people with their performances, which developed into a true national sport with a great number of variations and a firm set of regulations.

On Sundays, the *lienzo charros* are full to bursting, and the riders in their sumptuous tailor-made costumes have long since formed unions, just as the *voladores* have. Today there are even women performing the graceful mounted game *escaramuza charra*, riding side-saddle.

VOLADORES: THE FLYING MEN

When the tourists come streaming into the Plaza de la Pirámide in Acapulco for a nerve-tingling "show", only a few of them are aware that the *danza del volador* is among the oldest rituals in the western hemisphere. Since the early 1950s, the daring acts of the *voladores* have been steadily reduced – or should one say expanded into – to a spectator bit of show-business only.

Five men in traditional costume ascend a pillar, that stands at anywhere between 20 and 25 meters, and on the top of which is a round platform with a maximum diameter of 70 centimeters that can be rotated on an axle. Just beneath it hangs a wooden framework upon which four men seat themselves, each fastening a rope around his hips. The fifth man then ventures up to the platform and plays a

Above and right: Once a ritual act, the Dance of the Voladores is today no more than a tourist attraction.

flute, standing, while simultaneously beating on a drum. As he does so he bows to all four points of the compass. The other four men, hanging upside-down from the rope, let themselves glide down into the "abyss". By swinging his hips, the *caporal* on the platform causes the little platform to rotate, the ropes unwrap from the axle and the other four daring participants float down toward the ground in spirals. After exactly 13 rotations they touch down together, running in a forced circle while braking the rotary motion. Now sitting, the *caporal* ends his playing on the three-holed *puscol* and clambers back down the pillar.

Apparently, this fascinating ritual originated around 500 AD and was a fertility ceremony worshipping the god Xipe Totec, in the central regions of the modern-day state of Veracruz. To this day, the town of Papantla (in Veracruz), nearby the ruin-city of El Tajin, is considered the home of the *voladores* from the Totonac tribe. Over the course of time this ceremony spread throughout Meso-America.

In its original significance and execution, this ceremony is so complex and regionally differentiated that no single interpretation is even possible. In the course of its 1400- year-history it has experienced constant innovations, undergoing further influences in the wider world, with its multiplicity of deities.

Ever since the arrival of the conquistadors, the symbolism of the Dance of the Voladores has been the subject of speculation and differences in opinion. One widely accepted interpretation suggests that the man on the upper platform represents the sun; and the pillar the tree of life. The four "flying men" represent the rebirth of warriors and sacrifice victims, who float to the earth as birds, pay homage to the gods and ask the sun for its blessings. Their synchronous hovering symbolizes the unity between humanity and the cosmos. Four *voladores* and 13 revolutions yield the magical number 52, a completed cycle in the Aztec calendar, and indeed a complete year of weeks for Europeans.

The ceremony is a portrayal of a living myth, the symbolic answer to the eternal question of humanity's meaning and place in the history of creation. The conquistadors and their clergy never respected or grasped the symbolic character of this basic conception of the Indigenas' religion, with the result that this "heathen" custom was able to survive. Just as do the majority of tourists, they viewed it as more of an acrobatic stunt, although with veiled skepticism. But the Christians made concessions because they needed the Totonacs in an alliance against the Aztecs. The "flying men" responded by having one of their number hover to the ground with long hair as a tribute to Cortés and his native mistress Malinche.

The *voladores* have been organized for quite some time now. The *Union de Danzantes de la Región de Papantla* consists of twelve groups that go on tour and can be hired for private occasions, though they take care not to cross the inviolable territories of rival groups.

MACHISMO

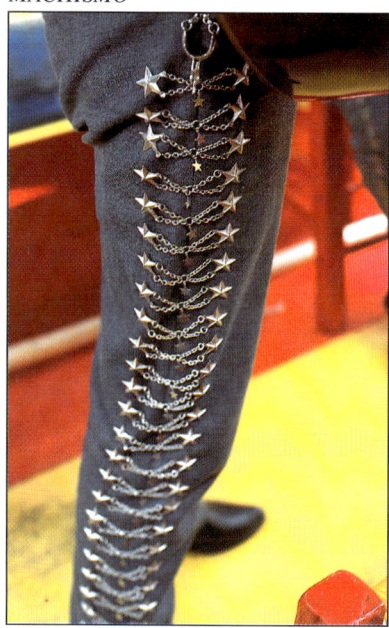

MACHISMO

In the archives of the Mexican Revolution, a photograph is kept of a group of revolutionary fighters heading off to some battle or other. They are proud and solemn, with double-rowed ammunition belts slung crosswise over their chests and their impressive hats, which protect them from the sun and cast a shadow over their eyes in such a way that they are invisible to the camera. They look as though they are all wearing black blindfolds, but their posture is such that they seem to know exactly where they are going nonetheless.

Running beside them are their women, veiled and loaded with baskets, laundry and provisions. With less protection, they march toward the same fate, accompanying the men and providing them refuge,

Above: Clothes make the man. Right: Particularly in the poorer classes it is the woman who bears the entire responsibility for keeping house and raising the children.

nourishing and comforting them. Naturally, things have changed since then. Women who live in cities often do not need a man to support them financially. They dedicate themselves with passion and success to politics, art, finance or medicine; they travel, handling their love-life freely and without inhibition; they socialize in locales where they were previously barred entrance, walking on the street any time of day or night without needing a dog, an attendant or a husband; they have no fear at the thought of living alone; contraception is a matter of course in spite of the ubiquitous Catholic church, and they consistently and unashamedly demand that their partner help with the everyday care of their children and households; they read and discuss with more élan than the men, and they converse with a freedom of thought and lack of inhibition that their grandmothers could only have dreamed of, or might even consider heresy.

Women who live in the countryside occasionally summon up the strength to set off with little more than their visions. They arrive in the cities full of hope, burning from within like a fire, as well as fear which they lay aside with their old shoes the moment they buy a new pair with their first pay. And many have the will and skill to succeed on their own. They are almost always quite young women, ready to do just about any work that liberates them from paternal authority and high-handedness; women who've had enough of grinding the corn and baking the tortillas, bearing children until their bodies fall apart and putting up with beatings and abuse.

This new attitude is based on a firm determination to reject the ostentatious masculinity and subjugation of women for which Mexico was once so renowned. Certainly, there have always been courageous and valiant women in this country, only earlier their heroism consisted more of extraordinary patience than rebelliousness, and not so much the enjoyment of their own freedom as in a sense of familial duty.

The demand for attention and nurture is perhaps the most prominent characteristic of Mexican machismo, which, considered from the other side, also makes these men vulnerable. Their supposed power was illusory, based on the servitude of women. To break the spell, it is quite sufficient to simply leave them; something the women have begun to do with little sense of guilt. After all, the more independent they are, the more they get an education and income of their own, then the more freely they are able to decide whether they love men or despise them. The second variety of machismo is the way women are treated as domestic animals – shouted at and often beaten – something not unknown in Europe and the other continents. Ever increasing numbers of women are denouncing such arbitrary acts, refusing mutely to suffer them any longer. 80 years have passed since that archive photograph was taken. Women are still standing by as their husbands go on benders, taking care of the drunkards and listening to their promises. But they no longer adapt their lives to the demands and loud-mouthed abuse of their menfolk although they still bemoan their infidelities and beseech their faithfulness. Perhaps it is here that we see the most pronounced transformation: The women of today have their own fields of activity, and there are ever more of them who march to their own drummer towards higher and more distant goals than those which the blinkered males of the species still stubbornly pursue. The women of today are no longer willing to leave their fate to the mercy of mens' unpredictable whims. They aren't even bothering to find out whether or not they even *live* in a macho society. Only recently have they realized the dream that had previously existed only in the mind of that woman on the yellowed photo, her body laden with baskets: In order to have a man, one need not follow meekly in his footsteps.

"VIVA LA MUERTE!"

It is indeed an odd cry, "Long Live Death!" – not only for its apparent contradiction, but also for city-dwelling Europeans and *gringos,* who do all they can to never think that every breath taken is a step closer to the grave. In Mexico, death is not a taboo – it is a part of life. In his essay *Labyrinth of Solitude*, Octavio Paz wrote: "For a Parisian, a New Yorker or Londoner, death is a word that one avoids because it singes the lips. In contrast, the Mexican seeks, fondles and teases and celebrates it; it is his favorite plaything and most faithful mistress..."

Death confronts us everywhere: in painting, literature, folk-songs and in everyday life. Death is the faithful companion of Mexican history, eradicating the Indigena culture, decimating society during the War of Independence, carrying off over a million Mexicans during the Civil War. It takes on great importance toward the end of October, when all of Mexico makes preparations for one of its most profoundly traditional festivals, the *día de los muertos* (All Souls' Day) on the 2nd of November.

For the non-Mexican, it can be disconcerting to encounter "death" on every corner, weeks before the festival, in most parts of the country. Colorfully decorated skulls of clay, plastic or paper maché grin out of display windows, skeletons swing merrily next to shop entrances, and department stores and stationery shops sell everything that could possibly be made in the form of a skull, skeleton or coffin: ashtrays, candle-holders, key rings and even costume jewelry.

Not to mention the *calaveras* at the bakeries. These brightly decorated skulls are little popular sweets that one presents to friends and children, often inscribed with the name of the recipient.

Right: Death, the inevitable part of life, holds no terrors for the Mexican.

Macabre! The origins of this special relationship with death go back long before christianization. As for many so-called "primitive" peoples, death was a natural continuation of life. Life and death were inseparably bound up with each other, an eternal cycle in which destruction must precede any rebirth. This dualism was one of the fundamental aspects of pre-Columbian belief.

In the Aztec world, life, with its inconsistencies and uncertainty, was more ominous than physical death. "Death is not the horror of this world, rather it is Tezcatlipoca (the god of calamities): the awareness that man can never be ruler of his fate." (Paul Westheim in *Death in Mexico*). This pagan belief has long since merged with Christian faith, creating a typically Mexican synthesis. Admittedly, death is no longer perceived as life-creating, but it no longer spreads the terror of purgatory and hell that it did at the time of christianization.

The festival to honor the dead, on November 1 and 2, demonstrates just how much of the Indigenas' spiritual heritage is still alive. These are the days and nights on which, according to folk-beliefs, the dead return to the earth to visit their relatives. It's customary, if not actually compulsory, to serve them their favorite meal and try to make their brief visit to this world as pleasant as possible. On October 30 and 31, the cemeteries are jumping with activity. The sometimes bombastic gravestones of the well-to-do receive a fresh coat of paint, just as do the Indigenas' plain wooden crosses. Bakers prepare the traditional "bread of the dead" (*pan de los muertos*) of sweetened dough, usually in the shape of bones; candles of every color and variety are hand-dipped, and the markets are one big sea of flowers. The *cempoalxúchitl* (flowers for the dead) are planted as early as June to make sure they are ready for this occasion. For the visitors from the other side, their relatives set up little

VIVA LA MUERTE

sacrificial tables on which, in the night before November 1, the *ofrendas* are laid out. Mountains of crisp *tortillas* tower next to pyramids of fruit, alongside them are bowls with *tamales, mole or atole* (a maize beverage).

Of course, there are also cigarettes, a glass of water and – hardly surprising – a ration of *tequila, mescal* or *pox*. Or perhaps Coca Cola, a drink that almost has cult status among the descendants of the Mayas.

The atmosphere is enhanced with candles and *copal* (incense). The sacrificial offerings represent the four elements of earth, water, fire and air. In front of houses and cottages, maize-stalks and flowers are woven into elaborate archways. A trail of yellow flowers leads from the grave of the deceased directly to the sacrificial table," so that they can find their way, since yellow is the only color the dead can recognize". At the same time these blossoms symbolize the sun, which is still (alongside Christ) the all-prevailing principle of life.

The customs vary from region to region. In some places the "guests" are welcomed home and then accompanied back to the cemetery later on; in others the families move right into the graveyards along with their offerings, spending the night from November 1 to 2 at the graveside. After the visitor from beyond has "eaten and drunk his fill", and has returned to the kingdom of the dead for another year, the family members and sometimes the entire village gathers together to eat up all the delicacies.

The most famous of these ceremonies is the *Día de los Muertes* in ritualistic Mixquic to the south of Mexico City and on the island of Janítzio on Lake Pátzcuaro (Michoacán). In more recent times, however, both towns now teem with tourists on these days; even the Festival of the Dead has fallen victim to tourism. In the smaller villages, especially in areas with a predominantly Indigena population, strangers are not exactly welcome. Unless they are *amigos* and not armed with cameras and flashbulbs...

SOCIAL CONFLICTS

SOCIAL CONFLICTS

Politics: In 1929, the predecessor of the PRI (Partido Revolucionario Institucional) was established by President Elías Calles, and with it, for all practical purposes, the one-party state. For 60 years, this Party of the Institutionalized Revolution has been in power, producing all of Mexico's presidents as well. Re-election may not be permitted, but the president determines his successor.

It's a widely-known secret that the head of state enriches himself and his own in no small measure during his six year term in office. First of all, he lines up lucrative positions in business and the state administration for himself, his relatives and friends. In turn, these people replace further occupants of high positions with their friends and fellow party members. They all try to pile up as much

Above: Rather than begging the Mexican will resort to the humblest activities to earn the pesos he needs to live on.

money and influence on the side as they possibly can in the time left to them.

Ex-President De la Madrid, who financed his 1982 PRI candidacy with $US 100 million and began his term with calls for a moral renewal and the fight against corruption, had a private fortune of $US 162 million at his disposal after leaving his office. The economy of corruption reaches its summit with the state-operated oil company PEMEX: In 1983 alone, oil "trickled away" into oblivion to the tune of $US 15 billion.

Among the general population these practices have slowly begun to provoke criticism and resistance. When discontent became evident in the gubernatorial and mayoral elections, the party responded by spoiling the ballot-papers. Riots broke out. Cuauhtémoc Cárdenas, the son of Lázaro Cárdenas, resigned from the PRI. In the elections of 1988, the party of Salinas de Gortari – the only president who couldn't be accused of abusing his office – won only 50,74 percent of the votes. As for 1994, for the first time, the assumption of the president's office by a PRI man is no longer a certainty.

Church and State: 95 percent of the Mexican population belong to the Roman Catholic Church. Benito Juárez' 1867 reform legislation established the separation of church and state, with this principle enshrined in law. However, conflicts of interest have arisen time and again due to the population's profound religious faith. All family planning programs have repeatedly been foiled due to the extremely powerful influence of the Catholic Church.

Although the government perceives the clergy as the successor to colonial rule – politically conservative and opposed to each and every change – it has had to learn to cope with them. This has resulted in the toleration of numerous constitutionally-banned religious holidays, the continuing existence of private parish schools, and, in 1976, the state treasury even had to finance the new Basilica of Guadalupe's construction.

Indigenas: 10 to 15 percent of the population (in other words eight to ten million Mexicans) are Indigenas. At the end of the Revolution they still composed over a third of the population. Right up to the present day, the number of Mexico's original inhabitants has continued to decline. Official sources talk of a higher rate of growth among the Mestizo population as well as the Indigenas' "wish to be assimilated" in the dominant population group as being one of the main reasons for this. But this decline also has other causes. The indigenous ethnic groups form the lowest class in Mexican society. As a result of expropriations and dam construction they have lost a large part of their communal farmlands, and this for a people who have virtually always survived from agriculture. What remained to them were useless lands, either in dried-up regions, on steep slopes or in the subtropical jungle. Most of them just manage to eke out a scanty living at a subsistence level. Infection and tropical diseases are aggravated by undernourishment, child mortality rate is high, and life expectancy is lower than that of the *mestizos*. Even an autonomous Indigenas' Institute (INI) hasn't been able to muster much more than souvenir workshops and sales outlets, despite the plans of founder Alfonso Caso. Thus it's really no surprise that increasing numbers of young Indigenas renounce their own culture and, by taking on the mestizos' clothing and life-styles, try to demonstrate at least externally their membership of the supposedly superior group.

Unemployment: 20 percent of the population is unemployed, with another 30 percent underemployed. On top of this, each year some 800,000 young people flood on to the job market, which only has 100,000 vacancies. It is no wonder that many of them try to find work across the border in the USA, passing through the so-called Tortilla Curtain illegally. Roughly five million are already working there, the majority of them as *braceros* (day-laborers). Attempts by state agencies to solve the problem have foundered. Even a 1986 amnesty program for Mexican foreign workers living in the USA without papers failed to induce them to crawl out of clandestinity.

Since economic progress is concentrated in its major cities and industrial centers, Mexico has long suffered from a heavy rural exodus. Slums expand around the edges of the cities, where people are living without water, electricity or sanitary facilities. Settlements are even developing at the garbage dumps, as their inhabitants try to live from recycling the metropolitan refuse. The primary causes of this misery are found in the inadequately executed land reforms, which result in a few large landowners on the one hand and a growing number of landless farmers, who are then forced to try to find a new life in the big city or the other, a perennial Mexican problem.

NELLES MAPS / NELLES ROAD ATLASES

Nelles Maps ...the maps that get you going.

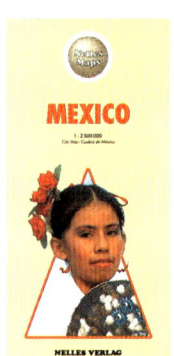

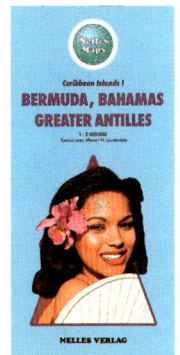

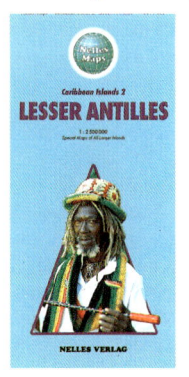

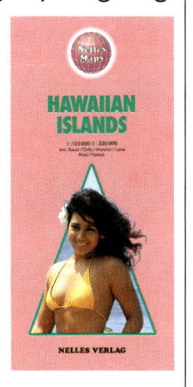

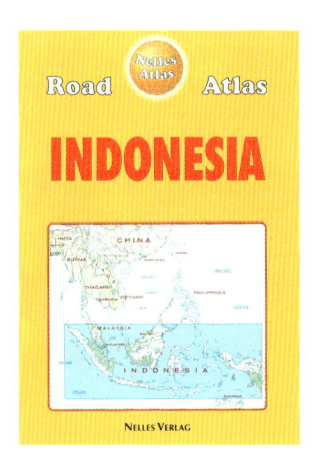

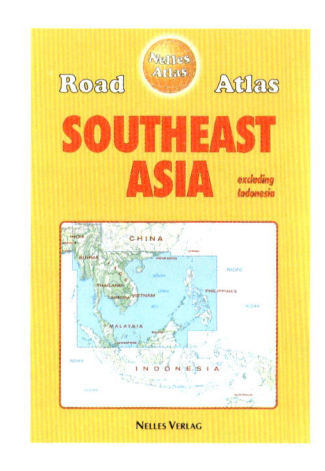

- Afghanistan
- Australia
- Bangkok
- Burma
- Caribbean Islands 1 / Bermuda, Bahamas, Greater Antilles
- Caribbean Islands 2 / Lesser Antilles
- China 1 / North-Eastern China
- China 2 / Northern China
- China 3 / Central China
- China 4 / Southern China
- Crete
- Egypt
- Hawaiian Islands
- Hawaiian Islands 1 / Kauai
- Hawaiian Islands 2 / Honolulu, Oahu

Nelles Maps

- Hawaiian Islands 3 / Maui, Molokai, Lanai
- Hawaiian Islands 4 / Hawaii
- Himalaya
- Hong Kong
- Indian Subcontinent
- India 1 / Northern India
- India 2 / Western India
- India 3 / Eastern India
- India 4 / Southern India
- India 5 / North-Eastern India
- Indonesia
- Indonesia 1 / Sumatra
- Indonesia 2 / Java + Nusa Tenggara
- Indonesia 3 / Bali
- Indonesia 4 / Kalimantan
- Indonesia 5 / Java + Bali
- Indonesia 6 / Sulawesi

- Indonesia 7 / Irian Jaya + Maluku
- Jakarta
- Japan
- Kenya
- Korea
- Malaysia
- West Malaysia
- Manila
- Mexico
- Nepal
- New Zealand
- Pakistan
- Philippines
- Singapore
- South East Asia
- Sri Lanka
- Taiwan
- Thailand
- Vietnam, Laos Cambodia

GUIDELINES

Travel Preparations 238
   Location / Climate / Travel Seasons 238
   Clothing 238
   Currency / Exchange / Foreign Money 239
   Immigration Conditions 239
   Health Precautions 239
Getting to Mexico 239
   By Air 239
   Departures 240
   By Ship 240
Travel within Mexico 240
   Buses 240
   Railroads 241
   By Air 242
   By Car 243
   Rental Cars 243
   Ferries 244
   Tours 244
Practical Tips 244
   Accomodation 244
   Banks 244
   Business Hours 244
   Customs 244
   Doctors 245
   Drinking Water 245
   Electricity 245
   Holidays and Festivals 245
   Illegal Drugs 245
   Mordidas 246
   Mosquitoes 246
   Museums and Art Galleries 246
   Pharmacies / Chemists 246
   Photography 246
   Press 247
   Radio and Television 247
   Rules for Behavior 247
   Shopping 247
   Telecommunications 248
   Time 248
   Tipping 248
   Tourist Information 248
   Weights and Measures 248
Language Guide 248
Authors / Photographers 250
Index 252

GUIDELINES

TRAVEL PREPARATIONS

Location / Climate / Travel Seasons

Mexico is composed of 31 states (*Estados Unidos Mejicanos*) and the Federal District (*Distrido Federal* or *D.F.*). This third-largest country in Latin America, with an area of nearly two million sq. km., has a population of over 70 million, of which about one-quarter live in Mexico City, the capital.

The land extends between Latitude 32 to 14 north, and Longitude 86 to 12 west. Its common border with the United States is 2597 km in length, and it also has frontiers to the southeast with Guatemala and Belize. The distance between these borders is roughly 6500 kilometers. At its narrowest point, at the Isthmus of Tehuantepec, Mexico is only 210 km wide. Its natural borders are the Gulf of Mexico and the Caribbean Sea (2611 km) and the Pacific Ocean (7427 km).

Due to the country's geographical situation between two oceans and its large altitude differences (two-thirds of the area consists of highlands between 1000 m and 2500 m altitude), its climatic zones vary drastically. They are roughly distinguished as the:

1. *Tierra caliente* (the hot regions up to 800 m), with an average annual temperature of over 25°C and high relative humidity (Tabasco, Yucatán, Chiapas, Quintana Roo);

2. *Tierra templada* (the temperate regions between 800 m and 1500 m), average annual temperature 18°C-22°C (the majority of the states, although they also have extremes);

3. *Tierra fria* (cold regions over 1800 m.), average annual temperature 15°C, cold winters, pleasantly warm in summer, great temperature differences between day and night (Mexico City and Chiapas, for example).

The rainy season occurs from the months of May/June until September/October, depending on altitude.

Mexico is a year-round travel destination, although along the coastal regions and in Yucatán winter is preferable.

Clothing

When you are packing your bags you shouldn't think only about the travel season, but also have a clear idea as to what altitudes your journey will take you.

Even in the middle altitudes it can get quite cold on winter evenings. It's a good idea to always take along some kind of raincoat on outings, since during the rainy season cloudburst can start at any time.

In general, light cotton clothing is advisable, while for the evenings a light sweater is not a bad idea. In the vacation towns (particularly in the coastal regions) it is quite normal to wear a short-sleeved shirt without a jacket, even in the better restaurants and hotels, whereas in Mexico City and other major cities this is not always appropriate. Official occasions and business dinners require the proper attire. In the hotter coastal regions, however, precious little attention is paid to "etiquette" in this matter – even important government officials may well appear at dinner in shirt-sleeves.

In the tourist-oriented hotel areas on the coasts (especially in Acapulco and Cancún) dress code is very informal though unfortunately it may offend the morals of the Mexican population. At private hotel beaches and their swimming pools, going topless is certainly tolerated, although it is elsewhere considered offensive. Nudism is forbidden throughout the country, but the guardians of public order have been known to turn a blind eye to it at a few thoroughly secluded beaches. On trips through the interior, particularly in regions with Indigenas populations, even shorts on men are viewed as bordering the indecent – a Mexican *never* wears shorts! On visits to religious buildings, women in particular should give attention to wearing conservative, modest attire.

GUIDELINES

Immigration Conditions

Travelers must have a passport that is valid for at least six more months. The "tourist card" required for stays of 90 days maximum is available at travel agencies, at the airport, on the aircraft, on arrival, or they can be obtained through the Mexican Consulate or state-operated Mexican tourist offices. Visitors from certain countries need visas, or even special clearance which can take up to three months. Check early with the Mexican Consulate. The "tourist card" (original and copy) must be canceled upon entering the country. The original is valid for entry, the copy for departing Mexico (keep it in a safe place!). Prolonging the "tourist card" is a both complicated and tedious procedure.

Currency / Exchange / Foreign Money

The Mexican unit of currency is the *peso* (or Mexican dollar). 1 peso = 100 *centavos*. There are bills in circulation in denominations of 500, 1000, 5000, 10.000, 20.000 and 50.000 pesos as well as coins of 1, 5, 10, 20, 50, 100, 200, 500, 1000 and 5000 pesos.

A recommendation: Take US$ in cash and/or US travelers' checks. Also, one can get into trouble without a credit card.

Generally speaking, all leading credit cards are accepted, although acceptance of American Express is on the way out, and a large number of hotels and shops greet them with a frown or simply refuse them altogether. Of course, they *do* have the advantage that one also can get cash with them in a few major cities. Visa, Eurocard-MasterCard and Diners Club are welcome everywhere. US$ can be exchanged for *pesos* in almost any hotel, but this is, of course, more expensive than at most banks and change-booths (*casa de cambio*). Exchanging other currencies is possible at only a few banks and usually involves a lengthy procedure. Caution: Larger hotels in the tourist centers also accept European currencies, but they ring up a commission for themselves of as much as 20 percent! Inflation is also constantly eating at the value of the peso.

As concerns foreign exchange, at present there are no regulations for foreigners; its import and export is unlimited. From time to time there are limitations on the handling of foreign currencies imposed on Mexicans, when a rather unpredictable black market develops, though the rate differences are not particularly notable.

Health Precautions

Vaccinations are not required, although a malaria injection is recommended for the tropical regions. The best treatments for "Moctezuma's revenge" (severe diarrhea) are *Kaomicyn* (with antibiotic) or *Kaopectate* (without antibiotic) as well as *Imodium*. With *Lomotil* (non-prescription in Mexico) it is possible to cure the illness at its onset. This digestive tract complaint, which is also called *turista* in the countries of Central America, can also be treated with a very simple-folk remedy: Eat watermelon and thoroughly chew the seeds. To counteract fluid losses caused by the disorder, accompanied by salt depletion, eat lots of (well-washed) fruit and drink a lot. Also, salt tablets can be obtained in any pharmacy before departure. The first symptom of salt deficiency is a headache.

GETTING TO MEXICO

By Air

Scheduled airline flights from Europe many of them non-stop to Mexico, are available from Aeroméxico, Air France, American Airlines, Continental Airlines, Delta Airlines, British Airways, Iberia, KLM, Lufthansa, TAESA and United Airlines. Visitors from Australia and New Zealand can benefit from numerous services operating from the USA.

239

GUIDELINES

Departures

On domestic flights an airport tax of Mex.$ 17,000 is charged (outbound and return flight), for international flights $US 12 (Current as this edition went to press in August 1992).

By Ship

With the age of the container ship the choice of ocean passages via freighter has decreased sharply. Nonetheless, there are still freighters bound for Veracruz from Antwerp, Rotterdam, Kiel, Hamburg and Bremen; these often dock in a number of harbors in the Caribbean Sea on the way to Mexico, taking a maximum of 12 passengers. The journeys take a long time and are comparatively expensive but certainly appealing.

Mexico itineraries are often incorporated into larger sea-cruise programs. Depending on the tour organizer, the following ports may be visited: the Yucatán coast on the Caribbean Sea with stops in Cancún or Cozumel as well as the Pacific coast. On several of the cruises both coasts are included (crossing the Panama Canal). In addition, certain of the world tours make calls to Mexican ports.

TRAVEL WITHIN MEXICO

Buses

A multitude of companies serve a dense route system. Due to the resulting tough competition it's worth doing some shopping around before departure.

Longer journeys should be taken with the *Rapidos* (first class). With these the principle of first-come, first-served applies (always with seat reservations). For travel during Easter week and during the Christmas vacation period secure your tickets long in advance. The buses are cheap (500 kilometers cost about US$ 24), comfortable, clean, have a lavatory and depart punctually as a rule. The personnel, both on the bus and in the *terminales*, are friendly and helpful. Warning: Pay attention to your luggage particularly during nighttime trips, and keep valuables and your passport on your lap, not between your legs.

When departing from Mexico City, be sure to check which bus terminal you want; in other towns they are almost always centrally located.

In Mexico City the four largest and most important bus stations are situated on the city's periphery. Their location corresponds to the direction of travel. Tickets must be purchased at the terminal, and there's no point in even bothering with telephone inquiries unless you speak fluent Spanish.

Toward the North, Northwest and Northeast: Bus Terminal North (*Terminal Central del Norte*), Ave. Cien Metros 4907 (by bus from Insurgentes Metro Plaza), Tel.: 587-1552. *Transportes Norte de Sonora* (Tel.: 567-9664 & 587-5633): Primary route Guadalajara-Nogales-Mexicali-Tijuana and buses to Cananea, Agua Prieta, Morelia, Uruapan, Puerto Vallarta, Manzanillo, Hermisillo, Ciudad Obregón, Ensenada. *Autobuses Estrella Blanca* (Tel.: 587-9219): Aguascalientes, Ciudad Juárez, Ciudad Reynosa, Ciudad Victoria, Chihuahua, Durango, Guadalajara, León, Matamoros, Matehuala, Mazatlán, Monterrey, Morelia, Nuevo Laredo, Poza Rica, Puerto Vallarta, San Juan de los Lagos, San Luis Potosí, Tampico, Torreón. *Tres Estrellas de Oro* (Tel.: 567-8426 & 567-8145): Primary route Querétaro-Guadalajara-Mazatlán-Tijuana and busses to Irapuato, Morelia, Zamora, León, San Juan de los Lagos, Puerto Vallarta, Culiacán, Ciudad Obregón, Mexicali, Reynosa, Matamoros, Celaya, Loredo, Monterrey, San Luis Potosí, Guanajuato, Uruapan, Ciudad Victoria, Manzanillo, Colima, Ensenada, Hermosillo, San Miguel de Allende, Dolores Hidalgo. *Transportes del Norte* (Tel.: 587-5400 & 587-5511); Tickets in the city office, Insurgentes Centro 137,

Tel.: 546-0032: Ciudad Valles, Ciudad Victoria, Durango, Laredo to Texas; Matamoros, Monterrey, Nuevo Laredo, Querétaro, Reynosa, Saltillo, San Luis Potosí, Torreón. *Omnibus de México* (Tel.: 567-7698 & 567-6756): Aguascalientes, Celaya, Ciudad Juárez, Ciudad Mante, Reynosa, Ciudad Valles, Colima, Chihuahua, Durango, Guadalajara, Irapuato, León, Matamoros, Ojinaga, Pozo Rica, Parral, Querétaro, San Luis Potosí, San Miguel de Allende, Tampico, Tepic, Torreón, Tuxpan, Zacatecas. THC *Transportes Chihuahuenses* TCH (Tel.: 587-5377 & 587-5355): Aguascalientes, Ciudad Juárez, Chihuahua, Durango, El Paso to Texas; Guadalajara, León, Parral, Querétaro, San Luis Potosí, Torreón, Zacatecas. ADO *Autobuses de Oriente* (Tel.: 567-8455): Alamo, Cerro Azul, Reynosa, Gutiérrez Zamora, Huachinango, Huejutla, Matamoros, Naranjos, Oaxaca, Pachuca, Pánuco, Papantla, Potrero, Poza Rica, Puebla, Tampico, Tantoluca, Tempoal, Tuxpan, Villa Juárez.

To the Southeast and Southwest: Bus Terminal East (*Terminal Central del Oriente*), Calzada Ignacio Zaragoza 200 (Metrostation San Lázaro), Tel.: 542-1582. ADO *Autobuses de Oriente* (Tel.: 542-7192-98): Agua Dulce, Campeche, Cancún, Ciudad del Carmen, Ciudad Chetumal, Ciudad Pemex, Coatepec, Coatzacoalcos, Córdoba, Cosamaloapan, Jalapa, Loma Bonita, Mérida, Minatitlán, Nautla, Oaxaca, Palenque, Puerto Ceiba, Tehuacán, Teziutlán, Veracruz, Villahermosa, Villa Isla. *Omnibus Cristóbal Colón* (Tel.: 542-7263/66): Acatlán, Ciudad Cuauhtémoc (Guatemalan border), Ciudad Ixtepec, Cuautla, Oaxaca, Salina Cruz, San Cristóbal da las Casas, Talismán, Tapachula, Tehuantepec, Tuxtla Gutiérrez.

To the South: Bus Terminal South (*Terminal Central del Sur*) Ave. Taxqueña 1320 (Metro station Taxqueña), Tel.: 532-0280. EDO *Estrella de Oro* (Tel.: 549-8520/29): Acapulco, Ciudad Lázaro Cárdenas, Chilpancingo, Cuernavaca, Iguala, Taxco, Zihuatanejo. *Líneas Unidas del Sur Flecha Roja* (Tel.: 672-3223), first class service to all destinations: Acapulco, Chilpancingo, Ciudad Lázaro, Cárdenas, Cuernavaca, Grutas de Cacahuamilpa, Iguala, Ixtapan de la Sal, Las Estacas, Puerto Escondido, Taxco, Tehuixtla, Zihuatanejo.

Bus Terminal West (*Terminal Central del Poniente*): Rio Tacubaya/ Ave. Sur 122 (Metrostation Observatorio), Tel.: 567-7131.

To a great extent, all the destinations served are the same as those of the Bus Terminal North, primarily to Morelia, Toluca, Guadalajara and Manzanillo as well as a great many smaller towns along the route or with transfers.

Turismo y Autobuses México-Toluca (Tel: 271-1433 and 277-2746) serves the route to Toluca exclusively.

Note: It is possible to make seat reservations for a service charge through the travel agency *Central de Autobuses* in Mexico City, Calle Londres 161 (Zona Rosa), Tel.: 533-2047/49); tickets are even delivered to the hotels.

Railroads

Mexico has about 24,000 kilometers of railroad lines. However, travel with the state-owned *Ferrocarriles Nacionales de México* requires a great deal of time, the trains are uncomfortable and frequently unpunctual though they are very reasonably priced. There is also frequently a very long wait when transferring from one train to the next. If you want to save hotel costs it's worth making overnight journeys by a sleeper-car (single and double compartments).

In Mexico City, the trains depart from the Buenavista Station; information can be obtained at Ave. Central 140, Tel.: 547-1084. Sleeper car reservations between Mexico City and Veracruz (9 1/2 hours), Oaxaca (15 hours), Palenque (26

GUIDELINES

hours) and Mérida (37 hours!): Chief Passenger Traffic Department, Buenavista Station, Tel.: 547-8971. Information on trains of the *Ferrocarril del Pacífico* between Nogales and Guadalajara: Mexico City, Ave. Jesús Garcia 140, Tel.: 547-6939; Guadalajara, Calle Tolsá 336, Tel.: 25-7984; Nogales, at the station, Tel.: 2-1680. Information on the *Ferrocarril de Chihuahua al Pacífico* ("Copper Canyon Express") between Los Mochis and Chihuahua: Mexico City, Ave. Jesús Garcia 140, 6th floor/Building C, Tel.: 541-5325, Chihuahua, Mendez/Calle 24, Tel.: 12-2284; in Los Mochis at the station and in the Hotel Santa Anita.

By Air

The local airlines (*Líneas Aéreas*), maintaining offices in their destination areas are: **Areocalifornia**, Aguascalientes, Tel.: 7-2153; Ciudad Constitucíon, Tel.: 2-1211; Colima, Tel.: 4-4850; Culiacán, Tel.: 16-0211; Guadalajara, Tel.: 26-1901; La Paz, Tel.: 2-1113; Loreto, Tel.: 3-0500; Los Cabos, Tel.: 3-0827; Los Mochis, Tel.: 5-2250; Mazatlán, Tel.: 83-2041; Mexico City, Tel: 207-1392; Puebla, Tel.: 32-0377; Puerto Vallarta, Tel.: 1-1444; Tijuana, Tel.: 34-1720. **Aerocancún**, Cancún, Tel.: 3-2144. **Aerocaribe-Cozumel**, Cancún, Tel.: 4-2111; Ciudad del Carmen, Tel.: 2-1203; Cozumel, Tel.: 2-0503; Chetumal, Tel.: 2-6675; Mérida, Tel.: 23-0002; Mexico City, Tel.: 660-4444; Minatitlán, Tel.: 2-9575; Oaxaca, Tel.: 5-9324; Tapachula, Tel.: 6-3245; Tuxtla Gtz., Tel.: 2-2032; Veracruz, Tel.: 35-0568; Villahermosa, Tel.: 4-3202. **Aeromar**, Ciudad Victoria, Tel.: 2-4511; Guadalajara, Tel.: 26-4656; Lázaro Cárdenas, Tel.: 2-2994; Mexico City, Tel.: 207-6666; Monterrey, Tel.: 44-6345; Morelia, Tel.: 2-8545; San Luis Potosí, Tel.: 17-7936; Tepic, Tel.: 3-5175; Uruapan, Tel.: 3-5050. **Aeromexico**, Acapulco, Tel.: 85-1625; Aguascalientes, Tel.: 17-0252; Huatulco, Tel.: 4-0328; Campeche, Tel.: 6-6656; Cancún, Tel.: 4-1186; Ciudad Juárez, Tel.: 13-8719; Ciudad Obregón, Tel.: 3-2190; Culiacán, Tel.: 15-3772; Chihuahua, Tel.: 15-6303; Durango, Tel.: 1-2813; Guadalajara, Tel.: 15-6565; Guayamas, Tel.: 2-0123; Hermosillo, Tel.: 16-8206; La Paz, Tel.:2-0091; León, Tel.: 16-6226; Los Mochis, Tel.: 5-2570; Manzanillo, Tel.: 2-1267; Matamoros, Tel.: 3-0701; Mazatlán, Tel.: 84-1111; Mérida, Tel.: 27-9000; Mexico City, Tel.: 207-8233; Monterrey, Tel.: 40-0617; Oaxaca, Tel.: 6-7101; Puebla, Tel.: 32-0013; Puerto Vallarta, Tel.: 1-1055; Reynosa, Tel.: 2-1115; Tapachula, Tel.: 6-2050; Tijuana, Tel.: 85-2230; Torreón, Tel.: 13-7593; Villahermosa, Tel.: 2-6991; Ixtapa-Zihuatanejo, Tel.: 4-2018. **Aero Sudpacifico**, Apatzingán, Tel.: 4-1577; Guadalajara, Tel.: 16-1119; Lázaro Cárdenas, Tel.: 2-3718; Mexico City, Tel.: 502-9208; Morelia, Tel.: 5-2413; Uruapan, Tel.: 3-7937. **Latur**, Mexico City, Tel.: 652-1104. **Litoral**, Ciudad del Carmen, Tel.:2-4976; Mexico City, Tel.: 207-8233; Minatitlán, Tel.: 4-9503; Monterrey, Tel.: 40-7979; Poza Rica, Tel.: 3-3525; Tampico, Tel.: 28-0857; Veracruz, Tel.: 35-0833; Villahermosa, Tel.: 4-3614. **Mexicana de Aviacion**, Acapulco, Tel.: 84-6890; Huatulco, Tel.: 7-0223; Cabo San Lucas, Tel.: 3-0411; Cancún, Tel.: 7-2513; Ciudad del Carmen, Tel.: 2-1171; Coatzacoalcos, Tel.: 2-6558; Cozumel, Tel.: 2-0157; Guadalajara, Tel.: 47-2222; Hermosillo, Tel.: 17-1103; Ixtapa-Zihuatanejo, Tel.: 3-2208; León, Tel.: 14-9500; Los Cabos, Tel.: 3-0411; Manzanillo, Tel.: 2-1972; Mazatlán, Tel.: 82-7722; Mérida, Tel.: 24-6633; Mexicali, Tel.: 52-5401; Mexico City, Tel.:660-4444; Minatitlán, Tel.: 4-0026; Monterrey, Tel.:40-5511; Nvo. Loredo, Tel.: 2-2051; Oaxaca, Tel: 6-8414; Puebla, Tel.: 48-5600; Puerto Escondido, Tel.: 2-0300; Puerto Vallarta, Tel.: 2-5000; San José del Cabo, Tel.: 2-0230; San Luis Potosí, Tel.: 14-1119; Tampico, Tel.: 13-9600; Tijuana, Tel.: 81-72211; Tuxtla Gtz., Tel.:

2-0020; Veracruz, Tel.: 32-2242; Villahermosa, Tel.: 3-5044; Zacatecas, Tel: 2-7429. **S.A.R.O.** (Servicios Aeros Rutas Oriente), Acapulco, Tel.: 84-0705; Culiacán, Tel.: 14-6766; León, Tel.: 29-0059; Monterrey, Tel.: 42-3597. Taesa, Mexico City, Tel.: 756-0832; Saltillo, Tel.: 16-4647. **Aeromonterrey**, Monterrey, Tel: 40-551. **Aeromorelos**, Acapulco, Tel.: 81-0852; Cuernavaca, Tel.: 17-5588; Huatulco, Tel.: 1-0055; Oaxaca, Tel.: 6-3010; Puebla, Tel.: 46-6622; Puerto Escondido, Tel.: 2-0734. **Aviacion del Noroeste**, Ciudad Obregón, Tel.: 3-9525; Culiacán, Tel.: 16-8899; Chihuahua, Tel.: 16-5146; Durango, Tel.: 2-6444; Hermosillo, Tel.: 17-3606; La Paz, Tel.: 2-7788; Mazatlán, Tel.: 84-1455; Mexicali, Tel.: 68-6635; Mexico City, Tel.: 564-4275. **Continua Aviacion del Noroeste, Monterrey**, Tel.: 44-7429; Puerto Peñasco, Tel.: 3-3555; San Luis Río Colorado, Tel.: 4-2494; Torreón, Tel.: 16-5679. **Aerovias Oaxaqueñas**, Mexico City, Tel.: 510-0162; Oaxaca, Tel.: 6-3833; Puerto Escondido, Tel.: 2-0300. **Aviacsa**, Cancún, Tel.: 7-4214; Chetumal, Tel: 2-7676; Mérida, Tel.: 26-9087; Mexico City, Tel.: 590-2624; Oaxaca, Tel.: 3-1809; San Cristóbal de las Casas, Tel.: 8-4384; Tapachula, Tel.: 6-3147; Tuxtla Gtz., Tel.: 2-6880; Villahermosa, Tel.: 4-5770.

By Car

Mexico possesses a well-developed road network (more than 75,000 km.). A good half of the system is surfaced. Some of the major highways are excellent. Patrolling the so-called "tourist routes" are the "Green Angels" *(Angeles Verdes)* of the Mexican Automobile Club (AMA) as a service of the Ministry of Tourism. These radio-equipped green-and-white vehicles are at the ready to provide assistance in case of breakdown 365 days a year from 8:00 am to 8:00 pm. The English-speaking mechanics are also trained in first aid, are prepared to provide tourist information and news on road conditions and can help with common replacement parts as well as emergency fuel and oil. Before and within towns there are frequently speed bumps *(topes)* or other "sleeping policemen". In these places keep the 30 km/hr speed limit! The usual speed limits are 30 or 40 kilometers per hour in towns and 80 km/h or 100 km/h on highways, while on several superhighways *(autopistas,* tolls must be paid) speeds of up to 110 km/h are permissible. Always fill up the tank at the state-operated PEMEX gasoline stations *(gasolinera)* it can take a long while before you reach the next one. Be sure to check that the pump is at zero before using it! Blue pumps have nova/81 octane; silver painted pumps extra/94 octane. Warning: Avoid driving by night, there are serious risks posed by rapidly changing road conditions, animals and hold-ups.

Rental Cars

An international drivers' permit is required to rent cars in Mexico. Minimum age is 24 years. All of the international car rental firms are represented, although certain of the usual conditions vary (they are franchises). This results in, for example, very high vehicle drive-back fees! Pay only with credit card, since otherwise a high security deposit is required. In general, it is possible to haggle over the rental rates, especially when several companies are lined up next to each-other (at airports, for example) and the rental period is to exceed one week. Price variations from region to region are very large in the tourist centers they often charge double what is usual elsewhere. In such place it's often worth doing a deal with a taxi driver for a day-rate. Always purchase accident insurance. Liability insurance doesn't even exist. Rentals run from $US 25 to 60 per day, plus 15 percent IVA (value-added or sales tax).

Central reservation offices of the larger companies in Mexico City are: Avis, Tel.:

578-1044; Budget, Tel.: 566-6800; Hertz, Tel.: 566-0099; National Car Rental, Tel.: 533-0375; Romano Rent-a-Car, Tel.: 250-0055; Quick Rent-a-Car, Tel.: 511-8928.

Ferries

Between Baja California and the west coast of Mexico: La Paz-Mazatlán (16 hours); Santa Rosalia-Guayamas (seven hours); La Paz-Los Mochis/Topolobambo (10 hours). Between Quintana Roo (Yucatán Peninsula) and islands in the Caribbean Sea: Playa del Carmen-Cozumel; Puerto Juárez-Isla Mujeres.

Information: Servicio de Transboradores, Juan de la Barrera 63, 06140 Mexico, D.F.. Tickets for the *transboradores* can be purchased in every case directly at the landing stages; cabin reservations for ferries between Baja California and the West Coast should be arranged well ahead.

Tours

People who want to wait until their arrival in Mexico before deciding on an organized tour are well advised to request a list of travel agency addresses in Mexico from the Mexican Tourist Office.

PRACTICAL TIPS

Accommodation

Mexico has some 8500 recognized hotels and motels, with a total of 330,000 beds. The majority of the better hotels belong to domestic or international chains. The quality standards vary sharply from region to region. Almost all of the luxury hotels are located either in the major cities or in the better-known vacation centers. Numerous haciendas have been converted into hotels; these are usually situated off the main roads and belong to the luxury class. A notable current trend is the growing number of small, intimate and upmarket lodges, for example the "Small Grand Hotels of Mexico". In Mexico, hotels are classified according to a different set of standards, not always corresponding to the common international categories.

Banks

Bank business hours are generally from 9:00 am to 1:30 pm; several branch outlets of the major banks are also open from 4:00-6:00 pm as well as Saturdays from 10:00 am to 1:30 pm. There may be further limits on the hours when currency is exchanged (US$ and travelers' checks). This is particularly true in the provinces, where in many places European currencies are not accepted at all (see also under Travel Preparations). Privately operated change-booths (called *casa de cambios* or *casa de monedas*) are open Monday through Saturday from nine to five; in Mexico City (Zona Rosa) occasionally one hour longer. The exchange rate for travelers' checks is lower at these than at banks, although usually about the same for the exchange of $US notes; the rate for other currencies is also below that of the banks. At the Benito Juárez International Airport in Mexico City there are several banks and change booths; one of them is always open 24 hours a day.

Business Hours

There are no state-sanctioned business hours, although they are commonly from nine or ten in the morning until 7:00 or 8:00 pm (with regional variations); Siesta from 2:00 to 4:00 pm (including most department stores). State agencies are frequently only open to the public from mornings until 2:00 pm, and it is generally pointless to appear earlier than 10:00 am. Business appointments should never be set for before 10 am or between 2:00 and 4:00 pm.

Customs

Adults may bring in 50 cigars, 200 cigarettes or up to 250 grams of tobacco, as well as three liters of wine or spirits. In addition, visitors are permitted 2 cameras and an 8mm-film or video camera, with 12 cassettes or rolls of film (no professional filming equipment).

Articles for personal needs, a travel typewriter, sporting gear (a surfboard or fishing rod, for example) and one musical instrument are also duty-free. A red/green "traffic light" indicates baggage clearance upon entering the country at the Benito Juárez International Airport in Mexico City. The export of gold or antiques, and especially archeological finds, is forbidden. Caution! At archeological sites there are almost always "genuine" finds offered for sale as souvenirs. Don't even think about them, because the customs officers are not necessarily able to distinguish between genuine and counterfeit articles.

Doctors

The health care system in Mexico is well developed. There is no shortage of hospitals nor of European or USA-trained physicians. The larger hotels in the tourist centers have a resident or on-call doctor. If medical attention should become necessary, treatment certificates are not accepted. One must pay cash and then present the diagnosis as well as the bill/receipt to the insurance establishment at a later date. Physicians' fees are comparatively low and often the doctor will say: "Pay me what you think is appropriate." If payment difficulties arise due to in-patient treatment, you should get in contact with your embassy or consulate as quickly as possible, as well as informing the insurance company. In case of high treatment costs that a traveler is unable to meet, there is an official way to arrange direct payment through the embassy/consulate or the insurance company. If you do not have a world-wide insurance policy, inquire before departure about a short-term travelers' insurance.

Drinking Water

Normal water from the tap should avoided at all costs ("Moctezumas revenge!"). It's best to purchase bottled *agua purificada* or *agua mineral.* Use this water for washing fruit and vegetables as well. Avoid ice-cubes in drinks except in better hotels or restaurants, since ice is made of purified water only in such establishments. In hotels, sealed bottles of purified water are left for the guests either in the bedroom or bathroom.

Electricity

110 volts; before leaving, pick up an adaptor for the American standard flat-bladed plug.

Holidays and Festivals

Hardly a day goes by without some kind of festival (see "Fiestas" chapter). The legal/religious holidays are: January 1st: New Year's Day *(Año Nuevo);* February 5th: Constitution Day *(Día de la Constitución);* March 21st: Birthday of Benito Juárez *(Natalico de Benito Juárez);* March/April: Easter Week *(Semana Santa);* May 1st: Labor Day *(Día del Trabajo);* May 5th: Anniversary of the Battle of Puebla *(Aniversario de la Batalla de Puebla);* September 1st: Report on the State of the Nation *(Informe Presidencial);* September 16th: Independence Day *(Día de la Independencia);* October 12th: Day of the Races, also called Columbus Day *(Día de la Raza);* November 1st and 2nd: All Saints' Day/All Souls' Day *(Todos los Santos / Día de los Muertos);* November 20th: Day of the Revolution *(Día de la Revolución);* December 12th: Festival of the Virgin of Guadalupe *(Día de la Virgen de Guadalupe);* December 25th: Christmas *(Navidad).*

Illegal Drugs

Mexico is a key transfer point for illegal drugs. The government takes the fight against drugs very seriously, and the pos-

GUIDELINES

session of even small quantities of hashish or marijuana can lead to fines or imprisonment; dealing and smuggling are punished very severely. Mexican criminal law does not distinguish between hard and soft drugs. The police and special units of the federal drug agency also conduct checks along the highways; furthermore, on arrival and departure luggage is occasionally searched specifically for illegal drugs.

Mordidas

If you are traveling by car, set aside an extra corner of your budget for various *mordidas* to be paid to the police. Without bribes one can wind up spending a long while in some rather suspenseful situations for little more than an minor parking infraction. Save yourself the time and unpleasantness. In case of traffic accidents one can easily be arrested and require legal assistance. In jail, only two telephone calls are permitted. There are no upper limits on the amount of a *mordida*.

Mosquitoes

In several coastal regions, particularly in Veracruz, Campeche, Yucatán and Quintana Roo, these can become a real torment. A *repelente* can help against them; these are available in any *farmacia*. There are a variety off sprays and lotions on the market, "Deep Woods-Off", a preparation from Canada and the USA, is very effective, though difficult to obtain.

Museums and Art Galleries

With few exceptions these are closed on Mondays. Usually admission is free on Sundays and holidays. Hours vary.

Pharmacies/Chemists

There are *farmacias* everywhere, including small towns, and they even appear as departments in supermarkets. Medications are generally cheap in Mexico and are sold to an astonishing extent without prescriptions, although this can be illegal without the *receta*. Many physicians operate *farmacias,* where they (or perhaps their assistants) make diagnoses. One can also receive injections *(inyecciónes)* then and there for a minimal "treatment fee". Blood is even analyzed in many pharmacies.

Important! Antibiotics *(antibioticos)* are also available prescription-free and are often used Mexico even when a less powerful treatment would suffice. When taking antibiotics, one should not discontinue as soon as the symptoms disappear, but continue the treatment to its conclusion at the recommended dose. A sudden discontinuation can bring about a worsened relapse of the illness.

Photography

Just about the only film that can be found in Mexico is from Kodak, of a quality that doesn't meet the demands of professionals; it is also expensive and seldom properly stored. Don't put your film in the sun (nor should it be stored in car boots). Beware when taking domestic flights! Despite inspection staff's assurances to the contrary, most of the x-ray machines are not "filmsafe". If possible try to limit your photography to the mornings and later afternoon due to the high intensity lighting conditions: No light-meter can really protect you from false exposures. Skylight and polarized filters are recommended. Exercise discretion and restraint when photographing people. Indigenas do not much like to have their pictures taken, in fact some aggressive reactions can even be expected. Throughout the country you will come up against local restrictions (in churches, museums and archeological sites, for example); these can either be an absolute ban, or the prohibition of tripods and flashes. A permit can be obtained from the INHA (Instituto Nacional de Antropología e Historia), Cordoba 45, Col. Roma, Tel.: 533-2263, Mexico City.

Press

The most important among some 25 daily newspapers in Mexico are the *Excelsior* (balanced/respectable), *Uno mas Uno* and *La Jornada* (both "leftist") as well as *El Nacional* (organ of the government). *La Prensa* is the largest-circulation sensationalist rag, while *The News* (in English) is read primarily by foreigners. *Time* and *Newsweek* can be obtained at kiosks in the tourist centers as well as the larger hotels. In Mexico City hotels there is almost always the *Daily Bulletin,* which features an odd mixture of news and tourist information, *The Gazer,* and *This Week – Esta Semana* (advertising magazines in English which are directed at a tourist audience, but offering negligible informative content).

Radio and Television

A large number of AM and FM radio stations cover the entire country. They play predominantly *ranchero* music, a sort of Mexican "country". Several stations specialize in rock or classical music. Radio VIP (associated with CBS) broadcasts news in English each hour on the hour on 1560 Khz AM and 86.0 Mhz FM. In addition there are commentaries on politics, economics and sports beamed in directly from the USA in the mornings and evenings.

The most powerful TV station is the privately-owned Televisa, with channels 2, 4, 5 and 8. Channel 11 belongs to the National Polytechnic Institute; channel 13 to the Mexican Institute of Television (both state-owned). They broadcast exclusively in the Spanish language. Many US series are run in the later evenings, either dubbed or with subtitles.

Rules for Behavior

Hospitality and warmth are typically Mexican characteristics, and one should take this at its face value. However, there are also particular expectations of foreign guests. The basic rule is "be polite and smile". At a bare minimum, the expressions *gracias, por favor,* and *con permiso* as well as a friendly *buenos días* or *buenas tardes* should be a part of your vocabulary. Mexicans are also very receptive to compliments. Do not expect punctuality *(mañana* is another day). The Mexicans are world champions at organized chaos. With this in mind, never lose your patience, don't get excited or upset and don't start complaining in loud or arrogant voice; you will either achieve nothing or else just the opposite of what you want. Injured pride and offended dignity can rapidly lead to aggressive behavior. Don't be stingy with tips, since, in view of the miserable salaries common in this country, they are the principal source of income for many. Mexican men often live up to their macho reputation. Women should react politely but firmly in uncomfortable situations, and generally avoid wearing provocative clothing, since it is taken the wrong way all too often.

Shopping

Mexico is a shoppers' paradise, with a truly great regional diversity in its handicrafts. The Indigenas' markets (haggling is customary) are particularly attractive. In addition, the urban *mercados* frequently offer a broad selection of locally-produced handcrafted items including pottery, leather goods, silver and basket wares, jewelry, sculptures, glass in various forms, Indigena paintings, traditional apparel and hammocks (see chapter on "Folk Art") alongside various foodstuffs, spices, fruits and vegetables and clothing. The largest markets in Mexico City are:

La Merced (La Merced Metro Station at the Anillo de Circunvalación), once the metropolis' main wholesale market, is very popular and the cheapest. The *Mercado de San Juan* (nearby the Salto del Agua Metro Station at the intersection of Ayuntamiento and Lopéz) is considered to have the best assortment; one can also

GUIDELINES

buy and eat a variety of delicacies there. *Tepito,* the "Thieves' Market", in the side-streets of the Rayón, is a key place where smuggled goods from the USA change hands, including televisions, radios and other electrical and electronic equipment, and clothing as well anything a heart could desire. There is also a Sunday flea-market *(La Lagunilla)* at the Rayón. It features antiques, jewelry, handcrafted articles and books.

Telecommunications

Mexico's postal service is certainly among the least reliable and most chaotic in the world, so important or urgent messages should only be exchanged by telephone, fax or courier services in both directions.

At postal counters, put the postage on personally, hand the item in, and then watch until the stamps *(timbres)* have been canceled. It's safer to send letters from the major hotels. The post offices *(correos)* are generally open Monday through Friday from 9:00 am to 6:00 or 7:00 pm and Saturdays from 9:00 am until noon or the early afternoon, though this can vary from region to region (see the guideposts at the end of the respective chapters).

Due to a 30 percent luxury tax, international telephone calls are extremely expensive. Hotels then slap a not-insignificant handling charge on top. Direct-dialed long distance calls are certainly cheaper. There are central offices for long-distance calls *(Casetas de Larga Distancia)* in the larger towns. You will be asked if you want to make a person-to-person call *(persona a persona).* If not, respond with a *quien contesta* (whoever answers).

Information for self-dialed calls: Domestic 02, International 09 (English). Information in Mexico City, 250-0404 and 533-0404, elsewhere 04. The prefix for domestic long distance calls is 91, International, 95.

Time

Mexico is divided into three time-zones. The time difference to Europe is between 7 and 9 hours.

During European summer time, one more hour can be added (Mexico does not observe a daylight savings time). The *Hora Central* applies in the entire highland region and Yucatán (Central European Time minus 7 hours); the *Hora de Montaña* in the northwestern states of Sinaloa, Sonora, Nayarit and Baja California Sur (CET minus 8 hours); the *Hora del Pacífico* in Baja California Norte from the end of October until the end of April (CET minus 9 hours).

Tipping

In restaurants and bars, tips of 15 percent are usual. Porters in hotels or at the airports expect about 3000 pesos per piece of luggage. Taxi drivers do not expect tips unless they have been exceptionally helpful.

Tourist Information

The state-operated Mexican Tourist Office has offices in many cities, and embassies or consulates can also help. Information for tourists already in Mexico City: Tourist Information (generally in English) Tel.: 525-9380; Tourism Hotline (for urgent situations), Tel.: 250-0123.

Secretaria de Turismo Presidente Masaryk 172 Col. Polanco/Chapultepec 11587 México, D.F. Tel.: 250-8158.

Additional telephone numbers can be found in the guideposts.

Weights and Measures

The metric system is used in Mexico.

LANGUAGE GUIDE

Monday . . . . *lunes*
Tuesday . . . . *martes*
Wednesday . . . . *miércoles*
Thursday . . . . *jueves*

LANGUAGE GUIDE

Friday	*viernes*
Saturday	*sábado*
Sunday	*domingo*
today	*hoy*
tomorrow	*mañana*
yesterday	*ayer*
in the morning	*por la mañana*
at noon	*al mediodía*
in the afternoon	*por la tarde(en las tardes)*
in the evening	*por la noche/en las noches*
0	*cero*
1	*uno*
2	*dos*
3	*tres*
4	*cuatro*
5	*cinco*
6	*seis*
7	*siete*
8	*ocho*
9	*nueve*
10	*diez*
11	*once*
12	*doce*
13	*trece*
14	*catorce*
15	*quince*
16	*dieciséis*
17	*diecisiete*
18	*dieciocho*
19	*diecinueve*
20	*veinte*
21	*veintiuno*
22	*veintidós*
30	*treinta*
40	*cuarenta*
50	*cincuenta*
60	*sesenta*
70	*setenta*
80	*ochenta*
90	*noventa*
100	*cien*
200	*doscientos*
500	*quinientos*
100 0	*mil*
single room	*habitación sencilla*
double room	*habitación doble*
(with bath)	*con baño*
(double)bed	*la cama*
air-conditioning, fan	*aire acondicionado/ventilador*
key	*la llave*
towel	*una toalla*
toilet paper	*papel de baño*
toilet	*baño*
men	*hombres/señores/caballeros*
women	*mujeres/señoras*
bill	*la cuenta*
Where is there a...?	*dónde hay*
closed	*cerrado*
open	*abierto*
Is this the way to...?	*Por aquí se va a...?*
straight ahead	*derecho*
to the right	*derecha*
to the left	*izquierda*
street	*carretera*
superhighway (four-lane highway)	*autopista*
path	*camino*
Do not pass	*no rebase*
danger	*peligro*
caution	*precaución*
Drive slowly	*disminuya su velocidad*
narrow bridge	*puente angosto*
detour	*desviación*
crossing/intersection	*crucero*
traffic light	*semáforo*
Keep right	*conserve su derecha*
breakdown	*derrame*
bus	*camión, autobus*
first/second class	*primera/segunda clase*
ticket	*boleto*
bus terminal	*central de camiones*
How long does it take/last...?	*Cuánto durará/ tarda...?*
Where does it go...?	*Adónde va...?*
Where does it come from....?	*De dónde viene...?*
good morning, good day	*buenos días*
good day, good afternoon (in the afternoon after 12:00 pm)	*buenas tardes*
good evening, good night	*buenas noches*
yes/no	*sí/no*
good-bye	*hasta luego. adiós*
excuse me, pardon me	*perdón*

with permission	*con permiso*
please	*por favor*
thank-you (very much)	*(muchas) gracias*
You're welcome/don't mention it	*de nada*
(as a response to thank-you)	
I need	*necesito*
There is/is there?	*hay*
How much does...cost?	*cuánto vale*
I don't understand	*no entiendo*
slowly, please	*despacio, por favor*
At what time...?	*A qué hora*
What time is it?/How late is it?	*Qué horá es/ que hora tiene?*
What's your name?	*Cómo se llama usted?*
ice-cubes	*Cubitos de hielo*
bottle	*Botella*
beer	*Cerveza*
wine	*Vino*
sweet	*Dulce*
dry	*Seco*
bottle opener/corkscrew	*Destapador*
post office	*Correo*
letter	*Carta*
address	*Dirección*
stamp/postage	*Estampillo, timbre*
post card	*Tarjeta*
airmail	*Correo aereo*
ordinary mail	*Ordinario*
registered	*Registrado*
duty/fee	*Impuesto*
weight	*Peso*
telegram	*Telegrama*
telephone	*Teléfono*
telephone call	*Una llamada*
telephone number	*Número*
long distance	*Larga distancia*
credit card	*Tarjeta de crédito*
hello!	*Ola! Bueno!*
money	*Dinero, lana*
exchange	*Cambio, feria, suelto*
check	*Cheque*
travelers' check	*Cheque de viajero*
bank	*Banco*
signature	*Firma*
physician	*Médico, Doctor*
hospital	*Hospital*
ill/sick	*Enfermo*
fever	*Fiebre*
headache	*Dolor de cabeza*
common cold	*Gripe*
medicine	*Medicina*
aspirin	*Aspirina*
toothache	*Dolor de muelas*
gas/petrol station	*Gasolinera*
gas/petrol	*Gasolina*
oil change	*Cambio de aceite*
oil	*Aceite*

AUTHORS

(In brackets you will find the respective contributions.)

Marilen Andrist lives as a freelance journalist and author in Hamburg. Her specialties are travel, international theater and the culture and religion of foreign peoples. ("Viva la Muerte")

Bob Brooke, a travel journalist and photographer based in Pennsylvania, is tand winner of the Real Award for Excellence in Travel Journalism. ("Toluca, the Spas, Valle de Bravo", "León, Aguascalientes, San Luis Potosì, Zacatecas", "Baja California", "Sun, Sand, Sea", "State of Veracruz", "Cancún, Isla Mujeres, Cozumel and the Coast of Quintana Roo")

Jim Budd graduated from Columbia University, left New York for Mexico City in 1958, and was an editor at the *Mexico City News* as well as foreign correspondent for the *United Press International* and *Time-Life*. ("Mexico City")

Ortrun Egelkraut, editor at a Berlin daily newspaper, has traveled in Mexico for many years as well as having penned her own travel guide on the country. ("Veracruz City", "Gems in the East of Veracruz", "Tabasco", "Campeche", "Literature")

Wayne Greenhaw lives in Alabama, was travel editor at *Pensacola Magazine* and *Alabama Magazine* and writes for the *New York Times*. ("Tula & Tepotzotlán", "Cuernavaca, Malinalco, Xochi-

CREDITS

calco", "Taxco", "Puebla", "Traditional Music", "Mural Art")

Arthur S. Harris, Jr., Harvard graduate and travel journalist from Vermont, has written travel guides on Boston and New York. ("Along the Coast")

Angeles Mastretta is one of the most renowned journalists and broadcast moderators/commentators in Mexico. ("Machismo")

Eleanor S. Morris, freelance travel journalist and photographer, lives in Austin, Texas. ("Monterrey", "Border States", "Mérida", "Puerto Progreso")

Birgit Müller, German sociologist whose main interest is the Third World, works as a freelance journalist. ("History and Culture", "Morelia, Uruapan, Lake Pátzcuaro", "Querétaro, San Miguel de Allende, Dolores Hidalgo, Guanajuato", "Oaxaca, Monte Albán, Mitla", "Chichén Itzá, Labná, Uxmal, Kabáh, Sayil, Cobá, Tulúm", "Social Conflicts")

Patricia Quintana-Fernandez resides in Mexico City. Her books *Cooking is a Game, Taste of Mexico* and *Feasts of Life* have become standards. She is columnist for *Novedades* and the Mexican edition of *Vogue*. ("Mexican Cuisine")

Volker W. Radke, this book's project editor, was for 12 years foreign correspondent in Southeast Asia and Africa for TV, radio and the press. He is now a freelance journalist and photographer. Since 1985 he has focused on Central America in general and on Mexico in particular, where he resided for some time. ("Teotihuacán", "Haziendas", "The Legend of Tequila" "Barranca del Cobre", "Peninsula of Ruins and Beaches", "Fiestas", "Bullfights and Mounted Games", "Voladores")

Jutta Schütz-Gormsen fell in love for Mexico in 1973. She produced a doctoral thesis on Mexican artisanry and two travel guides. ("Folk Art")

Anne Schumacher de la Cuesta resided in Mexico for over 16 years and is regional director of the state-operated Mexican Tourist Office in Frankfurt. ("National Museum of Anthropology")

Dr. Manfred Wöbcke is a Hamburg psychologist. His books include works on Mexico, Guatemala and Honduras. ("History and Culture", "Morelia, Uruapan, Lake Pátzcuaro", "Querétaro, San Miguel de Allende, Dolores Hidalgo, Guanajuato", "Oaxaca, Monte Albán, Mitla", "Chichén Itzá, Labná, Uxmal, Kabáh, Sayil, Cobá, Tulúm", "Social Conflicts")

PHOTOGRAPHERS

Archiv für Kunst und Geschichte, Berlin   14, 25, 28L, 28R, 31, 35L, 37, 38, 39, 40, 41, 43
Gross, Andreas   12, 18, 22, 45, 48/49, 50/51, 67, 72/73, 81, 87, 94, 100, 110, 127, 173, 186, 191, 193, 195, 206/207, 230, 233
Janicke, Volkmar   98, 229
Joerissen, Heinz   123R
Kaempf, Bernhard   8/9, 16, 151R, 174, 188, 192, 212
Kamphausen, Klaus / FLP   61, 187
Müller-Moewes, Ulf (Königswinter)   1, 64, 74, 112, 118/119, 129, 130, 156
Nelles, Günter   44
Radke, Volker W.   10/11, 17, 20, 29, 47, 52, 56, 59, 62, 63, 65, 66, 78, 82, 84, 88, 89, 99, 104R, 106, 107, 111, 125, 131, 137, 141, 152, 160/161, 167, 168, 169, 170, 175, 176, 178/179, 194, 198, 200, 201, 203, 208/209, 211R, 218, 219, 220, 221, 222, 227, 228, 231, backcover
Schiffl-Deiler, Marianne   126, 154
Skupy, Hans-Horst und **Hartl**, Helene   15, 21, 24, 26, 32, 33, 35R, 46, 76L, 76R, 101, 104L, 114, 134, 142, 144/145, 180, 185, 196, 211L, 214, 217L, 217R, 224, 234, cover
Teufelhart, Robert 85, 92/93, 123L, 132
Thiele, Klaus   80, 115, 146, 151L, 213

INDEX

A

Acapulco 135-138, 228
  Artesanias Finas de Acapulco (AFA) 138
  Ave. Costera Alemán 136
  Bazar del Arte Mexicano 138
  Cathedral 135
  CiCi 136
  Coyuca Lagoon 137
  Fuerte de San Diego 135
  La Quebrada 137
  La Roqueta 136
  Mercado de Artesanías 138
  Mercado Municipal 137
  Parque Papagayo 136
  Playa Caleta 135
  Playa La Condesa 136
  Playa Los Hornos 136
  Playa Paraíso 136
  Playa Pie de la Cuesta 137
  Playa Revolcadero 136, 137
  Plaza San Juan Alvarez 135
  Puerto Marques 136
  Teatro Netzahuacóyotl 137
Aguascalientes 112
  Cathedral 113
  Convento de San Diego 113
  Iglesia de San Antonio 113
  Iglesia de San Marcos 113
  Iglesia El Encino 113
  Museo de la Ciudad 113
  Palacio de Gobierno 113
  Palacio Municipal 113
  Plaza Principal 113
Aguilar, Gerónimo de 23
Aldamas, Juan 112
Alemán, Miguel, president 42
Allende, Ignacio de 32, 33, 34, 108, 104
Almoloya 88
Alvarado 169
Alvarado, Pedro de 25
Aztecs 15, 18, 19, 20, 21, 22, 23, 25, 27, 53, 56, 58, 65, 67, 68, 75, 80, 87, 88, 102, 112, 165, 210, 215, 222, 225
Azuela, Mariano 223

B

Bahia de Banderas 140
Bahuichivo 125
Baja California 29, **127-131**
Bajio 95
Ball courts 16, 19, 75, 156, 163
Ballet Folklorico 215
Barra de Navidad 140
Barranca del Cobre 122-126
Becal 176
Becán 175
Blom, Frans 155

Bonampak 157, 174, 220
Bullfight 224, **226-227**

C

Cabo San Lucas 132
Calendar 17, 22, 23, 67, 219, 229
Calixtlahuaca Arch. Zone 88
Calles, Plutarco Elias, president 42
Camacho, Avila, president 42
Camarena, Gonzalez 221
Campeche 174-176
Cancún 197-201
  Archeological Museum 198
  Playa Caracol 199
  Centro de Convenciones 197
  El Rey Ruins 198
  Playa Langosta 199
  Playa Las Perlas 199
  Mayan Observatory 198
  Mujeres Bay 199
  Paseo Kukulcán 197
  Playa Chac Mool 199
  Playa del Rey 199
  Punta Cancun 197
  Playa Tortugas 199
  Xel-há National Park 199
Cárdenas, Cuauhtémoc 45, 234
Cárdenas, Lázaro 42, 46
Carranza, Venustiano 40, 102, 167, 168
Carrillo, Julián 215
Castellanos, Rosario 223
Castillo de Teayo 163
Catemaco 170
Cerocahui 125
Chac, god 17, 192, 193
Chalkini 176
Champotón 176
Charreada 224, 227
Chávez, Charlos 215
Chelém 186
Chiapas 16, **153-157**
Chicanná 175
Chichén Itzá 16, 17, 19, 182, **187-190**
  Ball court 189
  Chac Mool sculpture 188
  Grupo de las Mil Columnas 189
  High Priest's Grave 189
  Holy Cenote 189
  Observatory 189
  Platform of the Jaguars and Eagles 189
  Temple of Jaguars 189
  Temple of Kukulcán 188
  Templo de los Guerreros 189
  Wall of the Death's Heads 189
Chichimecs 17, 19, 22, 75, 87, 104, 112
Chicomoztoc Ruins 115
Chihuahua 33, 41, 108, 121, 127

Chilpancingo 33
Cholula 87
Christianization 27, 124
Churrigueresque style 76, 98, 103, 107, 108, 114, 123, 127
City-States 16
Ciudad del Carmen 174
Ciudad Juárez 38, 122
  Arts and Crafts Center 122
  Misión de Nuestra Señora d. G. 122
  Museo de Arte e Historia 122
Ciudad Valles 162
Ciudad Victoria 123
Cobá
  La Iglesia 195
  Nohoch Mul Group 195
  Sacbe, cerem. causeways 195
Colombo, hot spring 113
Columbus 23
Comalcalco 172
Conquistadors 14, 23, 28, 30, 79, 87, 114, 123, 181, 215, 229
Copper Canyon 124
Cortés, Hernán 19, 23, 25, 28, 29, 58, 75, 79, 167, 172, 226, 229
Cortines, Ruiz, president 42
Cozumel 201-202
  Aquarium 202
  Botanical garden 202
  Chankanab Lagoon National Park 202
  Palancar Reef 201
  Passion Island 202
  Playa San Francisco 202
  Punta Chiquero 202
  San Miguel de Cozumel 201
  Tomb of the Snail 202
Creel 126
Creoles 31, 32, 34, 78, 181
Cruz, Juana Inéz de la 222
Cuauhtémoc 25, 26, 29, 61
Cubilete 105
Cuernavaca 79
  Cathedral de la Asunción 81
  Jardín Borda 81
  Jardín Juarez 80
  Museo Cuauhnáhuac 80
  Museo de la Herbolaria 81
  Palacio de Cortés 80
  Plaza de la Constitucion 80
Cupatitzio River 101

D

Desert of the Lions 88
Desierto Altar, desert 121
Díaz, Bernal 24
Díaz, Porfirio, general 36, 37, 38, 62, 107
Divisadero, railway station 126
Dolores Hidalgo 101, 105

INDEX

Dominicans 27
Dzibiltchaltún 182
Dzilam de Bravo 186

E

Eduardo Ruiz National Park 101
Edzná 176
El Arco 132
El Fuerte 124
El Límon 172
El Paraíso 172
El Tajin 19, 163
  Edificio de las Columnas 164
  Edificio de los Tuneles 164
  Plaza El Tajin Chico 164
  Pyramid of the Niches 19, 163
El Tamuin 162
Emiliano Zapata 173
Encomiendas 29
Ensenada 129

F

Fiestas 215, **224-225**
Folk Art 216-219
FONART 216, 219
Franciscans 27, 84, 98, 103, 105, 113, 115
Frente Democrático Nacional (FDN) 45
Fuentes, Carlos 223

G

Gachupines 31, 32, 33, 34
Grito de Dolores 33, 102
Guadalajara 30, 109
  Cathedral 109
  Mercado Libertad 110
  Museo Regional 109
  Palacio del Gobierno 109
  Plaza de Armas 109
  Plaza de la Liberación 109
  Plaza de los Laureles 109
Guanajuato 95, **105-109**
  Alhóndiga de Granaditas 108
  Basilica Nuestra Señora de Guanajuato 107
  Iglesia de Compañía 108
  Jardín de la Union 107
  Mercado Hidalgo 108
  Museo de las Momias 108
  Museo del Estado 108
  Pípila Monument 107
  Plaza de la Paz 107
  Teatro 107
  Templo Diego, church 107
  Valenciana, silver mine 108
Guaymas 121
Guerrero Negro 130
Guerrero, Vincente 34

Guzmán, Martin Luis 223
Guzmán, Nuno de 30, 109

H

Haciendas 29, 30, 36, **77-79**, 201
Hecelchakan 176
Henequén (sisal hemp) 78, 181, 182, 183, 186
Hermosillo
  La Presa Rodriguez, dam 121
  Museo Regional de Historia 121
Hidalgo del Parral 122
Saltillo 122-123
  Alameda 123
  Cathedral of Santiago 122
  Fortress of Carlota 123
  Plaza de Armas 122
Hidalgo y Costilla, Miguel 32, 33, 34, 95, 102, 104, 105, 106
Hieroglyphic script 16
Hombre de Tepexpan 13
Huaxtecs 22, 67, 120, 165
Huerta, Victoriano 39, 40
Humboldt, Alexander von 31, 84, 135

I

Indigenas 13, 20, 27, 30, 32, 35, 38, 67, 75, 77, 98, 102, 105, 113, 121, 124, 126, 142, 147, 153, 155, 163, 182, 214, 224, 229, 235
Inflation 43, 44, 47
Insurgentes 33
Isla del Carmen 174
Isla Mujeres 200
  El Garrafón 200
  Isla Contoy 201
  Playa Indios 200
  Playa Lancheros 200
  Playa Los Cocos 200
Isthmus of Tehuantepec 18
Iturbide, Agustín de 33, 58, 85
Itzam Na, god 17
Ix Chel, goddess 17
Ixtaccihuatl 86
Ixtapa 139
  Paseo del Palmar 139
  Playa del Palmar 139
  Playa Mahava 139
  Playa Quieta 139
Ixtapan de la Sal, spa 89

J

Jaguar 14, 16, 18, 19, 22, 75, 157, 170, 173, 188, 189, 214
Jalapa 164
  Cathedral 165
  Government Palace 165

Jardín Lecuona 165
Jardín Morelos 165
Museum of Anthropology 165
Parque Juárez 165
Janítzio, island of 233
Jesuits 27, 37, 76, 108, 115, 125, 127, 130, 131
Juárez, Benito 18, 35, 103, 107, 113, 149, 235

K

Kabáh 192
Kinich Ahau, god 17

L

La Antigua 167
Labná 182, **192-193**
  Archway 192
  Caves of Loltún 193
  Ceremonial Causeway 192
  Observation Tower 193
  Palacio 192
Laguna de Terminos 174
Lake Pátzcuaro 98, 99, 233
Lake Texcoco 56
Lake Vincente Guerrero 123
La Lazo 126
La Paz 129, 131
Lara, Agustín 169
Las Casa, Bartolomé de 28
Las Virgenes, volcano 130
La Venta 14, 15, 16, 172
León 112
  Nuestra Senora de la Luz 112
  Palacio Municipal 112
  Panteon Taurino 112
  Templo Expiatorio 112
Los Mochis 124

M

Machismo 230-231
Madero, Francisco 37, 38, 39, 40, 60
Madonna of Guadalupe, virgin of 27, 33, 37, 63
Madrid, Miguel de la 43, 234
Malinalco 82
Malinche 23, 29, 79, 172, 229
Manzanillo 139-140
  Avenida Cinco de Mayo 139
  Mercado Municipal 139
  Playa de Audienca 140
  Playa de Oro 140
  Playa Miramar 140
  Santiago Peninsular 139
Mariachi music 60, 65, 124, 166, 199, 215
Mastretta, Angeles 223
Matamoros 123

INDEX

Mateos, Alfonso López 42, 124
Maximilian of Habsburg 36, 61, 62, 66, 79, 81, 102, 103, 110, 121, 168
Mayas 15, 16, 17, 67, 80, 124, 157, 172, 174, 182, 187, 192, 194, 195, 210, 214, 220, 224
Mazatlán 142
   Acuario 142
   Cathedral 142
   Cerro de la Nevería 142
   Fishermen's Monument 142
   Old Spanish Fort 142
   Playa Olas Atlas 142
   Playa Sabalo 142
   Zocalo 142
   Zona Dorada 142
Mendoza, Antonio de 30
Mérida 30, 181, **182-186**
   Antique Bazaar 185
   Casa de las Artesanias 185
   Casa Montejo 184
   Cathedral 183
   Iglesia de Santa Ana 185
   Iglesia de Santa Lucia 185
   Jardin de los Compositores 185
   La Ermita de Santa Isabel 185
   La Pinacoteca 184
   Mercado Garcia Rejon 185
   Museo Antropol. e. Hist. 184
   Museo Nac. de Arte Popular 184
   Palacio del Gobierno 184
   Palacio Municipal 185
   Parque Hidalgo 185
   Parques Santiago 185
   Paseo Montejo 183
   Plaza de la Independencia 183
   Teatro Peon Conteras 184
Mérida, Carlos 221
Mescal 111, 233
Mestizos 30, 32, 36, 162, 235
Metepec 88
Mexicali 129
Mexico City 34, 35, 40, 44, **53-68**, 98, 226
   Alameda Park 61
   Avenida Francisco Madero 60
   Avenida Insurgentes 63
   Bosque de Chapultepec 62
   Casa de los Azulejos 60
   Chapultepec Castle 62
   Chapultepec Park 56, 62, 66
   Cuicuilco Archeological Zone 65
   Float.Gardens of Xochimilco 65
   Franz Mayer Museum 61
   Frida Kahlo Museum 64
   Great Temple of the Aztecs 56
   House of Tiles 60
   Iturbide Palace 60
   Latin American Tower 60
   Metropolitan Cathedral 56, 58
   Ministry of Education 59

Monument to Independence 62
Monument to the Revolution 61
Museum of Anthropology 13, 62
Museum of Modern Art 62
Museum of Technology 63
Mus. of the City of Mexico 59
Nat. Aut. University of Mexico (UNAM) 65, 221
National Art Museum 61
National Museum of History 62
Nat. Museum of Medicine 60
National Palace 56, 58
Nat. Mus. of Anthropol. 22, 66
Natural History Museum 63
Palace of Fine Arts 60
Palacio National 58
Paseo de la Reforma 56, 61
Pinacoteca Virreinal 61
Pink Zone (Zona Rosa) 62
Plaza de la Constitution 59
Plaza Garibaldi 60
Plaza Mexico 64
Plaza of Three Cultures 42, 57
Plaza Santo Domingo 59
Polyforum Cult. D.A. Siqueiros 63
Sagrario Church 58
San Angel 64
Sanborns 64
San Carlos Museum 61
Saturday Bazaar 64
Solidarity Park 61
Sunken Gardens 64
Tamayo Rufino Museum 62
Temple Museum 57
Tlatelolco 57
Torre Latinoamericana 60
Trotsky Museum 64
World Trade Center 63
Zocalo 56, 57, 58, 59, 61
Michoacán 28, 95, 100
Mitla 19, 67
Mixtecs 15, 19, 20, 22, 67, 147, 150, 151
Moctezuma 23, 24, 62, 67, 167
Mole 210, 233
Monte Albán 14, 15, 18, 19, 20, 67, 149
   Ball court 150
   Grave Number 7 150
   Los Danzantes 150
   Monticulo J 151
   House of the Dancers 150
Monterrey 120-123
   Bishop Palace 121
   Cathedral 121
   El Obispado 121
   Grand Square 120
   Museum of Monterrey 121
   Palacio del Gobierno 121
   Palacio Federal 121
Morelia 33, **95-99**

Aqueduct 99
Augustinian Convent 99
Casa de Artesanias 99
Cathedral 98
Museo de Michoacán 98
Palacio Clavijero 98
Palacio de Gobierno 98
Palacio de Justicia 99
Palacio Municipal 99
Plaza de Armas 98, 99
Morelos, José Maria, priest 33, 34, 38, 95, 98, 99, 100
Mulege 130
Mural Art 220, **220-221**
Murillo, Bartolome 109

N

NAFTA 47
Nahuátl 15, 23, 68, 114, 142
Nanauatzin, god 68
Netzahualcoyotl 214, 223
Netzahualpilli 223
Nevada de Toluca, vulcano 87
New Mexico 31, 35, 111, 121
Nogales 121
Nuevo Laredo 123

O

Oaxaca 26, 67, **147-149**
   Benito Juarez Market 149
   Cathedral 148
   Cerro del Fortin 149
   Church of Santo Domingo 148
   Museo Regional de Oaxaca 148
   Museum Benito Juárez 149
   Zócalo 147
Obregón, Alvaro, president 40, 41, 42
O Gorman, Juan 221
Ojinaga 124
Ojo Caliente, hot spring 113
Olinalá 217
Olmecs 13, 14, 15, 19, 67, 80, 87, 149, 162, 165, 169, 172, 174
Ordaz, Díaz, president 42
Orozco, José Climente 60, 109, 110, 121, 122
Ortiz de Dominguez, Josefa 102
Oxolotán 172

P

Palenque 16, 156, 174
   Museum 156
   Temple of Inscriptions 156
   Temple of the Jaguars 156
Papantla 163, 228
Paricutín, volcano 101
Partido Revolucionario Institucional (PRI) 42, 234

INDEX

Pátzcuaro 21, 100, 218
   Casa de los Once Patios 100
   Janitzio Island 100
   Museo de Arte Popular 100
   Píaza Gertrudis Bocanegra 100
   San Agustín 100
Paz, Octavio 43, 222, 224, 232
PEMEX 170, 234
Peninsulares 31, 32, 33
Petroleum industry 43, 170, 172, 173, 174
Pico de Orizaba (Citlaltepetl) 164
Piedras Negras 122
Playa Costa Azul 132
Playa del Amor 132
Ponce, Manuel M. 215
Poniatowska, Elena 223
Popocatepetl 86
Portillo, López, president 43, 45
Poza Rica 163
Puebla 84-87
   Casa del Alfenique 86
   Cathedral 86
   Church of San Francisco 86
   Iglesia de la Santo Domingo 86
   Museo Bello 86
   Museum of Popular Art 85
Puerto Angel
Puerto Ceiba 172
Puerto Escondido 153
Puerto Progreso 186
Puerto Vallarta 140-142
   Church of Guadalupe 141
   Cuale River Island 141
   Playa del Sol 141
   Playa de Oro 141
   Playa las Estacas 141
   Playa Mismaloya 141
   Playa Palo Maria 141
Punta Nimun 186

Q

Querétaro 32, 41, 79, 95, **101-104**
   Casa de los Condes de Ecala 102
   Casa Mausoleo 103
   Cerro de las Campañas 103
   Convento de la Cruz 103
   Los Arcos 103
   Monument de la Corregidora 102
   Museo Regional 102
   Palacio de Bellas Artes 102
   Palacio del Estado 102
   Plaza de la Constitucion 102
   Plaza de la Independencia 102
   San Francisco, church 102
   Santa Clara, church 102
   Santa Rosa de Viterbo 103
   Teatro de la República 103
Quetzalcóatl 19, 27, 67, 75, 82, 167, 187
Quintana Roo 202-203

Bacalar Lagoon 203
Banco Chinchorro 203
Chetumal 203
Kohunlich 203
Playa Akumal 202
Playa Chemuyil 203
Playa del Carmen 203
Underwater Museum 203
Quiroga 21

R

Rebozos 88, 114
Repartimientos 29
Revueltas, Femin 221
Revueltas, Silvestre 215
Río Bec, archeol. site 176
Río Bravo del Norte 122
Río Chinipas 125
Río Fuerte 124
Río Grande 122
Río Grijalva 153
Rivera, Diego 58, 60, 61, 64, 65, 80, 108, 220
Road of Independence 101
Romero, Carlos Orozco 221
Rosario 130
Rulfo, Juan 223

S

Sahagún, Bernardino de 214, 223
Salinas de Gortari, Carlos, president 45, 46, 47
Saltillo 122
San Andrés Tuxtla 170
San Cristobal de las Casas 154
   Na-Bolom 154
   San Jolobil (House of weaving) 154
   San Juan Chamula 155
   Templo de San Cristobal 154
   Templo de Santo Domingo 154
   Zinacantan 155
San Gil 79
San Ignacio 130
San Jose del Cabo 131
San Jose Purua 89
San Juan del Río 79
San Lorenzo 169
San Luis Potosi 95, **113-114**
   Cathed.d.l.Epectac.d.l.Virgin 113
   Convento de San Francisco 114
   Iglesia de San Francisco 114
   Jardin Hidalgo 113
   Mercado Hidalgo 114
   Museo Nacional de la Mascara 114
   Museo Regional de Art Popula 114
   Nuestra Senora del Carmen 113
   Palacio de Gobierno 113

Plaza de Armas 113
San Augustin 114
San Miguel de Allende 79, 101, **104-105**
   Casa de Canal 105
   Casa de los Perros 105
   Casa de Solariega 105
   Convento de la Concepcion 105
   Nigromante Cultural Institute 105
   Parque Benito Juarez 105
   Parroquia de San Miguel 104
   Plaza Allende 104
   Plaza de San Francisco 105
   Tercer Order 105
San Nicolas de la Cantera 113
Santa Ana, general 34
Santa Clara del Cobre 218
Santa Maria del Río 114
   Agua de Lourdes 114
   Cerro de San Pedro 114
   Gogorron 114
   Ojo Caliente 114
Santa Maria El Tule 151
Santa Maria Magdalena 125
Santa Rosalia
   Caves of San Borjita 130
   Mission Church of Santa Rosalia 130
Santiago Tuxtla 170
Sarapes 88, 114, 122
Sayil 193
Sea of Cortés 121
Sierra de la Giganta 129
Sierra de los Tuxtlas 170
Sierra Madre del Sur 147, 152
Sierra Madre Occidental 121, 123, 124, 225
Sierra Madre Oriental 121, 142, 162
Sierra San Pedro Martir 129
Siqueiros, David Alfaro 60, 65, 81, 121, 220, 221
Sonora 121
Spaniards 14, 17, 20, 22, 23, 25, 27, 30, 34, 56, 66, 68, 77, 95, 106, 135, 181, 194, 201, 224
Spratling, William 217
Sumidero Canyon 153

T

Tabasco 29, **172-174**
Taibo II, Paco Ignacio 223
Talud-Tablero system 18
Tamaupilas 123
Tamayo, Rufino 221
Tamazunchale 163
Tampico 123
   Aduana Maritimo 162
   Cathedral 162
   Huaxtec Museum 162

INDEX

Mercado Hidalgo 162
Palacio Municipal 162
Playa Miramar 162
Plaza de Armas 162
Plaza de la Libertad 162
Tarascans 20, 21, 100, 112
Taxco 82-84, 95
  Cable car 84
  Casa Borda 83
  Casa Figueroa 83
  Casa Humboldt 84
  Convento Bernardino 84
  Museo Guillermo Spratling 83
  Santa Prisca Church 83
  Taxco Viejo 83
  The Silver Mine 83
Teapa 172
Tecciztecatl, god 68
Temascaltepec 89
Tenancingo 88
Tenochtitlán 22, 23, 24, 25, 29, 56, 58
Teotenango 88
Teotihuacán 17, 18, 66, 68, 69, 75
  Citadel 69
  Court of the Four Small Temples 69
  Court of the Jaguars 69
  House of the High Priests 69
  Palace of the Sun 69
  Puma Wall 69
  Pyramid of the Moon 69
  Pyramid of the Sun 69
  Quetzalpapálotl Palace 69
  Temple of Agriculture 69
  Temple of Quetzalcóatl 66, 69
  Viking Group 69
Teotitlán del Valle 217
Tepatitlan 111
Tepotzotlan 76
  Chamber of the Virgin 77
  Iglesia d.l.San Francisc.Javier 76
  National Viceroy Museum 76
  Plaza Hidalgo 76
Tequila 110, 233
Texas 31, 34, 35, 38, 121, 122
Tianguistengo 88
Tijuana 129
Tlachtli, god 163
Tlacotalpan 169
Tlaquepaque 219
Tlatelolco 56
Toltecs 19, 66, 80, 87, 163, 188
Toluca 87-89
  Bridal Veil Waterfall 89
  Cruz de Mision 89
  Indigena market 87
  La Pena de Principe 89
  Charro Museum 89
  Our Lady of Tecajic, church 88
  Governor Palace 88
  Green Lagoon 89

Lake of the Moon 87
Lake of the Sun 87
Mercado Juarez 88
Mus. of Archeology/History 88
Museum of Fine Arts 88
Nevada de Toluco National Park 87
Parochial Church 88
State Museum of Popular Art 88
Tonala 219
Tonatiuh, sun god 22
Topolobambo 124
Totonacs 19, 22, 67, 163, 225, 228
Treaty of Córdoba 34
Treaty of Guadalupe 35
Tres Zapotes 14, 16, 169
Trotsky, Leon 64
Tula 19, 27, 66, **75-76**
  Museum of Aztec Pottery 75
  Palacio Quemado 75
  Templo de Tlahuizcalpantecuhtli 75
Tulum
  Castillo 194
  Temple of Frescoes 195
  Templo del Dios Descendente 195
Tuxtla Gutiérrez 153
Tzintzuntzan 21, 99

U

Uetepec 88
Urique Canon 125, 126
Uruapan 101
Uxmal 16, 182, **190-195**
  Casa de las Palomas 191
  Casa de las Tortugas 191
  Great Pyramid 191
  Kabáh Archway 192
  Palace of Justice 192
  Palace of Masks 192
  Palacio del Gobernador 191
  Pyramid of the Soothsayer 190
  Quadrangulo de las Monjas 191

V

Valle de Bravo 89
Veracruz 23, 40, 67, **162-170**
  Baluarte de Santiago 167
  Boca del Rio 168
  Cathedral 166
  Costa de Oro 168
  Faro Carranza 167
  Malecon 168
  Mocambo 168
  Museo de la Ciudad 167
  Palacio Municipal 166
  Plaza de Armas 166
  Plaza de la Reforma 166
  San Cristo del Buen Viaje 166

San Juan de Ulua 166
Victoria, Guadalupe 34
Villa, Francisco "Pancho" 38, 39, 40, 41, 120, 122, 124, 215
Villahermosa 173
  Lagoon of Illusions 173
  Museo Regional de Antropologia 174
  Parque Museo de La Venta 173
  Parque T. G. Canabal 173
  Tabasco 2000 173
  Zona Luz 173
Voladores 19, 137, 163, 225, 227, **228-229**

X

Xipe Totec 228
Xochicalco 82
Xonocatlán 88
Xpuhil 175
Xtacumbilxunan 176

Y

Yaxchilán 157
Yucalpeten 186
Yucatán 16, 26, 30, 35, 174, **181-203**

Z

Zaachila 19
Zacatal 174
Zacatecas 95, **114-115**
  Casa Moneda 115
  Catedral 114
  Convento de Nuestra Señora de Guadalupe 115
  El Eden, mine 115
  Iglesia de San Agustin 115
  Museo de Pedro Coronel 115
  Palacio de Gobierno 115
  Templo de Santo Domingo 115
Zapata, Emiliano 38, 39, 40, 41, 80, 215
Zapotecs 15, 18, 19, 20, 22, 35, 67, 87, 147, 150, 210
Zihuatanejo
  Isla Ixtapa 139
  Morro de los Pericos 139
  Playa la Ropa 139
  Playa las Gatas 138
  Playa Maderas 139
  Playa Municipal 138
Zuanga, king 21